eGovernment Management for Developing Countries

Dedicated to all the potential eLeaders and eChampions in developing countries who bear the torch of the future

AHMED IMRAN ♦ SHIRLEY GREGOR ♦ TIM TURNER

eGovernment Management for Developing Countries

First published 2013

This edition March 2017

Note to readers: Some papers have been written by authors who use the American form of spelling and some use the British. These two different approaches have been left unchanged.

ISBN: 978-1-911218-23-4

Printed by Lightning Source POD

Published by: Academic Conferences and Publishing International Limited, Reading, RG4 9SJ, United Kingdom, info@academic-publishing.org

Available from www.academic-bookshop.com

Contents

Preface

Management of eGovernment in Developing Countries

Information and Communication Technology (ICT) is now a source of value for many organizations, both public and private, across many industry sectors and in many countries, both developed and less developed. A gain in productivity across the whole economy that benefits all citizens can be shown to flow from effective use of ICT. Value is gained from ICT through new and improved services and products, information flows, increases in productivity, and implementation of strategic initiatives. Gaining value from ICT is not just the responsibility of technical staff, but requires the direct involvement of people at senior and middle management levels. Executive involvement is vital to ensure that ICT is used for the right purposes and that the introduction and use of ICT in the organization is well managed. Managers in the public sector have a critical role in overseeing the effective use of ICT in government organizations. The responsibility for managing ICT is known as ICT governance and involves directing, controlling, planning and monitoring the use of ICT in the organization.

Audience and Use of the Book

The audience for this book are government officers and post graduate students aspiring to work at managerial levels within the public sector organisations in developing countries. We believe, by virtue of their appointments, any public sector manager of this Information age in the 21st century will have to manage ICT based services or have to play the role as eGovernment Manager. Accordingly, we have designed the curriculum taking the perspective of practising managers. The development approach for the book has meant that the content and style take the characteristics of developing countries into account. However, the book also contains knowledge of eGovernment in general and may have a wider appeal beyond developing countries. It is expected that readers will come from different fields (such as arts, engineering, science, management) and will have already some tertiary education, plus basic ICT skills and knowledge (for example, word-processing and email).

We have tried our best to sift the important from the unimportant issues and pick the right level for target audiences, without burdening the readers too much with information that is not particularly relevant or is too technical or too specific for their use. We have also tried to maintain a balance between academic standards and practical needs with due attention and recognition of the past work done in this area. However, if there is confusion or any error has slipped through, we would appreciate receiving advice and suggestions to address any issues in future editions.

The book can be used as the text for a complete semester long course of instruction: that is, 13 weeks of 3 hours of lectures, tutorials, and workshops. The program could be offered in intensive mode in approximately 13 working days and subsets of the program could be used for short training programs. Instructors may make a selection of chapters to suit particular audiences.

In many ways, this textbook is a practical handbook that can be followed on-the-ground as a guide for managers not only in developing countries but managers in organisations elsewhere. We have included many checklists, bullet point lists and appendices to serve as accessible aids for practitioners in the field.

Background to the Book

This book draws upon many years of real life working experience in developing countries supported by strong theoretical knowledge in the area of the strategic use of ICT in organisations and in-depth research over an eight-year period. The production of the book was an outcome of an applied action-design research project funded by AusAID, the Australian Agency for International Development, in 2010-2013. The purpose of the AusAID project was to assist managers in the public sector in Bangladesh to be able to implement eGovernment more effectively, with the wider objective of improving transparency and efficiency in the public sector and enhanced benefits to citizens. The project was a follow-up of a prior AusAID-funded project in 2008, in which a strategic direction for eGovernment was developed (Imran, Turner and Gregor 2008), a shorter training program in eGovernment management was delivered to senior government officers, and 800 copies of a handbook for eGovernment were produced (Gregor, Imran and Turner 2008).

The diverse backgrounds and complementary skill sets of the authors were focussed on making the contents of the book relevant and useful in practice. Cross cultural knowledge sharing and best practices around the world were explored in great detail to provide the audience with the most up-to-date and cutting edge solutions supported by research and practice in the area.

This textbook has been a co-operative effort with many people making contributions. A principle has been to have active involvement with professionals from developing countries through all development phases. Colleagues and participants from the Bangladesh Public Administration Training Centre (BPATC) in Dhaka, who participated in our newly developed eGovernment Management course in 2011 and 2012, provided feedback and insights to improve successive versions of the manuscripts for the book.

One of the greatest challenges we faced was to properly manage the scope of the material. Many of the concepts and topics used in mature IT organisations in developed countries are difficult to translate and contextualise in the environments of developing countries that are at the early stages of IT adoption.

Another challenge was the use of popular terms, which have different connotations and use in different contexts and cultures. We have had to give significant attention to these issues to meet cultural norms, customs and use in presentation techniques, and the use of English language and style to suit the target audiences in the best possible manner.

Organization of the Book

The book is divided into five major parts:

Part I: Introduction. Part I explains the need for eGovernment and the importance of eGovernment for developing countries. The lifecycle approach to eGovernment management and the main components of eGovernment are also explained.

Part II: eGovernment Architecture. Part II covers ICT infrastructure and the core systems that are used in eGovernment. This part aims to give managers sufficient knowledge to be able to recognize opportunities and make informed choices about the types of systems that are available to government organizations. It is not intended, however, to provide an in-depth treatment of technical matters.

Part III: Implementing eGovernment Systems. This part shows how eGovernment systems are acquired or developed and how ICT projects are managed effectively.

Part IV: Managing eGovernment. This part covers the higher level topics of ongoing ICT operations management, ICT governance and people management and organizational issues. Political, legal, ethical and environmental issues associated with eGovernment are also examined.

Part V: Supplement. This part provides report templates that supplement the project management chapter.

Educational Approach

The book has been developed following an outcome-based approach to learning. Learning objectives (outcomes) are specified at the beginning of each chapter in the book. In specifying learning objectives we have made use of Bloom's taxonomy of learning objectives (Bloom 1956) as revised by Anderson et al. (2001). This taxonomy has six levels of learning and each level has "action" words associated with it, which indicate the explicit outcomes expected in terms of learning. An outcomes-based approach has many advantages: for example, both instructors and students know what is expected and assessment can be more easily designed.

Dr Ahmed Imran, Professor Shirley Gregor, Dr Tim Turner
June, 2013 Canberra, Australia

References

Anderson, W.L., Krathwohl, D.R., Airasian, P.W., Cruikshank, K.A., Mayer,R.E., Pintrich, P.R., J.,Raths and Wittrock, M.C., (Eds.) (2001). A Taxonomy for Learning, Teaching, and Assessing — A Revision of Bloom's Taxonomy of Educational Objectives; Addison Wesley Longman, Inc.

Bloom, B. S. (Ed.). (1956). Taxonomy of Educational Objectives: The Classification of Educational Goals; pp. 201-207, Susan Fauer Company.

Gregor, S., Imran, A. and Turner, T. (2008). ICT Management Handbook, A Guide for Government Officers in Bangladesh. Canberra, Australia: National Centre for Information Systems Research. ISBN: 978-0-9805777-1-6.

Imran, A., Turner, T. and Gregor, S. (2008). EGovernment for Bangladesh: A Strategic Pathway for Success. Canberra, Australia: National Centre for Information Systems Research.

Acknowledgements

The support of a number of organizations is gratefully acknowledged, especially AusAID, the Australian Agency for International Development, which was the primary funding body. Support was also provided by the School of Accounting and Business Information Systems at the Australian National University (ANU) and by the Bangladesh Public Administration Training Centre (BPATC).

We also acknowledge the students, faculty and management of BPATC who directly and indirectly supported the development and improvement of this edition. Also thanks to our friends and peers who agreed to be models for the many photographs we needed to enhance the understanding of the context. We are grateful for the contributions of the many researchers in the area whose work provided the basis of our work. Thanks to the many authors and organisations who have proved explicit permission to use their concepts, diagrams, photos and case studies in this book. We are particularly grateful to the Australian Government Information Management Office (AGIMO), which has provided us with support and permission to use some of its well-researched concepts and best practices.

Many individuals have provided willing assistance. The following individuals have made major contributions to the indicated chapters:

Dr Eric Kordt — Chapter 5
Adam Purtel — Chapters 6 and 8
David Avision — Chapter 9
Clive Rossiter — Chapter 12 and Chapter 17
Dr Idris Sulaiman — Green IT portion of Chapter 16

We also acknowledge others who provided their valuable support in different stages of development of this book in different ways. They are: Professor Neil Fargher, Deborah Veness, Tom Sear, Dora Gava, Rafiqul Islam Rowly, Ian Hirst, Dr Zillur Rahman, Afsana Hasan, Mehdi Hussain, Mallika Robinson, Bashir Hussain and our main copy editor Adam LeBroq. Special thanks to Kurt Barnett for the layout and initial cover design of the first printing of the book.

Finally, we extend our heartfelt thanks to Dr Dan Remenyi and his team from Academic Conferences & Publishing International (API) who came forward to publish this book and thus make it available for wider audiences across the world. We have received frequent requests for the book over the last few years and we hope this publication will fulfil the needs of readers and will benefit wider communities and countries, especially those who are on the other side of the digital divide.

PART I
INTRODUCTION

Part 1 - Introduction

One of the most important and challenging issues for eGovernment is establishing a clear concept, scope and motivation for its implementers. Part I addresses this issue with an analytical examination of eGovernment, focussing on the context of developing countries. It clarifies popular misconceptions and debates on eGovernment and explores the concept of a conducive knowledge atmosphere, which motivates readers and managers to recognise their potential in their organisations. Part I also describes the knowledge needed to be a successful manager of eGovernment. The two chapters in Part I cover the following:

Chapter 1, Introduction, ascertains the need and motivation for eGovernment in the digital world and also in the context of developing countries. It covers related terms and concepts on information systems, information technology and eGovernment components, and analyses the differences between traditional and ICT-based contemporary governments. The chapter demonstrates how information technology increases the value of a country's overall economy and the productivity of government organisations and shows both successful and failed information technology case studies.

Chapter 2, eGovernment, outlines the boundaries and scope of eGovernment with examples of its various applications, components and stages. It also describes the evolution and current status of eGovernment around the world with some examples of newer trends and developments. It further clarifies the application and relevance of eGovernment in the developing country context.

CHAPTER 1
Value of ICT and eGovernment

Learning Objectives

After studying this chapter, you will be able to:

- Explain the need for eGovernment in the digital world
- Define Information Systems, Information Technology, and eGovernment components
- Explain the difference between traditional and ICT-based modern governments
- Explain the value that information technology brings to economics, organizations, and citizens
- Explain the importance of eGovernment for least developed and developing countries
- Analyze cases of success and failure with information technology, and
- Describe the knowledge needed to be a successful eGovernment manager.

The Digital Citizen

(Photo credit: A. Imran)

Reyafet was born in Dhaka, Bangladesh, a time when personal computers emerged as a magic box with multipurpose functions, when Microsoft rolled over to its more user friendly Windows 3.0 version, and when mobile phones were about to become a common aspect of everyday life. He is now 21, a registered elector, and works in a bank and uses government services. Refayet expects that he should be able to deal with the government in the same ways he deals with many private organizations - electronically!

1.1 eGovernment in the Digital Age

Governments in the **digital age**[1] are interacting with a different kind of consumer - the **eCitizen** or **digital citizen**. Global Internet usage has grown dramatically (by 741% from 2000 to 2014[2]), and the number of current mobile subscribers exceeds 6 billion (equivalent to 87% of world's population)[3]. Social networking has become a global phenomenon making no boundary for digital reach. Thus, modern citizens, who have the habit of banking and buying tickets online, naturally expect similar services from their government. The changing pattern of citizens' expectations accompanying technological advances means that political leaders can no longer ignore information technology (IT) and eGovernment in their political agenda.

Rapidly changing technology and its increasing availability mean that government services can be modernized. For example, registering a business name that once involved a number of visits to the registration office for paper collection and submission can now be completed in a few minutes from the comfort of home. There are many examples that show how eGovernment can benefit customers and citizens by not only improving service delivery through **service transformation** but also indirectly by helping the country's overall economy and to achieve more productive, efficient and accountable management systems.

The hardware and software revolution that enabled mobile devices such as smart phones and tablets to operate has created new opportunities for more flexible and interactive engagement with governments.

[1] The digital age refers to the current age in which there is heavy reliance on digital devices and networks for information flow and economic and social activity.
[2] See http://www.internetworldstats.com/stats.htm
[3] See http://mobiforge.com/research-analysis/stats

(Photo credit: A. Imran)

For public sector organizations, eGovernment offers a number of potential **benefits**, such as increasing efficiency and effectiveness, and promoting transparent processes. Citizens can use **improved services** and can more easily provide feedback to their government and engage in decision making through online participation. eGovernment aims to achieve greater efficiency, **not a reduced workforce**. Instead, it aims to provide better tools to an existing workforce to provide better services. A recent trend is to speak of **citizen-centric** governments, which means governments that prioritize their citizens' needs and design their services accordingly.

However, for government institutions of different countries, transforming to eGovernment has never been easy or free from **challenges**. It is a massive task at many levels, and requires policy change, administrative reform, change management, and so on. Some countries respond to the challenges quickly, while some still struggle. Economic and **digital divides** have created a sharp difference between the countries that are the "haves" compared with those that are the "have nots". While the developed world reaps the benefits of information technology for economic productivity, many developing countries have fallen behind. For developing countries, using information technology is necessary to keep pace with the rest of the world in progress and prosperity.

1.2 Information Technology (IT), Information Communication Technology (ICT) and Information System (IS)

Information Technology (IT) refers to all the hardware and software that supports the "information systems" that a firm needs to use in order to achieve its business objectives (Laudon & Laudon, 2007).

Information Communication Technology (ICT) is a term used interchangeably with IT, but which has a wider meaning because it explicitly includes communications technology and networks. Henceforth in this book, we mostly use the term ICT rather than IT. The term ICT is more widely used in developing countries.

An Information System (IS) is the set of interrelated components involving collection, processing, storing, and distribution of data that communicate information, support decision making, and help managers and workers analyze problems, visualize complex subjects, and create new products.

People often struggle to explain information systems and their domain. For example, an eGovernment system does not comprise ICT alone, instead it includes many other essential elements of the total information system. ICT is only a portion of the information system's whole, which comprises hardware, software, and communication equipment (Figure 1.1).

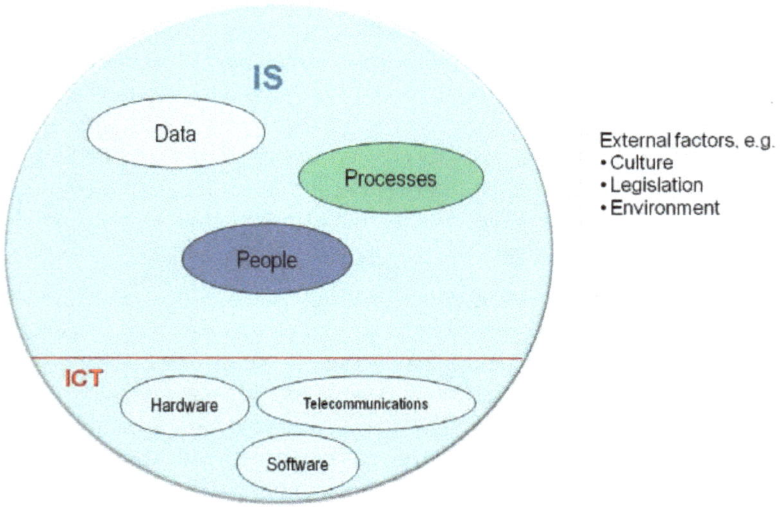

Figure 1.1. Elements of information systems (IS)

The other important elements of information systems include data, processes, and people. Further, an information system cannot function in isolation without external influences such as culture, legislation, environment, and so on that operate at different levels (e.g., organizational, national). Therefore, knowledge of all the elements of information systems is essential to understand any information system, which includes those in an eGovernment.

1.3 The Paradigm Shift

The 21st century's ICT revolution is also creating a "knowledge-based society" and "knowledge-based economy", which governments, organizations, and individuals around the world are increasingly recognizing the importance and value of. eGovernment has emerged as one of the most powerful and important means to drive the **transition toward a knowledge-based society and knowledge-based economy**.

The major ingredient and the by-product of a knowledge-based society is "knowledge". Knowledge is essentially processed "information" that originates from thousands of items of raw "data" that come from various sources (Figure 1.2). Information is an intermediary stage of knowledge and can be considered to be processed or value-added data.

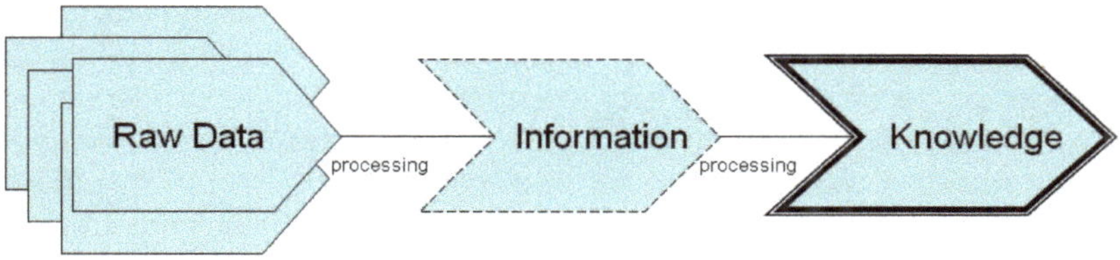

Figure 1.2. Knowledge processed from information and raw data

In the 21st century, knowledge and information are critical organizational and strategic assets, and can be regarded as the life blood of an enterprise. The more up-to-date and accurate the information and knowledge is, the greater the advantage one possesses. Thus, an organization's survival in the 21st century largely depends on their ability to process and capture information, transform it into usable knowledge, and disseminate it efficiently in the organizational chain. Appreciating the value of this vital commodity (knowledge), most developed countries are redesigning their strategies to use this important strategic resource more effectively. For example, the renaming of an Australian ministry to the "Ministry of Broadband, Communications, and the Digital Economy" emphasizes the close connection of ICTs and the knowledge-based economy. Also, the Australian Government's one billion dollar Digital Education Revolution aims to create a sustainable knowledge-based society. Internationally, the United Nations, the European Union, and the African Union run several initiatives, which reiterate the importance of knowledge societies in shaping the future.

If we critically examine the role and job of public servants, we find it is predominantly knowledge work. As such, **public servants are knowledge workers**. This term was introduced by Peter Drucker (1959), and implies well-educated professionals who create, modify, and synthesize knowledge to create value for their organizations (Jessup & Valacich, 2006). At the heart of all knowledge work activity is "productivity" - that is, the ability to create business value at the lowest cost. From this, the question of what contributes to productivity arises. For public service organizations, "efficiency" and "effectiveness" typically contribute to productivity (where efficiency means achieving the most output from a given input, and effectiveness means pursuing the goal or task that is appropriate for the given situation). The next question is how this knowledge work can be accomplished effectively. This is the role of ICT-driven smart "information systems", which play a vital role in the activities of knowledge work. The business environment is now much more volatile than in the past. A short timeframe can make the difference between profit and loss on the stock market. As such, smart information systems can provide a competitive advantage.

In the colonial era, governments used a strict hierarchical organizational model to deliver public services and to discharge public policies. Senior officials fulfilled their responsibilities by ordering staff to accomplish routine tasks under certain work restrictions. Today, in the complex and rapidly changing 21st century society, the traditional hierarchical model of government does not meet citizen's demands. While the hierarchical model still exists, its influence and effectiveness are gradually fading. Governments who still use this model are constantly being challenged by the need to solve ever more complex problems. Modern governments are thus gradually **shifting to a more people-centric and eGovernment-friendly organizational model** to produce public value. Newer organizations have developed distinct characteristics, which include being more result oriented, decentralized, and competitive, to survive in today's economy (Table 1.1).

Table 1.1. Characteristics of old and new organizations (adapted from Kernaghan, Marson & Borins, 2000)

Old colonial organizations	New organizations (eGovernment friendly)
Strictly hierarchical	Flat and collaborative
All power resides at the top	Distributed power & responsibilities
Rule-centered work processes	People-centered work processes
Top down/one-way information flow	Multidirectional information flow
More status quo oriented	More result oriented
Centralized structure	Decentralized structure
Teams work within individual departments, silos	Teams work collaboratively across departmental boundaries

Figure 1.3 compares the more traditional organization structure and a new organizational model (adapted from Post & Anderson, 2003, p. 826).

In the traditional model, lower-level managers deal with customers and citizens, and collect basic data. Middle-level managers analyze the data, create reports, and offer suggestions. In newer models, many organizations have moved toward a more decentralized form of management that removes the middle layers of management and replaces them with smaller teams.

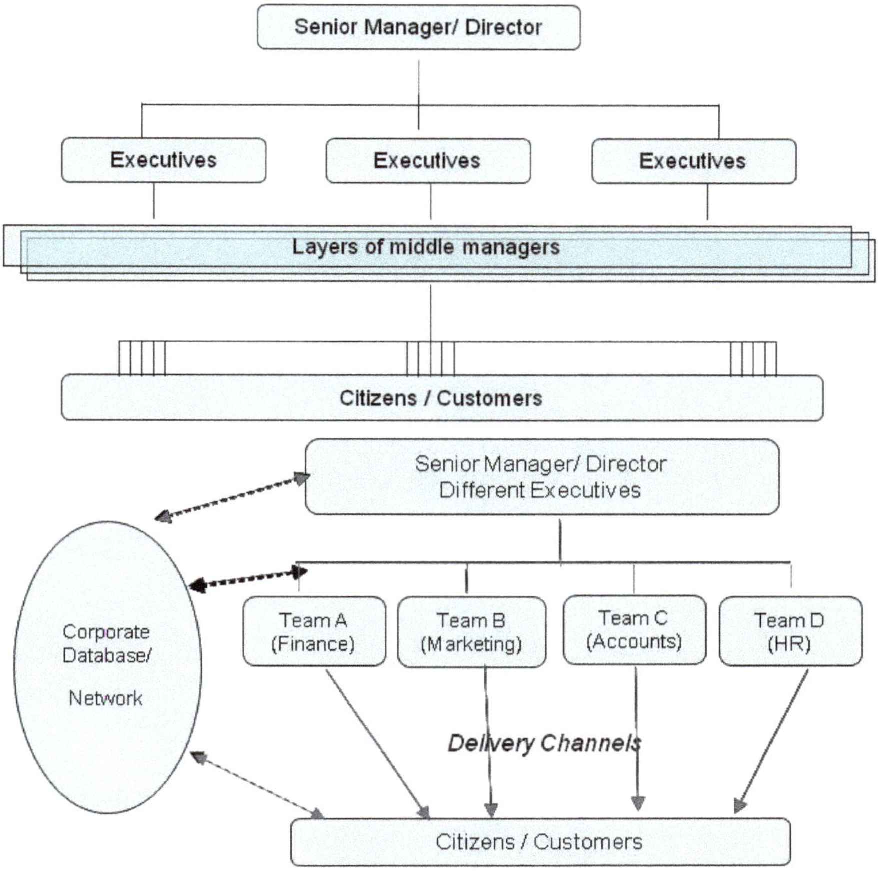

Figure 1.3. Traditional hierarchical structure vs. modern team-based approach

Information sharing, which occurs when teams communicate directly and share data across departments, becomes crucial in this environment. New models offer more eGovernment- friendly environments suitable for ICT-based business processes. eGovernment has opened up opportunities to examine the core function of processes and how they can be improved, such as reducing timelines and eliminating intermediaries where possible, with the aim of achieving greater effectiveness and efficiency.

Accordingly, public sector organizations' focus has shifted toward adding value through restructuring organizations to make them computer friendly, and toward implementing more appropriate procedures compatible with an ICT environment. This process involves reducing layers of traditional management, defining job roles and categories, creating teams, reengineering business processes, and amending rules and regulations.

The traditional government organizations are paper intensive and paper dependent. Official correspondence between sender and receiver involves a considerable amount of time and physical intervention. In an electronic world, using more secure and reliable means, this can be done in minutes. The time and effort wasted in traditional methods can be easily avoided through ICT-based processes. Thus, the eGovernment environment involves a transition in work patterns **transitioning from a traditional paper-based system to an electronic one.**

(Photo source: Imran, Gregor, & Turner, 2008)

1.4 Economic Value of ICT

The value of ICT-related initiatives is often difficult to measure because it cannot be determined by traditional cash flow analyses or by norms of economic rationality (Avgerou & Rovere, 2003).

In the past, tons of minerals or crops were the primary measure for the value of output. However, in today's economy, the sense of value generation has many dimensions such as product quality, timeliness, customization, convenience, variety, and so on. There has been a long debate about whether computers contribute to productivity growth. However, a number of studies show significant benefit from ICT adoption in an eGovernment framework (NOIE, 2003; OECD, 2003). Today, ICTs' widespread effects and linkages with the economy and society are well recognized. Research shows that ICT contributes to productivity growth if used in the right way and managed effectively (Litan & Rivlin, 2001; Pilat & Lee, 2001). Figure 1.4 shows the contribution of ICT to GDP growth among several OECD countries.

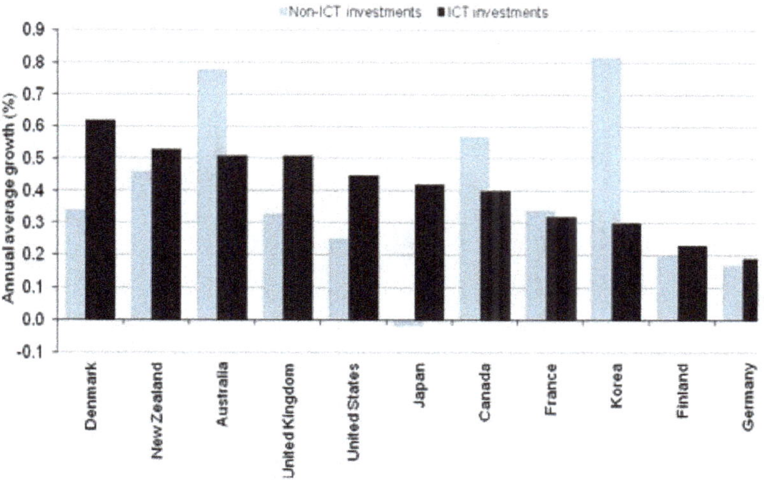

Figure 1.4. Contributions of ICT investment to GDP growth, 2000-09 (based on OECD Productivity Data, June, 2011[4]

1.5 Nature of Public Sector Organizations

The nature and characteristics of public sector organizations significantly differ from that of private organizations, both in developed and developing countries. This difference occurs primarily because of the differences in mission, structure, and statute of the two types of organizations. Unlike private organizations, the consumers of public service organizations (i.e., the citizens) cannot switch to a different service delivery organization. Hence, public service organizations are not pressured by competition to improve their services and business. Again, while earning profit is likely to be the key driver for private organizations, it could be entirely different for public sector organizations. For example, providing social welfare services to citizens does not necessarily aim to generate revenue. The public sector is an organ of the state - its rules and regulations are strictly bound, and change may require parliamentary intervention. Often there is a little scope for innovation from employees, where work patterns are often routine and prescribed. Another difference is that public sector service delivery is targeted toward a market larger than that of private organizations (Bozeman & Bretschneider, 1986; Bretschneider, 1990).

These characteristics add to the unique culture and constraints of least developed countries (LDCs). For example, most LDCs have inherited their public sector culture from the colonial era, which had a strict hierarchical structure and complex multilevel channels of bureaucracy, and where the relationship with citizens was mostly to govern and to be governed (Higgo, 2003). The old business proc-

---

[4] See OECD (2011), The Future of the Internet economy. A statistical profile. June 2011 update, OECD, Paris [http://www.oecd.org/internet/ieconomy/40827598.pdf]

ess is highly bureaucratic and too paper dependent. Even the term "public servant" in some LDCs appears to be taboo and unacceptable to government officials, who take their job as a privilege rather than as bounded with obligation to the citizens or the country.

A paper-intensive office environment (Photo credit A. Imran)

1.6 Value of ICT for Public Sector Organizations

Productivity growth does not come from working harder. Rather, it comes from **working smarter**, which implies **adopting new technologies and new techniques** for production (Brynjolfsson & Hitt, 1998).

ICT's impact is not immediate in nature like many other more tangible business resources and activities. Rather, ICT can require substantial time to see an effect, and often the results might appear in the form of a social change at the cost of some heavy initial investments (Weill & Ross, 2004; Williams & Williams, 2007). Furthermore, it is difficult to predict the precise nature of this impact in a complex network of political and organizational processes, especially in any government structure (Stanforth, 2006). By nature, the public sector is traditionally "reactive" rather than "proactive". eGovernment provides an opportunity to shift from this position to be more competitive in the modern world.

The key difference in public sector ICT value is that, while the private sector is primarily focused on creating private value, the public sector is concerned with creating public value (Moore, 1995). For example, a private firm offers goods and services in exchange for money, whereas a government department provides services, usually at no cost to the recipient (Donnelly, 1999). Thus, it is often argued that a public servant never sells the product rather they sell the benefits.

In summary, the overall public value of ICT can be grouped into four categories, which Liu, Derzsi, Raus, & Kipp (2008, p.90) outline as (Figure 1.5):

- **Financial value** implies impact on current or anticipated income, asset values, liabilities, entitlements, and other aspects of wealth or risks to any of the above.
- **Social value** implies impact on society as a whole or community relationships, social mobility, status, and identity. Social and psychological returns include increased social status, relationships, or opportunities; increased safety, trust in government, and economic well-being.
- **Operational (Foundational) value** implies impact in realized operations and processes and in laying the groundwork for future initiatives.
- **Strategic (Political) value** implies impact on personal or corporate influence on government actions or policy, on role in political affairs, or influence on political parties or prospects for current of future public office, including impacts on political advantage or opportunities, goals, resources for innovation or planning.

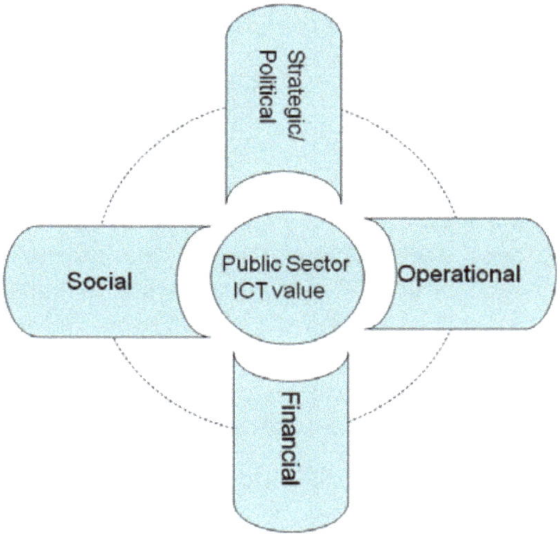

Figure 1.5. Public value of ICT

Access to quality and timely information is essential for a government's work. If an information network is not transparent and closed, decisions in the organization are likely to be based on misinformation or poor analysis, which can lead to severe consequences for the country (Schrage, 2003). According to Fountain (2001), technology has three roles to play in government: (1) to serve as a tool for managers for their communication, coordination, and work process; (2) to provide infrastructure to carry out program and administrative operations; and (3) to serve as a catalyst for organizational change to improve efficiency and productivity.

The major advantages of eGovernment can be listed as:

- Overall efficiency gains and cost reduction for the government
- Faster and quality service delivery to citizens

- Increased transparency and accountability
- Reduced corruption
- Reduced workload for staff
- Improved management of government resources
- Increased service capability
- Improvement in quality of decision making
- Simple and more integrated processes
- Less double handling and avoidance of human error
- Improved project management
- Avoid redundancy by using systems developed by other agencies, and
- Better diffusion and promotion of ICT in other sectors of the society.

1.6.1 Some real life examples

The following examples from employees of the Australian Public Service describe typical benefits that ICT provides in their day-to-day work. These employees were originally from developing countries, and thus were better able to appreciate ICT's value.

Time saving

> *ICT plays a strategic role in my department's output as it enables analysis of vast amounts of information in a short time. Most of the information storage, communication, business process and output delivery has become virtually paperless nowadays. One simple example of paperless work is a "Leave Application" through software, an employee simply needs to enter the leave dates and the leave reasons (from the pull down button) and directly sends that to his/her superior. The superior in turn can approve the application electronically. No one needs to fill out any paper and the whole process takes only a few minutes.*
>
> *- AN ECONOMIC ANALYST, DEPARTMENT OF THE AUSTRALIAN FEDERAL GOVERNMENT*

Timely response and inter departmental cooperation

> *Recently I received a call from the minister's office asking for some information that the Minister needed before going into the Chamber for Question Time. Question Time is the most important moment for a Minister when he/she faces unnoticed and unexpected questions from Opposition members on any issues in the Parliament, which is broadcast live across the country. As a result, we always remain alert to provide the most up-to-date information on Australian industry related issues. I had only a few minutes to prepare the advice. This advice needs to be succinct, polished and easy to understand. Within a few minutes with some help in gathering and retrieving the correct information from a few other sister organizations, I was able to email my advice direct to the Minister before he went onto the House floor. This would not have been possible without access to IT facilities*

- A SENIOR POLICY ADVISER TO THE AUSTRALIAN INDUSTRY MINISTER

Better management and control

I work in a large research organization for the government. We use IT in many different ways. Firstly, the organization has implemented SAP work-organization where all aspects of personnel and financial management are online. So matters such as pay, expenses, attendance, and leave are all recorded through IT. We also use IT for video conferencing as the organization has a number of sites spread all across Australia. This has reduced the need for travel and saved money and time. Personally, I have benefited most from the availability of journals on-line. This enables one to keep up with the relevant publications without having to make a regular trip to the library. This has enabled me to use the time to design and think about other aspects of my work.

- A SENIOR SCIENTIST, CSIRO

Cutting age solutions

We use SAP, which is a cutting edge business software package designed by a German-based software company and used by most of the Australian Federal Departments for Human resource, Financial Transactions, Inventory, Project Management and other day to day tasks. It has significantly benefitted the government and citizens. The SAP system helps to track and record financial transactions. The Department benefits through the availability of "real time" information, a flexible approach to departmental reporting, an ability to plan separately from budgeting and compare on-line and planning and monitoring across the life of the project, over several years. This software provides excellent controls around the department's financial transactions where any breach and fraud can be controlled.

- A PUBLIC SERVANT IN AUSTRALIAN FEDERAL GOVERNMENT

1.6.2 Success and Failure Cases with ICT

Many countries perform well on many indices of ICT use and eCommerce readiness. Yet all industries and enterprises are not at the same level. What distinguishes the winners? Talking about successful and failed case studies is useful because it helps determine the key factors in achieving success. What we want to understand is how to be "winners" and how to avoid outright failures. There is considerable evidence to show that **effectively managing ICT** can improve organizational performance and productivity regardless of the size of an organization or the industry in which it operates (Gregor, Fernandez, Holtham, Martin, Vitale, Stern & Pratt 2005). Managing ICT effectively means that managers in the organization are ICT aware. That is, they:

- Are knowledgeable about the opportunities that ICT can bring

- Understand that investments in ICT should be aimed at gaining clear and identifiable benefits for the organization, and
- Institute appropriate governance procedures in planning for ICT, managing ICT projects, and monitoring, controlling, and reviewing the use of ICT resources across their organization.

On the other hand, poor ICT management has led to some spectacular failures with ICT, which is often associated with the loss of large amounts of money and resources.

Table 1.2 shows one example: the case of the Sydney Water Board in Australia. It is believed that such a large loss in a private company could have brought about the end of the company. The auditor's review of the customer billing system at Sydney Water, which was developed under contract by a reputed firm, noted problems with ICT governance. They concluded that:

- The Sydney Water Board did not oversee the project properly.
- The responsibilities of the project-steering committee were not clearly defined.
- A proper analysis of the project beforehand could have stopped the project before it began.
- Contract administration was deficient. Much of the risk was transferred away from PricewaterhouseCoopers back to Sydney Water.

Table 1.2. The case of a failed project at Sydney Water (Avison, Gregor, & Wilson, 2006)

Organizational Characteristics	Observation
IT Background	Mixed success over some years
Revenue	AU$ 1.4 billion (2002)
IT Application	Customer information & billing
Project Costs	Original budget: AU$ 38.2 million
	Final estimate: AU$ 135.i million
Timeline	2000 – contract began
Decision	2002 – project scrapped

This text provides ICT managers with knowledge in key areas so that they can avoid ICT disasters and instead use ICT successfully.

An example of a successful eGovernment project is the Voter ID project in Bangladesh (Grönlund & Islam, 2010). In 2008, there was a need for a reliable database of voters for elections. The result was the largest biometric database in the world with the entire voting population of 80 million people registered. Key success factors identified are that there was:

- A controlled environment

- A highly structured management system, and
- A concrete and realistic roadmap.

1.7 Challenges for IT Management

For government institutions in many countries, transforming to eGovernment has not been easy or free from challenges. It is important to consider some of the challenges and difficulties that need to be overcome in managing ICT in organizations. These challenges include the following (Frenzel & Frenzel, 2004):

- Top-level organizational executives may have little understanding of, and little interest in, ICT.
- Managers need some knowledge of both ICT and the management skills needed for administration and managing people.
- The organization may be reluctant to resource ICT properly.
- The ICT may be critical to an organization's operations and reliability is essential, even if the ICT is not well resourced.
- ICT systems are often large and complex, which means that they are difficult to develop, install, and maintain.
- Globalization of ICT systems (e.g., Internet applications) means that the systems can have many links over a large geographic area, which creates more complexity.
- Rapid technological change in software and hardware means that it can be difficult to keep pace.
- Staff often have difficulty expressing their requirements for new systems because they may lack knowledge of what is possible and what can be achieved.
- People, in general, tend to resist change, and they may resist the changes brought about through ICT systems because they fear, for example, unknown things or a loss of power.

1.8 What Public Sector Managers need to know about eGovernment

Given the above challenges, it is important for all executives and managers who have any responsibility for ICT in their organizations to have knowledge that will enable them to ensure that ICT is used effectively and to deal with challenges. Thus, they should have knowledge of the following topics:

- ICT Governance
- Strategic planning for ICT
- Preparing business cases & evaluating returns
- Managing and controlling ICT projects
- Technology and industry trends
- Current application software packages
- ICT operational (service) management
- Managing human resources

- Change management, and
- The security of systems.

This book covers each of these topics in sequence.

"ICT is too important to leave to ICT people" (*Art by Rubayat Habib, 2012*)

Chapter Highlights

- Governments in the digital age interact with digital citizens because of the huge growth of the internet and mobile devices.
- The changing pattern of citizens' expectations accompanying technological advances means that political leaders can no longer ignore ICT and eGovernment in their political agenda.
- The 21st century's ICT revolution is creating a "knowledge-based society" and "knowledge-based economy".
- In complex and rapidly changing 21st century societies, the traditional, hierarchical model of government does not meet citizens' demands.
- The value of ICT-related initiatives is often difficult to measure because it cannot be determined by traditional cash flow analyses or by norms of economic rationality.
- The nature and characteristics of public sector organizations significantly differ from that of private organizations, both in developed or developing countries, primarily because of the differences in mission, structure, and statute of the two types of organizations.
- Productivity growth does not come from working harder; rather, it comes from working smarter, which means adopting new technologies and new techniques for production.
- The overall public benefits of ICT can be grouped into four categories; operational, financial, strategic, and social.
- There is considerable evidence to show that the effective ICT management can improve organizational performance and productivity regardless of the size of an organization or the industry in which it operates.
- It is important for all executives and managers who have any responsibility for ICT in their organizations to have knowledge that will enable them to both ensure that ICT is used effectively and to deal with challenges.

Review Questions

1. How can eGovernment increase productivity in government organizations?
2. List the benefits of eGovernment.
3. What is the definition of a "knowledge worker"?
4. What is the relationship between a "knowledge based society" and eGovernment?
5. What are the major differences between bureaucratic and post-bureaucratic (eGov friendly) organizations?
6. What is the difference between information technology and information systems?
7. What are the major differences between a public and private organization?

Discussion Questions

1. The value of ICT related initiatives is often difficult to measure - why?
2. Who will benefit most from eGovernment in a least developed country? Will benefits be gained more by some stakeholder groups than others?
3. What benefits will current public officers gain from new eGovernment systems? Could they feel threatened in some cases? Why?
4. What do you think are the most important factors for success with IT projects in a public sector organization? Think of an example in your own organization. Why did it work?

Exercises

1. Research the case studies of Sydney Water and the Bangladesh Voter ID project.
2. Do you agree with the factors identified as major contributions to failure at Sydney Water?
3. What other factors may have contributed to success in the Bangladesh Voter ID card project (not mentioned in the case study)?

References

Avgerou, C., & Rovere, R. (Eds.). (2003). Information Systems and the Economics of Innovation. Cheltenham: Edward Elgar.

Avison, D., Gregor, S., & Wilson, D. (2006). Managerial IT Unconsciousness. Communications of the ACM, 49(7), 88-93

Bozeman, B., & Bretschneider, S. (1986). Public Management Information Systems: Theory and Prescription. Public Administration Review, 46(Special Issue), 475 - 487.

Bretschneider, S. (1990). Management Information Systems in Public and Private Organizations: An Empirical Test. Public Administration Review, 50, 536 - 544.

Brynjolfsson, E., & Hitt, L. M. (1998). Beyond the Productivity Paradox. Communications of the ACM, 41(8), 49-55.

Donnelly, M. (1999). Making the Difference: Quality Strategy in the Public Sector. Managing Service Quality, 9(1), 47-52.

Drucker, P. (1959) The Landmarks of Tomorrow. New York: Harper & Row.

Fountain, J. E. (2001). Building the Virtual State: Information Technology and Institutional Change. Washington DC: Brookings Institution.

Frenzel, C. W., & Frenzel, J. (2004). Management of Information Technology (4th ed.). Cambridge, MA.

Gregor, S., Fernandez, W., Holtham, D., Martin, M., Stern, S., Vitale, M. and Pratt, G. (2005). Adding Value from ICT: Key Management Strategies. Department of Communications Information Technology and the Arts, Commonwealth of Australia.

Grönlund, Å., & Islam, Y. M. (2010). A mobile e-learning environment for developing countries: The Bangladesh Virtual Interactive Classroom. Information Technology for Development, 16(4), 244-259.

Higgo, H. A. (2003). Implementing an Information System in a Large LDC Bureaucracy: The Case of the Sudanese Ministry of Finance. The Electronic Journal on Information Systems in Developing Countries, 14(3), 1-13.

Jessup, L., & Valacich, J. (2006). Information Systems Today: Why IS matters. New Jersey: Prentice Hall.

Kernaghan, K., Marson, B., & Borins, S. (2000). The New Public Organization (Vol. 24). Toronto: The Institute of Public Administration of Canada.

Laudon, K., & Laudon, J. (2007). Management Information Systems: Managing the Digital Firm Global (11th ed.): Pearson Education.

Litan, R. E., & Rivlin, A. M. (2001). Projecting the Economic Impact of the Internet. American Economic Review, 91(2), 313-417.

Liu, J., Derzsi, Z., Raus, M., & Kipp, A. (2008). eGovernment Project Evaluation: An Integrated Framework. In M. Wimmer, H. Scholl & E. Ferro (Eds.), Electronic Government (Vol. 5184, pp. 85-97): Springer Berlin Heidelberg.

Moore, M. H. (1995). Creating public value: Strategic management in government: Cambridge, MA: Harvard University Press.

NOIE. (2003). EGovernment Benefits Study; Agency Case Studies. Canberra: National Office for the Information Economy, Commonwealth of Australia.

OECD. (2003). The EGovernment Imperative. Retrieved July 11, 2006, from http://www.oecd.org/gov/budgeting/43496369.pdf

Pilat, D., & Lee, F. C. (2001). Productivity Growth in ICT-producing and ICT-using Industries: A Source of Growth Differentials in the OECD? Paris: OECD.

Schrage, M. (2003). Perfect Information and Perverse Incentives: Costs and Consequences of Transformation and Transparency. SSP Working Paper. MIT. Retrieved from http://web.mit.edu/ssp/publications/working_papers/wp03-1.pdf

Stanforth, C. (2006). Using Actor-Network Theory to Analyze EGovernment Implementation in Developing Countries. Information Technologies and International Development, 3(3), 35-60.

Weill, P., & Ross, J. W. (2004). IT Governance: How Top Performers Manage IT Decision Rights for Superior Results: Harvard Business Press.

Williams, M. D., & Williams, J. (2007). A Change Management Approach to Evaluating ICT Investment Initiatives. Journal of Enterprise Information Management, 20(1), 32-50.

CHAPTER 2
eGovernment and its Evolution

Learning Objectives

After studying this chapter, you will be able to:

- Understand the application of ICT in government
- Explain the various components and stages of eGovernment
- Understand the relevance and application of eGovernment in the least developed and in developing countries
- Describe the evolution and current status of eGovernment around the world, and
- Describe new trends in eGovernment

ICT - The Life Line of a Modern Organization

(Photo credit: Marcel Mooij. Shutterstock.com)

ICT can be applied everywhere in government, from a simple gate-pass entry to a range of complex automatic business processes, which can often involve a number of government agencies. These days, it would be hard to find an area where ICT is not used in modern government organizations. A few minutes of ICT network downtime can mean the total cessation of office work because most business processes and activities are heavily dependent on ICT.

The first use of ICT or computers in many offices occurred when the word processor replaced manual typewriters. Organizations, dealing with financial accounts and statistics, also used computers as the advancement of the calculator. All such uses of ICT in government for the purpose of achieving organizational goals are known as eGovernment.

2.1 Inside eGovernment

2.1.1 eGovernment vs eGovernance

The terms "eGovernment" and "eGovernance" are used synonymously in various forums, but there is an important distinction between the two. That is, "government is the institution itself, whereas governance is a broader concept" (Perumal, Norwawi, & Muniandy, 2008, p. 95), which comprises forms of governing, decision making, and responsibility. Table 2.1 shows the differences between eGovernment and eGovernance.

Table 2.1. Differences between eGovernment and eGovernance

eGovernment	eGovernance
System and/or machinery including hardware, software and processes	An intangible status or condition
The means and tools to achieve eGovernance	The overall outcome through the implementation of eGovernment
A narrower discipline that deals with the development of ICT-based business processes or online services for government	A broader concept that defines the nature and operation of the government, including relationships between public servants and the wider society

2.1.2 The eGovernment domain and its influence

eGovernment is typically categorized into three main spheres (Figure 2.1):

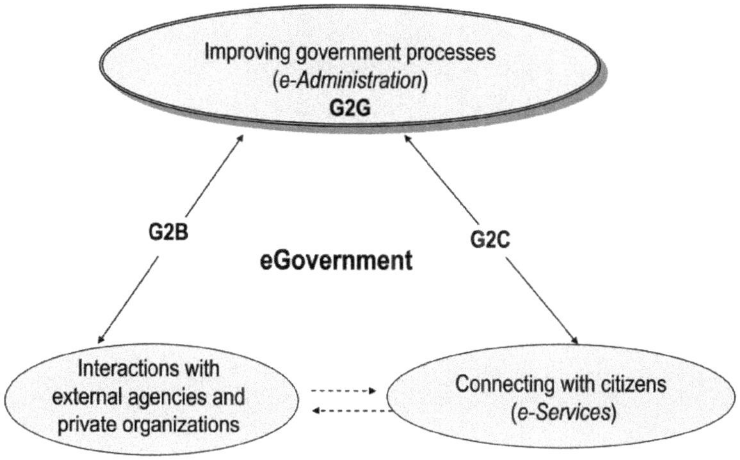

Figure 2.1. The spheres of public sector ICT (based on Backus, 2001; Heeks, 2004)

1. Government-to-government (G2G), where government agencies use ICT internally to interact in the organization or to interact with other governments agencies.
2. Government-to-business (G2B), where governments interact with businesses, agents, and other private organizations (e.g., when purchasing supplies).
3. Government-to-citizen (G2C), where governments engage with citizens by offering electronic services (eServices), such as information provision or online transactions.

There is still a **misconception that eGovernment** is about delivering government services to citizens via the Internet. This misconception can occur because this is often the main focus both in practice and in literature. In the academic world, Scholl (2005) calls it the "iceberg phenomenon" of eGovernment research. As he points out, most research, so far, is dedicated to the "above-surface phenomena"; that is, it focuses on G2C and G2B (Figure 2.2). These sections are the most visible occurrences and artefacts of eGovernment (e.g., government websites, and transactions between governments and private-sector businesses).

However, the majority of government activities take place in the other domains of eGovernment (mainly G2G); those that attend to internal effectiveness and efficiency (IEE). As Dawes (2002, p.1) points out, "While the citizen sees eGovernment from the public side of a website or email screen, the real work of eGovernment is on the other side, inside the government itself".

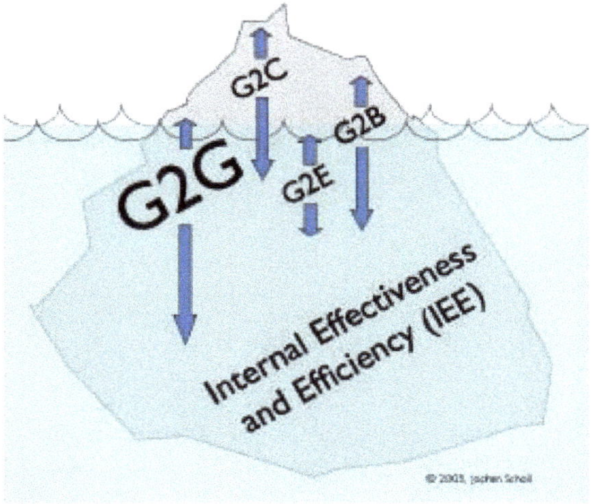

Figure 2.2. The iceberg phenomenon of eGovernment research (Scholl, 2005, p.7)

The G2G area of eGovernment has the highest potential impact in terms of productivity and change within government, yet often remains below the surface, and so attracts much less attention.

It is also often thought that all citizens need access to computers for eGovernment to succeed, which is not always true. For example, in Australia, only 35% of the population use the Internet to contact the government (AGIMO, 2011) despite 79% of its population being Internet users (ITU, 2012). Yet, Australia consistently maintains a leading position in world eGovernment rankings and in the public sector efficiency index, where the bulk of the internal government processes are driven by ICT.

G2G example - Criminal Justice Portal - Tennessee, USA

> *Law enforcement and officers of the court often have the onus of digging through various databases, conducting multiple searches, and accessing numerous systems to simply find the information and support they need to keep communities safe. The state of Tennessee partnered with NIC[1] to deploy a single resource for finding comprehensive law enforcement information on individuals that contains information from the state's driver's license, vehicle title and registration, orders of protection, wanted persons, and offender management system databases. Through integration and reengineering of process, the Law and Justice investigation was simplified into a one-stop viewing of information. Thus the portal provides:*
>
> - *Real-time means to disseminate data across the state.*

[1] NIC is the leading provider of official government portals in the US.

- *Economic efficiencies through a single portal and data sharing.*
- *Increased arrests and faster closure of criminal cases by uniting disparate databases.*

It turned into a level playing field for all law enforcement agencies across the state, regardless of population size or budget. After deploying the system, law enforcement agencies across the state have saved thousands of hours of staff time, which has created more time to enforce the law.

Source:http://www.egov.com/Insights/CaseStudies/Pages/TennesseeJustice.aspx (Republished with permissions of NICUSA, Inc.)

G2C example - Online claims and services, Centrelink, Australian Government

Centrelink provides health and welfare support services for Australian citizens and constantly strives for more reliable and robust services. The first online claim services in Centrelink were introduced for students claiming Youth Allowance and AusStudy in April 2005. Gradually, services were extended to Australian apprentices, claiming Maternity Payment and Family Tax Benefit.

Centrelink has also worked extensively behind the scenes to re-engineer the organization's business processes and revolutionize customer relationship management to support these online initiatives.

The development of online services involved the development of ICT architecture and technology, extensive user testing and customer consultation through user-centred design teams and customer research, service delivery through a combination of channels, strategic and targeted marketing of online claims and services, SMS and email reminders. Centrelink's online services brought a number of benefits to citizens: people can access their personal information online; correct inaccurate or out-of-date information, which ensures accuracy of their payments; lodge a new claim online without the help of a customer service; and, manage their Centrelink affairs without having to contact a customer service adviser - all from the comfort of their own home.

Source: Adapted from The Australian Government Information Management Office Archive, EGovernment Benefits Agency Case Studies, pp14–19, Available at: http://www.finance.gov.au/agimo-archive/__data/assets/file/0009/12330/ Casestudies.pdf

G2B example - eProcurement by Brazil's Federal Government

A government eProcurement system (COMPRASNET) was set up by the Secretariat of Logistics and Information Technology in the Brazilian Ministry of Planning, Budget and Management. The system is a web-based online procurement system used by more than 1000 federal government

procurement units. It enables online price quoting and reverse auction commodity purchases.

In this system, federal government organizations register their procurement needs (i.e., goods and services). The system automatically informs registered suppliers by email and the supplier may download the bidding documents.

The system was designed to reduce procurement costs and give more transparency to the process. Other objectives were to increase the number of government suppliers, which should also bring about cost reductions and better quality of goods and services acquired.

During the first two years of online use, Brazil's Federal Government is estimated to have saved up to US$1.5m. Besides this positive return on investment, the system enabled better and more transparent procurement, reduced participation costs for suppliers; increased competition among suppliers and most importantly reduced the red tape in the process. For example, while a normal procurement process takes more than two months, the online reverse auction process can be completed in less than 15 working days.

Source: Marcos Ozorio de Almeida (Author) at http://www.egov4dev.org/success/case/brazeproc.shtml.

2.2 Stages of eGovernment

The eGovernment development curve is traditionally described as commencing with initiation, followed by interaction, transaction, and finally integration (Baum & Maio, p. 828; UN, 2001). We extend these traditional stages by taking into consideration more recent developments, and the unique context of developing countries (Figure 2.3). For developing countries, the initiation stage largely involves the massive preparation required for this transformation. Before the technology adoption, preparation is an extremely important task for adopting eGovernment. This preparation includes training and developing readiness among the users, developing the appropriate mindset, organizational and procedural restructuring, and so on. In the initial stage, limited eGovernment occurs with one-way information dissemination by the organizations via static webpages.

In the interaction phase, exchange of information or services occurs with citizens through websites, where citizens can obtain information and resources from government databases and enquire about their needs and the services available.

In the transaction stage, citizens are able to perform financial transactions and have dealings with the government, such as paying government tax and bills, or obtaining social benefit schemes. At this stage, more sophisticated technological implementations that include secure payment gateways and reliable processing mechanisms are required.

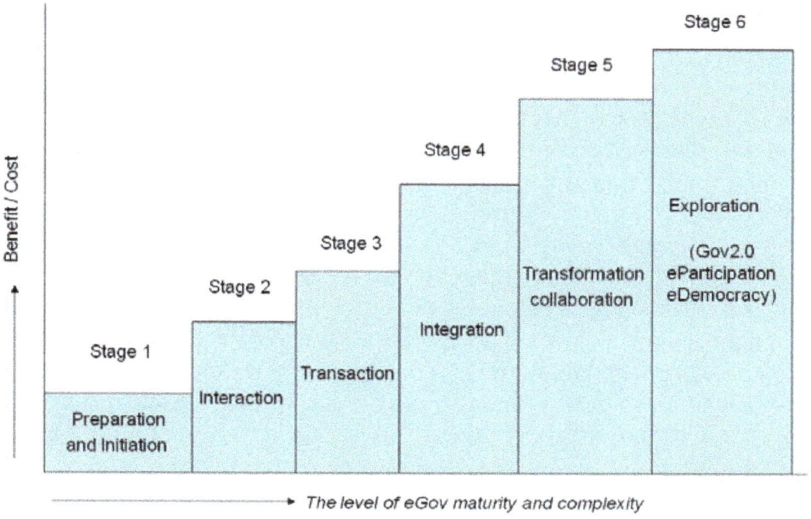

Figure 2.3. Stages of eGovernment

In the integration stage, eGovernment agencies start to integrate and collaborate between agencies to avoid duplication, and to work towards a one-stop contact point. When integration is completed, the real transformation in the organization begins, so as to accommodate the changes in organization structure, business processes, and the functioning of the government. While the investment cost and effort is high in the later stages, the benefits are also high because of the resultant effect of integration and automation.

At the final and most advanced stage (exploration), eGovernment reaches maturity. As organizations start reaping the benefits, they look for more innovative approaches to exploit new technology opportunities in order to provide government with a competitive edge over other organizations and countries. This is when new innovations and increased levels of citizen engagement are explored by using social media and other tools (Gov 2.0) in the form of eParticipation, eDemocracy, and so on.

> *"Technology is often not the challenge; it is the technological imagination that is in greatest scarcity"*
>
> *Malcolm Turnbull, (then) Shadow Minister for Communications and Broadband, Australia, 21 March 2012*

2.3 Relevance of eGovernment in the LDC Context

In many LDCs, universal access to the Internet and citizen-centric services may be unattainable. For example, in Cambodia, only 6% of households have Internet access (ITU, 2012). Yet there may still be scope for substantial improvements in the internal G2G processes, with significant potential outcomes in terms of improved productivity, efficiency, and transparency. Without personal access to the Internet, people can receive the benefit of eGovernment indirectly through the increased efficiency of automated government processes. For example, government to business (G2B) implementations have great potential to reduce costs through improved procurement practices and increased competition. G2G is the nerve center and engine of the government business process. Automation of G2G services brings substantial benefits in the form of increased productivity, efficiency, and transparency. Citizens ultimately enjoy the benefits, even without using the eGovernment services directly. So, in early stages of eGovernment, the primary concern should be to create an eGovernment environment in government organizations by automating selected business processes in the spectrum of G2G. This will make significant differences in terms of overall productivity and efficiency. A well-coordinated intergovernmental connection will gradually prepare the ground for smooth information access and greater service efficiency for customers and citizens at a later stage. This by no means implies that citizen access should be given less importance; rather, it should continue to progress in parallel as G2G structures become ready to deliver.

2.3.1 The use of ICT in LDCs' public sector

While the developed world is already dealing with advanced stages of this transformation through eParticipation, eDemocracy, and use of Web 2.0, only a few of the 49 LDCs are on the road to eGovernment progress. Others are lagging far behind, particularly those located in sub-Saharan Africa and South Asia. Despite initiatives at both international and national levels, eGovernment in LDCs is either failing or advancing at a slow pace. As Heeks (2003) reports, 35% of eGovernment initiatives in developing countries were total failures and 50% were partial failures. These outcomes occurred mainly because of the failure to recognize the complexity of each country's underlying issues (Avgerou, 2001; Heeks, 2002; Krishna & Madon, 2003; Nidumolu, Goodman, Vogel & Danowitz, 1996; Silva & Figueroa, 2002).

The public sector in an LDC is usually the largest user base of ICT systems and can play a leading role in ICT diffusion throughout the country. It can also exert influence through its policies and regulations (Nidumolu et al., 1996). Therefore, adopting ICT in government has the potential to bridge the divide between citizens and bureaucrats, which enhances mutual trust and lessens the digital divide (Bhatnagar, 2004; Curtin, Sommer, & Vis-Sommer, 2003).

Adopting and implementing eGovernment in LDCs is challenging because the process not only involves transferring machines, hardware, software, and skills, but also demands a change in attitudes and values (Heeks, 2002). Solutions designed for developed countries should not be applied to LDCs without adequate re-engineering because each country has a unique socio-cultural environment and different needs. However, despite the complexities that arise from different contextual conditions, a common strategy may be identified for adopting ICT in the administrations of many LDCs because they share some common characteristics.

2.3.2 eGovernment Process model

A study undertaken in Bangladesh, as an example of an LDC, showed that addressing knowledge and attitude issues among government officials was the key first step to take on the path to eGovernment. It was important to begin by addressing knowledge gaps and transforming attitudes, rather than by addressing other inhibitors, such as infrastructure and socio-economic conditions (Imran & Gregor, 2010). Uncovering "knowledge" as an underlying root cause of other problems is significant and addressing this issue led to an ICT-adoption process view of change. From a practitioner's perspective, the process model (Figure 2.4) can help educate agents to understand the dynamics of the adoption process and provide guidance on where and when to apply effort.

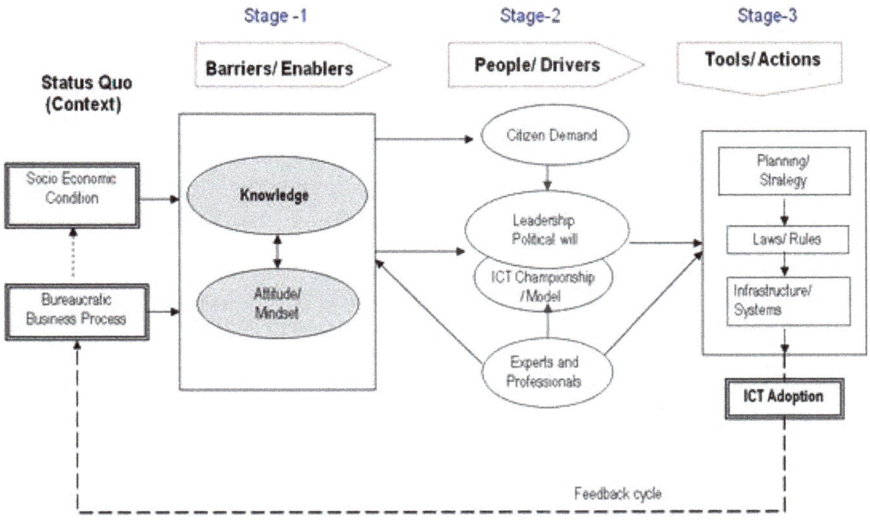

Figure 2.4. Process model for eGovernment adoption in LDCs (Imran & Gregor, 2012, p.339)

Bringing ICT innovation into the relatively rigid public sector organizations of a LDC is a cyclic process. The process begins with "ice-breaking" knowledge-building actions that are needed to initiate successful eGovernment. The study by Imran and Gregor (2010) showed that initially focusing on knowledge building has the potential to address other barriers, too, by creating an environment suitable for adopting eGovernment. Careful planning and innovation remain critical for success in eGovernment, but the research suggests that a knowledge-building process could avoid the failures that have been associated with more techno-centric approaches.

Further Reading

See Imran, A., & Gregor, S. (2012) *A Process Model for Successful EGovernment Adoption in the Least Developed Countries: A Case of Bangladesh. In F. Tan (Ed.), International Comparisons of Information Communication Technologies: Advancing Applications (pp.321-350)*

2.3.3 The way forward

Although ICT adoption brings potential for high returns and benefits, in order to derive these benefits government, employees and policy makers must understand what ICT can and cannot do; or, in other words, where efficiencies and productivity can realistically be achieved. Without such an understanding, a way forward is not likely to be realized. The following sub-sections, based on the findings from the Bangladesh case study (Imran, 2010), offer suggestions for the ICT- adoption process.

Planning and strategy

Understanding the problems and addressing them proactively through the right strategies is critical. The suggested long-term strategy for LDCs is built on four pillars that are aimed at directly tackling the barriers to adoption (Imran, Turner, & Gregor, 2008, p. 7). These pillars are:

- **Educate to innovate** - an education initiative, which starts with a program of training courses to immediately deliver needed skills and understanding to government employees. This is followed by a broader program to enhance the education and training opportunities for government employees, and then, eventually, all citizens, in order to prepare them for the information age.
- **Lead from the front** - a program of activities and approaches designed to generate visibility and commitment for eGovernment projects. The program is centered on key tactical eGovernment projects, which are identified and delivered by advocates within the government. These initial projects will inform future eGovernment activity, including reviews of policies, regulations, and laws that might be inhibiting the adoption and use of eGovernment.
- **Planning to succeed** - the ongoing management and review of the strategy and, more importantly, the careful planning and management of eGovernment projects across government.
- **Foundations for the future** - a series of information technology projects designed to invest in infrastructure for eGovernment operations by building on the energy and successes of the other programs.

Knowledge deployment and curriculum development

This strategy concentrates on knowledge development where the core of the problem lies. Education and training can positively influence and speed up the diffusion and awareness of ICT in government offices. The study also found a significant need for basic ICT skills and ICT awareness to become a component of the nation's education system and curriculum, and to prepare its citizens for 21st century conditions. "Digital literacy" should be a high priority in the education curriculum, which develops not only competencies and skills in ICT, but also the capacity to make judgments about the relevance of its use (Imran, 2008; OECD, 2001). Through skill development and effective and planned learning, people and decision makers can change their perceptions about ICT. This, in turn, could prevent resistance to change and accelerate ICT adoption. Education institutions and universities should devise industry-oriented curricula and training to meet the shortage of required human resources for ICT development.

Leadership with clear vision

Analysis of trends in developing countries shows that the success of eGovernment does not always depend on a long-term plan, but instead on good intentions, political will, and effective drive (Bhatnagar, 2004; Kumar & Best, 2006; UN, 2004; Wilson, 2004). A strong drive and willpower to accept the challenge for the greater interest is required - especially from leaders and people at the decision-making level. This is especially crucial for developing countries where notions of hierarchy are entrenched in the system, and where the leaders play the dominant role. Accordingly, the essence of the second strategic pillar (lead from the front) is to encourage and promote leadership and advocacy among the decision makers who are able to progress this innovation. ICT advocates at different levels can play a major role in promoting ICT, or can act as role models for others to follow. A conducive environment needs to be created, which can generate proactive, educated leaders with an informed long-term vision. These people are able to implement strategies for sustainable change (Sanford & Bhattacherjee, 2007). Top- level encouragement is also needed to create a risk-taking environment for innovators in the public service.

A top-down approach

In the LDCs, a majority of the population live below the poverty line, are deprived of education and knowledge, and are heavily dependent on government or their leaders (UN OHRLLS, 2012). Often, they tend to be good followers rather than exercising their own rights. As such, a top-down approach can be an effective way to bring about change.

In LDCs, one good government decision affects millions of people. These people would otherwise be difficult to reach through a bottom- up approach, which would also be a lengthy and time-consuming procedure. The vast majority of the population, who are mostly illiterate with almost no or little knowledge about ICT, will usually follow the trend of what the educated and the decision makers set for them.

eReadiness of the society

To achieve the greatest benefit from eGovernment, a society's eReadiness is important. Preparing a society to embrace the new way of doing business is an important institutional process that requires a re-orientation among citizens to be able to use government services electronically (Grant, 2005). "Readiness is the degree to which a community is prepared to participate in the Networked World", where the readiness of a country can be assessed broadly around the areas that are critical for ICT adoption, such as education, access, and affordability (CID, 2000, p. 1). Because the government is typically the largest employer in a country, it has the ability to create an information society hub through computerization of its agencies and services, which can gradually contribute to the expansion of a country-wide information society. Media and NGOs also can play a crucial role in preparing this eSociety. Through a knowledge and awareness program, interest should be generated among the population towards ICT-based business processes.

Injecting public sector value

Promoting and cultivating public sector values and good governance should be part of the institutional process as well. The idea that the role of government is to provide services for the public good is not a strong feature of existing cultures in LDCs. Although ICT or eGovernment has the potential to transform the public's negative image of government, in order to implement eGovernment effectively, the decades-old notion and perception of government services fi needs to be changed. Accordingly, necessary awareness needs to be raised in society. Successfully adopting eGovernment fi depends on changing the organization's values towards governance, accountability, and transparent processes before the technology adoption begins. Again, innovation needs to be compatible and workable with the existing values of the potential adopters. As Rogers (2003) stresses: "The adoption of an incompatible innovation often requires the prior adoption of a new value system which is a relatively slow process" (p. 15).

Massive administrative reform

A massive administrative reform, or crash program, is needed to remove the obstacles to the use of ICTs posed by redundant laws and regulations. A new public management (NPM) concept has to be introduced, and the existing one reformed with a disaggregation of public bureaucracies into agencies, which then fosters competition through contracting out services for greater output and cost savings (Reschenthaler & Thompson, 1996). Technology, structure, interpersonal relationships, and the goals of organizations must be carefully reexamined in light of the ICT-based business processes to create this new management culture. It is the government who needs to take the lead in establishing and reforming institutions, regulations, and structures incorporating the principles of ICT-based business processes.

Careful selection of business processes for innovation

Careful selection of business processes is of utmost importance, especially to begin with. An incorrect selection, or a failure, can discourage the launch of other initiatives. The cost of innovation versus profit is also an issue, despite the difficulty of such a value measurement in public sectors (described in Chapter 1). As such, selection of business processes should aim to achieve improvement in organizational performance and functions, which will immediately offer some return and visible impact. It is also important to develop locally relevant business processes and have appropriate automation of business processes. The social and legal compulsions of local societies often challenge technology directly imported from the West, where a mismatch and conflict hinders the expected outcome. Ambitious and complicated systems without much potential for a positive outcome must be avoided.

Design to suit local context

ICT in the government or eGovernment is a complex toolkit that must be custom designed for each organization (Heeks, 2006). Some social norms and values must be respected and addressed in the planning process. As Higgo (2003, p. 3) emphasises, "there is a need to ensure that social and cultural values and perceptions are usually receptive to the technology rather than opposed to it". Therefore, a good match of the system with the need is important, where all side effects are adequately addressed before initiating the project. A flexible but pragmatic approach can only tackle this issue after a careful and thorough consideration of various elements and their interaction with the processes of the organization. Often the changes to working procedures brought by ICT can directly result in cultural and political change. Due attention should be given to the impact and consequences of these changes, and they need to be dealt with during every step of implementation.

Supply-side pressure

In many developing countries, there is a significant lack of expertise, advocacy, and promotion from vendors, experts, and consultants. Also, inadequate knowledge from incompetent experts often leads to the costly failure of ICT initiatives. This may create a negative impression and lack of confidence among leaders and decision makers. The role of supply- side institutions, which includes vendors, innovators, and consultants, is crucial in improving intentions to use ICT (Agarwal & Karahanna, 2000; Attewell, 1992). Personal ICT innovativeness and personal motivation can influence perceptions towards ICT. This, in turn, affects behavioural intentions of organizations towards ICT use (Rahim, Shanks, & Johnston, 2002).

Embarking on eGovernment through the web presence

Many government departments in developing countries have initiated eGovernment efforts through a web presence. However, most of these websites lack clarity and purpose in addressing the needs of the vast majority of the real stakeholders. The process of eGovernment in publishing government information online should begin with something that adds value to the daily lives of the target group (e.g., citizens, farmers, and business), such as documents and forms, or rules and regulations, with a simple user-friendly design that is easy to navigate with limited knowledge. Information should be "accurate, complete, economical, flexible, reliable, relevant, simple, timely, and verifiable" (Stair & Reynolds, 2001, p. 192).

eGovernment websites need to be service delivery oriented instead of advertising or highlighting the organization itself with too much contents on its history, structure, messages, and so on. Obtaining people's trust and confidence is crucial, which can be obtained only by responding to people's requests and applications efficiently and promptly.

All these objectives can only be achieved with political stability, which is crucial for providing a conducive socioeconomic environment as a platform for broader participation in the domestic economy. As a final note, while there are no solutions that can be copied directly from another nation's situation, the innovative ways in which some countries address these challenges may lead to success, which will offer inspiration for other countries to follow.

Educating a single government official or decision maker can often mean educating millions because their one good decision could bring change to the lives of millions.

2.4 eGovernment Evolution

During the 1980s, efforts to computerize business processes began. With the rapid development of technology, particularly distributed processing and network computing, the concept of ICT use in the public sector changed dramatically. It was found that information technology started offering completely new ways of doing a job, which often emerged as the most crucial factor for transforming existing business processes.

Primarily, the developed countries were the first to take advantage of eGovernment. Canada, USA, Finland, and several European countries, were the pioneers in implementing eGovernment. Now we will look back to the history of some developed and developing countries to see how eGovernment evolved in those countries.

United States

The Advanced Research Projects Agency Network (APRANET), which was developed in 1960s and built in 1969, constitutes the first form of the Internet as it's known today. However, its use was restricted to some military and education institutions. In 1991, when the World Wide Web (WWW) was created, an opportunity arose to use the Internet as a means of communication between ordinary people. By about 1993, U.S. government agencies went online to communicate with citizens and businesses. However, this was limited to a web presence that provided sparse information. Over the next few years, a number of government agencies allowed citizens to interact with the government by paying taxes, renewing drivers' licenses, and so on. Gradually, during the late 1990s, an increas-

ing number of government websites started moving to a transactional model. By 2000, 89% of U.S. municipalities had websites, but only 58% allowed users to download forms and information. However, the number of financial transactions and online completion of applications was still low (8% and 31%, respectively). Initially, state governments were more advanced than the federal government. For example, in 1998, 14 states had a chief information officer (CIO) to coordinate and provide leadership for their technology efforts, and, by August 2002, this number rose to 34 states. Since then, the US has made exploiting the latest technologies and innovations to improve government automation and service delivery a high priority, which places the US as one of the world leaders in eGovernment adoption.

Source: Atkinson & Leigh, 2003, p. 821; West, 2005, p.823.

Singapore

Singapore has been a leader in eGovernment in the Asia Pacific. A high-level initiative in the early 1980s called The Civil Service Computerisation Programme (CSCP) built a solid foundation for eGovernment developments. Since its launch, the CSCP has progressively advanced and evolved alongside the changing technological, business, and social contexts to bring about exciting changes to the way the Singapore government serves the public. The first phase of the CSCP aimed to improve public administration by effectively using ICT to automate traditional work functions and reduce paperwork (G2G). The emphasis subsequently shifted to interagency communication and coordination in order to provide integrated services to the public. Various data hubs were created to streamline data capture and to promote data sharing in government agencies. The early 1990s saw the beginnings of an adaptive and robust civil service-wide network and the consolidation of computing facilities in a data center. Another outcome of the CSCP has been the build-up of a large pool of ICT-competent personnel in the public service. This group of ICT professionals is critical for conceptualizing and executing Singapore's eGovernment programs.

Source: Curtin et al., 2003, p. 21; Ke, W., & Wei, K. 2004.

Australia

Australia is an example of a country that has successfully and effectively adopted ICT in the government sector. Internationally, the OECD has highlighted Australia as an example of a country that has achieved high productivity gains without a large ICT-producing sector.

In Australia, concerns over ICT implementation were raised through different forums as early as 1980 when the "Information Technology Week" event successfully highlighted ICT's importance, and drew the attention of the Federal Government and the public. "Information Technology Week" was triggered as a result of various initiatives, such as the special committee formed by the Australian Prime Minister to examine and evaluate the technological innovation and change in Australian industry in order to maximize economic and social benefit. In the late 1990s, the Australian Government announced the Whole-of-Government Information Technology Infrastructure Consolidation and Outsourcing Initiative (also known as the ICT Initiative). The aim was to achieve long-term objectives in improving, sourcing, structuring, and integrating IT services across agencies and to realize significant cost savings. Until 1999, in Australia, ICT was mostly agency specific because there was no national body, such as Australian Government Information Management Office (AGIMO) available to monitor overall ICT activities.

The number of Australians increasingly relying on the Internet to access government services online grows daily, from 25% in 2006 to 37% in 2010. Amid political controversy, the present government is moving ahead to invest up to $47 billion to build a high-speed National Broadband Network (NBN) in order to maximize business and service delivery. The Australian Government Information Management Office (AGIMO) is implementing initiatives to ensure a stronger ICT workforce to serve its citizens. Australia has made successive improvements over the years in innovations and improvements of eGovernment services where its one stop citizen portal now offers an extensive A-to-Z list of interlinked eServices and forms, both at the federal and local levels. All these have contributed to raise Australia's position from 8th to 2nd in 2014 UN eGovernment Readiness Index.

Source: Cowen, 1981; OECD, 2003; AGIMO; 2012; ANAO, 2000 reports.

Samoa

Samoa has made impressive progress in ICT over the years among the LDCs. In 2002, the Samoa National ICT committee, which included the key ministry and industry officials, was formed to spearhead the development of National ICT policies and oversee their implementation. The committee established a national ICT framework that was very effective. The Government Wide Area Network (GWAN) for data exchange between government departments and systems was established to facilitate all eGovernment systems developed by different government agencies and a variety of smart applications, which has resulted in reduced business transaction costs and improved efficiency and productivity. In the education sector, a major development was the development of the "National Computer Studies Curriculum" for Year 12 and 13 in 2004, which played a key role in improving Samoa's eReadiness. On the infrastructure side, Samoa has been the front-runner in the region for deregulation by removing monopolies and liberalization of telecom markets. In July 2005, a new Telecommunications Act came into force, which became the cornerstone leg-

islation in resolving issues in competition, universal access, licensing and monitoring the telecommunications environment. Thus, the competition in mobile phones and Internet services have accelerated ICT development and benefited the consumer. In addition, the launch of the submarine cable in 2010 and the UNDP funded eGovernment project accelerated Samoa's progress to move to the top of LDCs in world eGov ranking of 2012.

Source: Ioana Chan Mow, Economic development in Samoa: The last 50 Years, National University of Samoa.

A personal reflection

When I think back to my twenty-odd years working for the Australian government, there are some things that really stand out as ICT changing the way we do things. I guess some of the following examples enliven the changes and differences made by technologies over the past 25 years or so.

Our original financial system was a very old 3270 green screen mainframe application that was built back in the early 80s by the clever people at Dun and Bradstreet. When we installed SAP R/3 ERP in late 1999 it was like we had moved forward about 40 years in technological terms! You see, underpinning the older systems was a "clunky" paper- driven process requiring three signatures and several hand changes of documents. The new web-based MySAP interface and smart backend allowed us to execute procurements and payments using electronic approvals and a seamless online process. We also saved countless pieces of paper in the workplace, and reduced our huge dependence on print consumables.

In saying this, our HR system was not much better. This was a typical "hand-raulic" system of signed and counter-signed paper forms that snaked its way to an antiquated scheduling system for staff. Although suffering some early teething problems, the Oracle PeopleSoft solution ensured that we could process the leave approvals, manage staffing records, and pay holiday loadings in the electronic domain, while minimising the use of print resources. In essence, the business process was smoothed and the administrative loads measurably lessened by a more sophisticated piece of ICT.

The other use of ICT that has really changed the look and feel of public administration has been in the area of records management. The Australian Archives literally holds 100s of tonnes of paper government files and records. In the bad old days, these were managed using paper-based recording systems, mostly founded on spreadsheets and written forms. Today, we operate DRMS (document records management systems) that support the administrative system rather than hinder it. The files are centrally catalogued and managed allowing for more complex logistics and storage solutions to be used. I guess this has really taken the burden out of the file management tasks.

ICT has made a real difference in government circles. Looking at the advent and advance of social networking, we can look towards Gov 2.0 with renewed enthusiasm and promise as public administration lets go of the past and allows the future in.

Source: Dr Nigel Martin, Former public servant at the Department of Defense, Commonwealth of Australia

2.5 World eGovernment Rankings

Several institutions rank countries around the world to gauge their progress and standing in eGovernment, such as the United Nations eGovernment Readiness Index, the Waseda University World eGovernment Ranking, the Eurostat rankings, The Economist, Brown University, and so on. However, different institutions use different scales and sets of criteria, which changes the order depending on the criteria used. For example, the UN Survey assesses the 191 member states according to a quantitative composite index of eGovernment readiness, which is based on website assessment, telecommunication infrastructure, and human resource endowment. On the other hand, the Waseda university rankings are based on a series of indicators which includes network preparedness, interface applications, eGovernment management capabilities, the existence of CIO, webpage, awareness and promotion and so on. While these may not represent the detail eGovernment development taking place within the countries, but provides an overall indication and snapshot of their status.

2.5.1 The top achievers

According to the UN eGovernment Survey Report (2014), Asia and Europe region significantly placed itself in the top five positions. The Republic of Korea has retained the top place in 2014 with its focus on eGovernment innovation. The United States ranked 7th and Canada ranked 11th from the America region. On the other hand, according to Waseda University's ranking, Asia region still is in the top five ranking with Singapore, Korea and Japan. USA is first in the total ranking (See Table 2.3).

Table 2.3. Top twelve positions in the latest eGovernment ranking

Rank	United Nations (2014)	Waseda University (2014)
1	Republic of Korea	USA
2	Australia	Singapore
3	Singapore	Korea
4	France	UK
5	Netherlands	Japan
6	Japan	Canada

Rank	United Nations (2014)	Waseda University (2014)
7	United States of America	Estonia
8	United Kingdom	Finland
9	New Zealand	Australia
10	Finland	Sweden
11	Canada	Denmark
12	Spain	New Zealand

2.5.2 LDCs status

eGovernment development in most of the Least Developed Countries (LDCs), continues to be slow with no countries in the top 100 of the global ranking. Amongst the 48 LDCs, 34 are in Africa, nine in Asia, four in Oceania and one in the Caribbean. A lack of a well-thought out strategy in their national development plans and a lack of human capacity remains a constraint for eGovernment innovation. Common lacking of access to modern technology and lack of legal and technical ICT infrastructure particularly telecommunication infrastructure still a hindrance in its progress. The LDC Telecommunication Infrastructure Index average is 0.0929 compared with the world average of 0.3650. Despite many initiatives by international and national bodies, many interventions have failed to yield desirable improvements because most of the eGovernment projects were short lived and ad-hoc. Some good initiatives failed to achieve a cumulative result due to a lack of synergy, coordination and long-term eGovernment planning. In addition, a lack of political stability and continuity often affected the implementation of long-term goals.

Nevertheless, it is noteworthy that all the 48 countries have now some online presence in comparison to previous survey where Central African Republic and Guinea had none. Some LDCs achieved pioneering initiatives and championship at various levels. Rwanda, Kiribati, Cambodia and Yemen made good progress in the last year, although most of the middle- and bottom-tier countries are failing to keep pace with the rest of the world. Table 2.4 shows UN eGovernment ranking of LDCs from 2008-2014.

Table 2.4. eGovernment rankings of LDCs (based on UN global eGovernment readiness data, 2008- 2012)

			eGov index	eGov. development ranking			
Tier	No	Country	2014	2014	2012	2010	2008
Top Tier	1	Rwanda	0.35888	125	140	148	141
	2	Kiribati	0.3201	132	149	184	N/A
	3	Tuvalu	0.3059	137	134	184	N/A

			eGov index	eGov. development ranking			
	4	Cambodia	0.29986	139	155	140	139
	5	Angola	0.29703	140	142	132	127
	6	Bhutan	0.28285	143	152	152	134
	7	United Rep. of Tanzania	0.27642	146	139	137	143
	8	Bangladesh	0.27572	148	150	134	142
	9	Yemen	0.27199	150	167	164	164
	10	Senegal	0.26657	151	163	163	153
	11	Lao People's Dem. Rep.	0.26588	152	153	151	156
	12	Lesotho	0.26294	153	136	121	114
	13	Sudan	0.26062	154	165	154	161
	14	Madagascar	0.2606	155	148	139	135
	15	Uganda	0.25926	156	143	142	133
	16	Ethiopia	0.25888	157	172	172	172
	17	Vanuatu	0.25705	159	135	155	154
	18	Timor-Leste	0.25276	161	170	162	155
	19	Togo	0.24463	162	178	165	160
	20	Zambia	0.23893	163	154	143	158
Middle Tier	21	Mozambique	0.23837	164	158	161	152
	22	Nepal	0.23442	165	164	153	150
	23	Malawi	0.23208	166	159	159	146
	24	Gambia	0.22851	167	161	167	159
	25	Equatorial Guinea	0.22675	168	151	138	145
	26	Sao Tome and Principe	0.20871	170	138	128	130
	27	Solomon Is-lands	0.20871	170	168	156	147
	28	Burundi	0.19278	172	173	174	174
	29	Afghanistan	0.19003	173	184	168	167
	30	Mauritania	0.1893	174	181	157	168

			eGov index	eGov. development ranking			
Bottom Tier	31	Myanmar	0.18694	175	160	141	144
	32	Haiti	0.18086	176	187	169	165
	33	Comoros	0.18077	177	171	160	170
	34	Burkina Faso	0.18043	178	185	178	176
	35	Liberia	0.17682	179	169	166	163
	36	Benin	0.1685	180	179	173	171
	37	Mali	0.16335	181	183	176	175
	38	Guinea Bissau	0.16085	182	182	179	177
	39	Democratic Republic of the Congo	0.15514	183	174	158	162
	40	Djibouti	0.1456	184	176	170	157
	41	South Sudan*	0.14184	185	175	N/A	N/A
	42	Sierra Leone	0.13286	186	186	177	178
	43	Central Africa Republic	0.12574	187	N/A	181	179
	44	Chad	0.1092	191	189	182	182
	45	Guinea	0.09543	190	N/A	180	180
	46	Niger	0.09456	191	188	183	181
	47	Eritrea	0.09075	192	180	175	169
	48	Somalia	0.01387	193	190	184	N/A

Note: In 2012, Central African Republic and Guinea did not have a web presence

*new member of LDC

2.6 Recent Trends in eGovernment

While the developing world focuses on making a presence in the eGovernment sphere with implementation of basic infrastructures, websites, human-capacity building and policy formulation, the advanced countries are moving towards innovations that exploit the opportunities offered by newer technologies and circumstances. Some of those newer tends are discussed below.

One of the new initiatives in eGovernment that advanced countries are increasingly adopting is the "single entry" point or "one-stop-shop" strategy. This aims to deliver government services to citizens more effectively through a single online access point. The single point access approach is a big shift from the traditional interaction between citizens and government. Instead of approaching respective departments to obtain particular services, citizens are offered one gateway from which all government departments can be accessed. For example, the single access point (government portal) www.australia.gov.au began to evolve by combining government services and personalizing them at the user level (Figure 2.5).

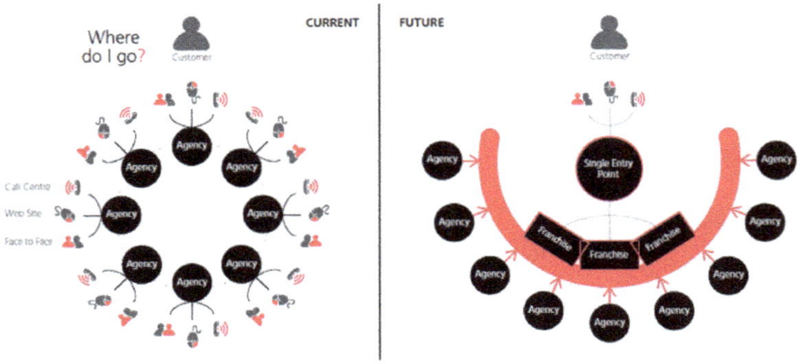

Figure 2.5. Single access point strategy (Government of SA Website, Ask Just Once)[2]

By typing simple queries and questions on any government matters, citizens can get the required information and services through a user-friendly platform. Similar approaches are being taken in many European countries and in the USA, Singapore, Korea, and Malaysia.

2.6.1 Government 2.0

Modern governments are exploring more open and transparent forms of government so that the public has a greater role in policy making. Newer social tools and media underlie this trend. Government 2.0 represents "a fundamental shift in the implementation of government - toward an open, collaborative, co-operative arrangement using two way communications between government and citizens"[3]. The characteristics of Government 2.0 are:

- Open consultation
- Open data
- Shared knowledge
- Mutual acknowledgment of expertise
- Mutual respect for shared values, and
- An understanding of how to agree to disagree.

---

[2] The original source is no longer available online. The National library of Australia holds records for it at: http://catalogue.nla.gov.au/Record/4237637

[3] Australian Government 2.0 Google Group http://www.gov2u.org/index.php/blog/164

Example: Gov 2.0

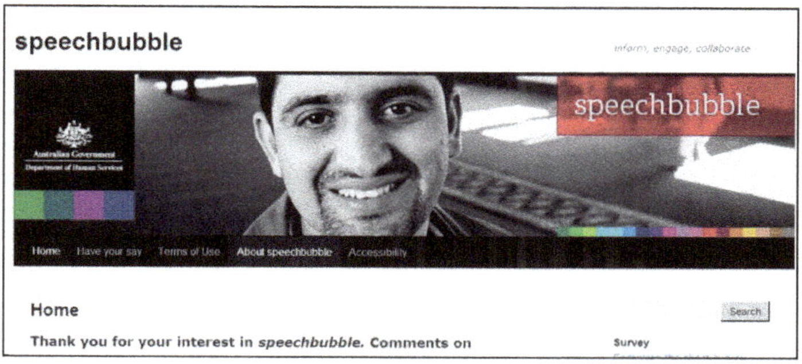

Speechbubble is an online discussion forum that was developed in 2010 to inform and engage with customers, staff and stakeholders on Department of Human Services' Initiatives (URL: http://speechbubble-blog.dhs.gov.au)

Speechbubble is an online collaborative platform where people can post comments, suggestions and feedback. It provides a less formal and more immediate way for the department to consult directly and widely with the public to develop citizen-centred products and services. Speechbubble provides a forum for anyone with access to a computer and internet connection to participate from wherever they are located and it can work alongside face-to-face forums such as workshops and focus groups, providing an alternative location for participants or a complementary platform for discussion.

In March 2011, the department used speechbubble as a means of providing consultation on Our Service Commitments, its new service charter. speechbubble was open for consultation for 10 days. Trained moderators and subject matter experts managed the discussion forum, both during and outside of business hours. During business hours, all comments were published immediately, while outside of business hours, moderators checked comments before being posted. Where moderation was required, the department did this in line with the Terms of Use, which are clearly available on speechbubble.

Source: http://showcase.govspace.gov.au/item/speechbubble/

2.6.2 Cloud Computing

More recently, cloud computing technology has opened up many new opportunities. One study shows that 75% of companies in the West either currently employ cloud computing solutions or plan to adopt them in the next five years (Savvis, 2010, p. 854). Cloud computing is the use of virtual servers, which are available over the Internet (Figure 2.6).

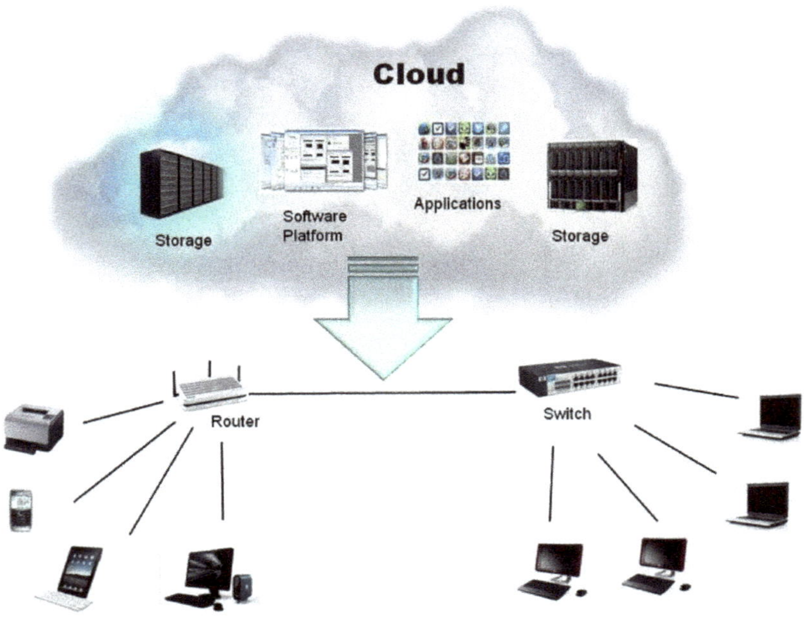

Figure 2.6. Using cloud or virtual servers over the Internet

The term is often used more broadly to imply any computing that is outside a company's firewall, which includes conventional outsourcing. Clouds can be run by third-party service providers where applications, storage systems, and networks are shared among different customers. The best example is Google, which offers web-based applications such as word-processing or online spreadsheets to many customers at the same time.

According to a McKinsey survey cited in The Economist (2008), on average, only 6% of the USA's server capacity is used. Resources such as infrastructure and IT services are not only costly to establish and maintain, but they also occupy a large space and pollute the environment. Under the cloud environment, exactly the same services and operation could be obtained by outsourcing infrastructure and services. The cloud computing domain can be classified into four categories:

- Platform as a service
- Infrastructure as a service
- Communication as a service, and
- Software as a service.

Based on its ownership, cloud computing can be public, private, or hybrid. For instance, many large, secure organizations can have their own private cloud.

While there are still some concerns about the ownership and security of data, the advantages of public cloud computing are many. These are:

- **Pay-as-you-go pricing mode**: public cloud computing can follow a "pay-as-you-go" system like other utilities such as electricity, and so on. As such, resources are not wasted because you pay for what you use.
- **Scalability and elasticity**: user organizations can obtain more or less processing power and storage when needed based on the organization's requirements. For example, when a business is running slower, it might scale down its storage requirements and pay less.
- **Shared infrastructure and software**: since infrastructure is managed by a third party, there are no overheads and expensive set-up required by the user organization. This arrangement also allows organizations to use costly enterprise software as a service shared by many other organizations.
- **Eliminates complex procurement cycles**: this allows users to focus on delivering business value instead of expending valuable resources on IT infrastructure.
- **High reliability**: the cloud application runs 24 hours per day, 365 days a year.
- **Low entry costs**: there is no long-term financial commitment.

To succeed in cloud computing, there should be a strong and clear understanding about the fundamental benefits of cloud adoption. For developing countries who are yet to embark on building large technological infrastructure, cloud computing presents an opportunity to skip the generations of technology that the western world has gone through. For many developing countries where large investment in infrastructure and resources is an issue, cloud computing could be the answer.

2.6.3 mGovernment

(Photo credit: A. Imran)

Mobile eGovernment and m-government are terms that have recently been talked about a great deal, especially in developing countries where large numbers of people adopting mobile technology has created new opportunities to provide government services and transactions through wireless mobile devices. mGovernment provides a viable alternative for the developing world where Internet access rates are low. This technology enables a larger number of citizens to access eGovernment services, and is more cost effective than other ICT applications.

With the evolution of 3G and 4G smart phones, the possibilities are continually increasing. Regardless of whether or not the entire government system could be brought under m-government, it will definitely occupy a significant portion of government service delivery in the future. Another key advantage is that this technology is convenient: it can be used, anywhere and anytime. For example, in the event of emergencies, innovative applications could be used to send out mass alerts to registered citizens via SMS.

Health workers can now enter data and reports directly from the field in real time using handheld terminals. M-government also encourages citizen participation in government affairs. For example, in the Philippines, citizens can help enforce anti-pollution laws by reporting smoke-belching public buses and other vehicles via SMS (Lallana, 2008).

However, m-government is not a replacement for eGovernment - rather, it complements it. Security is an issue for public networks and mobile devices. While mobile devices have many advantages in terms of ease of access and use, most devices are not ideal for transmitting complex information or large quantities of data. Despite the development and innovation of more sophisticated smart phones, they will have some limitation in terms of features and services compared with PC-based applications. Good mobile applications and services also rely heavily on appropriate back-office ICT infrastructure and work processes, which include data quality, procedures, and transaction recording processes (Lallana, 2008).

Case Study: mGovernment - EPurjee in Bangladesh

Traditionally, "purjee" is known as "supply order" to the sugar-cane farmer by the Sugar Mills during crushing season. In Bangladesh, there are 28 sugar mills and 2561 units of farmer groups comprising approximately 0.15 million farmers around the country. Mills normally maintains a passbook to record the supply of each farmer. However, the mills' authority was unable to reach 150,000 farmers quickly due to inadequate manpower to communicate with the farmers. Farmers are also not aware about the demand, price and time for delivery.

Purjee used to be sent to farmers through various centers and also by a farmer to neighbor farmer or by a third person. Often, either the Purjee did not reach the farmer in time to deliver properly, or it reached some middle man who bought from the farmer at lower cost and supplied to the mill the mill's rate. Mills also failed to collect required quantity and good quality of sugarcane. Farmer used to queue for days to finally deliver the products to the mill. It was not only flawed supply chain but was also inadequate for good quality sugar cane.

In year 2009 a project called ePurjee was launched by the A2I (Access to Information) program funded by UNDP. The project target was to replace the current supply process communications with a digitally based method. The project was executed by Bangladesh Sugar and Food Corporation (BSFIC).

Now the farmers get their purjee on their mobile phones. Mills have the full database of the 150,000 farmers with their cell number and delivery passport details. The mills are getting so much quality product that they can pre-announce the schedule of procurement. The farmers also don't have to live in uncertainty any more. They don't have to queue as they are requested to deliver at a particular day and time which is determined by capacity of receiving the consignment by mill authority. As the farmers are directly selling to mills they are getting a better price than selling to a middle man. They are financially better off.

Farmers are cutting the canes only just before their scheduled delivery date to avoid drying up. In 2010, two mills created a record output of their production by streamlining the supply of sugarcane. In 2009 the total production of all the mills was 62,250 metric ton, in 2010 the production went up to 118,925 metric tons, which is nearly double. It implies that farmer's income has also increased significantly by growing and supplying more sugar cane than they could do earlier. This has not only kept the consumer market price for sugar low, but has significantly reduced the import of sugar from other countries. Simple innovation through mobile services from government directly to a large number of individual suppliers made it possible.

Source: Rafiqul Islam Rowly

Chapter Highlights

- ICT has become an integral part of modern government organization, where brief ICT network disruptions or downtime may create a huge loss of productivity.
- The terms eGovernment and eGovernance are used synonymously, although there is an important distinction between the two. EGovernment is the tool or the means to achieve eGovernance, and eGovernance encompasses broader concepts about the governing mechanism, decision making, responsibilities, and so on.
- There is a misconception that eGovernment is about delivering government services online, whereas major government activities take place within the government to government (G2G) interactions, which impact on internal effectiveness and efficiency.
- Initially, in many developing countries where there are very low levels of accessibility to the Internet and computers, eGovernment implementation is a more viable proposition using G2G.
- Citizens can benefit from eGovernment without using a computer themselves through effective G2G implementation.
- For developing countries, eGovernment begins with the preparatory stage followed by the interaction, transaction, integration, transformation, and exploration stages, respectively.
- In developing countries, a large number of eGovernment failures are due to the failure to recognize the complexity of the underlying issues in their design.
- Adopting and implementing eGovernment in developing countries is challenging because the process not only involves transferring machines, hardware, software, and skills, but also demands a change in attitudes and values.
- In developing countries, it is important to begin by addressing knowledge gaps and transforming attitudes, rather than by addressing other inhibitors, such as infrastructure and socio-economic conditions.
- In order to derive the actual benefits, government employees and policy makers must understand what ICT can and cannot do - in other words, where efficiencies and productivity can realistically be achieved.
- To get the ultimate benefit of eGovernment, the society's eReadiness is important.
- A top-down approach can be effective in bringing about change in developing countries because one good government decision affects millions. These millions would otherwise be difficult to reach through a bottom-up approach.
- A lack of a well-thought-out strategy in their national development plans and a lack of human capacity remains a constraint for eGovernment innovation, along with lack of legal and technical infrastructures.

- Many of the good initiatives in eGovernment in the past failed to achieve a cumulative result due to lack of coordination, political stability, and continuity.
- Cloud computing has evolved as an opportunity for developing countries to skip the generations of technologies that the West has gone through during the last couple of decades.
- mGovernment provides a viable alternative for the developing world, where Internet access rates are low, but mobile phone adoption is rising.

Review Questions

1. What is the difference between eGovernment and eGovernanace?
2. When and how did ICT use in the public sector begin?
3. How were Australia's Centrelink online services developed?
4. What were the benefits achieved through Brazil's eProcurement initiative?
5. Why is the eReadiness of a society a precondition to become successful in eGovernment?
6. Describe a process model for eGovernment adoption.
7. How can supply-side institutions influence eGovernment adoption?
8. What are the critical success factors of Singapore, USA, Australia, and Samoa for excelling in eGovernment world ranking?
9. Enumerate the stages of eGovernment, with actions in each stage.

Discussion Questions

1. What are the major components of eGovernment? Discuss their relative importance?
2. Why is G2G implementation so important, yet difficult to accomplish?
3. What are the strategies used to implement a one-stop-shop service for eGovernment?
4. Are Facebook or other existing social network sites suitable for government transactions? Why or why not?
5. Discus the potentiality and possible application of cloud computing in your organization. Give a realistic example.
6. Discuss the limitations of eGovernment. How can these limitations be dealt with? What could be other alternatives?

Exercises

1. Investigate the eGovernment status of three developing countries of your own choice and make a comparative study. Find out critical factors for their progress or lack of progress.
2. In a group, discuss and prioritize the most critical barriers to eGovernment adoption in your country. Discuss the approaches and strategies to tackle those barriers. Justify your claims.

References

Agarwal, R., & Karahanna, E. (2000). Time flies when you're having fun: Cognitive absorption and beliefs about information technology usage. MIS Quarterly, 24(4), 665-694.
AGIMO.(2012). Australian Public Service Information and Communications Technology Strategy 2012-2015. Department of Finance and Deregulation, Australian Government Information Management Office. Canberra.
AGIMO. (2011). Australians' use of and satisfaction with eGovernment services. Canberra Department of Finance and Deregulation, Australian Government Information Management Office. Retrieved from http://www.finance.gov.au/publications/interacting-with-government-2011/ docs/interacting-with-government-2011.pdf
Attewell, P. (1992). Technology diffusion and organizational learning: The case of business computing. Organization Science, 3(1), 1-19.
Avgerou, C. (2001). The significance of context in information systems and organizational change. Information Systems Journal, 11(1), 43-63.
Backus, M. (2001). EGovernance and developing countries—introduction and examples. IICD Research Report No. 3. Retrieved from http://www.iicd.org/articles/IICDnews.import1857
Baum, C. H., & Maio, A. D. (2000). Gartner's four phases of eGovernment model. Retrieved from https://www.gartner.com/doc/317292/gartners-phases-egovernment-model
Bhatnagar, S. (2004). eGovernment, from vision to implementation, a practical guide with case studies. New Delhi: Sage Publications.
CID. (2000). Readiness for the networked world: A guide for developing countries. Center for International Development, Harvard University. Retrieved from http://cyber.law.harvard.edu/ readinessguide/readiness.html
Curtin, G., Sommer, M., & Vis-Sommer, V. (Eds.). (2003). The world of eGovernment. New York: Haworth Press.
Dawes, S. (2002). The future of eGovernment. An Examination of New York City's EGovernment Initiatives. Retrieved from https://www.ctg.albany.edu/publications/reports/future_of_egov/future_of_egov.pdf
Grant, G. (2005). Realizing the promise of electronic government (Editorial). Journal of Global Information Management, 13(1), 1-4.
Heeks, R. (2002). Information systems and developing countries: Failure, success, and local improvisations. The Information Society, 18(2), 101-112.
Heeks, R. (2003). Most eGovernment-for-development projects fail: How can risks be reduced? IDPM i-Government working paper no.14. University of Manchester. UK. Retrieved from http:// unpan1.un.org/intradoc/groups/public/documents/cafrad/unpan011226.pdf
Heeks, R. (2004). Basic definitions page. eGovernment for Development, IDPM, University of Manchester. Retrieved from http://www.egov4dev.org/egovdefn.htm
Heeks, R. (2006). Implementing and managing egovernment. London: Sage.
Higgo, H. A. (2003). Implementing an information system in a large LDC bureaucracy: The case of the Sudanese Ministry of Finance. The Electronic Journal on Information Systems in Developing Countries, 14(3), 1-13.
Imran, A. (2008). Bangladesh making progress in global eGovernment readiness. The Daily Star. Retrieved from http://www.thedailystar.net/story.php?nid=29536

Imran, A. (2010). ICT adoption in the public sector of least developed countries (LDCs): The case of Bangladesh. (Unpublished doctoral dissertation). Australian National University Canberra.

Imran, A., & Gregor, S. (2012). Uncovering the hidden issues in eGovernment adoption in a least developed country: The case of Bangladesh. Journal of Global Information Management, 18(2), 30-56.

Imran, A., Turner, T., & Gregor, S. (2008). eGovernment for Bangladesh: A strategic pathway for success. Canberra, Australia: National Centre for Information Systems Research, The Australian National University.

ITU. (2012). The State of broadband 2012: Achieving digital inclusion for all. Retrieved frm http://www. broadbandcommission.org/Documents/bb-annualreport2012.pdf

Krishna, S., & Madon, S. (Eds.). (2003). The digital challenge: information technology in the development context. Aldershot, UK: Ashgate Publishing.

Kumar, R., & Best, M. L. (2006). Impact and sustainability of eGovernment services in developing countries: Lessons learned from Tamil Nadu, India. The Information Society, 22, 1-12.

Lallana, E. C. (2008). mGovernment: Mobile/wireless applications in government eGovernment for Development. Retrieved January 7, 2012, from http://www.egov4dev.org/mgovernment/

Nidumolu, S. R., Goodman, S. E., Vogel, D. R., & Danowitz, A. K. (1996). Information technology for local administration support: The governorates project in Egypt. MIS Quarterly, 20(2), 197-224.

OECD. (2001). Learning to change: ICT in schools. Retrieved from http://www.oecd.org/document/2/0,3343,en_2649_34487_2466626_1_1_1_1,00.html

Osimo, D. (2008). Web 2.0 in government: Why and how? Spain: European Commission Joint Research Centre and Institute for Prospective Technological Studies. Retrieved from ftp://ftp.jrc.es/pub/ EURdoc/JRC45269.pdf

Perumal, S., Norwawi, N. M., & Muniandy, S. (2008). The success transmission model from governance to eGovernance. In J. Bhattacharya (Ed.), Critical thinking in eGovernance. New Delhi: GIFT.

Rahim, M., Shanks, G., & Johnston, R. (2002, August 1-3). Motivations for inter-organisational systems adoption: A tale of two organisations. Paper presented at the IFIP Working Group 8.6

Conference on The Adoption and Diffusion of IT in an Environment of Critical Change, Sydney.

Reschenthaler, G. B., & Thompson, F. (1996). The information revolution and the new public management. Journal of Public Administration Research and Theory, 6(1), 125-143.

Rogers, E. M. (2003). Diffusion of innovations (5th ed.). New York: Free Press.

Sanford, C., & Bhattacherjee, A. (2007). IT implementation in a developing country municipality: A sociocognitive analysis. Journal of Global Information Management, 15(3), 20-42.

Savvis. (2010), SAVVIS A CenturyLink Company. Retrieved from http://www.savvis.com/en-US/ Company/News/Press/Pages/SavvisStudyReveals75ofCompaniesWillUseEnterprise-ClassCloudComputingSolutionsWithinFiveYears.aspx

Scholl, H. J. (2005). Organizational transformation through eGovernment: Myth or reality? Paper presented at the 4th International Conference on Electronic Government, Denmark, Copenhagen.

Silva, L., & Figueroa, E. B. (2002). Institutional intervention and the expansion of ICTs in Latin America: The case of Chile. Information Technology and People, 15(1), 8-25.
Stair, R., & Reynolds, G. (2001). Principles of information systems. MA: Cambridge.
The Economist. (2008). Where the cloud meets the ground. Retrieved from http://www.economist.com/ node/12411920
UN OHRLLS. (2012). List of LDCs; United Nations Office of the High Representative for the Least Developed Countries. The Criteria for the Identification of the LDCs. Retrieved May 21, 2012, from http://www.unohrlls.org/en/ldc/164/
UN. (2001). United Nations Information and Communication Technologies Task Force. Retrieved May 9, 2009, from http://www.unicttaskforce.org/
UN. (2004). Global eGovernment readiness report 2004 - towards access for opportunity. Department of Economic and Social Affairs, Division for Public Administration and Development Management, United Nations. Retrieved from http://unpan1.un.org/intradoc/groups/public/documents/un/ unpan019207.pdf
Wilson, E. J. (2004). The information revolution and developing countries. London: MIT Press.

PART II
eGOVERNMENT ARCHITECTURE

PART II - eGovernment Architecture

Part II comprehensively describes the technology, infrastructure and systems required for implementing eGovernment. It enables managers to recognize opportunities and make informed choices about the types of systems that are available to government organisations. In-depth technological knowledge is significantly scaled down in keeping with the target audiences and their needs.

Chapter 3, eGovernment Architecture and Systems, describes an eGovernment architecture, the role of different components, and their interactions within the architecture. It distinguishes major types of eGovernment systems and describes their functionalities. It also identified and explains the main features of different types of eGovernment systems, and compares the critical differences between the systems. Lastly, it describes how these systems are applied in an eGovernment context.

Chapter 4, Data Networks, describes the different types of data networks that are common in a government environment. It identified four main eGovernment opportunities based on networks, and discusses the trade-offs that the governments of developing countries must make for network-based eGovernment.

Chapter 5, Data Management, explains the importance and function of data, the data lifecycle, business intelligence and enterprise content management. It outlines various control mechanisms to manage public data.

Chapter 6, Enterprise Systems, describes the different types of information systems in an enterprise, and discusses the importance of cross-functional systems. It also describes common functions of Enterprise Resource Planning (ERP) systems and important considerations when implementing an ERP in government. Lastly, it identifies the key elements of an eProcurement solution.

Chapter 7, Citizen Services, describes the key benefit of delivering government services to citizens online, and discusses the challenges associated with delivering services to citizens exclusively online. It also discusses the different roles that citizens play when they interact with government and the influence that this has on online service design.

Chapter 8, Security and Privacy, identifies how eGovernment changes the need for security, privacy and confidentiality in government processes. It demonstrates common approaches for securing eGovernment processes and identifies ways to manage the security risks of eGovernment.

CHAPTER 3
eGovernment Architecture and Systems

Learning Objectives

After studying this chapter, you will be able to:

- Understand the role and function of enterprise structure
- Describe the steps and approaches to development of enterprise architecture
- Describe eGovernment architecture, the role of different eGovernment components, and their interactions in the architecture
- Distinguish major types of eGovernment systems and understand their functionalities
- Identify and explain the main features of different types systems
- Compare the critical differences between the systems, and
- Describe how these systems are applied in eGovernment.

Why Architecture?

(Photo credit O. Hug)

An object's architecture, which refers to its design, construction, and orderly arrangement, is fundamental to its existence. Poor architecture may waste materials and time, or result in poor outcomes. For example, poor design and construction of a plane would most certainly jeopardize its ability to fly without crashing. This is no different for an enterprise solution - that is, the architecture of an organization or business.

If the necessary software and hardware are not designed to expand and be compatible, this may cause dysfunction later on. From a business perspective, this would result in a poor investment. Often, poor design and master planning hamper the quality and business goals of an organization, which may lead to its complete failure. Good architecture of an organization's business, assets, and operations can provide the pathway to achieve its long-term mission and objective, but still needs careful analysis of the past and future of the organisation and a substantial investment of time, effort and money

> *"Good enterprise architecture is vital to the vision, capability and healthy operation of today's modern organization"*
>
> *Dion HInchcliffe, 2009*[1]

3.1 Enterprise Architecture

The concept of enterprise architecture involves a blueprint or road map for an enterprise's[2] operations. In order to attain the best outcome, there should be a thorough examination, and careful alignment, of the enterprise's goal and strategy, structure, resources, and environment. Sound enterprise architecture helps agencies make decisions, implement strategy and policy, and improve service delivery, while also providing direction for further expansion and growth.

The term "architecture" can be applied to many areas. Enterprise architecture is large and complex, and can be subdivided into data architecture, technical architecture, network architecture, software architecture, and so on.

The term "enterprise architecture" (EA) rose to prominence in 1987 through the Zachman Framework for Enterprise Architecture[3], which was developed by John

---

1 http://www.ebizq.net/blogs/enterprise/2009/09/fixing_enterprise_architecture.php

2 Refers to organisation or business

3 http://www.zachman.com/about-the-zachman-framework

Zachman following the typical architecture of complex engineering projects, consisting of data, processes, and networks, represented as a two-dimensional matrix.

3.1.1 Essentials of EA

Before this, organizations used structured approaches such as Information System planning. Enterprise Architecture (EA) is a complex system which needs to take the following aspects into account:

- An organization's strategy, which describes its mission and expectations
- Information/data resources needed to perform its mission
- Technologies, business functions and processes, and the people needed to perform the mission
- Organizational structure and its physical distribution
- Relationships between the system elements and their environment/context
- Governance structure, standards, and design principles that guide and constrain its development
- Transitional processes for new innovations and additions
- Organization's future direction
- Right balance between innovation, risk, and cost, and
- Coordination and interface between ICT designers, planners, strategists, and business designers.

EA is extremely important because it reduces ICT costs by better aligning the organization's mission to its ICT investment. When enterprises use EA, they minimize potential information system problems and failures. Therefore, it improves the ability of organizations to achieve their missions.

3.1.2 Business architecture and IT architecture

Enterprise architecture includes various subcategories: for example, business architecture, and IT architecture - both of which are closely associated with each other. Creating IT architecture is a recursive process driven by the business architecture, which ensures that both categories are properly linked and meet the organization's long- term objectives (Figure 3.1). While business architecture contains organizational visions, objectives, policies, and the data and information required to support them, IT architecture ensures objectives are met effectively and efficiently through the use of the best ICT tools. As such, the potential use of ICT also plays a critical role in creating business architecture.

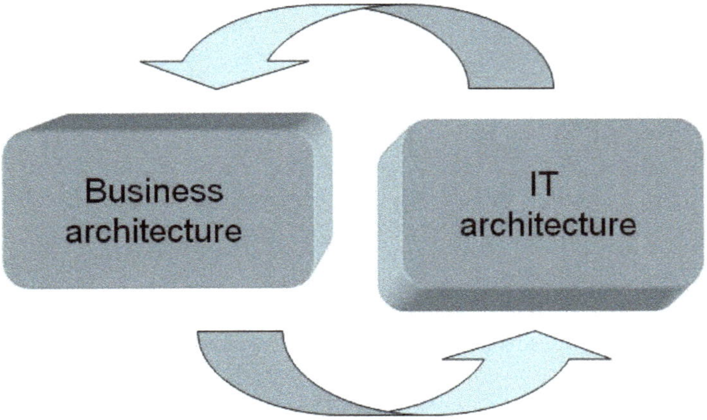

Figure 3.1. Relation between business architecture and ICT architecture

3.1.3 Enterprise architect

The person who develops enterprise architecture is called the "enterprise architect". Enterprise architects provide organizations a means to manage themselves more effectively and efficiently, and incorporate future planning for growth and success. An enterprise architect will set standards for components of IT and information infrastructure, so that ready-made program components can be used to reduce the time and cost of new application development. In small organizations, enterprise architects often perform the role of all associated architects; while in large organizations, ideally, enterprise architects oversee a plan that manages the enterprise more effectively, and specific architects are assigned to develop each architecture in the EA. For example:

- Business architect - deals with business model, process, organizational design
- Service architect - deals with service, data and application
- IT infrastructure architect - deals physical technology model

However, overall, it is the senior managers who must ensure that enterprise architecture is correctly implemented.

Further Reading

Buchanan, R., & Soley, R. (2002). *Aligning enterprise architecture and IT investments with corporate goals OMG and Meta Group.* Retrieved from http://www.bptrends.com/publicationfiles/META%20OMG%20WP%201-15-03.pdf

Hinchcliffe, D. (2009, September 3). *Fixing enterprise architecture: Balancing the forces of change in the modern organization. ebiz.* Retrieved from http://www.ebizq.net/blogs/enterprise/2009/09/fixing_enterprise_architecture.php

3.2 Development of Enterprise Architecture

3.2.1 EA frameworks

There are number of frameworks for the development of enterprise architecture that vary slightly from each other. Since our focus is government organizations, we will follow an approach based on a popular and widely used basic reference model, the U.S. Federal Enterprise Architecture (US FEA), developed by the U.S. Office of Management and Budget, Office of eGovernment in 1996 (Figure 3.2).

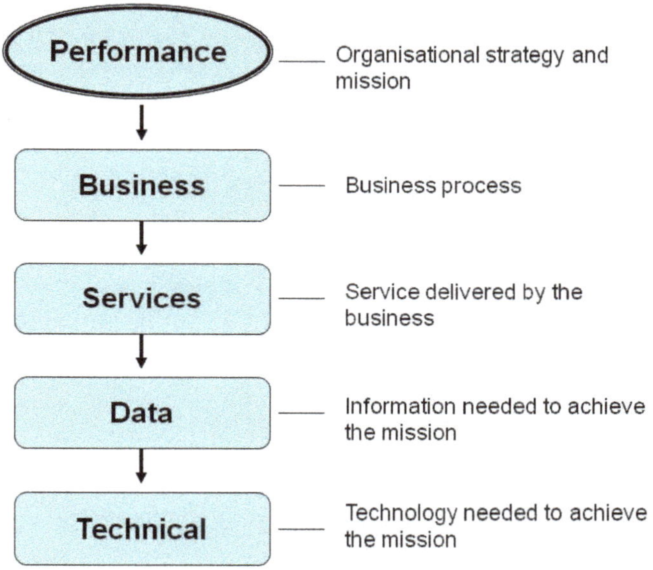

Figure 3.2. Chronological steps of enterprise architecture (based on US FEA[4])

Start with performance expectation

First, the functioning of any enterprise or organization revolves around its strategic goals and performance expectations. If we look at the big picture of an organization or an enterprise, the architectural framework will ideally originate from the organization's performance expectations, which are defined by its strategy and objectives. From these expectations, the detail architecture is designed hierarchically, taking into account all the required apparatuses and tools. Figure 3.2 shows the hierarchical steps of the areas of enterprise architecture derived from an organization's performance expectations.

Business architecture

Second, in this level, high-level business models and processes are drawn to describe the organization's ability to achieve the performance expectations. It also

[4] http://www.whitehouse.gov/sites/default/files/omb/assets/fea_docs/FEA_CRM_v23_Final_Oct_2007_Revised.pdf

examines the relationships among roles, capabilities, and business units and subunits, in order to achieve the organization's objectives.

Service architecture

In third level, business functions are split up into a set of services. Dividing the organization's functions into services helps maintain its distinct character without affecting the structure of technology, application, or data.

Data architecture

Fourth, at this level, all data/information necessary to fulfill the objectives are determined by examining and identifying the information currently available, and assessing what new information is needed. This outlines what data can or needs to be shared, stored, managed and delivered through multiple channels for the benefit of the organization.

Technical architecture

Finally, the technical requirements, both hardware and software, are formally assessed. Existing resources are inventoried, and the necessary upgrades and acquisitions are evaluated. In this step, the operating systems, transaction processors, and networking devices required to support the applications are worked out in detail.

Throughout the process, the human resources and procedures, including the legal, administrative, and financial constraints, should be examined. For example, a lack of certain ICT skills in the organization may require the hiring and retraining of personnel, or outsourcing. A constant environmental scan and assessment of the human resources' impact is also necessary, in order to choose the most suitable solution for the context.

3.3 EA Building Approaches

3.3.1 Big Bang approach

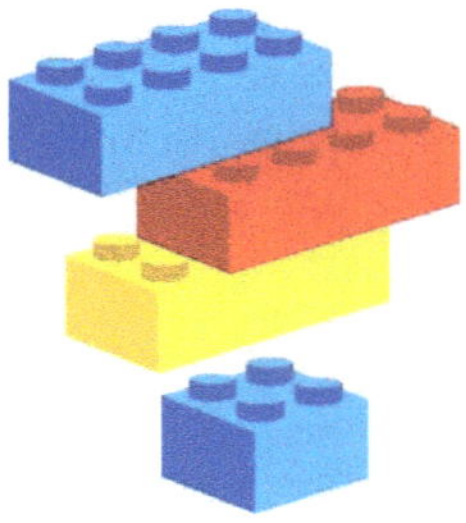

There are at least two ways to build enterprise architecture. One is the "big bang" method, which involves sketching everything, starting with the performance reference model, from scratch. For an established enterprise, this is a huge task because it could take years to understand and map all the business processes. The risk with this approach is that, due to organizational change, some of those processes may become redundant before the process mapping is complete. Moreover, the organization's strategy may also change over this timeframe due to the competiveness of the business, and the emerging technology and tools. Thus, the enormous effort to prepare the enterprise architecture with this approach may not be cost-effective or worthwhile.

3.3.2 Incremental approach

Another alternative is the incremental approach, which is more dynamic and provides greater flexibility. This approach is widely used, and begins with single building blocks. When a new project begins, its design follows the sequence in Figure 3.3. When another project subsequently starts, it is then developed by the same standards, so the two projects are compatible. In this way, separate projects can share resources while achieving the organization's overall objectives. Moreover, keeping common standards and sharing resources often results in fewer costs and better integration than duplicating processes. Thus, a single process architecture often leads to solution architecture, which addresses a specific problems and requirements. In turn, multiple solutions may then comprise building blocks for a segment architecture to meet specific needs of relatively larger business group area, which gradually erects the overall enterprise architecture (Figure 3.3).

For example, suppose an initiative has been taken in the enterprise to introduce a new payroll system. The enterprise architect, following the project management methodology, examines the business value and outcomes of the project, and whether it contributes to, and is consistent with, the overall performance of the enterprise. The systems are then developed according to the cost and expected standards in each level of business (including service, data, and technical) to ensure that they are compatible and develop the enterprise's value. Suppose that, after this, the enterprise introduces and develops another new system; for example, a leave processing system.

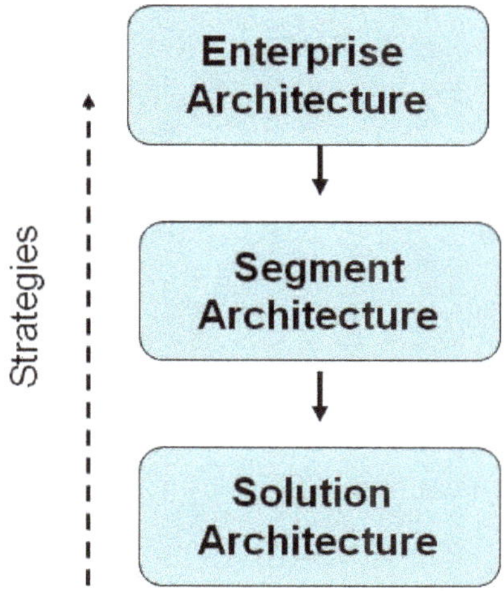

Figure 3.3. Flow of architecture at the lower level

Because of the initial efforts to ensure value and consistency, the leave processing system exploits the existing system at each level to avoid duplication and to maintain consistency. The process is dynamic and progressive. When the number of these projects increases, a standard EA for the organization gradually emerges. This method also allows existing processes to become a part of future development.

Further Reading

The common approach to Federal Enterprise Architecture. (2012). Executive Office of the President of the United States. Retrieved from http://www.whitehouse.gov/sites/default/files/omb/assets/egov_docs/common_approach_to_federal_ea.pdf

EA success stories: http://www.whitehouse.gov/omb/EGov/EA-Success

3.4 Examples of EA

There are many proprietary and non-proprietary frameworks in enterprise architecture. Some of the widely used and popular frameworks include:

- The United States Federal Enterprise Architecture (US FEA)
- Forrester pillars of Enterprise Architecture
- The Open Group Architecture Framework (TOGAF)
- Zachman Framework
- Gartner Enterprise Architecture Framework, and
- Australian Government Architecture (AGA).

Australian Government Architecture (AGA)

The Australian Government Information Management Office (AGIMO) established a government-wide enterprise architecture initiative in 2006, which drew from the US government's more established Federal Enterprise Architecture Framework (FEAF).

The AGA contains a set of interrelated "reference models", which are built chronologically. In order, they begin with the Performance Reference Model (PRM), the Business Reference Model (BRM), the Service Reference Model (SRM), the Data Reference Model (DRM), and the Technical Reference Model (TRM). These frameworks are used in a number of other countries and some state governments in Australia.

The aim of the Australian Government Architecture (AGA) framework is to:

Provide a common language for agencies involved in delivering cross-agency services

Enhance collaboration by identifying duplicate, re-usable, and sharable services

Assist with describing and analyzing ICT investments by providing a basis for their objective review, and

Assist with transforming government (citizen-centric, results-oriented, market- based) by enabling more cost-effective and timely delivery of ICT services. This is done through a repository of standards, principles, and templates that assist with the design and delivery of ICT investments and, in turn, business services to citizens.

Source: Australian Government Architecture Reference Models. More details about this AGA can be found at:
http://www.finance.gov.au/policy-guides-procurement/australian-government-architecture-aga/

3.5 Information Technology Infrastructure and Architecture

An **information infrastructure** comprises the physical facilities, services, and management that support all shared computing resources in an organization. Figure 3.4 shows five major components of an information infrastructure.

Figure 3.4. Components of information infrastructure (based on Turban & Volonino, 2010)

Information infrastructures not only include these resources, but also take account of their integration, operation, documentation, maintenance and management.

Information technology infrastructure (or ICT architecture) is essentially a master plan of the information assets in an organization, which includes the physical design and layout of where hardware components are placed. It is a plan not only for the ICT structures, but also for the integration of ICT resources and applications in the organization. In the Web domain, ICT architecture refers to the website content, organization, browsing interface, and search capabilities.

Again, **application architecture** in ICT architecture defines the software components. Applications are either developed or procured. Most of the major software vendors offer sophisticated readymade ICT application platforms that can significantly reduce the workload of application architecture.

3.6 A Typical eGovernment Architecture

In a public sector sphere, eGovernment architecture could be created to show all the possible components of an eGovernment system - to see where each component fits in and how they interact with each other in one big picture. Figure 3.5 is a typical example of eGovernment architecture, which encapsulates and combines the AGA, and several other existing models.

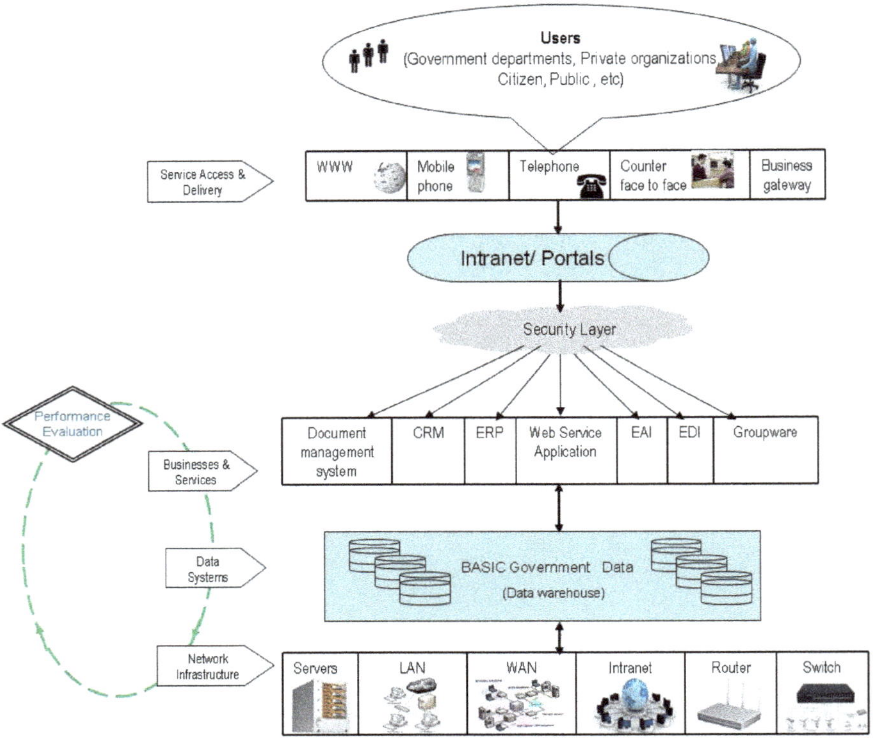

Figure 3.5. An eGovernment Architecture (based on AGIMO, 2009 p. 830, p. 825; Ebrahim & Irani, 2005)

Quick Quiz

1. What is the most important aspect of architecture design for an organization?
2. What differences can you note in the approach to enterprise architecture and segment architecture?
3. Of what is an information infrastructure comprised?

3.7 eGovernment Systems

3.7.1 What is a system

"System" is a common and widely used word often used to imply different things. The word system evolved from the Greek "systema", which implies a set of interrelated elements that perform some activity, function, or operation. More precisely, it is defined as "instrumentality that combines interrelated interacting artefacts designed to work as a coherent entity"[5]. A sub-system is a part of a larger system. For the purpose of this book, we are mostly concerned with "Information Systems" (as defined in Chapter 1), which carry out information-related functions or operations in government organizations. A system may encompass a number of levels in the architecture, which we discussed in the previous section.

Information systems

Information systems follow a development cycle similar to that used in software engineering, which is known as System Development Life Cycle (SDLC). This framework allows system designers and developers to follow a four-phase sequence of activities. We discuss further details of the system life cycle in Chapter 9. Once a system is built through this rigorous process, it is likely to function to perform a specific operation repeatedly without disruption.

Information systems in government

Government agencies are usually organized in a typical hierarchical fashion, starting from the head of the government down to different ministers, secretaries, mid-level officers, sections, and so on. This type of hierarchical structure and official business processes was formulated long before ICT's ability and role were understood. Government agencies only later used ICT and thus faced challenges to accommodate it into the well-established existing structure without disturbing the status quo. However, some negotiation and reengineering of the existing process had to be made at both ends to achieve better results and efficiency. A significant change to the structure and business operations of eGovernment is often inevitable to make it compatible with ICT-based business processes.

---

[5] http://wordnetweb.princeton.edu/perl/webwn?s=system

3.7.2 Levels of eGovernment Systems

Government agencies, like many other organizations, can be viewed as three-level entities, with each level representing a different level of control that have different data requirements and operations.

At the highest level, the government executives are responsible for the government's strategic policy and direction. In the middle level, managers control and organize the government's actions and perform supervisory activities to ensure correct procedures and quality processing. Employees are at the lowest, or operational, level and mostly process the actual and real-time transactions. This operational level is also where the organization receives most of its data. However, the scope is typically limited to specific activities. The operational domain primarily focuses on processing tasks, rather than functions and results. Figure 3.6 illustrates this.

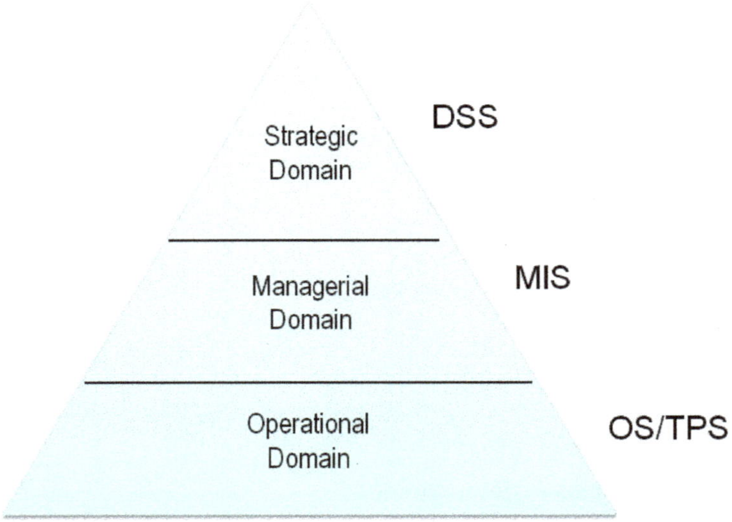

Figure 3.6. The pyramid structure and layers of government

Basic eGovernment systems are not much different from the information systems used elsewhere in private organizations for purposes such as accounting, human resource management, and so on. However, some system customization may occur to suit the specific purpose and requirements of the individual organization. Therefore, before building a customized mission-oriented system, it is important to know the different types of basic information systems (according to their functions) that organizations use. This knowledge is essential for selecting and analyzing appropriate information systems to achieve a particular organizational goal.

eGovernment systems can be divided into three different categories, which correspond with the three domains of government organizations: (a) operational systems, (b) management information systems, and (c) decision-making support systems. Table 3.1 describes the characteristics of each category and includes examples of the information systems used at each level. We discuss the details of those systems in the following paragraphs.

Table 3.1. Level of eGovernment systems and their use

Levels & Users	Characteristics	Systems
Operational: First line managers, operators, clerical employees, field employees, customer service.	• Repetitive activities, usually batch-oriented, • Specific inputs • Closest to citizens.	• Office automation • Transaction processing system • Collaborative systems • Document management and retrieval system
Managerial or administrative: Middle managers.	• Function and process dependent • Limited and fluid data • More dependent upon Information than data.	• Management information system
Strategic: Executives	• Mainly function oriented • Highly concentrated data • Complex analysis and programming involved	• Decision support system • Business Intelligence • Corporate Performance Management

3.7.3 Operational Level Systems

Office Automation Systems (OAS)

Office Automation Systems **(OAS)** provide effective and efficient ways of processing personal and organizational data, performing complex calculations, and generating desired reports and documents. These are essentially used to increase productivity and reduce an organization's paper trail. Examples of OAS include word processing, spreadsheets, file managers, personal calendars, presentation packages, and advanced communication and collaboration tools. OAS can be categorized into two types:

- Communication systems: these enable information to be shared in many different forms, such as teleconferencing (audio, video, and web), electronic mail, voice mail, fax, etc.
- Collaborative systems: these enhance teamwork through common document formats, shared systems, and controlling work flows.

Document Management and Retrieval Systems (DMRS)

Document Management and Retrieval Systems (**DMRS**) allow quick and efficient access and storage of all electronic and paper documents across the organization. It is the primary application for manipulating data across the organization.

DMRS provide users the flexibility to organize and view critical data in real-time. They also have the potential to manage the majority of information handled by any organization. DMRS evolved from the text indexing and retrieval systems, which were developed in the mid-1960s to support the bibliographic research of legal associates in the United States. DMRS have some limitations compared to the Database Management Systems (DBMS), which work, principally, with rigidly defined fields and records. Since document management is a big issue in any government, the development and application of DMRS is critical. It has been predicted that DBMS and DMRS will eventually merge as object-relational DBMS, as DBMS are becoming more popular.

Transaction Processing Systems (TPS)

Some of the earliest and elementary computerized information systems are transaction processing systems **(TPS)**, which involve software programs that record and report transactions. TPS support the monitoring, collection, storage, processing, and dissemination of the organization's basic business transactions. It processes large volumes of data and also provides the input data for other information systems (Figure 3.7). Sometimes, several TPS exist in one organization. Data collected at the transaction level is crucial because it provides the basic input for all other information systems, such as purchasing materials, billing, preparing a payroll, and transactions with citizens and businesses.

TPS continually collect data in real time. Most of this data is then stored in the corporate databases, which are available for processing as a group (referred to as batch processing). Some TPS provide immediate results, or real time data output, through online processing, especially when the customer or citizen needs immediate notification of the success or failure of a transaction.

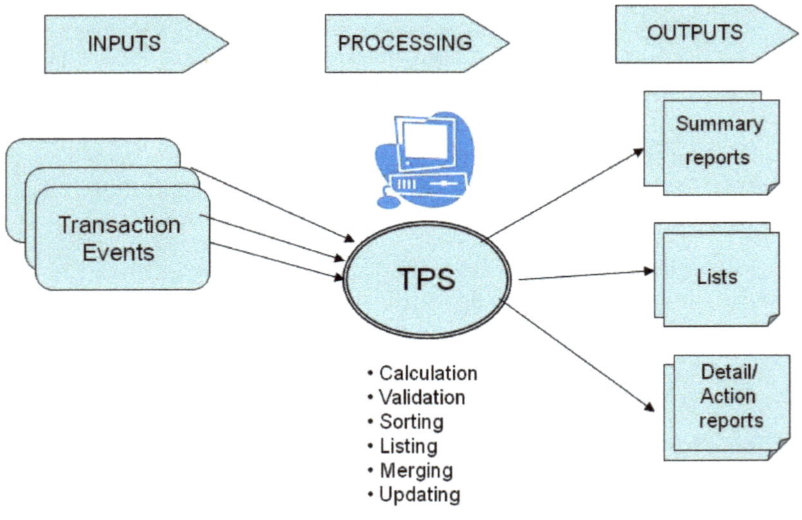

Figure 3.7. A transaction processing system

Examples of typical TPS in a government could be statistical data processing systems, payroll systems, accounting systems, payment processing systems, revenue systems, customs systems, and so on. TPS essentially provide source data for other information systems. For example, when someone launches a trade application, TPS data serves as an input for management information systems (MIS) to record all licensed traders in the country.

A good example of TPS is given in the Chittagong Custom house case study at the end of the chapter.

3.7.4 Managerial Level Systems

Management Information Systems (MIS)

Initially, computers were ideal for routine transaction processing. However, it was soon evident that their enormous capability for complex calculations and data analysis could provide important management information. Management information systems **(MIS)** have evolved out of transaction processing systems. Often, MIS are integrated with the TPS. For example, when processing a tax return, the transaction processing system records and updates each customer's account balance. Using this information, the related management information system can produce reports that recap daily tax return activities, list citizens who didn't submit a tax return, generate percentages and summary graphs, and so on.

Thus, MIS are information systems generate accurate, timely, and organized information, which assists managers in making decisions, solving problems, supervising activities, and tracking progress of work. Because they generate reports on a regular basis, management information systems are sometimes called management reporting systems (MRS).

MIS are mainly used by lower and middle-level employees to facilitate and control the day-to-day business of the organization. MIS support relatively structured decisions. Thus, they tend to be inflexible and have little analytical capacity. MIS deal with the past and present rather than the future. A typical MIS cycle is depicted in Figure 3.8.

Other examples for management information systems in a government are:

- Financial management systems (FMS)
- Personnel management systems (PMS)
- projects management information systems
- Land management systems (LMS)
- Police information systems
- Judicial information systems, and
- Information systems for national defence and security.

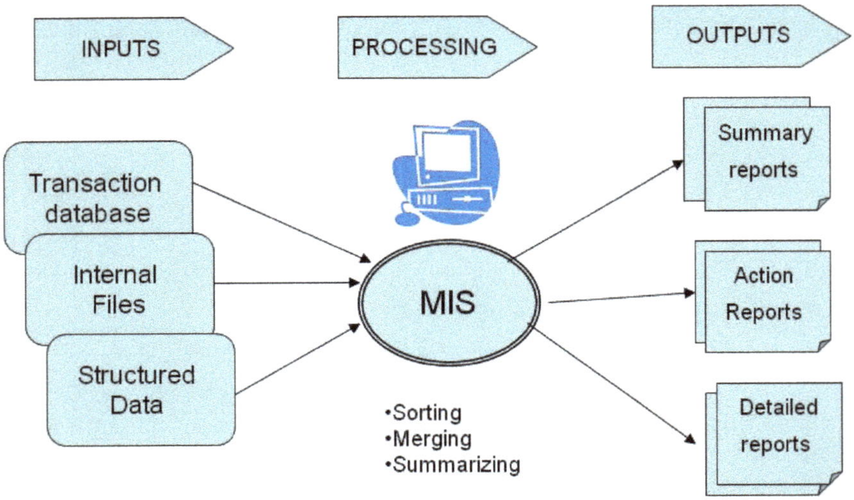

Figure 3.8. Management Information system

Case Study: RHD Success Story

The Roads and Highways Department (RHD) under The Ministry of Communications is one of the biggest departments in Bangladesh. It maintains about 21,000 km of roads and more than 18,000 bridges. As one of the major stakeholders of the annual budget, it directly employs 13,000 people.

The department maintains and improves its vast network of roads and bridges through field offices all over the country. Managing big numbers of employees, prioritizing works and managing projects - often at dispersed locations, political interventions - are some of the biggest challenges the department faces.

The U.K. Government's Department for International Development (DFID) funded technical assistance project introduced a suite of information systems to help RHD deal with some of its challenges, as part of an institutional reform. The introduction of systems, and reforms around them, started at 2001 and evolved over several years.

RHD now publishes promotions, postings and service history of all its employees on the Internet. It gives an insight into the condition of roads and bridges, and the progress made on different projects through its website. Before the RHD, this information was all on paper and required a lot of effort to obtain.

Field offices run small computer networks and spend an increasing amount of their day-to- day activities using purpose-built software that feeds information to central system.

Managers at different levels can now see every detail of projects running at the field offices, and are in a great position to monitor works and make informed decisions.

While there is still a long way to go, before the department's public image is improved and wastes are brought down, the system has significantly improved the way RHD does its business.

Source: Mohammed Salim, 2010.

Geographic Information Systems (GIS)

Geographic information systems (GIS) are a special type of MIS that originated in the mid-1960s that employ remote sensing technology. The rapid development of technology has accelerated the development and popularization of GIS. People soon realized that visualizing geographical information and data such as maps and charts helped the human brain to assimilate better. People discovered that GIS tools can be used to tie data to physical locations for numerous purposes at various levels of detail. As such, GIS, particularly through analyzing and examining data in their geographical context, are powerful.

GIS are becoming increasingly popular in public administrations. In addition to being an effective alternative to traditional surveying, GIS' applications are extended in other sectors such as environmental evaluation, natural resource management, urban planning, transport optimization, and so on. Examples of other GIS information include population levels, the number of doctors deployed, transportation routes/alternatives, vehicle allocation for transportation, and so on. This can be extremely helpful for planning and decision making.

However, despite their huge potential, use of GIS in developing countries will be difficult unless the country's infrastructure can support its application. It is also important for government agencies to recognize that GIS is a data-intensive system. If local data is of poor quality, GIS does not give the best value for money and effort. Thus, it is critical for government agencies to develop an overall plan that considers the characteristics, applications, data, and local context for implementing good GIS.

Case Study: A Land Licensing and Planning System for Beira City, Mozambique

Previously, the Land Registry consisted of an incomplete and inconsistent paper-based collection of dusty volumes, detailing plot usage, and dating back over a century. No definitive map existed - some showed groups of plots with duplicate or non-contiguous numbering systems, and plots overlaying others on different maps. Linking plots on the maps with the information in the Registry was sometimes difficult, providing insufficient information for both routine licenses and long-term strategic planning. Digitizing the maps and computerizing the Registry was a way of updat-

ing the system; namely, speeding it up and providing better quality information.

Land in Mozambique is owned by the state and divided into plots, according to a pre- determined structure plan for the city. Licenses for the development of vacant land are granted for a token fee on a first-come, first-served basis. Initially, licenses are for two years, after which they are revoked if no significant development has taken place. In most cases, such decisions should be purely administrative.

The local government authority of the city Beira, in Mozambique, implemented a decision support system, with a simple geographic information system interface. The data for the main database was based on the register of city land plots, their zoning (open space, industrial, or residential), and their status (vacant, under development, built on). The application produced information in two forms: a report with information on plot status, and a digitized map of city plots, which spatially represented the database. A common package was used to hold the database, which was run on two stand-alone PCs linked to a digitization tablet and two printers. A computer mapping/GIS product called "Data on the Map" was also used.

Operationally, the computerized application was intended to speed up decision-making by automating the processing of most license requests and revocations, leaving the Planning Department to concentrate on the few that warrant detailed consideration and negotiation. The application triggered warning letters and license withdrawal notices, in areas where legislation and regulations were not installed. For strategic land use planning, the application provided planners with information and trends, enabling them to better predict the future, and match developers with suitable plots.

However, the project failed to influence decision making. While Land Registry and Planning Department staff were keen, the political leadership was not happy with database results and found that the existing processing system was to its favor.

Source: http://www.egov4dev.org/success/case/beira.shtml

Further Reading

Bushell, S. (2003, October 7). *Spatial data to aid fire fighting efforts. CIO. Retrieved from* http://www.cio.com.au/article/110643/spatial_data_aid_fire_fighting_ efforts/?fp=4&fpid=2

Quick Quiz

1. What is the major incompatibility issue between a computer system and a government organization?
2. When can TPS be called MIS?
3. Give a few examples of GIS application in our day-to-day life.

3.7.5 Strategic Level Systems

Strategic information systems use ICT services and capabilities to gain advantages over the competitive forces that an organization faces in the global marketplace. A strategic information system can be any kind of information system that helps an organization gain a competitive advantage and meet other strategic enterprise objectives.

Decision Making Support Systems (DSS)

Often, it is said that 90% of our decisions rely on information. Modern information systems provide extremely rich data to decision makers, so people no longer dwell in a state of uncertainty when making a choice. In many cases in developing countries, people make decisions based on guesses, scattered and false information, or their own vested interests, which often leads to poor outcomes and mistakes at the national level. Information systems allow managers to use real-time data and analysis while making decisions.

Decision making support systems **(DSS)** are interactive computer systems that managers can use without help from computer specialists. DSS provide managers with the necessary information to make informed decisions (Figure 3.9). People typically use DSS to synthesize and manipulate data from MIS and TPS.

These systems usually project future trends based on the analysis of existing data. Data in DSS predict things, rather than accurately represent them. As such, it holistically overviews, instead of analyzing each individual occurrence. DSS typically involve lots of data analysis and modeling tools to help strategic decision-making.

DSS are often called executive information systems (EIS), though these tend to be highly personalized and custom-made for top-level executive use. As with normal DSS, EIS focus on predicting the future; however, they are also highly flexible and support unstructured decisions. A large number of ready-made EIS packages are available in the market. Also, all of the advanced enterprise systems include a customizable EIS module.

Decision-Making Support Systems have many applications in a government: in national or regional planning information systems, in social and economic information systems, in demography information systems, in manpower information systems, and so on.

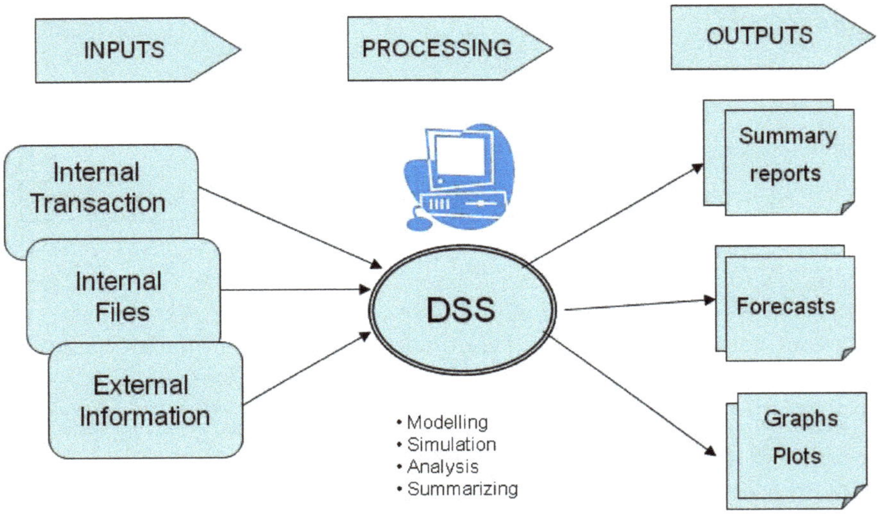

Figure 3.9. Decision-Making Support Systems

Quick Quiz

1. Give an example of strategic decisions for a government organisation.

3.7.6 Other Classifications of Information Systems

Expert Systems (ES)

An expert system (ES) is a knowledge-based information system that uses its knowledge about a specific area to act as an expert consultant to users. Knowledge is encoded as data in these systems as a form of files that are usually developed with the aid of experts in the field. While such systems do not often replace the human experts, they can serve as useful assistants.

Expert systems are being used in many different fields, such as medicine, engineering, the physical sciences, and business. For example, a disease recognition expert system can diagnose an illness, by asking questions about the patient's symptoms and analyzing laboratory results. These symptoms often overlap, which indicates several diseases. Thus, the system seeks to find a single pattern, or a disease from many overlapping patterns.

Other applications of expert systems include searching for minerals, analyzing compounds, recommending repairs, and planning of resources. Expert systems can support either operations or management activities.

Enterprise Information Systems (EI)

While other systems support isolated activities in a single department, enterprise systems support business processes that are performed by two or more departments. For example, evaluating a request for a loan is a business process, as is purchasing a part of, or conducting, an advertising campaign. The activities in the process are frequently done in sequence, but some can be conducted simultaneously. Enterprise systems usually integrate tasks done in different departments.

Enterprise Information systems **(EIS)** speed up communication throughout the company and make it easier for businesses to coordinate their daily operations. EIS are often also referred to as inter-organizational information systems (IOS). IOS enable computers to process the large amounts of information that flow between organizations. In addition, they enable computers to "talk" with other computers in different organizations.

One of the most popular enterprise applications is enterprise resources planning (ERP), which enables companies to plan and manage the resources of an entire enterprise. Other popular enterprise systems are customer relationship management (CRM), knowledge management (KM), and business intelligence (BI).

Enterprise Resources Planning (ERP)

With the successful deployment of ICT in manufacturing, forecasting and modelling, the opportunities arose to apply these techniques to other areas of business. Gradually, they were extended to total supply chain management, human resource management, accounting, finance, and marketing. Integrating all these functions into a single enterprise-wide system, to save time and resources and yield more business value, became known as enterprise resource planning (ERP).

ERP brings together the people, processes, tools, and resources across an entire organization to a single platform in order to facilitate decisions. ERP systems automate this activity with an integrated software application. These days, it is becoming increasingly difficult for a large company to remain competitive without a strong ERP system.

The best known ERP software, which comprises large modular integrated subsystems, is the German product SAP (the company name is System Anwedung Produkte[6]). This supports multi-site, concurrent business processes. However, converting from a traditional style of operation to ERP is not without risk, because the transition process is challenging and costly. We discuss ERP further in Chapter 6.

Supply Chain Management Systems (SCM)

Supply chain management (SCM) systems help businesses manage relationships with supplying agencies. These systems provide information to help suppliers, purchasing firms, and logistics companies share information about orders, production, inventory, and the delivery of products and services, so they can deliver services more efficiently. The ultimate objective is to get the right amount of products from the source to the point of consumption with the least amount of

---

[6] For a video on SAP, see http://www.youtube.com/watch?v=9_YY6z-_rsw&feature=related

time and cost. If the company and its supply network do not have accurate information, they are most likely to be burdened with excessive inventories, inaccurate manufacturing plans, and missed schedules. Inability to move products efficiently through the supply chain impacts negatively on customer service. A proper SCM ensures smooth business operations and supply resource management.

Knowledge Management Systems (KMS)

In many organizations, especially those in developing countries, when a top executive or key person retires or leaves, he/she leaves with all the important information and knowledge of the organization. There is no precise system to preserve an organization's important knowledge assets. As a result, organizations often cannot continue to grow. Moreover, scattered knowledge and information resources all through the organization and employees, which, individually, may not be so significant, can become immensely important when all these pieces are integrated together because it provides important business intelligence.

Knowledge management (KM) evolved from an increasing concern over how to manage the vast amount of knowledge resources that are produced everyday in the public sector. Managing this ever-growing, multi-dimensional information is a difficult and challenging task. We define knowledge management as "the management of activities and processes for leveraging knowledge to enhance competitiveness through better use and creation of individual and collective knowledge resources" (Chaffey, 2011, p. 563). A knowledge management system (KMS) facilitates the KM to capture, store, share, and apply knowledge where ICTs play a critical role (Alavi & Leidner, 1999). Technological solutions are important, but there is more to KM than just technology.

Because public administrations are knowledge-intensive organizations, the importance of knowledge management in eGovernment is enormous. Public sector officials, who are also known as "knowledge workers", create, organize, and share important business knowledge through their day-to-day work. Often, this important knowledge gets lost due to the lack of preservation.

While private sector organizations have reaped the benefits from the knowledge management system, public sector organizations are still catching up in response to growing customer demands, and the increasing possibilities of advanced information systems.

In modern public administration, it is extremely important to promote an integrated collaboration, a knowledge-supportive culture, and a common strategy to deliver services. A well-designed KM in public administration can make significant differences in terms of improving decision making, facilitating the public to participate in public decision making, building competitive social capital, and developing a competitive work force (Wiig, 2000). Knowledge management approaches may vary depending upon the specific needs. The public sectors of developed countries are investing a lot of resources and expending great effort to build strong KMS in the public sectors, which is becoming essential to gain competitive advantage.

Some case studies on Australian public service agencies show how KM is used to meet their strategic objectives. For example, the Australian Bureau of Statistics (ABS) uses workgroup-based databases to facilitate group information storage and sharing. Employees are encouraged to develop and practice sharing information, which helps staff collate and analyze huge amounts of statistical information valuable to organization. Another good example is Centrelink, where huge databases use advanced KM products to map common terms and phrases, monitor the performance of the entire organization, and form systems to simulate trends, in order to display data graphically on a small geographic area (AGIMO, 2004).

Further Reading

See Centrelink - *KM Principles and Lessons Learned*
http://www.finance.gov.au/agimo-archive/better_practice/km_case_studies/centrelink_-_km_principles.html

Case Study: Chittagong Customs House

Chittagong Customs House, located at the major seaport in Bangladesh, is one of the main sources of income for the National Board of Revenue (NBR). It processes 75-80% of national imports and exports. However, this important organization suffered from poor management and outdated procedures, which resulted in irregularities and the loss of national revenue.

The customs department spent significant sums of money to reform these legacies, but failed to gain any fruitful output, due to red tape barriers and the vested interests of different stakeholders. Because of the old-fashioned manual procedures, it used to take a long time to clear a consignment. The resulting bottleneck meant that doing business through Chittagong Customs was a time-consuming and costly process.

On the other hand, customs were also under pressure to become compliant with WCO standards by introducing world-class ICT infrastructure. In July 2007, customs department officials called for the automation of the Chittagong Customs House in order to mitigate the problems. For the purpose of automation, the customs house started collecting BDT[7] 70 per Bill of Entry. According to their estimate, it would require BDT 11-12 crore to fully automate the system. Chittagong Customs House had neither the budget nor the technical resources to perform the job. As a result, the Chittagong Chamber of Commerce and Industry (CCCI) stepped in with a

---

[7] BDT- Bangladesh Taka (Unit of currency); 1US$= 82 BDT (Approx)

task force. Considering the budget and resource limitations, the Chittagong Chamber of Commerce and Industry proposed to automate the Customs House in a Public Private Partnership (PPP) project, using the Build-Own-Operate-Transfer (BOOT) model. A local ICT firm, DataSoft, developed the automation system for Chittagong Customs House, which was officially launched on October 6, 2008. The government exchequer didn't have to pay anything for the automation project, and the stakeholders received returns on their investments through revenue generated from the Bill of Entry and other services.

The Chittagong Customs House Automation Project is one of the most successful government automation projects in Bangladesh. This automation, together with business process reengineering, has helped Chittagong Customs House double their revenue earnings, which now stand at Tk 15,000+ crore a year. It has also reduced the cost of doing business by at least 70%, reduced customs processing time by 80%, established transparency, leveled the playing field for businesses, and generated better risk management. One of the biggest challenges of the automation process was bringing in all the relevant stakeholders to develop a customized system.

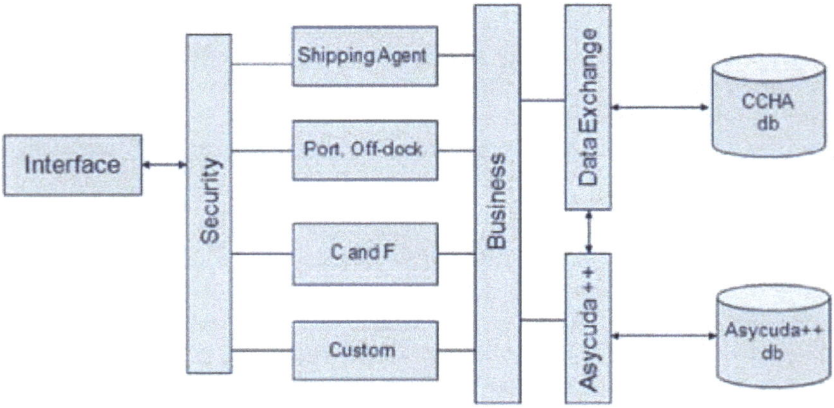

Figure 3.10. System Architecture

Further Reading

See Pryslak, J. (2009). *Why enterprise architecture? SYS-CON Media.* Retrieved from http://jeffpryslak.sys-con.com/node/909464

Table 3.2. A comparative scenario before and after introducing automation

Process	Before automation	After automation	Impact
Importing goods	42 steps	5 steps	Time spent by agent/ exporter/EPZ is reduced by 85%;
Exporting Goods	116 steps	5 steps	Significantly reduced scope for bribe transactions; Can submit BOE and other documents from own office
After submission of bills	Only 42% completed within 3 days of submission	70% is completed within the day and 90% within 3 days of submission	**Time span** Faster collection of Govt. revenue; No waiting for transaction of bill payments at Bank
Legal C&F Agent; Exporporter/Importer	Paid Tk. 70 per BOE	Only Tk. 50 (around 1 USD) per BOE	**Operational Cost** Agent/exporter no longer has to pay bribe of around Tk. 3000-4000 per BOE
Write petition of unsettled customs duty	Anomalies in file and document preservation	Database of scanned copy of around 12,677 files of Indemnity Bonds; Computerization of 10,033 writ petitions and related files	**Database of Indemnity Bonds** Registration and monitoring of the petitioner; NBR recovered around Tk. 125 crore in long-term outstanding revenue
Adjustment of the account	Took 4-5 hours to know the balance of revolving account	Stakeholder ca see balance minutes after logging on	**Online Account Balance of stakeholders** Escape to find out hundreds of ledger books by customs staff
Submission of documents	Had to submit up to 40 documents at Mercantile Marine Department	Online application process; Only have to submit 14 documents	**Port clearance by local agent** Reduced time
Informing about the status of stock	Companies avoided frequently measuring the real reserve	The real reserve is displayed at 90-minute intervals on a website	**Measure of the import amount and stock of soybean oil** The chance of customs evasion has been stopped

Rigorous 42 steps reduced to 6 steps

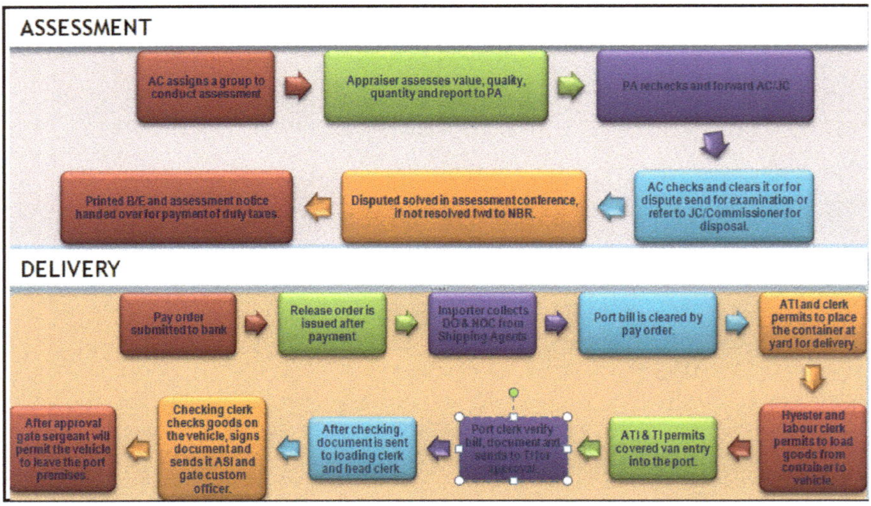
ASSESSMENT
AC assigns a group to conduct assessment
Appraiser assesses value, quality, quantity and report to PA
PA rechecks and forward AC/JC
AC checks and clears it or for dispute send for examination or refer to JC/Commissioner for disposal.
Disputed solved in assessment conference, if not resolved fwd to NBR.
Printed B/E and assessment notice handed over for payment of duty taxes.
DELIVERY
Pay order submitted to bank
Release order is issued after payment
Importer collects DO & NOC from Shipping Agents
Port bill is cleared by pay order.
ATI and clerk permits to place the container at yard for delivery.
Hyester and labour clerk permits to load goods from container to vehicle.
ATI & TI permits covered van entry into the port.
After checking, document is sent to loading clerk and head clerk
Checking clerk checks goods on the vehicle, signs document and sends it ASI and gate custom officer.
After approval gate sergeant will permit the vehicle to leave the port premises.

42 Steps (before automation)

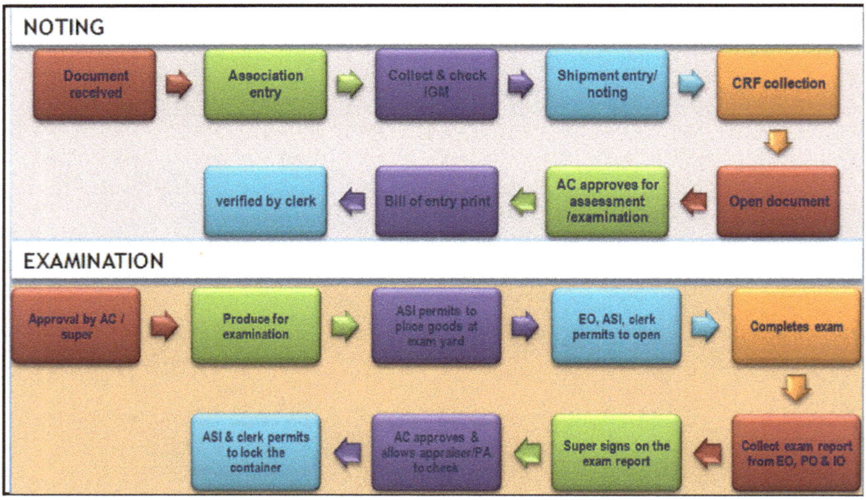
NOTING
Document received
Association entry
Collect & check IGM
Shipment entry/ noting
CRF collection
Open document
AC approves for assessment /examination
Bill of entry print
verified by clerk
EXAMINATION
Approval by AC / super
Produce for examination
ASI permits to place goods at exam yard
EO, ASI, clerk permits to open
Completes exam
Collect exam report from EO, PO & IO
Super signs on the exam report
AC approves & allows appraiser/PA to check
ASI & clerk permits to lock the container

5 Steps (after automation)

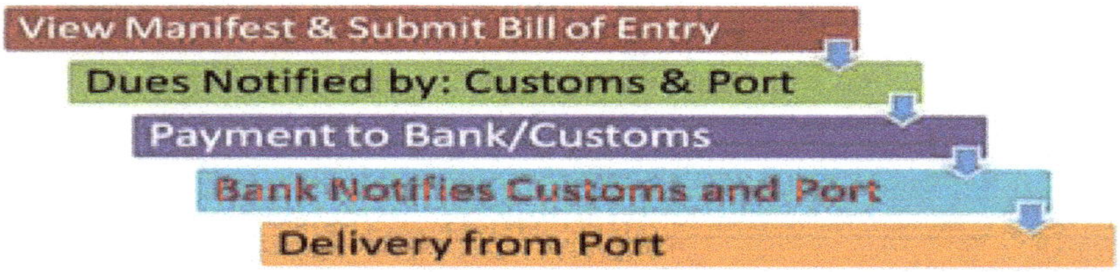
View Manifest & Submit Bill of Entry
Dues Notified by: Customs & Port
Payment to Bank/Customs
Bank Notifies Customs and Port
Delivery from Port

Source: Datasoft, Bangladesh, 2010

Chapter Highlights

- A large eGovernment system will typically combine several types of information systems.
- Most information systems are designed to manage and record business data/ functions to support decision making.
- An EA is extremely important as it reduces the costs of ICT by better aligning the organization's mission to ICT investment.
- There are at least two ways to build enterprise architecture. One is the "big bang" method, and the other is the incremental approach.
- Information technology architecture is essentially a master plan of the information assets in an organization, which includes the physical design and layout of where hardware components are placed.
- Government agencies, like many other organizations, can be viewed as three-level entities - each representing a distinct level of control, and each has different data requirements and operations.
- Some of the earliest and elementary computerized information systems are transaction processing systems (TPS), which support the collection, storage, processing, and dissemination, of the organization's basic business transactions.
- Management information systems (MIS) are information systems that generate organized information, so managers can solve problems, supervise activities, and track progress.
- Geographic information systems (GIS) can tie data to physical locations for numerous purposes at detail level, but are primarily used to analyze and examine data in their geographical context.
- A strategic information system helps organizations gain a competitive advantage and meet other strategic objectives.
- An expert system is a knowledge-intensive information system that uses its information about a specific area to act as an expert consultant to users.
- KMS refers to a system of managing knowledge in organizations that supports the creation, capture, storage, and dissemination of information.

Review Questions

1. What are the principles on which enterprise architecture is built?
2. What are the essential elements of an enterprise system?
3. What is solution architecture?
4. How does TPS output become the source for other systems?
5. Where and how does spatial data become important for decision making?
6. Explain what you understa nd by eGovernment system.
7. Explain the operational domain of the eGovernment system with examples.
8. What are the two types of office automation systems?
9. What is the difference between EIS and ERP?
10. Why is KM so important for government organizations?

Discussion questions

1. Why is alignment between business and IT so important, yet difficult to achieve?
2. What are the advantages and disadvantages of the two approaches of making enterprise architecture?
3. How does enterprise architecture help in future investment and growth?
4. What are the critical differences between the various information systems discussed in the book? How these systems can be effectively applied in eGovernment?

Exercises

1. Draw a transaction model based on a local government office in your state.
2. Draw solution architecture for a proposed eGovernment system in your organization, following the principles of EA.

References

AGIMO. (2004). APS KM case studies. The Australian Government Information Management Office Archive. Retrieved Jan 2, 2012, from http://www.finance.gov.au/agimo-archive/better_practice/ km_case_studies/centrelink_-_km_principles.html

AGIMO. (2009). Australian Government Architecture (AGA). Retrieved from http://www.finance.gov.au/policy-guides-procurement/australian-government-architecture-aga/

Alavi, M., & Leidner, D. E. (1999). Knowledge management systems: Issues, challenges, and benefits. Communications of the AIS, 1(2), 1-37.

Chaffey, D. (2011). EBusiness and eCommerce management: Strategy, implementation and practice. Italy: Financial Times Press.

Ebrahim, Z., & Irani, Z. (2005). EGovernment adoption: Architecture and barriers. Business Process Management Journal, 11(5), 589-611.

Turban, E., & Volonino, L. (2010). Information Technology for Management: Improving Performance in the Digital Economy (7th ed.). NJ: Wiley.

Wiig, K. M. (2000). Application of knowledge management in public administration. Paper presented at the Public Administrators of the City of Taipei Taiwan, ROC. Retrieved from http://unpan1.un.org/intradoc/groups/public/documents/apcity/unpan020329.pdf

CHAPTER 4 Data Networks

Learning Objectives

After studying this chapter, you will be able to:

- Describe the different types of data networks that are common in government work environments
- Identify when different types of networks are most likely to be used
- Describe the different uses of networks in government work
- Identify four main eGovernment opportunities based on networks and their uses, and
- Discuss the trade-offs that network-based eGovernments must make in least- developed countries.

Network Failure

Network availability is critical to government success

In January 2012, the Virginia State Police lost their network systems for five hours. The police were not able to access criminal records, gun licences, sex offender registers, or broader law enforcement systems such as the Automated Fingerprint Index System (AFIS). "At one point, those system failures affected 13 percent of the [Virginia] Commonwealth's file servers, hobbling agencies like [the department of Motor Vehicles], the Board of Elections and the Department of Taxation" (Holmberg, 2012). This affected public safety.

The availability of networks is usually so consistent and reliable that one forgets until they are not there that they are the critical linking element. Understanding what networks are, how they provide the communication backbone of computing, and what types are applicable in various circumstances is fundamental to eGovernment managers.

Source: http://wtvr.com/2012/01/19/virginia-state-police-network-down-for-several-hours/

4.1 Network Types

4.1.1 The simplest network

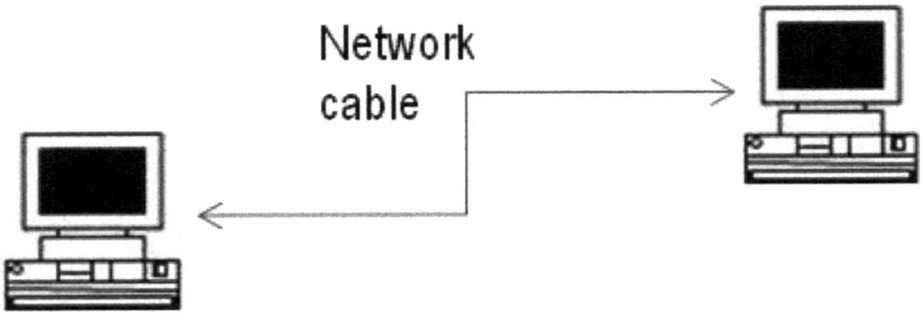

Figure 4.1. The simplest network: two directly connected devices

4.1.2 Personal Area Networks (PANs)

One computer is useful, but organizations rarely comprise one person. The simplest network connects two devices, usually so that data held on one can be shared with the other (Figure 4.1). One modern example of this simple network is connecting your Bluetooth-enabled phone to your computer to back up your phone's contact list. Another example is connecting your digital camera to your computer by USB cable to copy your photos onto the computer and manipulate them with software or attach them to an email. Sometimes, networks at this level are called personal area networks (or PANs).

But merely connecting two computers is not that helpful. The concept of the "network effect" deals with this issue. The network effect says that the more devices connected to a network, the more valuable the network is to each device. There is a downside to this, too; the more devices using the network, the more congested (slow) it becomes.

4.1.3 Local Area Networks (LANs)

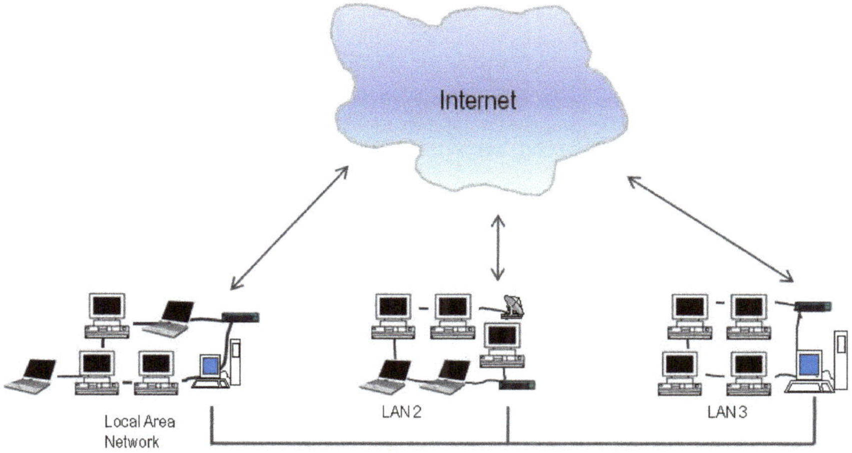

Figure 4.2. A campus area network made up of local area networks

In an environment such as an office or a school, computers that are networked together and sharing resources, such as printers, belong to a local area network (or LAN). An important difference between these networks and smaller ones used by individuals or families is that a dedicated computer, called a network server, is usually included in the network to manage the traffic and to share resources among the other computers.

Knowledge workers most commonly experience the LAN system. Resources such as Internet connections and large-scale software applications may be housed on other networks, but most often the knowledge worker accesses them through the LAN to which their computer is directly connected.

Figure 4.2 illustrates another approach that is common in larger organizations: many LANs connected together (e.g., one per division) to support the whole organization. When this occurs in a single (large) building or in a group of related and closely located buildings, the configuration is often called a campus area network or CAN.

Wide area networks (WANs) connect smaller-scale networks across large geographic distances. These networks allow organizations to share data and application systems across all of their offices (Figure 4.3).

4.1.4 Wide Area Networks (WANs)

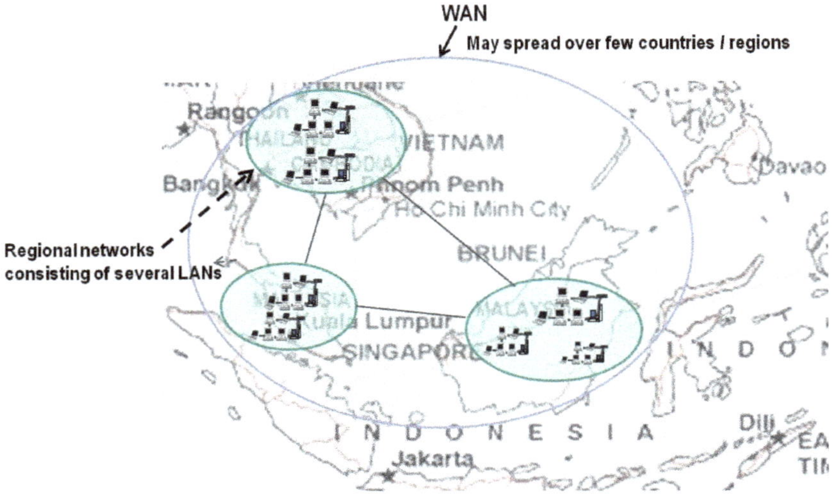

Figure 4.3. A wide area network

The majority of the physical networks on which WANs operate are owned and maintained by telecommunications companies. Most organizations that operate WANs lease their network capacity from telecommunications companies rather than build their own network. Increasingly, organizations are using the Internet as the carrier for their WANs; that is, they do not hold their own permanent network capacity but use whatever the Internet provides when they require it.

4.2 Network Carriers

There are two fundamental ways to create a network between computers:

- Wired - by connecting the computers using cables, and
- Wireless - by using radio signals to communicate between computers.

4.2.1 Wired networks

Wired networks use a variety of media to carry network data. The "simplest" and the one with the least capacity (usually called bandwidth) is twisted-pair wire, which is commonly used in telephone lines and for domestic network connections.

Once networks reach a larger, or more commercial, scale, the wire that carries the network data is coaxial cable. This cable is commonly used in buildings to host office LANs and for cable television connections.

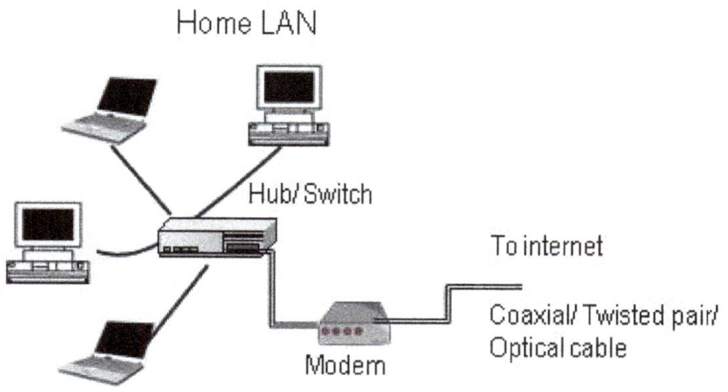

Figure 4.4. Devices connected by cables for networking

Large-scale network connections (or "backbones") are commonly carried on fiber-optic cable. Optical fiber is a special glass fiber material that transmits light pulses rather than electrical pulses and has huge bandwidth.

4.2.2 Wireless networks

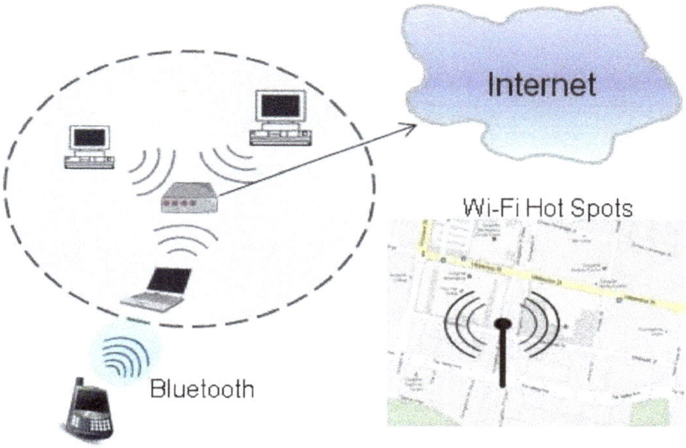

Figure 4.5. Illustrations of different wireless networks

Wireless networks are increasingly popular because of their installation convenience. Wireless networks differ in their ranges and capacities (Figure 4.5). Bluetooth is specifically designed to have a very short range (approx. 10 meters) and relatively low bandwidth (less than one mbps). Wi-Fi is a common domestic and office wireless network, and is based on standards promulgated by the Institute of Electrical and Electronics Engineers. Many cafes, libraries, airport lounges, and other businesses will offer a wireless connection, sometimes for free. These places are often called "hotspots".

WiMAX is a relatively new wireless protocol that allows large-scale wireless networks. WiMAX networks can cover up to 10 kilometers with data rates of up to 75 mbps.

Long Term Evolution (LTE) represents the leading edge in wireless network protocol development. Also called Mobile Broadband Wireless Access (MBWA), it is being developed for mobile phone companies to support wireless Internet access on smartphones and other handheld devices. The technology has the potential to reach 300 mbps, but, because the networks are shared among high numbers of devices, individual users will not directly experience this bandwidth speed.

4.3 Other Network Ideas

Two other important terms commonly occur when we discuss the use of computer networks in organizations and eGovernment:

- The Internet - the interconnection of WANs all over the world, and
- Virtual Private Networks (VPNs) - a special way of connecting a private network over a public network infrastructure.

4.3.1 The Internet

The Internet started in 1969 as a United States of America Defense research project called ARPANET. It focused on building resilient networks. Major U.S. universities conducted the research and immediately saw the value of being able to share data for research purposes. The

Defense wanted to ensure that the network would work in the event of up to 50% network destruction. The universities wanted to facilitate researchers communicating and working collaboratively. Then, in 1991, Tim Berners-Lee invented the World Wide Web while working at CERN. The Web was designed to make it much easier to connect information stored in different parts of the Internet. Suddenly, there were tools that allowed anyone to access information on the Internet.

The Internet does not belong to anyone, nor does it have a headquarters or controlling organization. Several organizations, such as the World Wide Web Consortium (W3C) and the Internet Engineering Task Force (IETF), coordinate the efforts of hundreds and thousands of businesses and individuals to set and extend standards for how the Internet and the applications running on it, such as email and the Web, will work.

In practice, these days, the Internet exists because Internet service providers (ISPs) sell customers access to the network capacity, which they lease from telecommunications companies. The customers (businesses, government agencies, and individuals) use that access to retrieve information, usually in the form of HTML web pages, stored on various servers belonging to other Internet customers. However, the single largest use of the Internet is still email, one of its very first uses.

4.3.2 Virtual Private Networks (VPNs)

Virtual private networks (VPNs) use special protocols and cryptography to send information over public networks. Although the data travels on networks that anyone could intercept, it is protected by the protocols and cryptography so that, if intercepted, it cannot be understood; that is, the data remains private.

Quick Quiz

1. Connect the acronym to the brief description of a type of network.

CAN	A network that connects devices over large geographic distances.
PAN	A network that connects devices in an office or school building.
WAN	A network that connects devices across several closely located buildings.
LAN	A network that connects devices that are close to each other.

2. If you were going to install a LAN in an existing building, which approach would be better: wireless or wired? Why?
3. What is the network effect? Can you explain why the network effect is important in network applications such as email?
4. What is a VPN? Can you explain why a government agency might use a VPN?

4.4 Uses of Networks

Computer networks can be used in many ways. A legitimate use is any arrangement of systems and the control of access to those systems or other networked resources. In many organizational contexts, meeting specific business requirements or supporting unique processing arrangements requires special approaches to network use.

Over time, many typical approaches have arisen. This section looks at these common approaches, namely:

- **Client/server** - the fundamental approach to resource sharing used on modern networks
- **Intranet** - an arrangement of resources and information, provided to support collaboration within an organization
- **Extranet** - an arrangement of resources and information and, particularly, access to those resources and information, provided to support collaboration between an organization and specific partners outside the organization, and

- **Website** - a presentation of information and systems (services) that an organization creates and manages to serve its customers and suppliers.

4.4.1 Client/Server

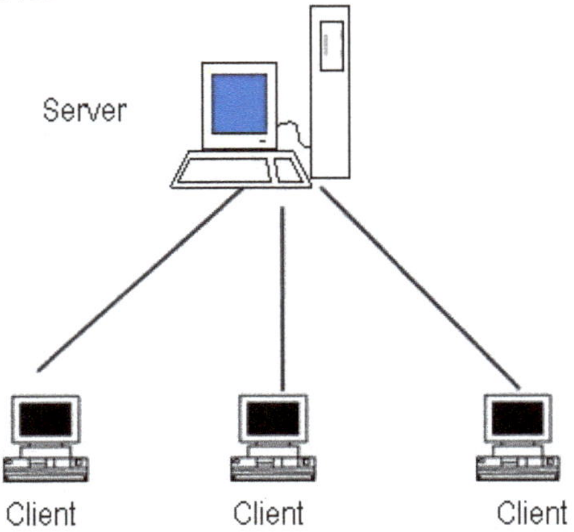

Figure 4.6. A simple illustration of a client/server architecture

In a client/server architecture, specific network devices are dedicated to managing certain resources; for example, printing, network routing, database storage, and file storage. These resources are called servers because they provide services to other network devices. Network devices that call on those services are called clients. A typical client is the user's personal computer. A client asks a server for the service they require and the server responds to the client (e.g., by sending data from a database the client is accessing) (Figure 4.6). Alternatively, the client might request the server do something with the data it has processed (e.g., print it or store it).

This separation of processing roles is now typical in networked computing operations. The extent to which the client is involved in processing data or performing other acts as a way for the user to interact with servers varies between architectures. When the client has significant processing power and only calls on the servers for fundamental roles (e.g., storage, printing, etc.), they are often called a "thick client". This is in contrast to a "thin client", which does little more than show the user whatever the servers send it; in other words, it does little actual processing.

4.4.2 Web-based Connections

The dominant approach to providing users with network-based services and information is using the technologies that underlie the Web. The Web operates with a client/server architecture and the client is almost always a piece of software called a web browser (e.g., Mozilla Firefox or Internet Explorer). Web browsers use certain technologies - primarily, Hypertext Markup Language (HTML), Cascading Style Sheets (CSS), and Javascript. These technologies form the basis of HTML5. Web browsers use Hypertext Transfer Protocol (HTTP) to request, receive, and interpret data from servers. So common is this approach that many people advocate web-based networks, because using them productively is thought to require little or no training.

This section looks at three important web-based uses of networks:

- Intranet - an Internet inside an organization
- Extranet - a system that allows specific people outside the organization to have access to the intranet, and
- Website - how the organization presents itself on the Internet.

Intranet

An intranet is a presentation of network resources (applications, information, and network devices) for users internal to an organization, and it uses the technologies that underlie the Internet (Figure 4.7). An intranet provides an Internet-like environment for information sharing, communication, collaboration, and workflow to support organizational processes.

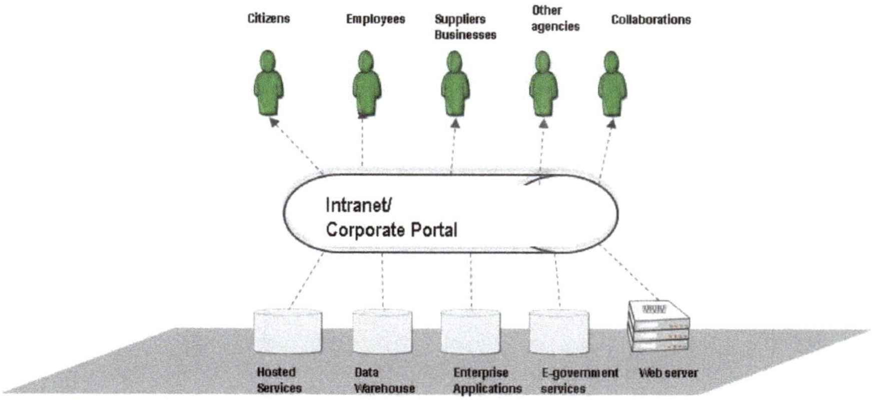

Figure 4.7. An intranet offers web-based access to corporate systems

Many intranets only require users to use a computer directly connected to their organization's internal networks, but some require further authentication to allow access to information and systems. An intranet is typically protected by network security to prevent people outside the organization from accessing it.

Specific opportunities that intranets can provide in an organization include:

- Communicating and collaborating - an intranet can host internal email, chat rooms, discussion boards, and websites. Some intranets can even send and deliver faxes without needing to print them on paper.
- Information publishing - one of the most valuable uses of the intranet is publishing corporate standards, policies, and guides. Everyone can access them and they are always up to date. The dynamic nature of modern web

presentation also allows for much richer presentation; for example, rather than print instructions on proper equipment use, an organization can embed videos showing the proper operation.

- Workflow processing - sophisticated intranets can also support organizational processes that may previously have been completed on paper forms, such as employees applying for leave or filing incident reports. Simple technologies such as webform processing can greatly enhance such routine operations.

Extranet

Organizations often arrange for partners, suppliers, and customers to make direct computer connections to transact routine business. When a connection provides access to a company's intranet, it is often called an extranet (Figure 4.8). When the connection is directly from one organization's computer system to another's (i.e., there are no human operators involved), it is typically referred to as electronic data interchange (EDI).

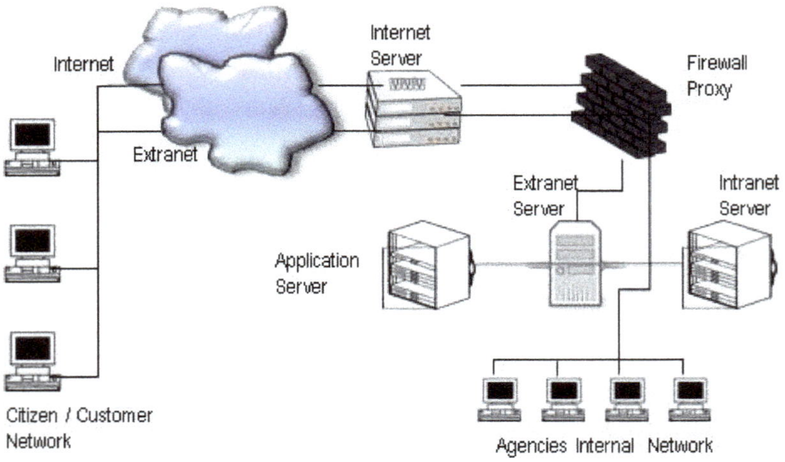

Figure 4.8. An extranet allows partners to access corporate systems

An extranet allows entities external to the organization to access its systems directly after passing necessary authentication processes. The connection provides those external parties with the opportunity to access the organization's intranet and use its services the way an employee would.

For example, take a situation in which an independent financial adviser received access to, say, an insurance company's extranet, allowing the adviser to prepare an insurance application on their client's behalf, as if the adviser were an employee of the insurance company. This arrangement would be beneficial to the insurance company (because it would sell insurance without involving any of its costly employees), to the adviser (because they could provide a more beneficial servicer to their client), and to the client (because the insurance arrangements would be made in one appointment and without forms).

Website

Through websites (Figure 4.9), organizations present information about themselves and their products, and often host systems and services for customers and other partners.

Most modern websites are dynamic, which means that they change their responses and the data they present on the basis of users' input and website navigation, or the device on which the browser is used (e.g., a mobile phone).

Figure 4.9. Websites present the corporate image on the Internet

The primary objectives of most company-operated websites are to:

- Generate new revenue from online sales
- Reduce costs through online sales and customer support
- Attract new customers through online marketing, advertising, and sales
- Increase the loyalty of existing customers through improved web customer service and support
- Develop new web-based markets and distribution channels for existing products, and
- Develop new information-based products accessible on the Web (Kalakota and Robinson, 2001).

4.4.3 Non-web Connections

As we mentioned previously, email remains the most common use of computer networks. Emails transfer across networks using a protocol different from web transactions. Email is such a common form of communication in personal and business correspondence that some postal services are reducing their number of letter delivery days because of the downturn in traditional means of correspondence (McDonald, 2012).

Inside organizations, file sharing is a common use of networks and allows many people access to a single version of information. The opportunity to share processing power and other scarce resources (e.g., printers, faxes, and scanners) also drives network use in organizations.

Quick Quiz

1. An intranet is used to support employees in their work. Which of the following is unlikely to appear on an intranet:
    a) Employee leave applications
    b) Standard operating procedures
    c) A shopping cart checkout function, or
    d) Internal e-mails
2. What can an organizational partner do on an extranet that they cannot do on the organization's website?
3. What is the biggest non-Web use of the Internet?

4.5 eGovernment over Networks

Networks implement connectivity. A fundamental tenet of eGovernment is connecting people and businesses to their governments. Clearly, networks are critical to successful eGovernment.

This desire for and value in connectivity is not limited to eGovernment: all businesses can benefit from increased connectivity with customers and partners. In this section, we discuss the benefits of networking and connectivity in an eGovernment context.

This chapter outlines some of the eGovernment opportunities presented by networked computing:

- Increased internal efficiency
- Increased reliability and control
- Increased flexibility and reach, and
- Increased coordination and outreach.

4.5.1 Increased Internal Efficiency

Government work routinely involves dealing with information, analyzing it as the basis for decisions, reviewing it as the basis for policy, collecting it as evidence of activity, or distributing it to manage the business of government. The more that individual public servants can work together in teams, and the more that those teams work together across agencies, the greater the efficiency they can attain in managing information.

Networks in government organizations promote:

- Sharing of data and information - when all individuals are connected to networks, those individuals can share information as data records in databases or as words and pictures in documents. Sharing this data is more efficient than making and managing multiple copies of it (e.g., by creating multiple photocopies of one document to circulate to each interested individual).
- More collaborative working arrangements - networks allow individuals in teams to work together more readily, and for different teams to work together to create and use information. They can collaborate without ever leaving their desks, and sophisticated teams can work across organizations and even around the world.
- Greater flexibility in communicating among teams and individuals - while much office work is still conducted in face-to-face meetings, network-based communication tools such as email, chat functions, and bulletin boards offer a range of alternatives for maintaining and recording communication.

The combination of networks and workflow support software can regularize and standardize efforts by automating the process of deciding what information to capture, in what form to capture it, and who should deal with it next. These kinds of systems introduce processing consistency and remove delays brought about by relying on particular individuals to keep all processing moving.

4.5.2 Increased Reliability and Control

Networks also offer greater control of the resources that individuals in an organization share. Typically, networks promote having a centralized collection of critical (data) resources.

A database should offer "one truth" that is always up to date. All parties concerned use this authoritative copy of important facts, and everyone is able to access the most recent version of a team's work. If everyone is using the same source of information, they will share a common view of what is happening and what decisions to make.

Centralized access to shared resources is also helpful in optimizing the use of high-value resources (e.g., mainframe computing, high-end printing, etc). An organization is more likely to receive real value from high-priced electronic resources if everyone is able to access them.

In the same way that organizations can make electronic resources accessible to everyone for infrequent use, networks can promote and support the development of centers of excellence - places where relatively small teams of experts become a resource drawn on across the organization.

Modern network management software can offer control of end-user devices. This control means that all end-user devices (e.g., workstations or mobile phones) have the same software and operate in a common way, which reduces support and increases consistency in employee productivity.

Case Study: Connecting All Government Agencies in New Zealand

In June 2006, the New Zealand State Services Commission (SSC) announced that it had secured approval to deploy the Government Shared Network (GSN). Laurence Millar, the SSC's Deputy Commissioner of Information and Communication Technologies, explained, "The GSN will provide a secure, controlled access network community within which government agencies can collaborate and better serve the needs of New Zealanders." At the time of the announcement, 17 agencies were expected to join the network in the first year of operation, and detailed planning was underway in seven of them.

IBM New Zealand Limited was selected as the GSN Service Manager, which meant that it was responsible for supplying network management and service delivery. Several other providers were in contract negotiations to provide the fundamental infrastructure.

The GSN was a NZ$14 million project expected to deliver high-speed services that included off-site disaster recovery, ICT telephony, and remote access. The GSN was expected to reduce the cost of voice and data traffic and to provide improved budgeting through fixed charging. These services were to be delivered to individual agencies at costs they would have been unable to negotiate individually.

The first users of the GSN, the Department of Labour and Maritime New Zealand, joined the network in October 2006. By February 2007, Archives New Zealand, Te Puni Kokiri (the ministry responsible for Maori affairs), and the SSC were also in the network. By September 2007, the Ministry of Education and Foreign Affairs had also joined. "Hub" agencies, those that other agencies interact with on a regular basis, were proving more reluctant. Inland Revenue, Statistics and Land Information New Zealand had signed letters of intent but not yet joined.

In a speech in September 2007, the then-Programme Manager of the GSN, Michael Foley, claimed bi-partisan support in Parliament. He stipulated the three main drivers of the GSN as, in order, improved security, increased collaboration and cooperation, and cost and efficiency gains.

Then, in February 2009, the new State Services Minister (a change of government occurred in late 2008 in New Zealand), announced that the GSN would be discontinued because it was financially unsustainable. The 16 agencies then using the GSN would be moved to a new provider in the private sector. That provider would be selected through a procurement process. "The project had been running at a considerable financial loss ever since it became operational in September 2007 - losing [NZ]$700,000 per month," said the Minister.

By July 2009, Government Technology Services (GTS) was managing the process of transferring agencies to a new service, and two separate reviews of the original project's failure were reported to have led to the resignation of New Zealand's first chief information officer, Laurence Millar.

The head of GTS claimed that the nine agencies participating in the GSN were sufficient demand for the new service provider, Datacraft, to cost-effectively provide the service. Further demand, of which much was claimed to exist, would add to that economy. The new service was dubbed "one.govt" (Open Network Environment). Running one.govt was seen as a marginal increase of the supplier's current demand, and hence could be offered at competitive prices. It was reported that the GSN's uncompetitiveness compared to private- sector alternatives was one of its main problems.

One.govt went live in December 2009. As of May 2011, Datacraft New Zealand was advertising that a dozen agencies were using one.govt and specifically named eight: the Department of Internal Affairs, the Department of Labour, the Ministry of Education, the Department of Conservation, New Zealand Trade and Enterprise, the National Library of New Zealand, New Zealand Police, and Archives New Zealand.

Sources:

Bell, S. (2009, July 6). Government IT service kicks off with GSN fix. Computerworld. Retrieved April 30, 2013, from http://computerworld.co.nz/news.nsf/ telecommunications/government-it-service- kicks-off-with-gsn-fix?Opendocument

Jackson, R. (2009, December 7). 110 sites cut over to new one.govt network. Retrieved April 30, 2013, from http://computerworld.co.nz/news.nsf/telecommunications/110-sites-cut-over-to-new- onegovt-network?Opendocument

State Services Commission. (2006). Government shared network deployment confirmed (Press release). Retrieved April 30, 2013, from http://www.scoop.co.nz/stories/BU0606/S00453/government- shared-network-deployment-confirmed.htm

State Services Commission. (2009). Government shared network to be discontinued (Press release). Retrieved April 30, 2013, from http://www.scoop.co.nz/stories/PA0902/S00035/government-shared- network-to-bediscontinued.htm

Review Questions

1. The adoption of GSN and now one.govt has never met their promoters' expectations. Discuss why this is the case.
2. If the GSN's primary driver was the delivery of a secure communications environment, why would a new provider be sought on the basis of cost effectiveness? Is there a point at which security costs too much?

4.5.3 Increased Flexibility and Reach

In the same way that networks promote a single, "central" collection of resources to share among all network users, they also provide the opportunity to locate that single resource anywhere on the network. This means that when a particular resource is in demand, all the network's instances of it can be drawn on to answer the demand. Examples are:

- Balancing loads across work teams - if all teams that process a particular type of application across a variety of offices are connected, then if one team develops a backlog of process requests, those requests can be transferred across the network to a team that is not under such pressure to process.
- Keeping everyone busy across the organization - in many customer-service-oriented organizations, highly skilled employees work in shopfront operations to better handle customer enquiries as they appear. These highly skilled employees can still process other complex tasks when they are not providing direct customer service, by accessing the relevant systems over the network from their shopfront station.
- Supporting work in places where customers appear - many organizations support customer service through complex systems for each customer need. Networks can allow a user to access those systems when a customer needs a service, rather than have to direct the customer to another office or employee because the system they need is only available on certain computers.

Thus, using networks means that all an organization's resources are available anywhere in the organization, not just where they were developed or implemented. The organization can therefore move work around to balance loads across teams (e.g., call centers, disaster response), and, when a customer appears at a shopfront, all services are available to them, even if processing is conducted elsewhere.

4.5.4 Increased Coordination and Outreach

Ultimately, networks can extend beyond organizations to allow benefits (similar to those mentioned above) to be developed across government agencies. In some countries, such as Australia and Canada, this approach has extended to establish agencies that are specifically created to bring together the services of a variety of departments in one place. In Australia, Centrelink's offices provide the services of several other government departments. Service Canada uses the same approach for Canadian government departments.

Networks can also promote partners interacting more efficiently. For example, in Australia, the Australian Border Force patrols the country's border entry points. In the process of checking each person who enters the country, the Border Force computer systems directly interact with systems in the Department of Foreign Affairs and Trade, and the Australian Quarantine and Inspection Service. This automated, computer-based checking streamlines the processing of arrivals and efficiently protects Australia's border interests. Such processing simply could not take place without networks connecting these agencies.

Case Study: Electronic Networking for a Ministry of Education in East Asia

Background

The national Ministry of Education is the apex body in charge of the country's education and employs around 400 staff. It is losing staff to retirement and the private sector, yet it needs to improve its operational and strategic effectiveness. Driven by this need, and the spread of ICTs in government, a networking project has been designed for the Ministry. This will join a series of existing internal and external networks, which will allow the ready exchange of documents, messages, and ideas. The intended benefits are improved decision-making and reduced time and costs for communication. Key internal stakeholders are the Minister, the other Ministry staff, and staff of the Management Data Centre. Key external stakeholders include regional education departments and all of the country's educational institutions.

Risk Assessment Through Design-Reality Gap Analysis

Along seven "ITPOSMO" dimensions, design-reality gap analysis compares the assumptions and requirements of an application's design with the existing reality of the public organization. The larger the gap, the larger the risk posed to the eGovernment project. The ITPOSMO dimensions of the network project are as follows:

- ***Information**: the design does not aim to significantly alter the reality of the content or the presentation of information the Ministry currently uses. What it does assume is that that information will flow more quickly and easily around the organization than it does at present.*

- ***Technology**: the design is based on the concept of inter-networking - linking four networks that already exist (the Ministry intranet; the Ministry website; the National Education Network website, which links educational institutions around the country; and the Government Na-*

tional Network website, which links government organizations). The only changes between reality and design are the addition of new servers, Internet links, and document-sharing and knowledge-management software.

- ***Processes**: the design builds on the reality of current communication and decision- making processes. It does not aim to radically reengineer these processes, merely to support them in order to improve their effectiveness. The design does assume more sharing of data and, hence, some new forms of decision-making that add to those currently found.*
- ***Objectives and values**: the design assumes a relatively open organizational culture in which information is shared quite readily; it also assumes an objective of improving the quality of decision-making in the Ministry. While, in reality, key stakeholders share the objective to some degree, there is an "information is power" culture at present that discourages the open sharing of many types of information.*
- ***Staffing and skills**: the design assumes a range of competencies to be present. These include network installation and operation skills, basic computer literacy among all staff, and skills in the interpretation and use of information up to an understanding of knowledge management. In reality, ICT-related skills are present in the Ministry, with almost all staff already computer literate. However, information- and knowledge-related competencies are weaker at present.*
- ***Management systems and structures**: the design enables a flexible range of systems and structures to operate, including those already present in reality. However, there is an assumption that the network will also support a more decentralized mode of operations than found in reality at present, and some cross-unit teams are planned that will require far more lateral communication flows.*
- ***Other resources**: the design assumes a whole set of capital and recurrent costs for the network. In reality, the Ministry has available sources of such revenue. Design assumptions about timescales - allowing for three to five years to fully operationalize the inter-network - do not appear to clash significantly with current realities, although a few users have other calls on their time.*

Overall Risk Assessment and Recommendation

The overall gap analysis of the project suggests some chance of partial failure unless action is taken. The recommendation is to proceed with the project, but to undertake action to reduce some of the larger design-reality gaps.

The three largest gaps occur in the dimensions of objectives and values, staffing and skills, and management systems and structures. Therefore, these dimensions should be addressed first.

Review Question

1. Suggest risk mitigation actions that might be applied to the three largest gaps, identified above. Do not be too concerned about accuracy; the case is fictional for this purpose.

4.6 Concluding Remarks

Networks involve much technical detail that we have not mentioned here. We have adopted a managerial view that does not include the details of technical network implementation. We view networking as a technology essential to eGovernment. The intricacies of network implementation are consistent and well understood among network technicians.

Managers attend to the types and uses of networks. Table 4.1 summarizes how the different types of networks and their uses might be deployed to achieve the benefits for eGovernment that networking promises. The table is a simple summary of the ideas in this chapter. Networked computing can offer much more complex services and functionality than we discuss here.

Table 4.1. Summary of network uses to achieve eGovernment objectives

eGovernment objective	Network type	Network use
Increased internal efficiency	LAN	File sharing Intranet
Increased reliability and control	LAN WAN	File sharing Intranet
Increased flexibility and reach	WAN (Internet)	Extranet Non-web connections
Increased coordination and outreach	(WAN) Internet VPN	Extranet Website Non-web connections

4.6.1 Balance Efficiency and Effectiveness

Like most technology deployments, the use of networks must balance efficiency and effectiveness. Efficiency arises when computers talk to each other rather than when pieces of paper are used for communication. Therefore, non-web connectivity between government agencies and between agencies and their suppliers is an area in which using networks can increase efficiency. Similarly, using web-based communication to allow citizens to self-serve offers efficiency to both government and citizens.

These arguments carry significant weight in developed countries' discussions about eGovernment. Indeed, the idea of being interconnected through networked computers is so fundamental that it is not even discussed; what is discussed is only how computers will operate together over such networks. But these assumptions are not always practical in least-developed countries (LDCs). LDCs face several inhibitors, particularly the following:

- There is little routine connectivity in LDCs - where developed countries claim very high rates of Internet connectivity, LDCs have very low levels of networked computing capacity, Internet- connected or otherwise.
- ICT literacy in LDCs is still relatively low - educational achievement is usually limited by the demands on people to provide for themselves and their families in low socio-economic conditions. Widespread ICT literacy is necessary for a sufficient number of people to become interested in adopting ICT-based services, and hence to create the beneficial network effect.
- The acceptability of electronic signatures is contentious - most government services require definitive authentication to prove that the individual receiving the service is entitled to and did receive it. This is customarily documented by recording the recipient's signature (to record their identity and acceptance of the service). Even in developed countries, digital versions of signatures are contentious. Ultimately, networked government services are limited, to the extent that a user will need to sign something at some stage.
- The collection of physical evidence (plans, samples, etc) is sometimes necessary - similar to the signature issue, many complex government services require physical evidence as part of the process. This evidence will always lie outside the networked government service and ultimately limits the efficiency that networked government services can attain.

In the context of networking government services to seek efficiency, the primary efficiencies arise from reducing employees' involvement (i.e., less staff time means less staff salary to pay). Most governments do not have reduction in their employment levels as an overarching objective. Indeed, in LDCs, government employment is often a strategic economic lever to achieve socio-economic policy objectives. This often means that the key primary efficiency of reduced staff levels cannot be achieved.

However, other important efficiencies arise in networked computing. Efficiencies arise from more accurate data (reduced or no need to re- work because of mistakes, reduced or no incorrect work because of accurate data collection), data being collected more quickly (more people are served more quickly by the same staff), and consumption of opportunities increasing (i.e., a reduction in opportunity cost).

Finally, LDCs may benefit from leaping over conventional connectivity approaches - that is, wired networks. In most LDCs, the level at which wired networks penetrate citizens' homes and businesses is relatively low. However, in those same countries, demand for connectivity is high and is being addressed by 3G mobile and other forms of wireless connection. Focusing on delivering networked government services to handheld devices (e.g., smart phones) through these networks may offer opportunities for LDC governments to leap forward in eGovernment solutions for their citizens.

Group Activity

In a group, imagine that you have the opportunity to establish a new LAN for an area of your organization that, to date, has either not had computers or has only had simple computing facilities.

Develop a prioritized list of network functions that you would seek to install in this hypothetical situation:

1. *Assuming that there are three teams of 20 individuals working in this area, what equipment would you estimate is required? What does each person need? What might be shared in the teams? What might be shared across the teams?*
2. *If you had to prioritize the installation of software, what software would you install in what order, and would it be on each person's desk or only available through the network?*
3. *What functions would you like to make available, through the network, to the team from outside the organization? In what order would you implement these functions?*

Prepare a timeline that shows the implementation of functions for individuals and for teams on a month-by-month basis over two years.

Be prepared to defend the equipment that you define and the order in which you decide to implement the functions.

Chapter Highlights

- Computer networks increase the power and usefulness of computers. In general, the more computers connected by networks, the better, according to the "network effect".
- A network is typically named according to its scale, from local area networks (LANs) in a building or building floor through to wide area networks (WANs) that span cities and countries, and the Internet, which is global.
- Networks may be implemented using wires (network cables) or by radio signal (wireless).
- Organizations can use "public" networks (e.g., the Internet) for their private business, through various network security measures (primarily involving cryptography) and the creation of virtual private networks (VPNs).
- Networks can improve the efficiency and collaboration within an organization by making it simpler to share information and resources.
- Networks between organizational partners can also improve efficiency.
- The majority of network activity in organizations and governments is not web browsing. Email and direct communications between computer applications form the majority of network activity.
- eGovernment relies on networks, and particularly public networks such as the Internet, to "reach out" to other government agencies, businesses, and the citizens to deliver services and information.
- eGovernment offers governments and citizens many benefits that directly relate to the benefits of networking computers.
- Networked services for citizens rely on citizens' access to those networks. In least-developed countries, that access might be more readily available through telecommunications (mobile phones) than through personal computers connected to the Internet.

Review Questions

1. Define the term "computer network".
2. Describe the principles that underlie client/server architecture.
3. What is an intranet? Who uses it?
4. What is an Internet service provider? What service do they provide?
5. What is the most heavily used application on the Internet?
6. How can a government benefit from network connections between government agencies?
7. Identify three key ways that networking can benefit businesses in their interactions with government.

References

Holmberg, M. (2012). Virginia State Police network down for several hours. WTVR.com. Retrieved from http://wtvr.com/2012/01/19/virginia-state-police-network-down-for-several-hours/

Kalakota, R., & Robinson, M. (2001). eBusiness 2.0: Roadmap for success. Boston: Addison Wesley.

McDonald, P. (2012, June 9). NZ considers halving mail deliveries. ABC News. Retrieved from http:// www.abc.net.au/news/2010-06-09/nz-considers-halving-mail-deliveries/860478

CHAPTER 5 Data Management

Learning Objectives

After studying this chapter, you should be able to:

- Understand the importance of data
- Identify the data lifecycle
- Understand the importance of business intelligence and enterprise content management, and
- Identify controls to manage public data.

Data.gov.au

Protecting Data

Advances in technology have allowed the Australian Government to deal with large amounts of personal and commercially sensitive data. To protect this data, successive Australian Governments have introduced secrecy laws. These laws have had a significant impact on the relationship between citizens and government. In particular, citizens have felt that public data protected by these laws should be made available to hold the government to account for its decisions.

Shift to Open Government

In response to these citizen concerns, the Australian Government made a Declaration of Open Government to release public data, subject to privacy, security, and other relevant concerns. Under this declaration, in 2011, the Australian Government established data.gov.au to open up government data to citizens. Data.gov.au provides an easy way for citizens to discover, access, and reuse data from the Australian Government and state/territory governments.

Fostering Innovation

Citizens can use data provided by the government on data.gov.au in all sorts of ways. This may range from simple analysis and research to the creation of innovative 'mashups' that combine data from different sources. For example, a mashup combining government crime and census data could be used to compare and contrast suburbs by a range of economic, education, safety, and socio-economic indicators. Figure 5.1 shows the data of a Canberra suburb, Yarralumla, combining a number of publicly available online resources, such as the Australia Bureau of Statistics, Australian Institute of Criminology, the NSW Bureau of Crime Statistics, and Google. Citizens could use this mashup to analyze various issues, such as crime trends over time, to see whether government law enforcement policy changes are effective.

Citizen Empowerment

Data.gov.au represents a successful initiative by the Australian Government to empower citizens with data that they can use to hold the government to account for its decisions. It also represents a Whole of Government approach to releasing data and making it discoverable through a central access point. With more citizens making requests to have data released on data.gov.au the future of open government in Australia looks promising.

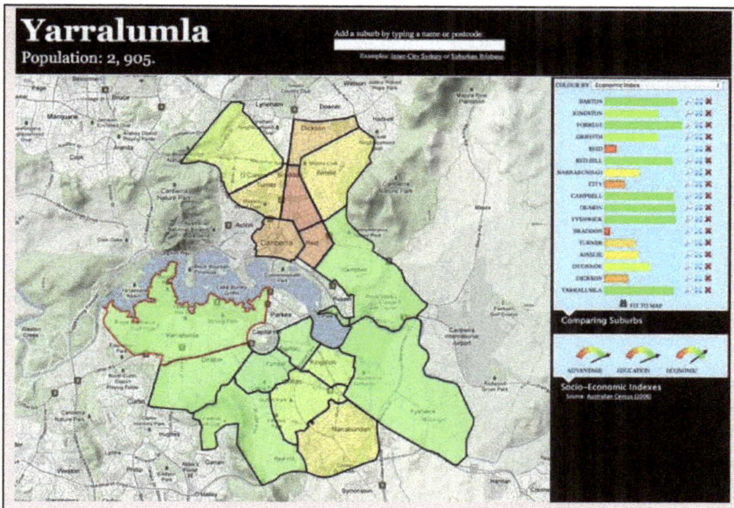

***Figure 5.1**. Screenshot of suburban trend data (Source: http://www.suburbantrends.com.au created by Alejandro Metke-Jimenez and Michael Henderson.)*

Source: http://data.gov.au

5.1 Introduction

5.1.1 Data, information, and knowledge

Data is the foundation of information and knowledge, which can lead to informed actions being taken by a decision maker, as illustrated in Figure 5.2.

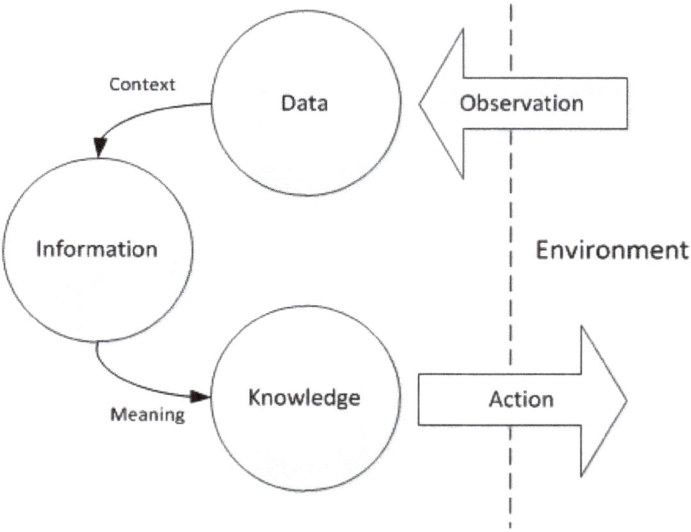

Figure 5.2. Data, information, and knowledge

Data is the representation of facts, such as values or measurements. Data can be either qualitative, where it describes something, or quantitative, where it involves numbers, as illustrated in Figure 5.3.

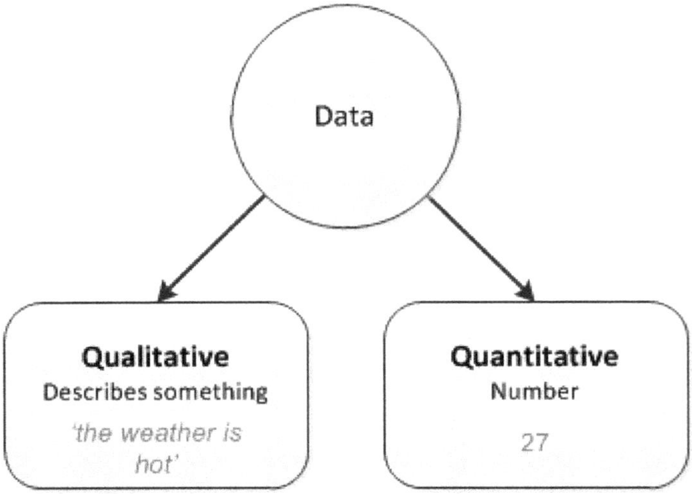

Figure 5.3. Data is qualitative or quantitative

Information is data that has been processed for a specific purpose or context to become meaningful. In this process, information is inferred from data by taking into consideration factors that include:

- The business meaning of the data
- The relevance of the data for a specific purpose, and
- The quality of the data.

For instance, the number 3 is quantitative data that alone is meaningless (e.g., 3 bicycles or 3 days). However, if this number's business meaning was the change in temperature over the past hour, it would be meaningful for answering what changes in the weather are occurring outside, as illustrated in Figure 5.4.

Knowledge is information combined with skills and experience. Knowledge may be expressed and recorded as words, numbers, codes, mathematical and scientific formulae, and musical notations (explicit knowledge), or as unwritten and unspoken intuitive thoughts (tacit knowledge).

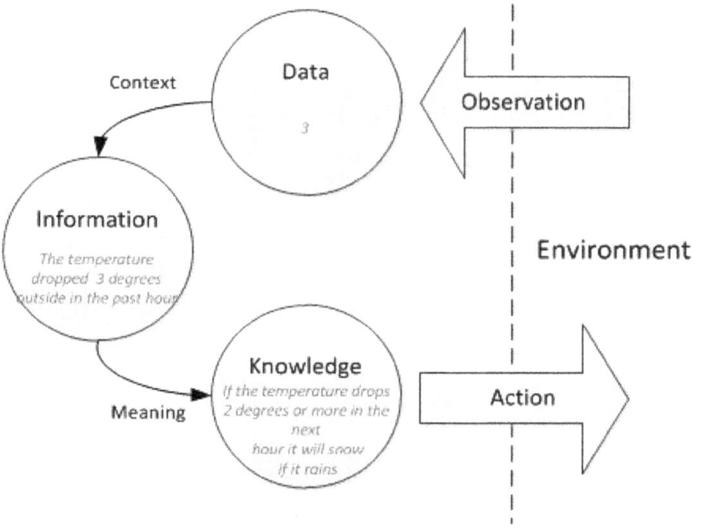

Figure 5.4. Converting weather data to knowledge

5.2 Data

Governments need data to guide their operational, tactical and strategic activities. **Data has value**, which means it is an asset that is just as important, if not more important, than physical government assets, such as schools and hospitals.

Data must meet the needs of Government. While the value of data is largely recognized by governments, operational effectiveness is still impacted by poor data quality or gaps in the data. Increasingly, governments are focused on ways to allocate time, funds, and resources to better manage their data.

5.2.1 Data lifecycle

The data lifecycle is the flow of data from identifying a business need through to no longer having that need. Like any asset, data has a lifecycle that commences with planning what data is needed, its collection, maintenance, use, and finally to the data being disposed, as illustrated in Figure 5.5.

When data is effectively managed, the data lifecycle begins in the planning phase, before data is even obtained.

Plan

The data that is needed and the standards to apply in its capture and storage are important elements of the planning phase. By describing these requirements, data management will be more efficient and effective.

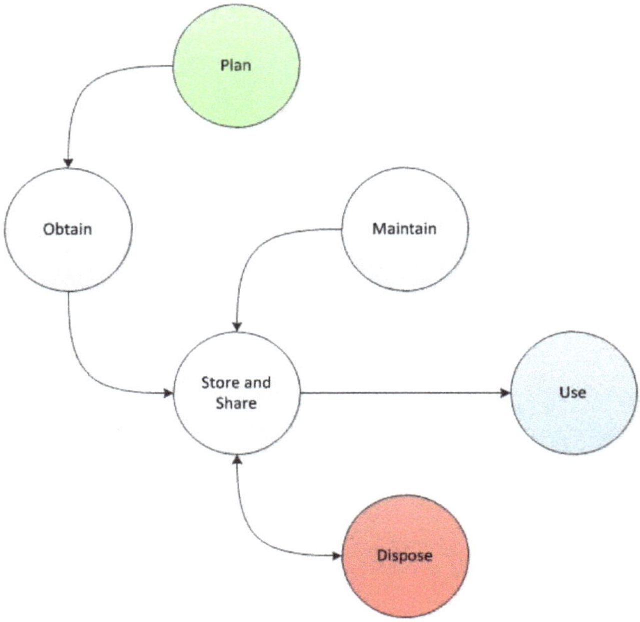

Figure 5.5. Data lifecycle

Agency data requirements can be identified through many ways that include:

- Internal documents that outline requirements, and
- Interviews that identify requirements.

Ensuring that data requirements are understood is important, as it will provide users' confidence that the data obtained will actually meet their needs. It is wasteful and frustrating to spend valuable time and money obtaining data, only to then discover it is the wrong data.

Data standards describe the expected meaning and acceptable representation of data for use within a defined context. This is important as it allows data to be discovered, shared, and exchanged easily. Where data is not defined appropriately, problems can emerge, such as it being misunderstood or hidden from decision makers.

The Australian and United States Federal Governments use a Whole of Government data reference model to define data. This model provides a structured approach to defining data to ensure it can be found, understood, and shared, as illustrated in Figure 5.6.

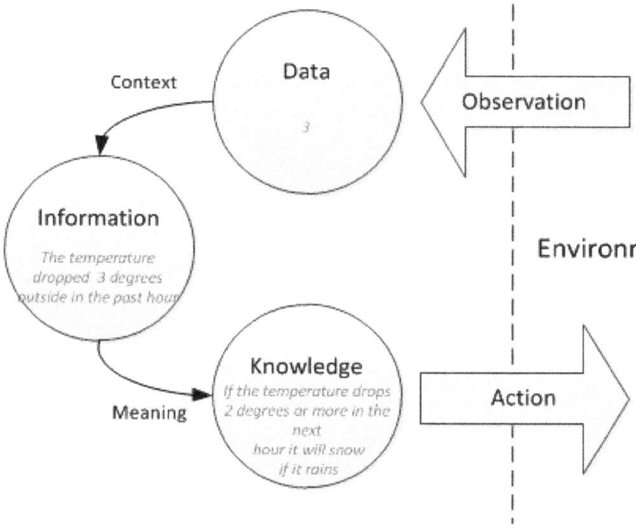

Figure 5.6. Data reference model to define data across government

Using the data reference model enforces:

- Defining the data context - placing the data into one or more categories, which explains the purpose to which the data may be put. Grouping data into categories helps in finding data for reuse and identifying data that may have been duplicated.
- Defining a data description - this can include a description of the data, creator of the data, the format of the data, and the date the data was created.
- Determining what data sharing is required - the data context and data description are defined in a way that allows data to be found and understood by people and systems.

Defining the data promotes better understanding of the data available and the extent to which that data meets the business needs, and contributes to designing efficient solutions that deliver data to all necessary and appropriate people and systems.

Obtain

With a plan and agreed data definitions, data can be reliably collected to meet the identified business needs. Data collection involves identifying available data sources, both internal and external to the organization, and assessing the extent to which those sources meet the identified needs. Establishing a new source of data (i.e., creating data with a new process) should be a last resort, adopted only when no internal or external data sources can be identified, or they fail to meet the identified needs.

Internal data sources are those that collect, store, and maintain data in the existing operations of the organization. Two ways to obtain data from internal data sources are:

- Share or exchange - identify other areas in the organization that may have the needed data, and
- Modify, convert, or transform - identify existing data that can be modified, converted, or transformed to meet the new business needs.

Identifying internal data sources can be difficult, as data is likely to be in a lot of places, spread across data repositories maintained by many parts of the organization. This often results in data being hidden from other parts of the organization. However, it is important to try to find this data, as it will prevent future data quality issues arising, such as unwanted duplication of data across systems. Ways to find this data include talking to people in areas likely to use the data or looking in data catalogues that provide a record of all data in the organization.

External data sources are those that originate from outside the organization. The two main ways to obtain data from external data sources are:

- Purchase - identify and purchase from an outside source or other government agency that has the needed data.
- Share or exchange - identify and share with other organizations that have the needed data.

When using external sources, you will need to be aware of conditions attached to using the data. For instance, it may be illegal to share data with citizens if the data is purchased from a commercial provider.

Once **data sources must be assessed** for the extent to which they meet business needs. This will involve assessing the data for:

- Fit - whether the data fits the needs of the business
- Accuracy - whether the data is correct
- Timeliness - whether the data is current or out of date
- Completeness - whether there is missing data, and
- Consistency - whether all the data is in the same format.

Where data is not obtained from internal or external data sources, the **data must be created** to meet the identified needs. Typically, a new information system, or an extension to an existing system, will be required to support the processes that will generate the data.

With governments wanting to reduce paperwork and increase efficiency, web forms offer opportunities for convenient data creation. Web forms are webpages that allow a person to enter data on the Internet (e.g., a license application) and have that data submitted electronically to the organization for processing. Web forms resemble paper forms and can have rules to enforce that forms are filled out correctly before being submitted for processing. Benefits of web forms are that they:

- Capture data from a reliable source (e.g., the citizen) directly
- Reduce costs of having paper forms printed and manually processed
- Reduce errors caused by incomplete or incorrect data being entered in the form, and
- Decrease delays in processing the data.

When using web forms, critical and sensitive data that is entered on the Internet must be kept secure. Ways that you can make web forms more secure include:

- Identification and authentication - check the user is who they say they are, and
- Entitlements - provide access to data in forms only where the user is allowed access.

Making sure web forms are secure for people entering data is important. Breaches of security can damage the government's reputation.

Store and Share

Once the data has been obtained, it must be stored safely and made available to authorized users. Data storage may be internal or external to the organization. Sharing the data will require determining how and when users may access the data and for what purposes they may use the data.

Data can be stored internally and externally to the agency. The location of the data storage is typically dependent upon where the users of the data are located. In particular:

- Data shared only with other people in the organization is usually stored internal to the organization (i.e., within its internal network), and
- Data that is shared with people external to the organization is stored on a server that sits immediately outside the organization's network, often called a Demilitarized Zone (DMZ).

Data stored on the internal network is inherently more secure than data stored in the DMZ because of concept of 'security in depth'. Security in depth reflects the greater number of layers of security that are present to protect data from unauthorized users, typically from outside the organization, as illustrated in Figure 5.7. These layers of security include the use of firewalls that attempt to block unauthorized access from the Internet.

Data stored in the DMZ has fewer layers of security to permit authorized external users access to the data. However, this means fewer layers of security for unauthorized users to overcome. Consequently, data stored in the DMZ should not be sensitive or likely to affect the organization's reputation or the privacy of citizens if compromised.

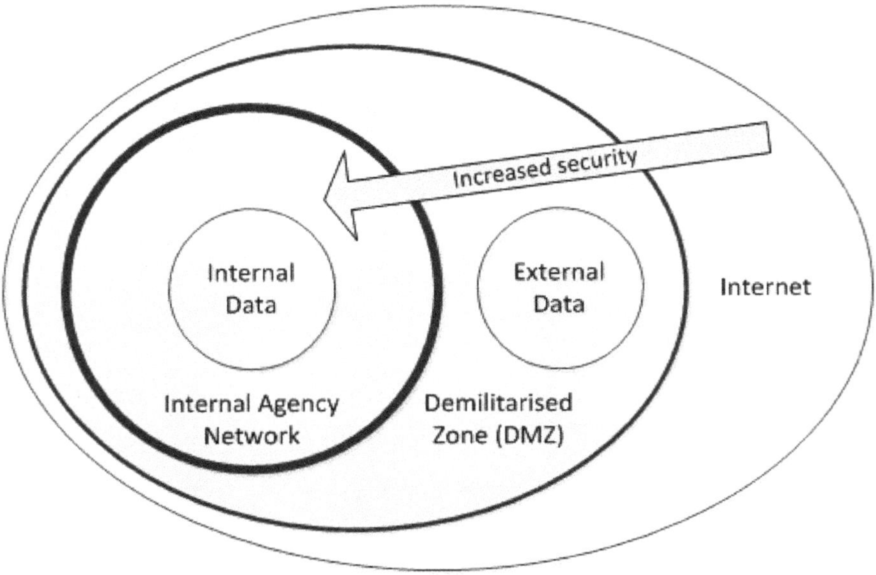

Figure 5.7. Security in depth

The value of stored data is only released when it is shared. However, **sharing must be controlled** to ensure that the data is properly used and not damaged or destroyed. Control is usually managed for groups of users through granting permission to:

- Read - view and access the data
- Write - edit or modify the data, and/or
- Delete - delete the data.

Access is controlled through granting either none of these permissions (not share the data), one of these permissions (i.e., read, write, or delete) or some of these permissions (e.g., read and write).

Use

Once the data has been shared, it is available for use. Data used by the agency needs to be meaningful, and so it is generally converted into information needed by the agency or citizens to support decision making, metrics, compliance, automated processes, and other objectives. One technique that can be used to obtain meaningful information from data is data mining.

Data mining inspects data to discover patterns and trends. These patterns and trends may not have been detectable from different individual data sources. For example, luxury car purchases registered by a transport agency could be used to identify people not paying the correct income tax to the taxation agency.

An important challenge with data mining is ensuring that the privacy of citizens is protected. This is important, as a relationship between a piece of data and a particular citizen could potentially be established that might breach that citizen's privacy. To protect a citizen's privacy, agencies should consider what information is shared for use and also advise citizens what the data will be used for when collected (e.g., that it might be disclosed to third parties).

Maintain

Stored data must be maintained to ensure that the data continues to meet business requirements. This will involve ongoing processes that continually improve at least the six most common dimensions of data quality:

- Completeness - data is complete and nothing is missing
- Validity - data is within the accepted values specified by the business
- Accuracy - data reflects true values or a verifiable source
- Consistency - data is consistent between systems and duplicates do not exist
- Integrity - data that is related to other data is correctly associated with that data, and
- Timeliness - data is provided in a timely manner and available when needed.

Data quality key performance indicators should be established to help monitor whether the processes to improve data quality are working. Refer to Chapter 13 for more details on establishing performance indicators.

Defining and monitoring data quality key performance indicators will allow the organization to identify problems, plan actions to correct any problems, and implement those actions.

Dispose

Once the data has delivered value to the organization and is no longer of use, it can be discarded either by archiving it or deleting it. However, many times the option to delete data is not available to government organizations because of laws and government policies that require data to be archived. This is particularly true for data that has been used to make decisions.

Data archiving is the process of moving data that is no longer actively used to a separate long-term storage where it can still be accessed. Data archiving is essential as it provides:

- Increased speed accessing current data - archiving reduces the size of search catalogues used to find data that is stored and frequently used by the business
- Reduced data growth - data archiving typically involves compression. Less frequently accessed data that is archived and compressed reduces data growth
- Compliance with government policy - government agencies typically need to archive data used for decision making for a specified period of time

(e.g., seven years in Australia). It is a criminal offence to delete data before this time period has elapsed, and

- Data reuse at a later time - data that has been archived can be reused in the future to meet business requirements. This involves moving the data from dispose to storage.

Archiving data requires policies about what data is archived, when, and for how long. Typically, government policy mandates that all data used for making decisions must be archived. The time to archive data will typically be driven by business needs. For example, will data be archived if it is no longer being used after a certain period of time (e.g., two months)? Or, will it be manually archived by somebody who is allocated that responsibility in the organization?

Data deletion is where data is permanently deleted. Once data has been deleted it can never be reused. Clearly, the decision to delete data must be made carefully.

Data deletion is important because it provides:

- Increased storage space - data that is no longer deleted is removed, freeing up storage space
- Decreased data duplication - removes duplicates that are not necessary or may be confusing, and
- Reduced ability to access sensitive data - sensitive data may be deleted after it has been analyzed and details that might impact a person's privacy have been removed.

Data that has been archived can also be deleted after it has been archived for a specified period. Deleting this archived data can free storage space for future archives.

Quick Quiz

1. What are the different types of knowledge?
2. What is the difference between data, information and knowledge?
3. What is data mining?

5.3 Information

Data is converted into information during the data lifecycle. To ensure information meets the needs of the organization and citizens, many organizations pursue enterprise information management.

Enterprise information management is the bringing together of business and technology so that information can improve operational efficiency, promote transparency, and enable decision making across the organization. To achieve this, enterprise information management combines business intelligence and enterprise content management.

5.3.1 Business Intelligence

Business intelligence is the use of technology to gather information from data to support strategic, operational and tactical decisions. Business intelligence technologies have the ability to provide:

- Real-time monitoring of performance metrics
- A visual representation of data
- Predictions on performance results, and
- Ability for decision makers to drill down deeper into high-level performance metrics (e.g., education levels and locations of the unemployed, instead of just the total number of unemployed).

Data warehouse

There are many different ways to implement business intelligence in agencies. One common approach is illustrated in Figure 5.8. This approach uses data gathered from a data warehouse. A data warehouse is a large store of data sourced from many data stores across the agency. Data warehouses are well suited to business intelligence because all the data is in one central data store, which makes data analysis and reporting easier.

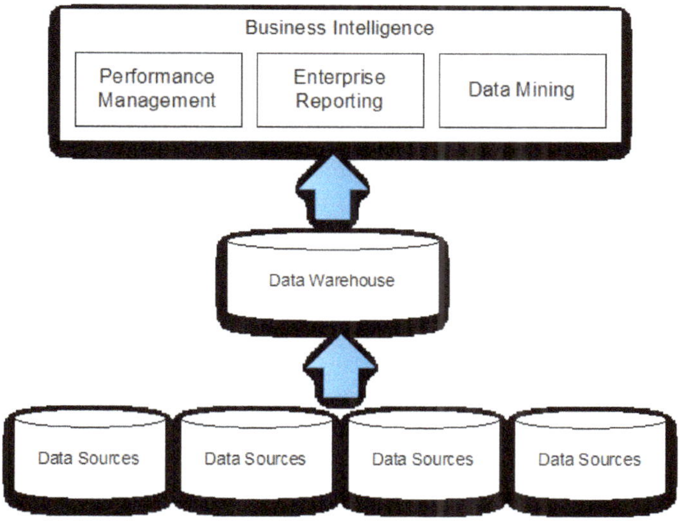

Figure 5.8. Using data to gather information to support decision making

Business intelligence applications

Using data stored in the data warehouse, business intelligence technologies provide:

- Performance management - metrics for benchmarking that can inform decision makers about progress towards goals

- Enterprise reporting - complex data in simplified reports to guide strategic decision-making, and
- Data mining - the discovery of trends and patterns in data to inform decision making.

The use of business intelligence is growing in government and private organizations worldwide.

5.4 Enterprise Content Management

Enterprise content management encompasses the technologies and methods that allow an organization to capture, store, manage, and deliver information. This information can include:

- Documents - written, printed, or electronic material that provides information or serves as an official record
- Records - evidence about the past, such as an account of an act or occurrence kept in writing or some other permanent form
- Images - visual representations of people or things, and
- Web content - textual, visual or audio content that is delivered on an intranet or the Internet.

Enterprise content management systems can provide employees of organizations quick access to this information through keyword and full-text searching using a computer.

The four main parts of an enterprise content management system are capture, store, manage, and deliver.

5.4.1 Capture and Store

To be useful, information needs to be captured in an enterprise content management system. This typically involves:

- Converting information into electronic format - to search documents and avoid having to find paper documents in filing cabinets they need to be converted into a digital format. This may involve scanning paper documents into a digital format such as portable document format (PDF)
- Adding metadata to the information - metadata is data that describes things about the information (e.g., author, date created, contact officer); these data items can then be used in searches to enhance data retrieval, and
- Storing the information.

Information stored in an enterprise content management system needs to be managed. The way that information is managed within an enterprise content management system will vary depending on the system.

5.4.2 Manage

Three common enterprise content management systems that have different ways to manage information are:

- Document management systems - used to track and store electronic documents. These systems typically require a user to check-in and check-out documents for editing
- Web content management systems - used to create and manage web pages. These systems typically are based around a workflow that requires another person to approve edits made to content before being published, and
- Records management systems - used to capture, classify, and manage records. These systems typically do not allow users to edit official records.

5.4.3 Deliver

Enterprise content management systems provide information. A good system will allow users to find information using a simple and easy-to-use search function. Searching for information is typically faster than find information by manually navigating through a hierarchical structure. For instance, finding information on Subtopic C3 in Figure 5.9 would require navigating from the home page to topic C to subtopic C3. In contrast, a search for subtopic C3 would retrieve the information directly.

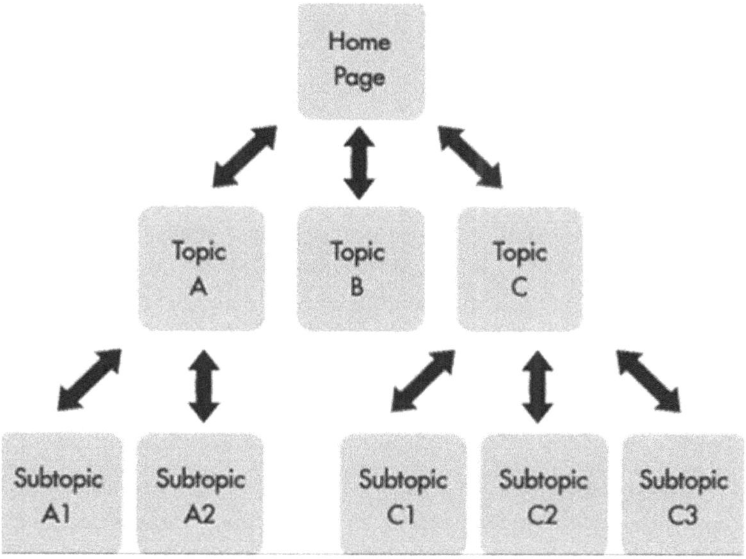

Figure 5.9. Hierarchical structure

For instance, finding information on Subtopic C3 in Figure 5.9 would require navigating from the home page to topic C to subtopic C3. In contrast, a search for subtopic C3 would retrieve the information directly.

5.5 Managing Public Data

Government agencies collect and disseminate a lot of data and information. Advances in technology such as data mining and cross- organizational data warehouses now provide agencies even more opportunities to use the data. However, the use of this data must be balanced against the rights of the citizen. This means providing access to information while respecting the privacy of the citizen and keeping their details secret.

To ensure that agencies protect the privacy of citizens, governments typically pass laws. For instance, in Australia, under Freedom of Information Act 1982 (Cth) agencies may refuse access to information if it contains personal information. Personal information is defined under this act in section 4(1) as "information or an opinion . . . whether true or not . . . about an individual whose identity is apparent, or can reasonably be ascertained, from the information or opinion".

To ensure agencies comply with the law and manage public data appropriately, they can use a combination of three controls. These controls are:

- Administrative - written policies, procedures, standards, and guidelines
- Logical - use of software to monitor and control access to data and information, and
- Physical - use of physical measures, such as locks, to control the workplace and computing facilities.

The use of these three controls can help agencies mitigate the risks associated with managing public data.

5.5.1 Administrative Controls

Administrative controls (also called procedural controls) consist of policies, procedures, standards, and guidelines. Administrative controls that can be implemented in an agency include:

- Policies and procedures that establish an organizational structure in the agency with lines of authority and responsibility for data management
- Performance standards that identify whether the agency is meeting its obligations to manage public data (e.g., number of privacy breaches), and
- Personnel policies and procedures that ensure proper training of staff to handle confidential data.

Administrative controls form the basis for logical and physical controls.

5.5.2 Logical Controls

Logical controls (also called technical controls) use software to monitor and control access to data and systems used to store the data. Logical controls limit what data a user can access and restrict their access on a system to only what is appropriate to their role. Logical controls must be carefully implemented to ensure that they do not prevent authorized users from accessing data they require in their role.

5.5.3 Physical Controls

Physical controls monitor and control the environment of the workplace. These controls include lockable filing cabinets to secure information.

An important physical control in the context of managing public data is the separation of duties. The separation of duties ensures that an individual cannot complete a critical task alone. For example, an employee who handles backups on a computer system with confidential data should not be able to view the confidential data.

Chapter Highlights

- Data has value, which means it is an asset like any physical asset of the organization.
- Data is the foundation of information and knowledge, which can lead to informed actions being taken by a decision maker.
- Data is converted into information during the data lifecycle to meet the needs of the agency and citizens.
- Information is inferred from data through the consideration of its business value, relevance and quality.
- Operational effectiveness is impacted by poor data quality or gaps in the data.
- Data standards describe the expected meaning and acceptable representation of data for use within a defined context.
- Data mining allows you to use the data to discover patterns and trends from different data sources
- Data archiving is essential, and involves the process of moving data no longer actively used to a separate long-term storage where it can still be accessed.
- Business intelligence is the use of technology to gather information from data to support strategic, operational, and tactical decisions.
- Data warehouses are well suited to business intelligence because all the data is in one central data store, which makes data analysis and reporting easier.
- Enterprise content management encompasses the technologies and methods that allow an agency to capture, store, manage, and deliver information
- The use of government data must be balanced against the rights of the citizen.
- To ensure agencies comply with the law and manage public data appropriately, they can use a combination of three controls- administrative, logical, and physical.
- Understanding of the data lifecycle and enterprise information management help managers to appreciate ways that can influence data quality and provide methods to better manage public data.

Review Questions

1. What is the difference between knowledge and business intelligence?
2. What is the data lifecycle?
3. Why do you need to maintain data?
4. What are the six common dimensions of data quality that need to be addressed?
5. What is metadata?
6. What are three controls that you can use to manage public data?

Discussion Questions

1. It is widely considered that data is an asset. Do you support this view?
2. Why might business intelligence technologies impact citizen privacy?
3. Why would you add it to data stored in an enterprise content management system?

Further Resources

Australian Government. (2011). The Australian Government Architecture Reference Models (Version 3.0). AGIMO. Available at: http://agimo.gov.au/files/2012/04/AGA_RM_v3_0.pdf

US Government Data Portal - Data.gov http://www.data.gov/ Australian Government Data Portal - http://www.data.gov.au/

Office of the Australian Information Commissioner: http://www.oaic.gov.au/

CHAPTER 6 Enterprise Systems

Learning Objectives

After studying this chapter, you will be able to:

- Describe the different types of information systems in the enterprise
- Discuss the importance of cross-functional systems
- Describe the common functions of Enterprise Resource Planning systems
- Describe important considerations in implementing an ERP in government
- Identify the key elements of an eProcurement solution
- Discuss the benefits of eProcurement, particularly in terms of better business practices that it encourages, and
- Discuss the considerations for an implementation of eProcurement in a government organization.

6.1 Why Enterprise Systems?

eGovernment is a key enabler of organizational ability to improve delivery of information and services both in government, and from the government to the public. Enterprise systems enable the delivery of key business outcomes and the supporting services of any large organization. Chapter 3 covers these ideas at a high level. This chapter looks more deeply into enterprise systems that are applicable in government organizations.

Enterprise Systems is a term that covers a broad range of corporate support functions, both ICT and non-ICT. Enterprise systems enable business units to deliver their outcomes by supporting customer management, payroll and leave, stores and inventory management, project management and financial allocation and tracking. This broad range of business functions can be supported by one or many different products using a variety of system architectures.

As an example, people management functions are supported by transaction-processing functionality that will calculate pay for time worked, ensure the accrual of appropriate leave allowances, and advise managers of excessive leave, overtime, or possible areas of underperformance. Grouping together transaction processing systems that are in a related business area produces a functional system (e.g., human resource management).

This chapter will explore types of enterprise systems and how they support the delivery of an eGovernment outcome.

6.2 Types of Enterprise System

Enterprise systems are as different as the enterprises that they seek to support. At the root of any automation product supporting business activities is a cluster of transaction processing systems, each designed to do one activity over and over again. Once separate products, these transaction processing systems are no longer recognizable as separate entities, but embedded as functions in the enterprise system.

Functional systems are not "one size fits all"; scalability is key to cost, usability, and functionality. Aggregation of the transaction processing systems to support a particular business function created the first recognizable enterprise systems. Many of these products started out supporting financial systems in business; for example, spreadsheet packages to speed reconciliation of money and receipts within a retail or services supply business. Examples of systems like these at the smaller end of the spectrum are Quicken, MYOB, and Attaché. These smaller functional products are commonly found in small and medium businesses and deliver labor-saving record keeping functionality that assists in the operation of the business and comply with taxation or excise obligations. These functional systems are not designed to operate in larger business entities because they lack the capacity for the increased scale of activity implicit in a large company or government department.

Effective systems architecture lays the foundation for successful use of enterprise systems throughout an organization. Functional systems support aggregated business functions very well, but often fail to integrate with other functional systems. Without an effective systems architecture, many organizations allow the finance department to choose the finance system, the human resources department to choose the people management system, and the warehousing department to purchase the system they felt serve their needs well. This independent procurement frequently results in situations where finance systems cannot communicate with the people management systems or the stores systems. Senior management soon recognizes a need for some form of integration to deliver the business intelligence they require to make informed management decisions. Integration substantially raises the risk profit and cost allowance for any project. Successfully integrating two disparate functionally based enterprise systems can be a costly activity that may not achieve the desired outcome.

Modern enterprise systems remain functionally based, with the offering usually split into finance functions, people management functions, stores functions, and so on, but have an architecture that scales effectively to deal with thousands of employees and tens of thousands of transactions per day across a wide geographic area (Figure 6.1).

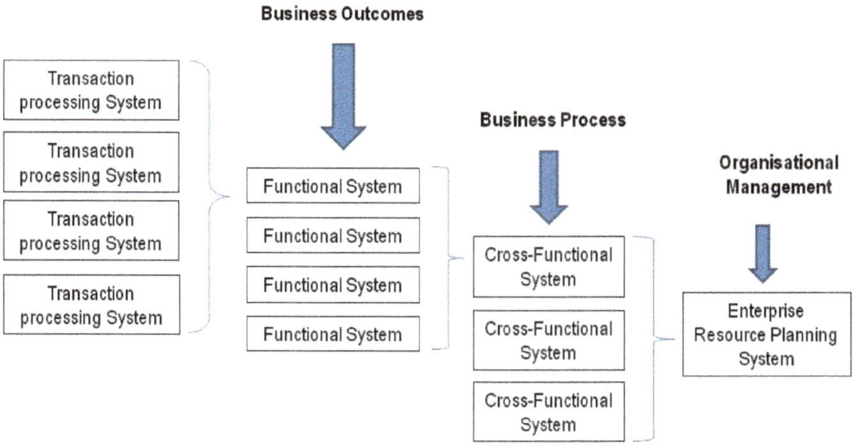

Figure 6.1. How an enterprise resource planning system supports all elements of the business

Five basic functional systems combine to cover the majority of functions supporting a business organization:

- Sales and Marketing
- Operations Information
- Manufacturing Information
- Human Resources Information, and
- Accounting Information.

Despite being functionally based, modern systems include integration products, aggregate reporting, and planning functionality, and are designed to be deployed across the organization and its functions.

Activity

Functional Systems of Health Department

Each government department is assigned specific outcomes to achieve on behalf of the population. Commonly, the health department is responsible for the provision of hospitals, clinics, essential equipment and supplies and suitably skilled people to staff the medical system.

Write a list of your ideas for answers to these questions:

1. What functional systems would be essential to the operation of a hospital?
2. What functional systems would the health department need that a hospital does not need?

6.2.1 Cross-functional Systems

Bringing functions together into a cross-functional system enhances their inherent functionality and creates a product generally known as an Enterprise Resource Planning (ERP) suite.

Cross-functional systems deliver an agreed process chain from one section to another. Traditional cross-functional systems support a complete business process across the whole organization and may sometimes be called process-based systems as they rely upon the implementation of a process flow to support workplace activities. Most cross-functional systems come with a number of pre-defined processes that are often distilled from the needs of many other customers. Processes to manage personal leave, pay variations, or purchasing are quite common with similar legislative and behavioural influences. Modern enterprise systems leverage this commonality to offer a core of best practice processes that are almost a complete fit for many organizations.

Issues arise when implementing these cross-functional systems, as some business units within the organization may have unique processes that the common system cannot facilitate. When the pre-defined process is not supported by the business, the implementation team has hard choices to make. Changing the product to facilitate a special workplace process is costly and has inherent risk; it is always worth considering changing the workplace processes to conform to those offered by the product. If it is sensible to change the product to facilitate a workplace process, close attention to definition and implementation is necessary.

The typical basis on which the decision to accept the "standard" approach or to tailor the enterprise system lies in the competitive advantage the organization derives from the process in question. If the process is a common one (e.g., most of the "corporate" activities like finance, people management, or asset management), there is rarely sufficient business advantage in retaining the organization's unique approach over that of the best practice standard in the enterprise system. However, if the process is closely tied to the organization's value chain, perhaps a clever stock management process, then tailoring the system to support that may cost less than the competitive advantage gained by the clever approach.

Changing these products can be completed using two quite different approaches. **Configuring the product** uses existing components to provide the desired business functionality. This is a low-risk, and less costly approach. **Customizing the product** changes the basic product and introduces higher risks and often significant costs. Most configurations will roll forward into new versions of the basic product. Customizations often present barriers to upgrades, as they require the customization to be implemented in the new version.

Activity

Cross-Functional Challenge

The military is an organization that involves many people, high levels of expenditure, and a substantial equipment inventory that it must manage effectively. Managing just these issues presents a challenge worthy of the best ERPs, but for a military organization, they are simply supporting the primary business outcome of the organization.

The primary business process of the military is to take action in line with government wishes: make war, participate in peacekeeping operations, protect vital assets or territory, conduct search and rescue, or work with the community to deliver non-military outcomes. This is not a functionality traditionally offered by commercial cross-functional systems, yet it draws upon every element of common ERP products.

Write a paragraph or two to answer these questions:

1. What are the high level functions unique to a military cross-functional business support system?
2. What traditional cross-functional outcomes would need to feed into this unique business system?

6.3 Enterprise Resource Planning

Enterprise resource planning (ERP) systems are business management systems that integrate support for a wide range of business functions to allow a more coordinated approach to managing the whole business. ERPs originated in the manufacturing industry and have grown and evolved into valuable tools for all large business organizations. The advantages that ERPs brought to manufacturing were:

- Efficient business processes
- Inventory reduction
- Lead-time reduction
- Improved customer service
- Improved insight into the organization, and
- Higher profitability.

These improvements delivered higher management maturity for the organizations, reducing overheads, focussing on profitable product lines, and improving planning and development. By implementing and following ERP processes, many manufacturers found it easy to obtain and retain ISO 9001 quality certifications, which led to larger contracts, including government contracts.

6.3.1 Core Functionality

Modern ERP solutions contain four core functionality sets. This section outlines the typical modules within each area that make up the functionality provided.

Financial and Accounting

- Financial and management accounting - provides analysts, managers, and accountants with a robust, integrated platform for management and financial reporting.
- Financial supply chain management - helps streamline customer-to-cash processes, improve control of cash flow, and reduce working capital.
- Treasury applications - to achieve greater control over cash, liquidity and financial risk to improve profitability and compliance.
- Corporate governance - helps reduce the administrative costs of achieving compliance.

Human Resources Management

- End-user service delivery - direct access by end-users to multiple ERP services along with business content.
- Workforce analytics - delivers real-time insight into the workforce to manage human resources more effectively and track costs and ROI associated with HR projects.
- Talent management - supports the development of people through their career with the organization from recruitment to training, development, and retention.
- Workforce process management - streamlines and integrates essential workforce processes.
- Workforce deployment - deploy the right people based on skills and availability, monitor scheduling and progress on projects, track time, and analyze results for strategic decision making.

Operations Management

- Procurement and logistics execution - manages end-to-end procurement and logistics business processes for complete business cycles, from self-service requisitioning to flexible invoicing and payment.
- Product development and manufacturing - supports the entire life cycle of product development and manufacturing from production planning, through manufacturing execution integrated with shop-floor systems, and product development with life-cycle data management.
- Sales and service - manages customer-focused activities, from selling products and services, to managing professional- services delivery and internal processes such as calculating incentives and commissions.

Corporate Services Delivery

- Real estate management - offers a means to avoid vacancies and reduce costs associated with real estate development, rentals and property management.
- Enterprise asset management - manages preventive and predictive maintenance, maintenance cost budgeting, maintenance execution and work-clearance management.
- Project and portfolio management - from strategic portfolio management to project planning, execution and accounting.
- Travel management - streamlines travel administration processes, monitors compliance with travel policies and manages changes in compensation and pricing models from suppliers, global distribution systems and travel agencies.
- Environment, health, and safety management - allows the organization to implement EHS strategies to address regulatory compliance and take an integrated approach to managing operational risks related to environment, health and safety.
- Quality management - delivers a unified approach to total quality management, delivering efficiencies that result from fewer product returns and improved asset utilization.
- Global trade services - help secure the organization's supply chain, connect and communicate with partner systems and promote the use of shared data.

Each of these core functions deliver the process and common storage that enable the organization to act in synchrony, with strong management information systems informing senior managers on the position of the organization.

6.3.2 Enterprise Resource Planning Implementation

ERPs are expensive and complex products that should be implemented carefully. Offsetting the organizational improvements delivered by an ERP are the costs of implementing an ERP. The product vendors have invested a great deal of work in their products, and they seek to recover some of these costs with every sale. The

SAP, Oracle, and Infor product suites are generally ranked as the top three ERPs globally. Their scale and complexity are staggering, with the financial costs of simply purchasing an ERP often more than many expect, but the organizational and financial costs of implementing the ERP are higher still.

Implementing an ERP will generate corporate change - is the change sponsor up to the demands? An implementation program will spend the majority of time and money working through business process re-engineering, data cleansing, intensive training on the new processes and tool, and then will spend a little money on purchasing the tools and supporting IT systems. Implementing an ERP must be approached as a corporate change programme, not an ICT implementation. Leadership by both the business and ICT organization is essential for a successful outcome.

Case studies in failed ERP implementations have identified these common themes as the major contributor to the failure of the implementation program:

- Poor advice and work from consultants engaged to enable the implementation
- Inconsistent or minimal business process re-engineering leading up to the implementation, and
- Poor project management.

The chapter on Project Management looks at the means and methods for managing a complex project. Many organizations find that engaging a consulting team to assist the vendor and the organization through the planning and implementation process is beneficial. Care must be taken to ensure the consultants are familiar with the vendor's products, yet remain loyal to the organization, not the vendor. Specifying the contract and choosing these consultants can provide more influence upon the success of the implementation than any other variable.

6.3.3 Signs that an ERP implementation is not proceeding correctly:

- No milestones - key implementation deliverables and milestones are needed to measure progress, identify stalls and ensure a smooth conclusion. A lack of checkpoints with periodic deliverables is a sign of future trouble.
- Missed milestone and deadlines - project deadlines can slip for many reasons, such as staff turnover or unforeseen events. However, a team that repeatedly misses its deadlines exhibits a lack of discipline, which dramatically increases project risk.
- Shifting priorities and specifications - scope creep and shifting requirements will affect the project's timeframe, cost and risk
- Infrequent or weak executive sponsorship - employees take their cues from the leaders of the company. If the organization's leaders haven't demonstrated the project is a priority, it isn't a priority and user adoption will be extremely difficult.

- Staff turnover - while some project team turnover may be unavoidable, repeated or constant turnover can doom the project, and
- Poor incident management and spotty reporting - open issues which linger eventually escalate. The inability to recognize and resolve issues or an absence of management reporting tools almost guarantees that problems are not being reported or are not being communicated to the extended project team.

Source: http://www.erp.asia/erp-failures.asp

6.3.4 Government Enterprise Resource Planning

ERPs in government offer unique challenges but also deliver exceptional opportunities. The implementation of ERPs in government organizations traditionally lagged behind industry, but the benefits observed in manufacturing have also become evident in government implementations. The benefits that governments could derive and the ensuing interest from other governments ensured that ERPs for government have become a unique development line for the vendors, alongside their traditional commercial market developments. Government organizations are less concerned with profit/loss, but are vitally interested in customer service, value for money, and improved efficiency within the organization. To cater for this, many larger ERP vendors have created processes and functionality that meet the challenges of implementing an ERP in government service.

Challenges for ERPs in government service include non-commercial elements such as:

- Military Service conditions
- Large customer service obligations
- Differing levels of availability
- eGovernment initiatives, and
- Specific recruitment, redeployment, and retention requirements.

ERPs in government service have evolved from the simple pay system, the store's inventory, and the accounting register through an evolutionary approach. This evolution has occasionally been challenged by radical change driven by external forces such as the Y2K bug. This challenge granted an opportunity for many organizations to move from independent functional or cross-functional systems into an ERP implementation for many common business processes in the organization.

The potential benefits of implementing ERPs in government agencies depend upon the level of the government agency. Central government agencies that focus on policy and regulation can derive management benefits from efficiency in the use of functions related to corporate services (e.g., finance, human resources, purchasing, and corporate governance). Agencies with more direct implementation responsibilities, often in state, provincial or local governments can derive benefit from other functions too, such as asset management, real estate or property management, and sales and distribution functions. By leveraging the pre-defined processes, government agencies can readily achieve improved management and operating cost reductions.

Activity

Implementing an ERP in Government

Your department seeks to implement an ERP to support as much of its business as it can but is unsure of what can be achieved within a reasonable budget.

Write a short answer to the following questions:

1. If your team was appointed to plan how this implementation would proceed, who else in the department would add value to the planning team?
2. What difficulties do you think will arise during the implementation?
3. What controls should be in place to ensure the implementation is tracking correctly?
4. What benefits will you be able to measure when your department implements the ERP?

6.4 eProcurement for Government

An offshoot of many ERPs that has delivered exceptional value to many government organizations is functionality that permits Electronic Procurement (eProcurement). eProcurement involves a number of inter- related methods for improving the procurement process through the use of electronic systems and processes. eProcurement relies on established policy and legislative frameworks to be effective. Government organizations must ensure the implementation of these methods complies with all relevant financial policy, and legislative provisions of established government procurement policy.

One eProcurement solution will not work for all organizations. eProcurement is not a one-size-fits-all solution, and a targeted implementation approach that focuses on tangible business benefits will ensure a government organization focuses their activities on those areas where the highest return on investment exists.

Agencies that have implemented eProcurement projects have realized benefits such as:

- Accelerated time to market for sourcing and procurement activities
- Better buying power through managed purchases and reduced "rogue" purchases

- Improved governance and probity through maintaining an electronic record of activity, and
- Reduction in resources associated with administration of procurement processes.

eProcurement adds value by simplifying low-complexity purchases. Automating any part of the procurement process is an implementation of eProcurement. Common implementations of eProcurement in government are:

- Travel
- Stationery and office supplies, and
- Payment of suppliers using electronic funds transfer (EFT).

Advanced uses of eProcurement include invoice-less payment systems, automation of the entire procurement process, and publishing RFTs and RFQs through an established tendering portal.

The Australian Government Department of Finance breaks eProcurement into three distinct streams. These streams identify the three stages of a procurement cycle (Table 6.1):

- Planning the purchase
- Executing the purchase, and
- Payment.

Table 6.1. Streams of eProcurement (Source: Commonwealth of Australia (2006))

Planning	Procurement	Payment
Request for Quote (RFQs) Request for Purchase (RFPs) Contract and Supplier Management Tender Evaluation Tools Electronic Auctions	Catalogues Electronic Purchase Orders (EPOs) Automatic Approval Work-flow Financial Management Information (FMIS) systems Vendor Managed Inventory (VMI) systems	Credit or Purchasing Cards Expense Management Systems Evaluated Receipt Settlement Electronic Funds Transfer (EFT) Recurring Payments Electronic Invoicing

A business case, benefits map, and a targeted implementation will get the best value for money out of eProcurement. By mapping out these processes and targeting specific implementations within the procurement cycle, a government organization can deliver significant benefit without implementing full eProcurement. These targeted implementations should be considered in relation to the demands of the organization. Successful implementations of eProcurement have been assisted through:

- Establishing metrics to measure the potential benefits and tangible outcomes

- Developing a robust business case and tracking the progress against that business case
- Appointing a single point of accountability to assume responsibility for the project
- Managing stakeholders in order to obtain and maintain buy-in to the project
- Providing clear communication to employees, stakeholders and suppliers, and
- Understanding suppliers' concerns and ensuring their continued support.

In summary, eProcurement success can be achieved by combining an understanding of the purchasing profile of your organization with an appreciation for the different eProcurement tools available, and implementing the appropriate tool to suit the business case and/or any identified business problem. This is described in Table 6.2.

Table 6.2. Drivers of Success in eProcurement Implementation (Source: Commonwealth of Australia (2006))

Governance Focus

Increased benefits from Automation →

Spend by Category	Low (Frequency of Activity)	High (Frequency of Activity)
High	Governance Focus Sourcing Electronic Purchase Orders Electronic Funds Transfer (EFT) Recurring Payments **Mitigate Risk**	Dedicated Solution Electronic Purchase Orders Evaluated Receipt Settlement Direct Connect eSourcing Tools **Invest in Systems**
Low	Provide Enablers Catalogues Electronic Purchase Orders Purchasing Cards Electronic Request management **Streamline**	Rationalise & Reduce Purchasing Cards One Time Vendors **Minimise**

↑ **Increasing need for Governance and Control**

Frequency of Activity
Sourcing/Contracts; Transactions/Purchases; Payments/Invoices

> **Further Reading**
>
> *A quality guide for eProcurement implementation can be found at:*
> http://www.finance.gov.au/publications/strategic-guide-to-eProcurement/index.html

Group Activity

eProcurement

Your government department has chosen to implement an eProcurement system, but some elements of the department seek to implement less automation than other areas. The "technology champions" and the "cautious businessmen" cannot agree on the procurement processes that will be incorporated in the eProcurement specification.

1. *Divide your workgroup into two teams, the technology champions and the cautious businessmen. Each team is to consider the processes and define the functionality they seek to include in the scope, and then build a short-form business case for their proposal. The business case should also document why certain functionality has been excluded from the scope.*
2. *Once the business cases are complete, present to the other team.*
3. *As a complete group, work through both business cases and negotiate an agreed scope for the eProcurement proposal.*

Chapter Highlights

- Information systems within government agencies can be considered as transaction processing systems, clustered together to create functional systems. Clusters of functional systems are sometimes called enterprise resource planning (ERP) systems.
- ERP systems are business management systems that integrate support for a wide range of business functions to allow a more coordinated approach to managing the whole business.
- The four core areas that ERP systems support are: finance and accounting; human resource management; operations management; and corporate services delivery.
- Implementing an ERP in government requires careful planning. Not all functions of an ERP are useful or relevant to all government agencies. Decisions to tailor ERPs can be expensive.
- eProcurement involves a number of inter-related methods for improving the procurement process through the use of electronic systems and processes. Common implementations of eProcurement in government support travel, stationery and office supplies, and the payment of suppliers using electronic funds transfer (EFT).

Review Questions

1. The text lists a couple of typical transaction processing systems (payroll and leave accrual). What other transaction processing systems apply in government?
2. The selection of ERP modules to implement can be influenced by the level of government; for example, a national-level government agency might implement different modules of an ERP compared to a large local government agency. Discuss this statement.
3. Do you think ERPs are better suited to supporting centralized or devolved corporate services (human resources, finance, purchasing, and so on) arrangements? Why?
4. Can you think of government purchases that are not well suited to eProcurement?

References

Commonwealth of Australia. (2006). Strategic guide to eProcurement. Retrieved from http://www. finance.gov.au/publications/strategic-guide-to-eProcurement/index.html

Kroenke, D. M. (2009). Using MIS (2nd ed.). New Jersey: Pearson Prentice Hall.

CHAPTER 7 Citizen Services

Learning Objectives

After studying this chapter, you will be able to:

- Describe the key benefits of delivering government services to citizens online
- Identify typical stages of eGovernment development that focus on citizen service delivery
- Identify inhibitors to delivering services to citizens exclusively online
- Discuss examples of eGovernment initiatives that have delivered citizen services online in several countries, and
- Discuss the different roles that citizens play when they interact with government and the influence these have on online service design.

In the past, "obtaining an import or export licence in Singapore required an applicant to fill out 21 different forms and then wait 15 to 20 days for 23 government agencies to process the request. But, since the government launched TradeNet, applicants have had to submit only one on-line form, and they receive a licence as soon as 15 seconds later." (Al-Kibsi, de Boer, Mourshed, & Rea, 2001)

Moving citizens from "in line" to "online" (Photo credit: O. Huq, A. Imran)

7.1 Improving Citizen Access to Services Through eGovernment

> *"The greatest benefits and value of eGovernment, however, will be realized over the longer term in the context of enhanced citizen engagement, better citizen services, increased public participation, renewed trust in government, and overall greater participatory democracy."*
>
> *Curtin, Sommer, & Vis-Sommer, 2003, p. 15*

Governments in developing countries have frequently centered eGovernment strategies on delivering services to citizens electronically, a focus motivated by the idea that this will allow better government service delivery at less cost. More specifically, the motivation for electronic government services is the belief that they will permit more inclusive services to be delivered to more people, which offers greater choice and flexibility, and provides more responsive services tailored to the increasingly disparate needs of citizens. At its grandest, the promise of electronic government service delivery has:

> *within it the potential for changing the nature of democracy, citizenship, control and power in the state. In principle, new information and communications capabilities will widen access to public services, enhancing consumer knowledge and enriching consumption. Greater equity of provision, the empowering of citizens and the strengthening of the political competence of citizens are all potential consequences of the application of ICTs (Bellamy & Taylor, 1998, p. 67).*

In this context, electronic government services, usually called government-to-citizen (G2C) services, are an important part of all eGovernment thinking. However, the priority of electronic government services in developed countries is driven by the many years of ICT development in government and the private sector, and by the high and increasing levels of Internet connectivity in government constituencies. Almost by definition, these circumstances are not present in least developing countries. Hence, this text places a priority on developing government-to-government ideas to enhance the efficiency and effectiveness of government itself. However, once that initiative is in place, moving attention to the delivery of services directly to the citizens through the Internet or, increasingly, mobile telephone platforms is a proper priority for government. This section deals with the broad issues of designing and implementing G2C services.

7.1.1 The Impetus for Online Service Delivery

Government organizations, especially in developing countries, are often large, rigid, and powerful. Hierarchical structures in cultures with high power distance create an invisible wall between general citizens and government authorities. It is often difficult to get in touch with government officials, and to do so involves long queues and long waiting times. G2C offers the paradigm shift from "in line" to "online" (Al- Kibsi et al., 2001) as a service strategy in delivering services to citizens. Through online interactions, citizens can directly build confidence and trust in their governments because no third party is involved. This directness and transparency are major strengths of G2C. Citizens also feel empowered to be able to participate and directly integrate themselves in the government process with a more "touch and feel" experience.

The fulfilment of total eGovernment is accomplished through delivering services to citizens online. The citizens of this digital age are increasingly IT dependent, with ICT enabling many of their daily activities. Citizen expectations are thus changing. Innovative, ICT-driven service delivery is critical to meeting these expectations.

Although G2C is not the core function area of eGovernment operation (see Chapter 2), it is the most visible and the aspect where the government's main stakeholders (i.e., citizens) can directly participate. Service delivery through G2C, facilitated by a robust G2G implementation, might be seen as the end-point of eGovernment.

However, most developed countries have focused first on their online presence, largely for political reasons. But, to harness the full potential of eGovernment through online delivery, the backend infrastructure is essential (Imran & Gregor, 2012; Scholl, 2005). Governments that have reached mature stages of eGovernment with a solid infrastructure and streamlined business processes are able to derive real benefit from eGovernment by extending computerization at the service-delivery level.

7.1.2 Advantages of Delivering Services Online

The benefits of delivering government services to citizens online could be manifold to both organizations and citizens. The advantages are discussed below (adapted from APSC, 2010; NOIE, 2003; OECD, 2003).

Organizational benefits

- Citizen satisfaction: this is an important measure of public sector performance. It can be improved through online service delivery because of the efficiency and transparency typically offered by eGovernment services. Services can be more flexible and responsive to better match citizens' expectations, which increases their satisfaction.
- Low-cost channels of communication: online channels offer an additional means to communicate with people, one that is usually far more cost effective than other forms of service delivery.
- Overall cost saving: through combined savings, the government's overall productivity can be increased. According to AGIMO (2003), about 65% of government service costs are reduced through improved business processes, which include savings from advertising, printed material, staff costs, and client management costs.
- Increased resource efficiency: organizations are able to use their resources more efficiently by sharing citizens' information and transaction records with other organizations via electronic means, subject to privacy considerations.
- Service efficiency: at any given time, more citizens can be served online than through any other channel. Importantly, this increased volume of service requires no additional staff. Online services can also reach citizens in places where other delivery channels are too expensive to offer (e.g., remote locations).
- Reputation and image: delivering better services to citizens is often a key part of the political agenda that earns government votes and popularity. Online services help to build a government's image by providing cutting-edge technology and services to citizens. Online services also help to portray the government as progressive, transparent, and accountable.

Citizens' benefits

There are three main areas in which citizens derive benefit from electronic government service delivery:

- **Access**- the availability of government information and services "anytime, anywhere" is usually considered more convenient and less costly for citizens (Figure 7.2). Citizens frequently complete electronic services online, which reduces the number of times that they must interact with the government and the associated costs they must deal with. These access benefits are felt particularly keenly by those who are traditionally excluded from accessing government services: the remotely located and the disabled.

- **Flexibility**- electronic service delivery allows citizens to access and complete services when they are ready, often in their native language. Usually, the online delivery allows easier discovery of all service options, possibly in combinations that make sense to citizens who are not necessarily related to the government's internal structure.
- **Social benefits**- electronic government services and the initiatives that deliver them often include opportunities for citizens to learn new skills and to improve their IT capabilities. Other social benefits are the ready availability of government information and the increase in government transparency, efficiency, and accountability.

Online services allow interaction with the government 24/7 from the comfort of one's own home (Photo credit A. Imran)

7.2 Inhibitors to Delivering Services to Citizens Exclusively Online

Despite their lucrative potential and strong appeal, online services are still struggling to compete with other channels of service delivery, even in the most developed countries. There are many reasons for this, which include socio-cultural habit, lack of ICT skills in the populace, ease of conducting business by other means (e.g., telephone), and privacy and security issues. These limitations will add to the constraints typical of developing countries, such as accessibility, affordability, and Internet penetration rates (Wilson, 2004).

Below, we discuss the challenges faced by various eGovernment efforts around the world.

7.2.1 Accessibility and affordability

Accessibility of online services for the majority of a population is a fundamental issue. If it is only able to serve a small portion of the population, the online option will increase the digital divide. A government must ensure access to any online initiative among the majority of its citizens through a variety of means, including information centers, kiosks, and the promotion of affordable, national Internet access.

7.2.2 Financial viability

Adding the online delivery option must be financially viable when considering other channels. Introducing a new channel means adding to government costs because existing channels need to be maintained. It is only when a critical mass of users migrate to the new channel and when the old channels can be scaled down or closed that major savings can be realized.

7.2.3 Employee resistance

Government employees' resistance to changing the existing process is a critical barrier. Many employees will think that they will lose their job with computerization. Fear of the transparency and accountability offered by automated systems threatens a section of employees who exploit inefficient and non-transparent systems. These challenges have to be carefully managed through adequate training, awareness, and a change-management strategy.

Employees' fear and uncertainty need to be managed carefully
(Photo credit R. Islam)

7.2.4 eLiteracy

A basic level of ICT literacy and an understanding of how to operate online services is essential to achieving the expected outcome. Digital literacy, training, and awareness campaigns through schools, community organizations, and the media are necessary to bridge this gap.

7.2.5 Motivation and incentives

Without motivation and incentives, citizens are not likely to adopt innovations that involve some degree of learning effort. The government should give financial or other incentives to encourage online transactions.

7.2.6 Trust

Establishing citizens' trust on online services is very important. The credibility of the service will be questioned if it is not regularly updated or if it provides flawed data and remains out of service for significant periods of time. Citizens will need to be completely assured that their data is preserved securely and that transactions are completed correctly. Hacking incidents and software bugs in government websites can quickly reduce citizens' trust. A large number of people still have superstitions and hesitations about using the Internet. Many are concerned about virus attacks, data loss, and breaches of privacy. While it is difficult and time consuming to build trust, it is easy to destroy it in a few seconds when such breaches occur.

(Photo credit A. Imran)

7.2.7 Failure to meet expectations

In terms of information and services, there are often substantial gaps between citizens' expectations and what is actually delivered. Citizens will always compare online services to other channels in terms of time taken, cost, and service quality. Monitoring services to maintain standards and to meet customers' changing circumstances and demands is critical. If citizens do not get what they want from an online service, they will quickly switch to other channels and may not return to this option.

7.2.8 Administrative and legal barriers

The implementation of new online services will challenge most existing administrative and legal procedures and regulations. Administrative and legal reforms that support the smooth operation of online service delivery are crucial and often time consuming. Strong leadership is required to overcome this barrier.

7.3 Development of Online Citizen Services

> *"Citizen-centered Government will use the Internet to bring about transformational change: agencies will conduct transactions with the public along secure web-enabled systems that use portals to link common applications and protect privacy, which will give citizens the ability to go online and interact with their Government ... around citizen preferences and not agency boundaries"*
>
> *A blueprint for new beginnings, US Government (2001, p. 179)*[1]

7.3.1 An Overview of eGovernment Service Development

New technologies and innovations create new opportunities for the government to improve services offered to citizens. Regular innovations and effort from the government is necessary to reap the best results. For developing countries, the best way to begin this journey is to learn from the practices and experiences of others. There is an opportunity for developing countries to skip a generation of technologies used by others and adopt newer offerings, such as cloud computing, that may be more cost effective and efficient.

Online services do not justify investment if the majority stakeholders (i.e., citizens and businesses) do not use them. For this reason, their target audience has to be carefully determined so that the online services address their needs. A government service must serve the entire population, whether that service is economically viable or not. Indeed, governments often provide services where a market has failed to deliver. Consequently, selecting service audiences and targeting their needs is not simply a matter of determining who can afford to pay.

Overall citizen need and the capability to adopt online services is sometimes described as a society's eReadiness. Preparing the society to embrace a new way of doing business is an important task of eGovernment implementation. The media and non-government organizations can also play an important role in preparing people. Awareness campaigns can educate and empower citizens to handle ICT-based business processes. In parallel, the telecommunications and network infrastructure must be developed so that services can be taken to the citizens' doorsteps. Initiatives that encourage businesses to adopt electronic commerce can also foster a societal environment of adopting electronic approaches to service delivery and consumption.

While eGovernment is built on the same principles and technologies as eCommerce, it is also quite different because of the public nature of government. Designing and delivering services that meet citizens' expectations is a major challenge for government organizations. It is not good enough to deliver services online without incorporating citizens' perspectives into service design and deliv-

---

[1] http://www.gpo.gov/fdsys/pkg/BUDGET-2002-BLUEPRINT/pdf/BUDGET-2002-BLUEPRINT.pdf

ery. This requires thorough market research of the prospective audience; that is, citizens and businesses. Careful design and planning, followed by a good business case, can create financially viable online service delivery. It is also important to remember that "not all [government] services are amenable to the electronic mode of delivery, because of issues such as bulky submissions, interview requirements, and submission of physical samples and so forth" (Alan Siu, Deputy Secretary of Information Technology & Broadcasting Bureau, Government of Hong Kong, quoted in Deloitte Research, 2001, p. 17).

7.3.2 Important factors for online development

The following factors are of central importance in online service development.

1. Putting citizens at the centre

Citizen-centered services place the citizen at the heart of the entire public service delivery system (Figure 7.5). That is, services are designed to achieve citizens' objectives, not merely to be more convenient for government agencies. This can sometimes lead to radical restructuring of services, and it can even shift responsibilities for some services between different agencies and different government ministers. Such radical change requires an active commitment to engaging and empowering all stakeholders along the service delivery chain (APSC, 2010).

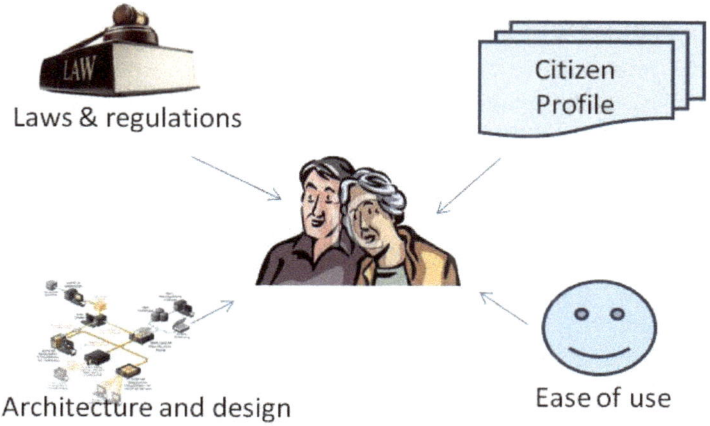

Figure 7.5. Designing services focused on the citizen

Care should be taken so that the newly designed services address the needs of a majority of people and not just a section of those who are already in advantageous positions. Failure to do so may increase the digital divide. The profile of a general user should be drawn from the bell curve of the entire population, and the online service delivery should be designed and implemented with the use of this profile. Stakeholder groups that represent different sections of the community should also be consulted during eGovernment service design activities.

2. User friendliness and simplification of the service process

Creating an online service does not mean merely applying existing processes. Creating an online service offers the opportunity to reengineer the existing business process to eliminate unnecessary intermediaries, to simplify and speed up the procedure, to consider whether other value-adding elements can be included, and to ensure that citizen users are able to handle the process with ease and without assistance. Whereas government employees can be trained to use a new system and a new process, citizen training is usually unattainable. Processes must be simple enough to be understood and used by untrained users while not compromising the accuracy of the data collected or the service's proper decision-making process.

3. Collaboration

Another important factor in achieving success in online service delivery is collaborating effectively with other government agencies. Collaboration offers stakeholders insights and resources, and presents the opportunity to add value to new online services by combining the interests of different agencies in a single service. Services that have previously been two separate processes in two different agencies may now become a single service for citizens, yet still collect the data that both agencies require. Solutions that combine services across agencies create efficiencies both for the agencies and for citizens.

At a broader level, a coordinating body across a government that takes into account the interests of government agencies, non-government organizations, communities, and individual citizens can define common standards and systems. Establishing whole-of-government standards that are based on a common enterprise architecture offers the opportunity for services to present the same "look and feel" to users and to share data between the agencies offering the services. eGovernment initiatives often offer opportunities for greater collaboration with industry stakeholders through approaches such as public private partnerships (PPP). Industry partners can sometimes bring skills and other resources to the development of eGovernment services that would take a government much too long to develop by itself. In the context of a least-developed country, these industry partnerships may be aid programs.

4. Administrative and regulatory reform

Where necessary, laws and regulations associated with the relevant business processes should be reviewed and amended, and new regulations enacted to accommodate and facilitate online business processes. The legal status of online transactions and digital records is a critical area of electronic government. Many governments have enacted laws specifically to recognize digital records, digital signatures, and the validity of online submissions so that eGovernment initiatives can be delivered. Strong leadership and top-level commitment is required to make the necessary changes in parliament and the judiciary system.

7.3.3 Tips for eGovernment Websites

> *"It is all too easy to build a website without actually improving service."*
>
> *(Al-Kibsi et al., 2001, p. 70)*

An eGovernment's online interface is invariably a website. Government websites provide citizens and businesses with their first impressions of a government's online initiatives. A poorly designed interface or website can diminish the expectation of a good online service delivery and reduce the level of adoption by citizens. At a minimum, users expect a government website to be technically robust, load quickly, and have intact links with good navigation and search aids.

Early examples of government websites presented information in the form that governments used. The content was written for public servants trained in the relevant policies and procedures. The websites were structured along the lines of their agencies' hierarchical structures. In short, they were not designed for citizens' ease of use, although this failing was not a deliberate objective of the website designers. The important lessons that early eGovernment website developers learned were threefold:

1. Citizens expect to be able to find information on government programs and initiatives to assist them with their concerns in terms that they, the citizens, understand. Simply making the information present on a website is not enough. Citizens must be able to discover it, and it must be written using terms that they understand.
2. Citizens do not typically think about their government as a collection of agencies. Consequently, they do not necessarily know what part of the government, or what branch of an agency, is responsible for assisting them. Citizens generally prefer government websites that are structured in terms of their concerns or "life events".
3. Whatever is displayed on a government website must also be what citizens are told in offices or on the telephone. Nothing will dissuade citizens from using online services more quickly than feeling that the service is not the correct one because it says something different from what people in the organization told them.

(Photo credit Wrangler, shutterstock.com)

A good design is indeed like a great artwork: expressive and relatable to almost everyone. The KISS - "Keep It Simple, Stupid" - principle is also a handy rule of thumb for website design. The World Wide Web Consortium's Web Accessibility project has produced an extensive list of guidelines for web designers. Consistency, clarity, and user friendliness are the key design issues for government websites (McGovern, 2003).

7.3.4 Essential elements of a good government website

While citizens will expect government websites to use modern technologies, the application of many attributes and features is not the only determinant of a useful government website. A good design helps a visitor to focus on and understand what the designer intended to convey to them (McGovern, 2003). When a design is kept simple by following a few basic rules, the reader's ability to use the website increases (Nielsen, 2000). Below, we discuss some essential elements of a good government website.

Content

A well-designed webpage is meaningless without good content. Information must be accurate, complete, economical, flexible, reliable, relevant, simple, timely, and verifiable (Stair & Reynolds, 2001). Websites need to be service-delivery oriented instead of advertising or highlighting the organization itself. Obtaining users' trust and confidence is crucial, and this can be done by delivering correct and up-to-date information and by responding to queries and applications efficiently and promptly.

Structure

The structure of a website will largely depend on its type of audience. The structure must be recognizable from the citizen user's point of view, which may be quite different from that of the agency hosting the website. It is recommended that all government organizations have common standards for terminology, presentation, and technology use to define the structures, graphics, and navigation of government websites (Nielsen, 2000).

Visual Appeal

Websites must also be visually appealing, although not at the expense of ease of use. It is said that "a picture is worth a thousand words". Experienced graphic designers can use graphics to enhance the message of a website and to increase its usability. Often, a good graphic (e.g., a chart or graph) can convey a great deal of information in an economical way. However, incidental pictures, too many colors, and too many different fonts will simply clutter up a website and reduce its effectiveness.

Navigation

To a user browsing the Internet, "time" and "easiness" are the two most important factors. Users want to reach their expected location in the shortest possible time and without any confusion: this is the standard rule of navigation. Designers are increasingly trying to enhance websites' interactivity and to establish innovative ways of navigating and accessing websites. Deviations from users' expectations will impede communication and performance.

Further Reading

For more about website design issues, see the following:

Lynch, P., & Horton, S. (2002). *Web style guide (2nd ed.).* URL: http://www.webstyleguide.com/index.html

Nielsen, J. (2000). *Designing web usability: The practice of simplicity. New Riders.* URL: http://www.nngroup.com/

W3C Web Accessibility Initiative. URL: http://www.w3.org/WAI/

7.4 The Citizen's Role in eGovernment Services

Government services should be aimed at particular recipients as much as possible. It is common wisdom that the government serves four broad markets: citizens, businesses, other government agencies, and employees. The citizen market segment is regularly referred to by a variety of names: citizens, customers, clients, the public, and so on. Sometimes, these are used interchangeably; for example, "The emancipated citizen is a highly demanding client, who wishes to be treated in a customer-friendly way" (Lapre & van Venrooij, 2001). However, the terms should not be used interchangeably (Mintzberg, 1996; Scholl, 2001) because they can have different implications for service design, as we discuss below.

One approach to thinking about eGovernment service design proposes that government constituents can be classified into four groups: customers, clients, subjects, and citizens (Turner, 2006). Each of these roles takes a different view of government. An individual acting in a particular role will expect particular outcomes and behaviors from their government. The roles categorize all people that a government serves, placing them into segments on the basis of their intent as they access a service. The following descriptions of the different segments are drawn from Turner (2006), based on earlier work by Mintzberg (1996), and offer some insights into the different design decisions that might be made when developing eGovernment services.

Customers are people who purchase commodities (e.g., utilities or lottery tickets) from government agencies. These interactions are usually brief, and the relationship between the customer and the government is a commercial one. Customers often conduct similar interactions with non-government entities. Some developed countries have considered implementing policies that stop governments offering these kinds of transactions or services because a government agency offering the service adds no value when the service is also being offered by commercial organizations. However, addressing market failures and managing public goods are two reasons for government participation in selling commodities.

When a government interacts with customers, the focus is on driving the cost out of a transaction. The government must respond to commercial pressures or lose its customers to competitors; for example, private- sector companies or other local-level governments that might attempt to lure away businesses and citizens.

A customer, by definition, adopts the approaches and attitudes of a typical online shopper. Online shoppers use the Internet as a time- saving device, a convenient means of accessing a service, and as a research tool to determine the "best" match to their needs. They usually compare various product (service) characteristics and prices. They usually complete the transaction online and in one session. With this level of research and comparison, online shoppers can be expected to be fickle, and so developing an ongoing relationship with them requires careful soliciting.

Therefore, eGovernment service customers will consider the service as one of a range of alternatives, seek initial information with which to make a decision, and transact their business online. If the services they are offered do not receive careful attention, the customers cannot be expected to return. We can deduce that the characteristics of eGovernment services that would meet their needs are either:

- Transactional in nature (i.e., they receive, or at least initiate, the service online) or informational about the services
- A commodity, or at least mass-produced (i.e., some selection from a "menu" of pre-defined alternatives), with the nature, scope, and cost of the services unaffected by the personal circumstances of the recipients, or

- Commercial in nature, implying the likely presence of a fee and the presence of competitive offerings or substitutes from other (possibly non-government) suppliers in the market.

Clients are constituents who purchase or receive professional services (e.g., health services, education, or job-locating services) from the government over a period of time (possibly their whole lifetime). These interactions are similar in character to commercial professional service offerings where the longer the relationship goes on, the more complex and tailored the service becomes for the individual client. The nature of the relationship, particularly its longevity and its value to the recipient, means that these services are only a government monopoly when the government has determined they should be (i.e., nationalized services). Nevertheless, the government is frequently, but not always, the first-choice provider of such services.

In interactions between governments and clients, the focus is on delivering a professionally appropriate, quality outcome to the individual. Governments frequently deliver such services (e.g., legal aid and education) as a lower-cost alternative to commercial offerings to cover "market failures". These services are offered to guarantee access for all government constituents, regardless of their ability to pay. Governments attempt to ensure that clients receive the correct, appropriate, and complete service that they require at the minimum government cost. Interactions of this type are enhanced by eCommerce technologies, although there are clear potential benefits from eBusiness techniques.

Clients, by definition seek professional, long-term services - those meeting a complex need or set of needs that cannot be satisfied with a single transaction. The need will be unique to the client - although the service they receive may not be - and they will consider a range of alternatives when looking for the service that most closely matches their requirements. Information that pertains to the nature of the service, to the client's eligibility to receive it, to discounts on the cost of the service, or to how to apply for and receive the service would also interest the client.

We can deduce that the characteristics of eGovernment services that would meet client needs are:

- Both transactional (either for initiation or for ongoing steps in an overall service) and informational about the services, their parameters, and client eligibility
- Individually tailored; the nature, scope, and cost of the services would be significantly affected by the personal circumstances of the recipients
- Routinely interactional; once a relationship was established, there would be further, regular interactions (e.g., medical check-ups, rent payments, etc.), and

- Commercial in nature, which implies the likely presence of a fee and competitive offerings or substitutes from other (probably non-government) suppliers in the market.

Subjects are constituents who receive a mandatory service from the government without the opportunity to influence the parameters of the service's provision (e.g., prison inmates, tax and rate payers, and national service conscripts). These interactions tend to be personal to the extent that the service is tailored to an individual's circumstances; however, the relationship is not equal or balanced. That is, the government compels the subject to accept the service because the government deems that it should be received. The delivery of these services is generally seen as a government obligation, although there are examples of these services being delivered by outsourced providers under the guidance and monitoring of governments.

The focus of interactions between governments and subjects is to seek a fair, consistently applied service delivery. These services are a direct expenditure of government funds and, consequently, must be expended with utmost regard to efficiency and probity. The nature of these services demands that attention should also be paid to the correctness or appropriateness of their delivery. Mechanisms that support this focus lie in the realm of eBusiness. Electronically enabled internal processes provide greater efficiency in delivering these services, and provide the necessary management information to ensure that the services are efficiently and appropriately delivered to the relevant constituents.

To a large extent, the electronic services that pertain to subjects will focus on improving internal communication and operations in the relevant government bureaucracy (i.e., G2G), rather than on delivering services to subjects directly. However, any service that helps constituents to comply routinely with their obligations under law falls into subject- targeted service. The characteristics of services that subjects seek are:

- Frequently informational about obligations and means to comply, but can include transactions such as paying rates
- Individually tailored; the nature and scope of the services will be substantially affected by the personal circumstances of the recipients
- Routinely interactional; transactions will occur on a regular, if not frequent, basis, and
- Specifically sourced from the government, although some services may be provided by third parties under contracts or other arrangements (e.g., tax accountants).

Citizens are constituents who receive services from the government at a broad level; for example, the provision of infrastructure, such as sewerage, roads, or air traffic control. These interactions tend to be more impersonal, and are generally provided in a one-size-fits-all manner. The relationship between a government and its citizens is essentially one of benefactor and beneficiary, although this is not a strict definition. The government is generally accepted as the appropriate deliverer of these services. It also maintains the role of policy setter and regulator where these services are delivered by non-government bodies.

There are some more direct services available to citizens. However, services that allow citizens to occasionally carry out their civic responsibilities fit into this group; for example, providing the means for a citizen to acquire a fishing permit. The permit has a limited life and the citizen may not ever acquire a second one, but they will feel and be obliged to acquire one if they want to fish. In this example service, the government's management approach is to act to preserve the value of the public good of fish stocks by limiting access to them and requiring each fisher to seek permission.

Citizens also have another important relationship with their government that of "owner" (Swedberg & Douglas, 2001). Governments act to address citizens' needs as expressed through actions such as voting, lobbying, and using agencies and elected representatives to provide direct feedback. Citizens interact among themselves to form and promote the needs governments seek to address. These activities can also be enhanced by electronic interaction, an area often called eDemocracy or eParticipation. As early as 1996, Tapscott described "Internet-worked Government", which includes the idea of government "foster[ing] the launching of 'virtual interest groups', which can contribute to societal well-being" (Tapscott, 1996).

The focus of government interactions with citizens is to ensure a consistent, equitable, and appropriate outcome from large-scale services delivered to everyone. These interactions seek to facilitate citizens and government collaborating to determine the nature, delivery means, and outcomes of the services that government provides. For example, the consultation process to determine, say, parking arrangements in a local council area would be a citizen service. Leighninger (2011) elaborates on this idea. The level of sophistication that such interactions might ideally achieve would require significant complexity in any underpinning information technology.

The majority of services that citizens receive are in the nature of public goods and are rarely delivered electronically. However, there are some services that citizens might seek electronically, such as information on government operations, or details of current or proposed legislation or policy. These examples point to the characteristics of eGovernment services that citizens seek, which are:

- Largely informational in nature, although providing feedback on policy or legislation might be considered transactional
- Either a commodity or a "menu" selection; the nature of the services is unaffected by the personal circumstances of the recipients, and
- Specifically sourced from the government, both as the originating source and as the authoritative provider.

7.5 Some Examples of eGovernment Initiatives

During the early phases of eGovernment in developed countries, the concept of a "one-stop government" was formulated to integrate public services into citizens' perspectives. This portal integrates all the services offered by various government departments and acts as a single platform for citizens and businesses to access their services. These portals help government departments to improve the transparency and accountability of their functioning and to reduce the cost of delivery. Citizens no longer need to search various government agencies for a service; rather, they can access all services through one doorway. Some examples of such national portals are in Australia (www.australia. gov.au), Singapore (http://www.ecitizen.gov.sg/), and Malaysia (http:// www.sarawak.gov.my/). This approach is also called a "single entry- point strategy" (discussed in Chapter 2), which promotes high levels of citizen satisfaction and can help to develop long-lasting relationships between a government and its citizens.

Three case studies from three countries demonstrate practical examples of several governments' successful online service delivery initiatives.

Case Study: eGovernment Portal Solution: Manipur State Portal

With a population of 2.72 million, Manipur is one of the eight states in India's northeast region. Access to government services, such as form submission, status tracking, placing a request for a public distribution system card, registering with the employment exchange, etc. for citizens at Manipur is complicated. Citizens need to rely on the assistance of government officials to locate the correct office or channel. They may need to travel with difficulty through rugged landscape and heavy rainfall. Similarly, the move from the state for young people to study or work can complicate the situation.

To setup and deliver the State portal, the Department of Information Technology (DIT), Government of Manipur partnered with Accenture. Accenture started this three and half year project worth more than US $3 million on July 19, 2011 including a ten month systems implementation and testing period. In its first six-month phase, Accenture offered 20 services by four government departments. In the second phase, 22 services by five government departments were added. The main challenges that the project faced were a lack of standardization for the provision of services across departments and districts, incomplete applications, collating data from different forms to make informed decisions, and a lack of necessary computing infrastructure.

The Accenture team offered an end-to-end IT solution carrying out adequate planning to ensure sufficient delivery through an onsite-offshore model. The DIT, Govt. of Manipur, uses resources from Accenture's Offshore Delivery Centre in Gurgaon to compliment the onsite team located in Imphal, Manipur's capital city. The team developed a common bilingual (English and Manipuri) grievance form for all departments, with a user guide for first time user's filling out the form. In addition, they contributed to the setting up of content management tools that help arrange, store and display content to the portal users in a structured manner. The Accenture team also tested the information exchange through text messages and the ePayments of the integrated application for conformance with Open Web Application Security Project (OWASP) standards. To ensure efficient delivery, the team considered several factors: weather, road conditions, local festivals, cultures, dependency on partners, subcontractors, a few flash strikes, and the need for a graphic designer's involvement to meet the local taste and sensitivity. The Accenture team also made an advance assessment to ensure a one month deadline of setting up computing infrastructure and connectivity across the state.

Citizens started reaping the benefits getting easy access to government. They only need to make a final visit to get the desired services: collect the certificate or document, furnish original documents, or make payments. They can get started with a simple self-registration process online and keep the unique tracking identification code which is sent for each request. Users also receive updates by text or email at every stage from logging of a request or processing.

Source: Accenture. 2013. Manipur State Portal. Public Service for the Future: Enabling eGovernance for efficient and affordable services. Retrieved from https://www.accenture.com/in-en/success-manipur-state-portal-eGovernance-efficient-affordable-services.aspx

Case Study: Pre-filling of Income Tax Returns in Australia

This initiative enables individual income tax returns to pre-fill information held on Tax Office systems and information reported by third-party data providers. It helps taxpayers to meet their tax obligations by supplying information they need to complete their tax returns, verify their records, and resolve any discrepancies between the pre-filled information and their own records before they lodge. Since the service went into full production in July 2008, more than 1.5 million eTax users (of 2.2 million potential users) have accessed pre-filling, and tax agents have downloaded over six million pre-filled reports through the Tax Agent Portal. Over 100 million data items were made available in 2008.

Taxpayers first suggested having access to their personal data during the Tax Office's Listening to the Community initiative in 2002-03. Thus, in line with its commitment to consultation, co-design, and collaboration, the Tax Office worked closely with data providers, tax agents, taxpayers, and other government agencies to develop this concept.

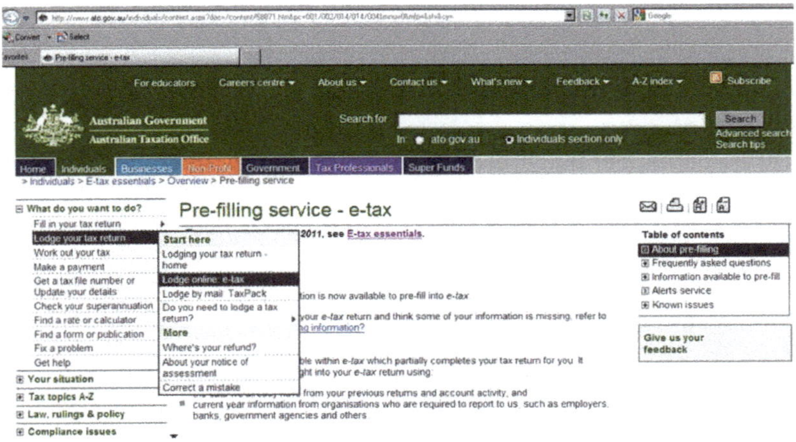

In developing this initiative, the Tax Office built on two existing, successful products - eTax and the Tax Agent Portal. The eTax user interface was modified to accommodate pre-filling data, while a pre-filling report was added to the existing suite of reports on the Tax Agent Portal. The report was developed from its original, view-and-print format to a multi-format that can be integrated, via web services and mark-up languages, with proprietary tax agent recordkeeping and return preparation software.

The pre-filling service delivers information from third-party data providers directly to taxpayers and tax agents. It also includes reminders and prompts on data included in previous years' returns and about some Tax Office letters a taxpayer may have received during the year.

Taxpayers using eTax have the added benefit of having their pre-fill data downloaded directly into their tax return at the relevant labels. Some taxpayers with simple tax affairs may only need to check their pre-filled data before lodging their return, without adding any information.

Pre-filling also offers an "alerts" subscription service, whereby the Tax Office will advise taxpayers by SMS or email when new data becomes available. Although built for pre-filling, this was designed as a reusable and scalable service for the Tax Office.The pre-filling service benefits not only taxpayers but also data providers, tax agents, and the Tax Office. For taxpayers, having pre-filled data provided on their tax returns makes preparing their returns easier and enables them to clarify any discrepancies between the pre-filled information (provided to the Tax Office by third parties) and their own records before they lodge, thus avoiding inadvertent omissions or errors. This initiative also reduces the number of compliance cases and helps to make the Tax Office appear to be proactive, transparent, and living up to its values and the Taxpayers' Charter.

Source: http://www.finance.gov.au/agimo-archive/seminars_and_events/2009/excellence- in-eGovernment-awards-2009-finalist-case-studies/ATO_TaxReturns.html

Case Study: Citizen Service Centers in Bahia, Brazil

The state government of Bahia has created Citizen Assistance Service Centers (SACs) that bring together federal, state, and municipal agencies in a single location to offer the services that citizens most frequently need and use. The centers have been placed in locations convenient to the public, such as shopping malls and major public transportation hubs.

As in much of the world, Bahia's public services have traditionally been delivered by disparate government agencies, at different locations, and with very different service standards. Sometimes, to receive a single service a citizen would have to visit multiple agencies. Often a citizen would learn of the information and documentation needed for a given service only after visiting multiple government agencies on multiple occasions. Typically, citizens were treated with less courtesy and professionalism than in the private sector.

In 1994, the Government of Bahia hosted the first of several annual technology fairs in the state capital, Salvador. A few government services were offered there, using new ICT systems (e.g., issuing identification cards). These services were far more efficient and well received by the public. The idea was then raised: why not deliver services this way on a regular basis?

The centers bring multiple government services together in a single location. As of June 2001, 29 different service agencies are part of the SAC system. Participating agencies include the State Department of Motor Vehicles, the Social Security Ministry, the Secretary of Agriculture and Agrarian Reform, the Municipal Public Services Secretariat, Labor and Social Action, Public Safety, the Federal Police, small claims court, the State Water and Sanitation company, and Bahia's private electric company. Now a citizen can register their vehicle or obtain a driver's license at the SAC. During the same visit, they can obtain a national identification card, apply for unemployment benefits, look for a new job, obtain a labor identification card, submit a legal case in small claims court, obtain a passport, register a business complaint, check on their retirement eligibility and benefits, and so on. Over 500 separate services are offered by the participating agencies.

Not all services are available at all centers. The SACs come in different sizes. Three large SACs each house over 20 agencies. All of these are located in Bahia's capital city, Salvador. There are 15 medium-sized SACs, with between eight and 20 government agencies. There are also five

small SACs, with fewer than eight agencies. Within the SACs, each of the multiple government agencies occupies a separate space with signs clearly indicating the names and locations of different agencies. A publication is available at the reception desk of each center, detailing which agencies are present. Citizens can also obtain the same information by calling a toll-free SAC information hotline.

A Mobile Documents SAC was also developed to reach the most remote and deprived communities in Bahia. This Mobile SAC is a large, 18-wheel truck equipped with air-conditioning, television, toilets, and a covered waiting area. Inside the truck, four basic citizenship services are provided: issuance of birth certificate, identification card, labor identification card, and criminal record verification.

The first SAC was inaugurated in Salvador in September 1995. By April 2001, nearly 32 million services had been delivered through the SACs (two-thirds in the eight SACs of the capital, and the remaining one-third in the Mobile SACs and 14 fixed SACs of the interior).

It used to require multiple visits and long lines for a citizen to receive an identification card, but now it can be done in 20-30 minutes at the SACs. While business owners must still go in person to a government office to register a new business for the first time, registration documents can be renewed in just minutes at a center or through the Internet. (The initial registration can be completed in approximately one day.)

Case study author: Jeffrey Rinne, Ana Benvinda Teixeirra Lage and Elba Andrade.

Source: http://web.worldbank.org/WBSITE/EXTERNAL/TOPICS/RMATIONAND COMMUNICATIONAN DTECHNOLOGIES/T/0,,contentMDK:20486008~ is-CURL:Y~menuPK: 702592~pagePK:148956~piPK:216618~theSite PK:702586,00.html

Chapter Highlights

- Government-to-citizen (G2C) services offer a paradigm shift from an "in-line" to "online" service strategy for communicating and interacting with the government.
- Online services empower citizens to participate and directly involve themselves in the government processes that serve them.
- To harness the full potential of eGovernment through online delivery, the internal processing in government (G2G) must be ready.
- Online services help to build a government's image by providing cutting-edge technology and services to its citizens, which also helps to portray the government as more progressive, transparent, and accountable.
- Access to information is a key human right. Providing citizen services through eGovernment helps to ensure people's democratic and information rights through online participation and direct access to government information.
- Despite their strong appeal, online services still struggle to compete with other channels because of socio-cultural habits, the difficulty of finding correct information, citizens' lack of ICT skills, the ease of conducting business by other means, and privacy and security issues.
- Regular innovations and effort from a government are necessary to reap the best results. For developing countries, the best way to begin this journey is to learn from the best practices and experiences of other countries.
- Preparing a society to embrace this new way of doing business is also an important task of eGovernment implementation.
- Designing and delivering services that meet citizens' expectations is a major challenge for government organizations.
- A poorly designed website can diminish the prospect of online service delivery success. The design of eGovernment services should begin with seeking what adds value to the daily lives of the target groups.
- One approach to identifying target groups when designing eGovernment services is to categorize the public by their intent when they seek services from the government. This can be done using four segments: customer, client, subject, and citizen.

Review Questions

1. What are the organizational benefits that online services provide?
2. What are the benefits that citizens can obtain from online services when compared to other channels?
3. "Not all government services are amenable to the electronic mode of delivery." Why?
4. What are the new approaches toward more user-friendly citizen services in the West?
5. Why is collaboration between government and other agencies so important to online service design?
6. What are the characteristics of a good website?
7. What are the stages or levels of the online sophistication model?
8. What is a proactive website? Give an example.

Discussion Questions

1. Discuss the challenges of online services in the context of your country.
2. There is a fear that online services will create redundancy and job loss in government departments. How do you counter this argument?
3. Discuss the circumstances of when an online service will be able to add real value to the overall efficiency and productivity of public service organizations.

Exercises

In a group of three or four, select three different government department websites and critically examine their design issues in light of each website's purpose and expected target audience.

In a group of three or four, explore three government department websites to find:

1. What kind of services are available and at what level?
2. How the services are structured and arranged (process map)?
3. Design a citizen service model for your organization, based on the principles and lessons you learned from this chapter.

Further Reading

Booz Allen Hamilton. (2005). Beyond eGovernment: The world's most successful technology-enabled transformations. INSEAD. Retrieved from http://www.boozallen.com/ media/file/151607.pdf

This report was commissioned by the eGovernment Unit of the United Kingdom Cabinet Office. It presents a series of country-based case studies on achievements in eGovernment in the then-leading eGovernment (developed)

countries. Most of the examples involve eGovernment services for citizens and all offer suggestions and models for eGovernment.

Al-Kibsi, G., de Boer, K., Mourshed, M., & Rea, N. (2001). Putting citizens on-line, not in line. Mckinsey Quarterly, 2, 64-73.

This article describes the "ideal" implementation of eGovernment services for citizens envisaged at the peak of the "Internet bubble". While optimistic, the article's fundamental ideas and objectives for eGovernment remain at the heart of eGovernment initiatives today.

Economist. (2003, January 2). EGovernment? No, thanks, we prefer shopping. The Economist.

This brief magazine article summarizes the frustration faced by the UK government (and governments all around the world) in encouraging citizens to adopt eGovernment services once they are created.

Cullen, R. (2005). EGovernment: A citizens' perspective. Journal of eGovernment, 1(3), 5-28.

This article describes a research project that investigated what citizens really thought of eGovernment services offered online and what could be done to increase the acceptability and use of those services. The research identified a number of factors that must be managed to make eGovernment services useful and therefore used by citizens.

Turner, T. (2006). Introducing a novel market segmentation for eGovernment services. Journal of eGovernment, 3(4), 5-38.

This article describes a novel way of segmenting citizens that allows the design of eGovernment services to more closely match the expectations of citizens.

References

Al-Kibsi, G., de Boer, K., Mourshed, M., & Rea, N. (2001). Putting citizens on-line, not in line. Mckinsey Quarterly, 2, 64-73.

Australian Government Information Management Office (AGIMO). (2003). EGovernment benefits study. Retrieved from http://www.finance.gov.au/agimo-archive/__data/assets/file/0012/16032/benefits.pdf

Australian Public Service Commission (APSC). (2010). Delivering better services for citizens. State of the Services Report 2009-10. Canberra: APSC.

Bellamy, C., & Taylor, J. A. (1998). Governing in the information age. Buckingham: Open University Press. Curtin, G., Sommer, M., & Vis-Sommer, V. (Eds.). (2003). The world of eGovernment. NY: Haworth Press.

Deloitte Research. (2001). eGovernment's next generation: Transforming the government enterprise through customer service. Retrieved from http://www.deloitte.com/assets/Dcom-Global/ Local%20Assets/Documents/DTT_DR_eGovNextGen.pdf

Imran, A., & Gregor, S. (2012). A process model for successful eGovernment adoption in the least developed countries: A case of Bangladesh. In F. B. Tan (Ed.), International comparisons of information communication technologies: Advancing applications (pp. 321-350). IGI Global.

Lapre, L., & van Venrooij, A. (2001). Bridging the gap between citizen and administration. Paper presented at the European Conference on eGovernment (ECEG), Dublin.

Leighninger, M. (2011). Using online tools to engage - and be engaged by - the public. Deliberative democracy consortium. IBM Center for The Business of Government. Retrieved from http://businessofgovernment.org/report/using-online-tools-engage-public

McGovern, G. (2003). Websites require flexible not fixed design. Retrieved from http://www. gerrymcgovern.com/nt/2003/nt_2003_09_29_brochure.htm

Mintzberg, H. (1996). Managing government, governing management. Harvard Business Review, 74(3), 75-83.

Nielsen, J. (2000). Designing web usability: The practice of simplicity. Retrieved from http://www.nngroup.com/

NOIE. (2003). eGovernment benefits study: Agency case studies. Canberra. Retrieved from http://www.finance.gov.au/agimo-archive/__data/assets/file/0009/12330/Casestudies.pdf

OECD. (2003). The eGovernment Imperative. OECD eGovernment Studies. OECD publishing. pp.204.

Scholl, H. J. (2001). Applying stakeholder theory to eGovernment: Benefits and limits. Paper presented at Towards the ESociety: ECommerce, EBusiness, and EGovernment, The First IFIP Conference on ECommerce, EBusiness, and EGovernment, Zurich.

Scholl, H. J. (2005). Organizational transformation through eGovernment: Myth or reality? Paper presented at the 4th International Conference on Electronic Government, Copenhagen.

Stair, R., & Reynolds, G. (2001). Principles of information systems (5th ed.). MA: Cambridge.

Swedberg, D., & Douglas, J. (2001). Transformation by design: An innovative approach to implementation of eGovernment. Paper presented at the European Conference on eGovernment (ECEG), Dublin.

Tapscott, D. (1996). Digital economy. New York: McGraw Hill.

Turner, T. (2006). Introducing a novel market segmentation for eGovernment services. Journal of eGovernment, 3(4), 5-38.
Wilson, E. J. (2004). The information revolution and developing countries. London: MIT Press.

CHAPTER 8
Security and Privacy

Learning Objectives

After studying this chapter, you will be able to:

- Describe the key elements of IT security
- Identify typical stages in implementing IT security systems
- Identify the stages in risk assessment for applications and eGovernment processes, and
- Discuss the concept of trust online and why it is particularly important in eGovernment.

Case: Private and Personal

Jane works in the kitchen at Central Hospital, a government-run public health facility. She was married last year to Frank, and both Jane and Frank want to start a family as soon as they can. Unfortunately, Jane is not yet pregnant.

Jane visits the government doctor at Central Hospital several times for tests and examinations. The doctor sends samples off to the laboratory for testing and assures Jane that the results will come back to her privately. He is aware of her employment in the hospital.

The doctor is very busy with other patients over the next two weeks and is often away from his office. When the results come back from the laboratory by the eGovernment system, they are mistakenly printed by the doctor's office assistant and placed in Jane's employee notices folder in the break room. This folder is open to anyone who passes by. Consequently, her results are open to anyone visiting the room.

Jane is very embarrassed by this and is now upset that several of her fellow workers know as much about the problem as she does. She does not want to use the electronic system anymore. Other women in the community are concerned that the hospital does not care about their privacy. They also refuse to use the new system.

Review Questions

1. Why is this information important to Jane? Why does that mean it should be kept private?
2. What could the breach of privacy mean to the hospital?

8.1 Why worry about security and privacy?

Electronic government frequently extends government activity beyond the physical boundaries of the government agencies delivering the service. This "reaching out" is never more true than when services are offered to citizens and businesses directly. The movement of activity outside the controlled environment within an agency immediately raises issues of security for the processes and data within those services. Simultaneously, transactions over the Internet are notorious for being unsafe or risky. The message of vulnerability is reinforced by frequent reports in the media of large-scale breaches of security at some key Internet sites. The success of eGovernment has been tied frequently to overcoming concerns of security and privacy.

Familiarity with the Internet has grown around the world since the mid- 1990s. Sometimes, it seems as if literally everyone is comfortable using online services for activities like shopping and communicating with friends. However, in 2012 the adoption of such services is far short of 100% and there are still large portions of the world's population with no Internet connectivity at all. A lack of familiarity with the Internet is most prevalent in least developed countries, almost by definition.

Over time, a series of explanations for these relatively low adoption rates has developed. Key issues including security, privacy, accessibility, and discoverability have been identified, although with diminishing impact over time in countries with high-levels of Internet adoption (AGIMO, 2005, 2006, 2007, 2008). In summary, inhibitors to eGovernment adoption largely involve matters of trust (Al-adawi, Yousafzai, & Pallister, 2005; Carter & Bélanger, 2004; 2005; Colesca, 2009; Teo, Jiang, & Srivastava, 2008; Warkentin, Gefen, Pavlou, & Rose, 2002).

Arising from the growing work on online trust is a small body of literature on trust in eGovernment adoption (e.g., Al-adawi, et al., 2005; Colesca, 2009; Huang, D'Ambra, & Bhalla, 2002; Teo, et al. 2008; Warkentin, et al., 2002).

The contrast of the need for trust in online activity with non-government bodies and with government is important. When interacting online with commercial vendors, the user may choose another vendor if they do not trust the one they are using and still interact online. However, that luxury is not available when interacting with government. If the user (citizen or business) does not trust the online interaction with their government, they will not use the online services and rely upon offline modes (e.g., face-to- face, or by telephone). Clearly, the establishment of trust in eGovernment is "an absolute necessity" (Srivastava & Teo, 2009, p. 360).

Importantly, there is also a small but growing body of work investigating whether eGovernment is increasing trust in government (e.g.,Tolbert & Mossberger, 2006; Welch, Hinnant, & Moon, 2005). If eGovernment increases trust in government (Tolbert & Mossberger, 2006), and increased trust in government reinforces satisfaction with, and increases adoption of, eGovernment (Al-adawi, et al., 2005; Colesca, 2009; Hung, Chang, & Yu, 2006; Teo, et al., 2008; Warkentin, et al., 2002; Welch, et al., 2005), a virtuous circle is built. Clearly, increasing and maintaining trust in the context of eGovernment services is important to increase adoption of those services.

8.2 Building and Maintaining Trust

Trust is about feeling sure, confident, and comfortable. Much of what embodies trust in an online environment centers on transactions. They must operate as expected, and must operate that way every time. There is a significant discipline of well-understood techniques for maintaining and repairing data when errors occur, but those technologies cannot repair the trust that is lost when a transaction "goes wrong". Even if the transaction has worked flawlessly thousands of times in the past, that one erroneous transaction can destroy the trust developed, and it may never be recovered.

The citizen's trust in an eGovernment service starts with the offline reputation of the government. The more that the agency is seen to be one that deals fairly with people, that treats each citizen's issues with respect and concern and in a timely and efficient manner, the more that citizens will trust the agency.

Agencies seen to be trustworthy in offline transactions can translate that trustworthiness to their online services by implementing the same ideas: consistency, consideration of individual issues, and efficiency. Continued confidence in the agency, both online and offline is based on the belief that the agency is concerned about and can maintain the reliability and integrity of its systems (Keen, Balance, Chan, & Schrump, 2000).

There are three focal areas for trust development: integrity, confidentiality, and privacy.

Integrity in eGovernment services is about ensuring that the service and the data it generates are not in error. In error here means both incorrect values, but also possibly the wrong values for the circumstances. Integrity leads to certainty in the transaction and the agency offering it (Keen et al., 2000).

Confidentiality is about ensuring that only those people who need to handle information do so and that they do so in the context of the transaction in which it was collected. Confidentiality ranges from the highest levels of national security, through legal considerations (e.g., commercial confidentiality) and on to issues of personal privacy (Keen et al., 2000).

Privacy relates to personal data and the control of how that data is used (Keen, et al., 2000). The use of "private" data is subtly different to issues of confidentiality. Privacy breaches might arise when data collected in one process is used in another process without the knowledge or consent of the person who provided the data, even if this is done without any third party being made aware of the data.

8.3 Implementing Security in eGovernment

This section will consider the core security themes and identify some of the methods used to secure systems. Generally, security involves the overlapping application of three security themes:

- Physical security
- Technical security, and
- Personnel security.

Employing all of these three themes can create an effective defence-in- depth that protects the eGovernment system.

Security is largely implemented through controls. Controls are actions that the agency takes to manage the ICT environment to lessen the likelihood of threats eventuating, or to minimize the losses when a threat does occur. Controls have three broad categories:

- Threat Avoidance Controls - these controls seek to prevent the threat having an effect, or to reduce the likelihood of the threat occurring
- Threat Tolerance Controls - these controls seek to reduce the impact of the threat when it does occur, limiting the extent of the damage caused, and
- Threat Mitigation Controls - these controls seek to re-establish normal service as quickly as possible after a threat has damaged operations.

8.3.1 Physical Security

Physical security is the primary security measure for any government business, including eGovernment. It is probably safe to say that since the start of civilization, farmers have put fences around their crops to keep animals away. Securing eGovernment starts with this oldest form of security - controlling or denying physical access. For ICT systems, physical security means protecting the technology from malicious or accidental physical harm and limiting access to the technology to only authorised users (Slay & Koronis, 2006).

A crucial part of any ICT security plan is to protect the technology and systems from natural disasters: fire, flood, earthquake, or other natural catastrophe. Typically, these disasters cannot be controlled. Controls tend to focus on damage limitation (e.g., fire sprinklers in server rooms) and recovery (e.g., regular off-site backups). Protection from unauthorized people often takes the form of securing server rooms to control access, installing alarms, and other active or passive boundary security measures.

Table 8.1 summarizes physical security controls that can reduce the risk of damage to information technology or limit the damage done when unavoidable catastrophes occur.

Table 8.1: A summary of physical IT security controls

Threat Avoidance Controls
Environmental controls - appropriate location of computer center and orientation on its site; conditioned environment and anti-static protection, and so on.
Threat Tolerance Controls
Power line remedies - Electrical problems can be endured through power line conditioners, uninterruptible power supplies, and backup generators.
Distributed systems - a system with operating elements that are geographically dispersed is inherently less vulnerable to physical threats; the drawback is the coordination required to maintain data integrity.
Media precautions - using higher-quality media and storing them in fireproof, environmentally controlled locations all increase media life.

Threat Mitigation Controls
Siting - locations near emergency response centers can diminish the effects of some hazards.
Alarms - monitoring of environmental conditions can allow rapid response.
Hardware diagnostics - self-monitoring equipment can alert operators before the system degrades to an unacceptable level.
Performance monitors - similar to above, monitors of system performance can detect degradation before it becomes problematic.
Back-up - alternative plant, equipment, and personnel to replace that which fails, or degrades in performance to unacceptable levels.
Insurance - can provide the necessary costs to restore operations after a failure.

Case Study: Physically Securing Information

Martin is a doctor employed at Central Hospital who specializes in treating infections. He often works late into the night taking care of his patients, working with doctors elsewhere in the world to identify an infection and determine the best way to treat it. To facilitate this communication, Martin has bought his own laptop computer and a mobile phone. He uses these devices to consult with other doctors, often from the bedside of the patient.

One afternoon Martin is working on his laptop, trying to identify a nasty infection in the foot of a farmer when he receives a call on his phone. As it is about another patient, Martin steps out of the room into a nearby office to complete the call.

While Martin is out of the room taking the call, the farmer's eldest son uses the doctor's laptop to check out the score on the World Series Cricket. He notices that the doctor has kept patient details on the laptop. As he can hear the doctor talking in the other room, he looks through the files.

Review Question

1. Identify some measures Martin could have used to prevent this security breach.

Technical Security

Technical security can provide high levels of assurance, yet can also be expensive to implement and maintain. The very nature of eGovernment systems ensures that it is not possible to extend physical and personnel security out to every terminal or phone used to provide eGovernment access. For this reason, a manager considering eGovernment service delivery will consider adding a technical security layer to ensure adequate security.

Technical security is often the theme many people think of first when they consider ICT security in support of eGovernment. Technical security includes measures like:

- Secure communications (e.g., HTTPS and virtual private networks [VPNs])
- Strong authentication (e.g., digital certificates and electronic key generators), and
- Data encryption (e.g., DES, TripleDES, WEP, WPA).

These methods will provide security for the most important information, ensuring that it cannot be used by any but those who are explicitly permitted access. The drawback with some of these technical security measures is that they are expensive to purchase, expensive to maintain, and are often only suited to high-quality ICT systems and communications. They also tend to rely upon system users cooperating with the technical requirements (e.g., digital certificates).

Choosing to employ technical security must seek to strike a balance between security and accessibility. Table 8.2 offers a summary of technical security controls with which to draw the balance between security and accessibility.

Table 8.2: A summary of technical IT security controls

Threat Avoidance Controls
Trusted computer base - systems that have undergone formal verification of the correctness of their security mechanisms; this can be expensive.
Database management systems - provides more structured and consistent security than non-database file/data management.
Statistical database privacy - statistically valid errors or additional random data can overcome individual identification.
Application controls - data entry checking, direct data capture (e.g., scanning), and multi-part covered output forms; correct and comprehensive system design and documentation.
Design audits - check of the application's correctness and the robustness of its controls prior to implementation.
Call-back - a modem that receives your call, authorizes you (by user ID and password) and then hangs-up; it calls the authorized number assigned to that user ID.
Eavesdropping controls - tactical-level controls restrict information from an eavesdropper for a limited period, strategic controls prevent eavesdropping without significant expense and elapsed time. Best-known control for eavesdropping is encryption.
Threat Tolerance Controls
NB: Data tends to be either good or bad, not something that can be partially "damaged" and tolerated.

Data cross parity checks - horizontal and vertical parity systems can restore data that is damaged through cross-reference.

Database complexity - inherent in database management systems and complex relational table designs is the privacy maintenance of data separation; if raw data is browsed the relationships between data items may not be readily identifiable, and therefore tolerable.

Communications redundancy - alternate communication channels.

Robust configurations - either the use of front-end processors (FEP) for communication management (which can be switched to the main computer if the FEP fails) and network topologies that permit node failures without whole network failure.

Threat Mitigation Controls

Operating systems - some security software facilities can also monitor system use and performance to ensure that data is not lost or compromised through identified threats; password expiry fits into this category too.

Application controls - controls such as check digits, field validation routines, and digital labelling of secondary storage media to ensure correct operation.

Seals - similar to a digital signature for the file; cannot prevent damage, but will reveal the fact.

Auditing - systematic review by independent authorities to verify correct operations of the system.

Recovery - checkpoints, transaction logs, and roll-back processes allow recovery of data to a predetermined "safe" point after a failure.

Insurance - again, cover the cost of restoring lost data, or reimburse for lost business.

Signatures - use of public key encryption can secure the message but also provides a "signature" of the sender (as only their public key will decrypt the message).

Authentication - the same techniques can be applied to authenticate the message; a separate "hash" value is calculated using a secret key; if the recipient generates the same hash using the agreed key, the message is authentic.

8.3.2 Personnel Security

Personnel security ensures that the person accessing the information should be able to access that information. Personnel security is about ensuring that the people who have access to the eGovernment systems have demonstrated they can be trusted. In essence, there are two types of eGovernment system access:

- People who manage and maintain the system, and
- People who use the system.

The people who manage or maintain the system should have their backgrounds checked to ensure that they are who they say they are, do not have criminal backgrounds, and are the type of person trusted by the public to hold personal information. This "vetting" process is common to government departments and large companies. Vetting a person to manage or maintain an eGovernment system is crucial to the integrity of the system. The end-users of the eGovernment system are often quite difficult to fully identify. It is common in Western societies for these people to be identified by a specific sequential number when they deal with the government or specific government agencies. In the US, the Social

Security Number is a singular identifier in government. In Australia, though, citizens are identified by their Tax File Number with some agencies, with their Medicare number with other agencies, and by their Driver's Licence at state government level. Even with this approach, it is still difficult to adequately validate the identity of the person using the eGovernment system without additional information that is often known only by the individual.

Even in countries where a single identifier is issued to each citizen, there is still no guarantee that the person interacting with the system with that identifier is the person being identified. Secondary tests of identity such as questions about personal facts (e.g., date of birth, mother's maiden name) can help to confirm a user's identity. Table 8.4 lists the controls available to manage the security of IT systems when considering the personnel who operate or use the systems.

Table 8.4. Summary of personnel ICT security controls

Threat Avoidance Controls
Physical access controls - limited entry points controlled by ID cards and visitor tracking.
Segregation of duties - prevent a single individual from exercising control over a complete process or transaction (e.g., developers cannot access Production; Operators cannot program).
Personnel - appropriately selected and screened individuals only.
Operating system controls - typically user ID and password access to systems; only effective if good password management is in place.
Threat Mitigation Controls
Application controls - controls such as check digits, field validation routines, and digital labelling of secondary storage media to ensure correct operation.
Audit trails - comprehensive logging of transactions and data used allows identification of the extent of problems and rectification.
Signatures - use of public key encryption can secure the message but also provides a "signature" of the sender (only their public key will decrypt the message).
Authentication - the same techniques can be applied to authenticate the message; a separate "hash" value is calculated using a secret key; if the re-

cipient generates the same hash using the agreed key, the message is authentic.

Case Study: Common security mistakes

Central Hospital keeps all medicine locked up to stop it being stolen. Unfortunately, the hospital has not secured the doctors' rooms, believing that a camera system and security patrols would prevent theft.

Bill is a cleaner in the hospital. When he was employed the hospital administrator decided that Bill did not need to be vetted before starting work, as he couldn't steal anything from the hospital because of the security cameras in all public places and the security patrols. What the hospital administrator does not know is that Bill has had problems with drug use in the past, even selling drugs to others.

As Bill cleaned the corridors he was often asked into doctors' rooms to clean the floors. Even though this was not a part of his job, Bill was happy to help out, as he wanted to keep his job.

After a few months, Bill finds that he has access to the doctors' rooms at any time. He notices that the doctors are able to print out orders for drugs from their computers. One day, while cleaning, Bill watches when one of the doctors enters their password into the system to prescribe morphine for a patient with extreme pain from a broken shoulder.

Some months later, the Central Hospital's administrator notices that the hospital is using a lot more morphine than might normally be expected. When the administrator reviews the logs of drug dispensing, it appears that one doctor has been prescribing morphine for many patients - even those who should not need it. The doctor denies making the orders and the nurses have not logged administering the drugs to many of the patients. The administrator cannot work out what is going on, but he suspects the pharmacy staff of cooking the books.

Bill is now a supplier of top quality drugs in the local community, a fact he works hard to hide.

Review Questions

1. What security measures could have stopped Bill?
2. The hospital clearly has some security controls in place (e.g., drug dispensing logs). What more might the systems be made to do to prevent incorrect system use?

8.4 Security Risk Assessment

Deciding what controls to put in place to maintain IT security is called Risk Assessment. There is an international standard for the conduct of risk assessments (ISO 31000, 2009). It provides the principles and guidelines for risk management, including proper risk assessment approaches. This standard and its various national-level antecedents (e.g., AS/NZS 4360:2004) form the basis of much advice on ICT security risk assessment.

There are typically three key questions to ask for each system when considering how to secure it:

1. What could happen (what threats exist)?
    a. If it happened, how bad could it be (threat impact)?
    b. How often could it happen (threat frequency)?
    c. How certain are the answers to the first three questions (recognition of uncertainty)?
2. What can be done in response to each threat?
    a. What can be done to avoid its occurrence?
    b. What can be done to mitigate the damage of the threat?
    c. What can be done to remedy the damage if the threat occurs?
3. What priority does the threat have?
    a. Is the balance of the likelihood of the threat and the damage it can do worthy of attention?
    b. Is the damage that the threat can do of more value than the cost of preventing the threat?

The evaluation of these three questions will lead to a prioritized list of threats and preferred controls that will secure the system. A qualitative risk analysis will help to identify threats to the system and essential features that introduce vulnerabilities that may be exploited by the threats. These vulnerabilities can then be assessed, and critical system components can be built with suitable controls to reduce the threats, vulnerabilities and criticalities.

The key outcome for any system is to provide appropriate security while retaining usability. Some systems will have a long list of threats and accompanying controls because the value of the integrity of the system is very high. Others will only need to be protected from the most obvious, easily managed threats because more security would cost more than the value of the system.

Case Study: Applications of Security

The Australian eTax system requires very specific information for access, yet most library systems do not.
(https://www.ato.gov.au/Individuals/Lodging-your-tax-return/Lodge-online/)

The taxation system deals with billions of dollars each year. Compromise of the system would be a major problem for the Australian government. The designers had to provide a system for the general public to access, yet they needed to positively identify each person, secure the information that they submitted, and ensure the central system could not be breached.

In contrast, a public library system deals with a large number of books, each of relatively low value. Compromise of the library system would be annoying, but would deliver no lasting damage. Information available on the system is of little or no value outside the library and is not normally targeted.

In the design of both systems, choices were made to accept certain vulnerabilities necessary to provide the service, but these are balanced by measures implemented to provide a level of security appropriate to the role of the system.

Review Question

1. How do the threats differ between a library system and a tax assessment system?

8.5 Dealing with Security Breaches

Eventually, even the most sophisticated eGovernment system will be breached. This may occur as a result of a deliberate attack, an accidental act by a trusted person, or failure of an implemented security measure. After the breach is discovered there are four main considerations any person charged with the system must consider:

1. Do I need to preserve evidence for a police investigation?
2. What has been compromised?
3. Who needs to know about the breach?
4. What caused the breach?

Only after these questions have been answered, is the next question asked: Can I restore the eGovernment system?

8.5.1 Preserving Evidence

Attempts to restore an eGovernment system, or even identify what has been compromised, will often destroy electronic evidence that may be necessary to identify and prosecute the person who caused the breach. Good practice is to develop a simple set of standard operating procedures (SOPs) for dealing with a suspected breach. These SOPs should include information about the system to help identify if the breach should be treated as a criminal act or not. The SOPs should also have steps to preserve evidence for a police investigation.

8.5.2 Determining Compromise

Consider the information stored in the system; the breach may not have compromised anything. Knowing what is managed by the eGovernment system is as critical as understanding how the system security controls are constructed. By tracing through both of these, it is possible to estimate the extent of damage incurred by the system.

8.5.3 Informing Stakeholders

If the breach is considered to be a criminal one, then the police must be informed as soon as possible. Beyond this, system managers are faced with difficult choices. One side of the dilemma is that public confidence in the eGovernment system could be destroyed by disclosure of a security breach. On the other hand, the public may have been affected by the breach and need to be notified to remedy possible further damage (e.g., by changing their passwords). It is usually better that affected stakeholders find out from the system manager than by other means (e.g., the media). The answer to this question is difficult and, with eGovernment systems, can often be a political question as much as a practical one. Again, a risk management approach is commonly used to determine who needs to know about the breach.

8.5.4 Investigating the Cause

Once the preservation of evidence is in place, the extent of the breach is identified, and the notification of stakeholders is underway, it is time to work out the mechanics of the breach.

If the incident is "natural" in cause (e.g., a flood), then further ideas about how to prevent or limit damage may be developed. If the incident involves a malicious act, earlier detection or greater limitation options may arise by understanding the details of security breach.

Chapter Highlights

- Security and privacy are never more important than when developing and delivering eGovernment services.
- Unlike eCommerce with commercial vendors, citizens can only interact with government; if they do not trust the online offering they must interact offline.
- Building trust with citizens and businesses will promote adoption of eGovernment services; good eGovernment services will build trust with citizens and businesses.
- There are three key elements of trust online: integrity, confidentiality, and privacy.
- Security for ICT systems and eGovernment involves three themes: physical, technical and personnel security.
- Security is implemented through controls. There are three broad classes of controls: threat avoidance controls, threat tolerance controls, and threat mitigation controls.
- To determine what security is required, a risk assessment is needed.
- Risk management is guided by an International Standard (ISO 31000:2009), which has direct applicability in ICT security assessments.
- Not all systems require the same level of security. The extent to which security is implemented is a reflection of the value of the contents (usually the data) within the system.
- Eventually, a security break will occur. There is a recommended priority of actions to follow in the event of a breach.

Review Questions

1. Why are security and privacy particularly important in the context of eGovernment?
2. What are the three key themes of ICT security?
3. What are the three main types of security controls?
4. What are the important things to do when you realize that there has been a security breach?

Discussion Questions

1. What elements of eGovernment service contribute to a feeling of trust-worthiness?
2. Are there eGovernment services that would not require security?
3. Are there some government services that cannot be properly secured for eGovernment implementation?

Exercises

1. Imagine that you are a new ICT security person at Central Hospital (from the case studies). Carry out a high-level security risk assessment of the hospital from what you know through the case studies and your personal experience of hospitals in general.
2. Visit the online headquarters of CERT (http://www.cert.org). Review the CERT Resilience Management Model. Using this framework as a guide, conduct a high- level review of the security arrangements in your place of work.

References

AGIMO. (2005). Australians' use of and satisfaction with eGovernment services. Commonwealth of Australia. Retrieved from http://www.finance.gov.au/sites/default/files/eGovt_services_lowres_8Jun.pdf

AGIMO. (2006). Australians' use of and satisfaction with eGovernment services. Commonwealth of Australia. Retrieved from http://www.finance.gov.au/sites/default/files/2006_Measurementreport_final.pdf

AGIMO. (2007). Australians' use of and satisfaction with eGovernment services. Commonwealth of Australia. Retrieved from http://www.finance.gov.au/sites/default/files/31576_AGIMO_Satisfaction-ALL.pdf

AGIMO. (2008). Interacting with government: Australians' use and satisfaction with eGovernment services. Commonwealth of Australia. Retrieved from http://www.finance.gov.au/sites/default/files/interacting-with-government-report.pdf

Al-adawi, Z., Yousafzai, S., & Pallister, J. (2005). Conceptual model of citizen adoption of eGovernment. Paper presented at the The Second International Conference on Innovations in Information Technology, Dubai. Retrieved from http://www.it-innovations.ae/iit005/proceedings/articles/G_6_IIT05-Al-Adawi.pdf

Carter, L., & Bélanger, F. (2004). The influence of perceived characteristics of innovating on eGovernment adoption. Electronic Journal of eGovernment, 2(1). 1-74.

Carter, L., & Bélanger, F. (2005). The utilization of eGovernment services: Citizen trust, innovation and acceptance factors. Information Systems Journal, 15, 5-25.

Colesca, S. E. (2009). Understanding trust in eGovernment. Economics of Engineering Decisions, 3, 7-15.

Huang, W., D'Ambra, J., & Bhalla, V. (2002). An empirical investigation of the adoption of eGovernment in Australian citizens: Some unexpected research findings. Journal of Computer Information Systems, 43(1), 15-22.

Hung, S.-Y., Chang, C.-M., & Yu, T.-J. (2006). Determinants of user acceptance of eGovernment services: The case of online tax filing and payment system. Government Information Quarterly, 23(1), 97-122.

ISO. (2009). International standards organisation risk management: Principles and guidelines 31000.

Keen, P., Balance, C., Chan, S., & Schrump, S. (2000). Electronic commerce relationships: Trust by design. New Jersey: Prentice Hall.

Slay, J., & Koronis, A. (2006). Information technology security & risk management. QLD, Australia: Wiley, Milton

Srivastava, S. C., & Teo, T. S. H. (2009). Citizen trust development for egovernment adoption and usage: Insights from young adults in Singapore. Communications of the Association for Information Systems, 25. Article 31.

Teo, T. S. H., Srivastava, S. C., & Jiang, L. (2008). Trust and electronic government success: An empirical study. Journal of Management Information Systems, 25(3), 99-131.

Tolbert, C. J., & Mossberger, K. (2006). The effects of eGovernment on trust and confidence in government. Public Administration Review, 66(3), 354-369.

Warkentin, M., Gefen, D., Pavlou, P. A., & Rose, G. M. (2002). Encouraging citizen adoption of eGovernment by building trust. Electronic Markets, 12(3), 157-162.

Welch, E. W., Hinnant, C. C., & Moon, M. J. (2005). Linking citizen satisfaction with eGovernment and trust in government. Journal of Public Administration Research and Theory, 15(3), 371-391.

PART III
IMPLEMENTING eGOVERNMENT SYSTEMS

Part III - Implementing eGovernment Systems

Drawing on the knowledge of the concepts, dimensions and technologies of eGovernment from previous chapters, managers may now feel ready for implementation. Part III helps readers to acquire the knowledge required to physically implement an eGovernment initiative or project through step-by-step procedures, best practices, guidelines and checklists. These chapters were developed from examination of existing practices, literature and practical experiences of the authors to provide the best possible functional knowledge for the developing country context or in organisations where eGovernment uptake has yet to reach a mature stage. The chapters are particularly important from a management point of view.

Chapter 9, eGovernment Systems Lifecycle, holistically overviews the whole eGovernment Life Cycle and describes the stages and activities that occur in the eGovernment Systems Life Cycle for ICT systems. It also describes how the rest of the chapters in this part are organised in terms of the eGovernment Life Cycle. Lastly, it describes the role of different stakeholders in the eGovernment Life Cycle.

Chapter 10, Feasibility Study and Preparation of Business Case, describes the activities that occur in the first phase of the eGovernment Life Cycle. The chapter presents all the steps from understanding the need to make a formal Business Case for an ICT investment, through analysing ICT investment options, costs and benefits, to justifying the decision to select, acquire and implement an ICT solution. The chapter also presents typical contents of a Business Case and suggests how to prepare such a document.

Chapter 11, Build or Buy, covers the second and third phases of the eGovernment Life Cycle; Requirements Definition, and Build or Buy? The chapter highlights the important steps of specifying exactly what the system is to achieve through Requirements Definition. It also discusses the different approaches to acquiring a system, either by constructing it in-house or by acquiring a system through outsourcing.

Chapter 12, eGovernment Project Management Methodology, covers Project Management, which is required throughout the eGovernment Life Cycle from Phase 2 (Project Approval) through to the end of Phase 5 (System Delivery). The chapter describes all the elements of a project, how to scope and schedule a project and what steps to take to ensure that the project delivers its objectives. The chapter also discusses control and monitoring of projects, dealing with change, and points to a range of sources for additional information on project management.

CHAPTER 9
eGovernment Systems Life Cycle

Learning Objectives

After studying this chapter, you will be able to:

- Describe the stages and activities that occur in the eGovernment Systems Life Cycle for ICT systems, and
- Describe the role of different stakeholders in the eGovernment Systems Life Cycle.

Customs' Cargo Management Re- engineering Project, Australian National Audit Office (ANAO)

The Australian Customs Service (Customs) recognized the need to re-engineer its cargo management processes in 1996 and published its Cargo Management Strategy (CMS) in 1997. The strategy sought to fully integrate the people, processes, and technology associated with cargo management. The CMS was further progressed in the Cargo Management Re-engineering (CMR) Business Model. The model outlined the CMR project's objective to introduce new cargo management processes and systems to improve the effective delivery of services to government, industry, and the community.

The CMR project was a large and complex information communication technology (ICT) project that spanned many years. It was to improve import and export processes, increase cargo management efficiency for industry, and improve targeting of high-risk cargo. Key aspects of the project were:

1. *Re-engineering Customs' business processes*

2. *Legislative change to support this new business environment, and*

3. *Developing the Integrated Cargo System (ICS) to replace Customs' transaction processing systems.*

Electronic Data Systems (EDS) Australia began developing the CMR applications in 1998 under Customs' existing information technology (IT) outsourcing arrangements. In October 2001, Customs and EDS agreed that EDS would continue to manage the infrastructure, desktop and voice, and data aspects of the project, with remaining analysis and development to be done by one or more third parties. In early 2002, the Computer Associates Consortium (the Consortium) was engaged to develop the ICS, and separate contracts were established with IBM and Secure Net to develop the Customs Connect Facility (CCF). Given the scope of the work to be undertaken, Customs was under considerable pressure to meet the legislative implementation date of July the following year.

The CMR project encountered delays, and costs increased significantly. In 1999, Customs estimated that the project would cost $30 million. The total reported cost of the CMR project as at the end of February 2006 was $205 million. Between February and June 2006, Customs made additional payments of $7.7 million for further developments and support of the ICS and CCF. The ICS was implemented in three releases: Release 1a was a trial with industry during March and April 2003; Release 2, the exports component, was implemented on 6 October 2004; and Release 3, imports processing, was implemented on 12 October 2005.

The implementation of ICS Exports (Release 2) was relatively successful. This was in contrast to the implementation of ICS Imports (Release 3), which had a significant impact on Australia's supply chain and international trading environment. Problems with the functionality and performance of the ICS and CCF resulted in substantial disruption to the movement of cargo, particularly in the sea cargo environment. As widely reported, Australia's major ports were congested with a backlog of containers awaiting clearance and delivery for many weeks.

Audit findings and overall conclusion

The management framework that Customs had in place to support this project lacked many of the basic fundamentals necessary to successfully implement a large ICT project. The outcomes to be achieved and the expected benefits from the project were never clearly defined. There was no overall CMR project plan, financial management plan, project budget, or proper assessment of the risks facing the project. There was also a lack of supporting documentation surrounding contractual arrangements. Delays in the early years of the project had major repercussions for the latter stages of the project. Project teams were continually under pressure to meet tight deadlines, which were not achieved. Delays with the project necessitated three amendments to the legislated implementation date.

Customs underestimated the complexity and the risks associated with the project and failed to properly respond to emerging issues and changes in risks. The implementation was not supported by a coordinated implementation strategy or adequate business continuity planning. Insufficient time was allowed for system testing, particularly end-to- end testing. Customs did not have quality assurance mechanisms to assess the readiness of third party software providers, the quality of their software, or the preparedness of industry participants. Problems with the Cargo Risk Assessment system also impacted on Customs' ability to clear cargo and to target and assess high risk cargo, increasing the risks to Australia's border security and Customs' revenue collection responsibilities.

The CMR project involved significant changes in system design, operating procedures, working relationships, business processes, skill levels and attitudes. A lack of understanding of industry's business processes contributed to the problems that occurred in October 2005 when ICS Imports was introduced.

Source: Australian National Audit Office (2007).

9.1 eGovernment Systems Life Cycle

Life Cycle approaches

Like any other system, it is important to understand the "life cycle" of an eGovernment system from its inception to the delivery of the final product. It is common to talk about ICT applications and systems having a life cycle, because they come into being, are in use for a period of time, then grow outdated when they are retired or superseded by a new system.

In this chapter, we describe the life cycle approach to the acquisition and development of eGovernment systems.

The idea of a "Systems Development Life Cycle" (SDLC) dates back to the early days of large-scale data processing in the 1960s. There are many variations on the SDLC with different numbers of steps or stages in the life cycle and different names for each step. However, there are commonalities among the different versions, and most include much the same activities arranged a little differently.

Figure 9.1 shows the eGovernment Life Cycle Framework followed in this book. This framework provides an organizing device for materials covered in different stages and chapters of this part of the book. Stage 1 (feasibility study) is covered in Chapter 10. Stage 2 and 3 (requirement definition and build vs. buy, respectively) are covered in Chapter 11. Stage 6 (performance management and benefits realization, which occur after the system is handed over to users) is in Part IV on managing eGovernment systems.

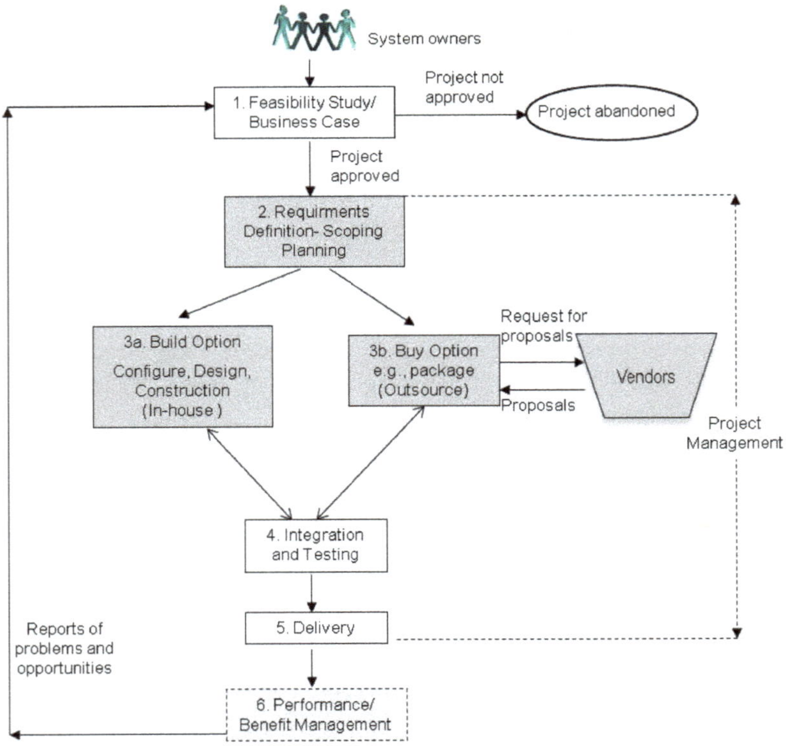

Figure 9.1. The eGovernment Systems Life Cycle Framework (adapted from Whitten & Bentley, 1998, p. 83).

9.1.1 eGovernment lifecycle framework

This framework is a modified form of other popular versions of the SDLC (see Avison & Fitzgerald, 2006; Whitten & Bentley, 1998). The SDLC arose when many systems were developed in-house, whereas today many systems are purchased off-the-shelf as packages. Thus, the EGovernment Life Cycle Framework shows that systems can be acquired by purchasing them rather than being designed and built by programmers in organizations. Note that, even when a system is bought as a package, it is still necessary to carry out a requirements analysis before the purchase and to test it after the purchase.

The life cycle presented is a general framework, and the steps and activities in it can vary with the size and nature of the project. The first stage, the feasibility study, is usually done in-house. However, stages 2-5 can be outsourced.

9.1.2 Managerial Motivation

As this book primarily targets managers, it may be surprising that we include a section on information systems development. The assumption may be that managers are not going to write computer programs, and, therefore, that this topic is not important to them. But systems development is important for a number of reasons.

Managerial responsibility

Even if the computer applications are going to be developed by specialist systems analysts and programmers who are part of the IT department (or equivalent), it is important to inform them of any requirements, to keep in touch with them as the system progresses, and to ensure that the system is what you asked for and will be able to use once it is operational. At the very least, this means that you know something of the process, the terminology, and the people involved.

Meeting requirements

Even if the application is implemented using an application package supplied by an external company, you will need to know that the package is appropriate and that you are involved in the implementation process to ensure that it is tuned for your company or department.

User expectation

Figure 9.1 (above) shows systems owners and users as being mainly involved in the early stages of initiation and requirements analysis. However, as discussed further below, managers and users need to participate in all stages.

9.1.3 eGovernment Systems Life Cycle Stages

The stages in the framework are as follows. The stages are described briefly, because the more important stages are covered in more depth in subsequent chapters.

Stage1: Feasibility Study (Chapter 10)

A project is initiated when someone realizes that there is an opportunity to improve organizational performance in some way. An old system may no longer fulfil requirements, new technology may promise benefits, or the organization may have changed needs.

It is necessary to carry out a high-level analysis (the most macro-level of analysis) of needs, identify options for going forward, and prepare a business case (project proposal) for management decision making.

On completion of this stage, a decision is made whether to proceed with the development project and which option is to be pursued. If the decision is made to go forward, the project management process should be initiated.

Stage 2: Requirements Definition (Chapter 11)

The scope of the project is defined, user needs are analyzed, and the requirements specified. Some of the activities in the feasibility study may need to be repeated in more detail. This step is also called “scoping” or “systems analysis”.

Stage 3: Acquisition, Sourcing and Development (Chapter 11)

In this step, the important decisions about whether to purchase the system as a package or to design and build it in-house is taken; that is, to decide whether to build or buy after due consideration of long- term advantages and disadvantages. In this stage, the actual design, construction, and implementation of the system are done either through in-house developers or through vendors. Both follow similar development strategy and procedures. However, for the buy option, a ready-made off-the-shelf package may be purchased from vendors.

Stage 4: Integration and testing

All the components of the system are brought together and tested in the operational environment to ensure that the subsystems function together as a system.

Integration includes:

- Planning the sequence in which components will be integrated
- Creating scaffolding to support interim versions of the software
- Determining the degree of testing and quality work performed on components before they are integrated, and
- Determining points in the project at which interim versions of the software are tested.

Stage 5: Delivery

The system goes live and performs organizational functions. The key activities are:

- Planning for deployment and use of systems
- Preparations for use of system, which include user training
- Systems deployment and software release management, and
- Post-deployment verification.

Deployment and transition to use include:

- Determining deployment sequencing, packaging, and timings
- Identifying key deployment roles and responsibilities
- Preparing and distributing information about the new (or changed) systems
- Training and briefing users and stakeholders

Preparing and approving business continuity plans

- Reviewing deployment readiness and obtaining approval to deploy/implement, and
- Deploying the new (or changed) systems.

Stage 6: Operation and Maintenance, Performance Management and Benefits Realization (Chapter 13)

The system goes into a regular operational stage, but will require ongoing updates and modifications. This stage is often the longest and may take several years. Performance management is needed on an ongoing basis. This occurs after the project delivery and physical implementation, and, as such, it belongs to the ongoing management of eGovernment in Part IV.

Project Management: Stages 2 to 6. (Chapter 12)

Project management is an ongoing activity that occurs across stages 2 to 6. Once the system becomes operational, responsibility is usually handed over to the IT department for ongoing maintenance (Stage 6).

Group Activity

Consider the opening case study of Australian Customs.

1. *What problems occurred during the Feasibility Study stage?*
2. *What was the development strategy here? In-house or external sourcing?*
3. *What problems occurred during the implementation stages (requirements definition through to delivery)?*
4. *What problems arose from inadequate project management?*

9.2 An eGovernment System as a Project

Implementation of any new eGovernment system follows the characteristics of a "project". It is thus a good idea for eGovernment managers to be aware of the standard project management methodologies and project lifecycles along with the system development lifecycles.

There are many definitions of a project. According to Gray and Larson (2003, p. 5): "A project is a complex, non-routine, one-time effort limited by time, budget, resources, and performance specification designed to meet customer needs".

Generally speaking, a project can be any work with the following characteristics:

- Has a defined purpose, with established goals (ultimately seeking to deliver benefits)
- Has a defined life-span - a beginning and an end
- Introduces a change to the organization
- Involves interrelated activities
- Requires resources (people, materials, etc), typically with a range of capabilities and from across a range of functions within the organisation
- Produces defined products (deliverables) against agreed quality criteria
- Has specific time, cost, and performance requirements or constraints
- Has an element of risk, and
- Has an element of uniqueness (generally, something that has not been done before).

In most organizations, activities are typically classified as either part of an ongoing operation or part of a project. For example, any developmental effort, particularly systems development, is usually classified as a project, whereas a routine financial record-keeping activity is part of an operation. In contrast to projects, normal business operations are ongoing and repetitive and generally have consistent resources. Projects are essentially about creating change in order to deliver benefits.

9.3 Stakeholder Roles

We will now look at people who are likely to be involved in the development of a computer information system. Note that there is further discussion of ICT staff in subsequent chapters. We mention important roles in development here, because they are important for understanding the development cycle.

We identify a number of groups or stakeholders. First we identify the "ICT experts":

9.3.1 ICT Experts

- **Programmers**: These are people who code and develop software systems in a computer programming language.
- **Systems analysts**: These are people who specify the requirements for a system and the outline designs and solutions that will meet the requirements. Typically, they are the interface or liaison between the business users/analysts and the programmers.
- **Business analysts**: These are people who understand the complexities of the business and its needs and liaise with the systems analysts. They are typically from the business side but adopt the business analyst role in the context of a particular development project for a specific period.
- **Project managers**: These are the people who manage the project with particular emphasis on people, schedules, and resources. The role of project manager is crucial to the success of total system implementation. Hence it is discussed further in the next section.
- **Senior ICT management**: These are the people who are responsible for managing ICT in the organization.
- **Chief information officer (CIO)**: This person is responsible for ICT and information strategy, which should be aligned to the needs of the business as a whole (The CIO's role is discussed further in Chapter 15).

The above stakeholders may not be identifiable as distinct groups in all organizations. The boundaries between them have become blurred over the years. In some circumstances, one person may undertake a number of roles, or a group may flexibly undertake all roles as needed.

Next, we identify those in the business or organization for whom the system is required. This group is often generically known as the "users", but this is misleading because they are not homogeneous, and there are a range of different types of user. Indeed, users can also be "developers". We break this category down as follows:

9.3.2 Users

- **End users (staff)**: These are people who use the system in an operational sense. They may be an intermediary between the system and the business users.
- **Business users**: These are people in a particular business function who have a need for the system. They might or might not physically interact with the system itself. They are interested in its functions and output, the knowledge of which they use to achieve their business objectives.

- **Business management**: These are people who are responsible for the business function that the system addresses, and for commissioning the system and financing it from their budget. They are responsible for the strategic use of ICT in their business unit.
- **Business strategy management**: These people are responsible for the overall strategy of the organization and the way that information systems can both support and enable that strategy.

Again, we describe roles for people here. They may be combined or separated. Sometimes different categories of user are identified; for example, regular user and occasional or casual user. This categorization is important for determining what type of user interface is required in a system and what type of training is needed. Clearly, these needs will be different for regular users and occasional users. A regular user may require little help, explanation, or interaction, whereas an occasional user will require detailed help and guidance when using the system.

9.3.3 External Users

Our next category is external users. These are stakeholders outside the boundaries of the organization in which the system exists:

- **Citizens or potential customers**: These are people who use the system to find services or search for information that relates to services. They are not employees of the government agencies and, thus, have a different relationship to the earlier categories of users. Too often, citizens' views are ignored when systems are being designed and developed, but they are the most important stakeholders and have varying requirements.
- **Trusted external users**: These are people who have a particular relationship with the organization and may be given special privileges in the system. Suppliers are examples of such users. There are likely to be specific design requirements and security implications for this category of user.
- **Shareholders, other owners, or sponsors**: These are people who have invested or collaborated with the organization. They may be only peripherally concerned with the information systems in the organization, but they will want to ensure that ICT is contributing to their mutual objectives.
- **Society**: These are people who may be affected by the system without necessarily being regular users in any way. This is a broad category and relates to people or a society as a whole who may be potentially affected by the system in some way. People may be put out of work by a system, or it may disseminate inaccurate or private information. It might be that a system refuses credit to someone based on old or inaccurate information, or makes mistakes with payments that are due, or disrupts industry because of inefficiencies. Society is an important stakeholder in systems development and societal impacts need to be considered.

In general, we believe that it is desirable for all stakeholders of a system to be involved in the development process. They all have some kind of stake in the success of the information system.

9.3.4 IS strategy group

In the information systems development process, some stakeholders might be part of a group, such as the information systems strategy group, the steering committee, or the development team.

The aim of the information systems strategy group is to develop a plan for information systems development in the organization and ensure that the plan is carried out and tuned as circumstances change. It is a high-level group, perhaps meeting monthly, and represents top management, heads of the various divisions, and the head of the information systems function.

9.3.5 Steering committee

A steering committee will oversee each project in the overall plan to ensure that the wishes of the information systems strategy group are met. The committee will also give guidance for the project, which includes providing performance requirements, approving the personnel working on the project, and approving the final system.

9.3.6 Systems development team

The systems development team will concern itself with the day-to- day development of the information system and include the analysts, programmers, and users working on the project. The composition of the team will differ as the system progresses through the stages of the systems development life cycle, although there will normally be one project team leader who ensures continuity throughout the process.

9.4 The Role of the Project Manager

The project manager is accountable to the project board or senior management for the end-to-end delivery of the project. The project manager has the responsibility and authority to manage the project on a day-to-day basis. The project manager is also responsible for the well-being and performance of the project team. It is part of the job of the project manager to lead the team and establish a culture of commitment, trust and shared responsibility.

Consequently, the project manager requires significant people management and leadership skills, in addition to excellent process management abilities. The challenges faced by the project manager vary significantly depending on the size and complexity of the project, and hence, the skills and experience of the project manager must be matched to the requirements of the project.

Specific responsibilities of the project manager include:

- Preparing, maintaining, and archiving the project documentation
- Managing the production of the project deliverables

- Leading, managing, and motivating the project team
- Identifying and obtaining any support or advice required
- Maintaining the project's focus on the outcomes to be delivered
- Identifying stakeholders and establishing appropriate communications
- Managing the use of resources
- Tracking the project schedule and budget
- Providing regular reports to the project board and seeking approvals, as appropriate
- Controlling the project scope, including negotiating any changes with the project board
- Managing project risks, issues, and quality
- Raising project risks and issues with the project board, where appropriate
- Capturing lessons learned throughout the course of the project, and
- Bringing the project to a complete and controlled close.

While the project manager is ultimately responsible for delivering the project, project managers are not expected to perform their role in isolation. The project manager should seek input and support from other members of the project team and the broader organization, as required.

9.5 Participation

Here we are concerned with the active role of the people involved in the development of an information system, particularly users and other stakeholders. In the traditional systems analysis approaches used in the early days of computing, the computer professional was the person who was making the real decisions and driving the development process. The end user (the person who is going to use the system) frequently felt resentment, and top management did little more than pay lip service to computing. The users were rarely satisfied with the end result.

If the users are involved in the analysis, design, and implementation of information systems relevant to their own work, particularly if this involvement has meant users being involved in the decision-making process, these users are more likely to be fully committed to the information system when operational. This will increase the likelihood of its success. However, top managers who overly interfere on system development may be counterproductive because it may discourage and limit the capability of the developers. A balance is needed.

Some information systems may "work" in that they are technically viable, but fail because of "people problems". For example, users may feel that the new system will make their job more demanding or less secure, will change their relationship with others, or will lead to a loss of the independence that they previously enjoyed. As a result of these feelings, users may do their best to ensure that the computer system does not succeed. This aggression may show itself in attempts to "beat the system"; for example, by "losing" documents or even by more obvious acts of sabotage. Frequently, it manifests itself in people blaming the system for causing difficulties that may well be caused by other factors. This problem is sometimes referred to as projection; people project their problems on to the system. Some people may just want to have nothing to do with the computer system, an avoidance tactic. In these situations, information systems are unlikely to be successful or, at the very least, will fail to achieve their potential (people and environmental issues are discussed further in Chapters 15 and 16).

Chapter Highlights

- The eGovernment Systems Life Cycle framework has 6 stages: (1) feasibility study, (2) requirements definition, (3) build or buy systems, (4) system integration and testing, (5) delivery, (6) operation and performance management.
- Managers must understand system development, because they have responsibility for its success.
- Stakeholders in the development cycle include: ICT experts, management, and internal and external users.
- An implementation of new eGovernment systems can be seen as a "project", an effort with a defined purpose and life span.
- The role of project manager is complex and demanding.
- Participation by management and users throughout the development cycle is vital.

Review Questions

1. What are the 6 stages of the eGovernment Life Cycle?
2. Why do managers need to know about systems development?
3. Who are the important people involved in systems development or purchase?
4. What is an IT project steering committee? Why do users need to be involved in the eGovernment Life Cycle? In which stages do they have most involvement?

Discussion Question

Who is the prime stakeholder in an information systems development project? Is it the developer, user, customer, or management? Provide a case for each one.

Exercise

A traditional way of depicting the systems development process is the "systems development life cycle" (SDLC). Find an article that describes the SDLC and compare it with the eGovernment Life Cycle Framework described in this chapter. How different are they?

Glossary

Systems development life cycle (SDLC) - The traditional model for the development of ICT systems, with a number of stages or steps, such as: feasibility study, systems analysis, development, integration and testing, deployment, and maintenance.

The "system" in the SDLC could be software, such as an accounting system, a new email system, new hardware, a website, or one of many other types of system.

eGovernment Systems Life Cycle Framework - A modified form of the SDLC that recognizes that a new system may be acquired through purchase rather than being developed in-house.

ICT project - An activity with a defined purpose that occurs within a specific timeframe that brings about change with ICT. A project is contrasted with routine activity, such as recordkeeping that is part of ongoing operations. The project usually starts with a go-ahead decision after a feasibility study and concludes with the hand-over of a production system to users.

References

Australian National Audit Office. (2007). ANAO Audit Report No.24 2006-07: Customs' Cargo Management Re-engineering Project. Commonwealth of Australia. Retrieved from http://www. anao.gov.au/uploads/documents/2006-07_audit_report_24.pdf

Avison, D., & Fitzgerald, G. (2006). Information systems development: Methodologies, techniques and tools (4th ed.). Berkshire: McGraw-Hill Education.

Gray, C. F., & Larson, E. W. (2003). Project management. New York, NY:McGraw-Hill Irwin.

Whitten, J., & Bentley, L. (1998). Systems analysis and design methods (4th ed.). Boston, MA: McGraw- Hill Irwin.

CHAPTER 10
The Feasibility Study and Preparation of a Business Case

Learning Objectives

After studying this chapter, you should be able to:

- Describe the activities that occur in the first phase of the eGovernment Systems Life Cycle, the feasibility study
- Understand the need for making a formal business case for an ICT investment
- Analyze ICT investment options, costs, and benefits
- Justify an investment to select, acquire, and implement an ICT solution
- Describe the contents of a business case report, and
- Prepare a business case report.

Building a Compelling Business Case

(Photo credit A. Imran)

Maximizing value for the enterprise, for its shareholders, and for its customers - this is at the core of corporate governance. And making this happen by extracting value from investments is what management is all about. Yet, managers continue to pour billions of dollars, pounds or Euros into projects with uncertain outcomes. Studies continue to show a scary high number of project failures, missed delivery goals and cost overruns. While the information technology sector seems to be leading the pack, many other investment areas are less openly scrutinized. Many of us feel we are playing roulette with our decisions - or could actually get better odds in our decision making process doing exactly this.

Most enterprises do not yet have the necessary organizational capability, know-how, and experience to put together such compelling business cases that effectively support them to select investments and justify their decisions. They need to:

1. *Increase the likelihood that projected investment benefits will actually be reaped in;*
2. *Decrease the time and effort in preparing investment decision papers;*
3. *And last but not least, reduce politics and friction through stakeholder involvement, as well as increase the senior management buy-in through objective reasoning.*

Hence, investment justifications through business cases are multi-faceted. They are both about careful mathematical calculations and percentages, as well as about politics, psychology, and conversations with stakeholders. They need to obsessively focus on turning perceived intangible benefits into hard numbers, bold but verifiable, and holding the commitment of the organization.

Source: GloBus Business Research, http://www.globusresearch.com/business-case.aspx

10.1 The Feasibility Study Phase

The chapter describes the activities that are performed in the first phase of the eGovernment Systems Life Cycle, a phase that is termed Project Initiation or Feasibility Study or Project Selection Phase or Business Case Phase or the Project Proposal Phase.

The chapter explains the activities undertaken to ensure that an acquired ICT solution or service will support business objectives, will be useful to the acquiring organization, and will be selected using robust and effective processes.

10.1.1 Feasibility Study Activities

The activities in this step include:

- Problem or opportunity recognition
- Environmental analysis and identification of business needs (also called situation analysis)
- Proposal of options for proceeding (do nothing versus alternatives for change)
- Cost/benefit analysis of alternative options
- Documenting findings in a business case report
- Decision on how to proceed, and
- Formation of project team if decision is to proceed with change.

Effective performance of these activities will assist an organization to understand and manage the challenges associated with making ICT investments. This is particularly important in situations where a significant commitment in terms of money, time, and resources is being made to acquire ICT solutions and services.

Impact of failure

When an ICT project fails, the acquirer may incur impacts to their business that seriously impact its ability to function. For commercial organizations, this may lead to loss of income and reputation and exposure to legal action. For not-for-profit organizations, significant loss of reputation and trust can occur. Suppliers are also exposed to business and legal risks when an ICT project fails.

Reviewing business case

Although feasibility study activities are routinely conducted prior to committing to an ICT project, many organizations have learnt that it is wise to regularly review progress against strategies, plans, and business cases throughout the project lifecycle. It is appropriate, then, that acquirers take a holistic full lifecycle approach to managing ICT investments when planning for and managing ICT acquisitions and investments.

Discussion

It may seem strange to talk about making a "business" case for public sector organizations, when a public sector organization is not a business, in the sense that the organization is not expected to make a profit, but instead aims to serve the purposes of government and citizens. The use and interpretation of the word business in a Western context often implies "any activity or work undertaken in an office or home environment", whether it is public or private. So the word business has a broad meaning. What is your view? Is the "business case" terminology appropriate?

10.2 A Feasibility Study

An important activity in the Initiation Phase is the feasibility study. In simple terms, a feasibility study is a justification for undertaking a course of action, such as an investment or a project.

10.2.1 Current situation assessment

It is important to understand the existing business process of an organization when attempting to implement an ICT intervention for greater business benefits. It is important to be aware of current and projected business objectives, activities, and organizational structures. It is also important to understand the external forces that may act on an organization because these may drive or constrain ICT investment decisions.

This understanding should include appreciation of the scope, effectiveness, and potential for constraining or enabling new solutions and services. It is also important to understand the extent to which existing systems, services, and contracts will expire, or be terminated or retired during the timeframe of interest because these factors may impact the success of a proposed initiative.

10.2.2 Feasibility study aims

A feasibility study:

- Provides the information needed to make a fully informed decision on whether an investment should proceed
- Provides cost, benefit and risk impact information
- Documents key information in a business case report, and
- Should be reviewed at various stages in the project to confirm that the justification is still valid and that the project will deliver acceptable business benefits.

Activity

As a prerequisite of a business case it is important to develop the skill in writing a "situational assessment and problem statement". Consider the example of the Chittagong Customs House that was given in a previous chapter. Read this case study and prepare a "situational assessment and problem statement" for a business case report. Assume you were looking at the situation before the project began.

10.2.3 Benefits of a Business Case Report

The key information in the feasibility study is documented in a formal business case report. Note that this document will have different names in different organizations. The amount of analysis and documentation necessary will vary according to the size of the proposed project, the volatility of the organization and its environment and the degree of risk associated with the proposed project.

In the remainder of this chapter we will focus discussion around the production of this report, as it provides a structure for the feasibility study.

Benefits of a business case

The benefits of having a business case report are:

- It helps decision makers to make informed decisions about initiating and continuing ICT projects
- It provides a foundation for competition for allocation of scarce resources within an organization
- It provides a basis for technical risk and business impact analysis
- It provides benchmarks for evaluation of project progress and success
- It forms part of the evidence that appropriate ICT governance has been applied by an organization, and
- It also serves as a legal protection for any future audit.

10.3 Contents of a Business Case Report

A business case on a case-to-case basis could range from two to three pages to a hundred pages, based on the nature and scale of the project. For a small purchase, a business case could be a simple memo or email. However, an ideal business case should have the following components:

- A summary of the current situation, the strategic issues, and a rationale for making a change
- An explanation of how the proposed investment addresses the organization's interests and priorities
- A proposed course of action (or a set of alternatives)
- A summary of expected outcomes, benefits, and impacts
- A whole-of-life, whole-of-implementation cost/benefit analysis, and
- When necessary - supporting data, analyses, strategies, and plans.

A suggested format for a business case is given in Appendix 10A.

Group Activity

Before proceeding, examine the format of different types of business case reports. Some examples are:

- A Project Management Docs business case template, with examples completed in each section for a web platform project (Piscopo 2013).
- A blank template provided by the Tasmanian Government (2008).

Activities:

1. Compare the different examples of business case reports. What important differences can you see?
2. The example given in the Project Management Docs template has only quantifiable costs (in dollars) in the cost/benefit analysis. Yet the Tasmanian Government template says: "For many initiatives the benefits/disbenefits are not directly quantifiable or financial, for example improvements in service delivery or achievement of government policy objectives." Their suggestion is to assign qualitative ratings of high, medium or low for both positive and negative impacts for each concerned stakeholder. Which approach is better, the quantitative or qualitative? Or should both approaches be used together, where appropriate?

References: Piscopo (2013), Tasmanian Government (2008).

10.4 Developing a Business Case

A well-researched, prepared, and maintained business case will enable ICT investment decision makers to make well-informed decisions so the investment time and effort in preparing a business case is both necessary and justified. The business case report as described above is the outcome of a detailed investigation and step-by-step process. But how can this process be performed effectively?

10.4.1 Business case process

There could be a number of formal processes for developing business cases. Below is a suggested business case development process adapted from AGIMO (2008, p. 19).

Step One: *Preparation.* A business case development team needs to be formed that includes people with different skill sets in the organization, such as technical, financial, business analysis, and so on. However, the team size will depend on the scale of the project. Issues to consider at this stage are the rationale, assumptions, benefits, risks, and broad cost of the ICT initiative. The most important question to answer is "Whether an ICT intervention is the most cost-effective way to support the government's policy and service delivery objectives, or whether a non-ICT capability would better address the costs and risks involved?" The costs, benefits and risks of the non-ICT options would then need to be compared to the ICT options.

Step Two: *Demonstrate Strategic Alignment.* A business case should begin by stating the practical business problem or limitation that a new ICT capability could help to overcome, and help to achieve the government's policy and service delivery objectives. These objectives can include stakeholder priorities and business needs, and enhancing the level of service delivered to stakeholders.

Step Three: *Clarify Demand.* A business case should provide a comprehensive assessment of demand sources and characteristics, particularly among citizens and end-users. The assessment should include as much quantitative and qualitative evidence of demand as possible. Sources of demand may include feedback from citizens and end users of the current system, other related agencies and business groups, advocacy groups, or community lobby groups.

Step Four: *Establish Benefits and Key Performance Indicators.* Clearly articulate a "statement of success" and broad performance indicators for the ICT component based on the demand set out in the previous section. An example of statements of success for an eProcurement system proposal could be:

The agency will benefit through:

- *Increased single-point access to 70% of government tenders*
- *Secure 24-hour-a-day, 7-day-a-week, geographically independent tender lodgement, and*
- *Increased procurement transparency and accountability.*

Once the benefits and key performance indicators are documented, explain how those measures will be achieved.

Step Five: *Clarify ICT Baseline and Gaps.* This step documents relevant components of the organization's current ICT baseline. For example, the section should briefly describe: ICT infrastructure (both hardware and software), voice and data communications facilities, workforce skills and numbers, and security. The section must describe any gaps that the project must address to meet the statement of success and performance indicators. The purpose of this step is to clarify the ICT environment as it stands and identify shortfalls.

Step Six: *Prepare for ICT Options Analysis.* The business case must consider a number of alternative options, which range from minimal technology upgrades to more innovative ICT business solutions, and includes those that may challenge prevailing culture and service delivery habits. This step ensures that all options are considered objectively on their merits. The outcome will be a shortlist of options for analysis and comparison in the initial cost- benefit analysis. Normally, this shortlist will include a base, do nothing case (maintaining existing arrangements), a do minimum case (to address only urgent and unavoidable requirements), and two to three other options after screening out options that are not feasible.

Step Seven: *Identify Practical ICT Options*. Step Six will identify a shortlist of practical options. Step Seven describes each option in the following terms: high-level benefit objectives, costs and risks, functions performed, capacity to integrate with the existing system, potential constraints and limitations of the option, the market's ability to deliver the required products or services, any critical organizational or business environment assumptions / impacts (particularly from external environments). This step must set out how each option will perform over a period (e.g. five years) against the statement of success, benefits and performance indicators (outlined in Step Four). At this early stage of analysis, solutions that are not feasible should be analyzed and discarded. When options are discarded, the reasons for elimination should be recorded. In cases where the analyst does not have the authority to discard an option, a more comprehensive record of analyses and justification for recommending removal of the rejected options may be required. It is important that all parties in the options analysis process understand the information needs of the decision authorities so that the documentation is sufficient for effective decision making.

Note: **Base Case Option**. One option that is often overlooked is the "do nothing" option. This option is sometimes called the "Base Case" option. It should be analyzed so that there is a benchmark to compare both benefits and risks against. This option estimates the costs and benefits of maintaining the current operation, and takes into account known external pressures for change, which include changes in demand for services, budgets, staffing, and business direction.

Do Minimum Option. This option presents the minimum possible solution in terms of cost and effort required to meet only urgent and unavoidable requirements. The solution must be genuine and have a reasonable prospect of achieving most of the elements of the statement of success: benefits and performance indicators developed in Step Four.

Step Eight: *Clarify Schedules and Governance*. Indicate how long each option is likely to take to be fully operational and deliver the planned benefits. It is important to be realistic in planning and to explain the logic and assumptions that underpin each element of the schedule. For example, to allow sufficient time for software development, testing and evaluation, and user training and acceptance, you should look to similar work recently performed elsewhere in your agency or in another agency. You should use this knowledge to question informal schedule advice from potential industry partners. Governance activities must be explicitly shown in the schedule for each option and must cover activities required in your agency with stakeholders and reporting back to the government.

Step Nine: *Identify Risks and Mitigation.* A robust and reliable approach to risk analysis for ICT proposals can be developed based on the concepts and principles of risk management. A good reference for further information is the web site of the Project Management Institute. Appendix 10B provides a list of common ICT project risks. The risk management documentation will give a close account of several risk mitigation strategies and exit points.

Exit Points. The business case must establish potential exit points in the schedule for each ICT option. For each exit point, the business case must list the approximate exit cost and any other significant consequences. It must also identify the conditions that could trigger a recommendation to terminate. Some examples of triggers are: anticipated benefits of the proposal are no longer sufficient to warrant further expenditure, changes in stakeholders, their requirements have reduced support for the proposal, and so on.

Step Ten: *Develop Cost Estimates.* ICT-related costs are both expense and capital costs, including infrastructure, software, administration, maintenance, and resourcing costs. The costs are associated with the business transformation delivered by an ICT enabled project and the processes associated with the planning, design, development, change management, training, and evaluation of the project. The cost analysis focuses on the benefits of each option from the perspective of end users and of the agency. As part of the cost/benefit analysis, you should consider each option in terms of the inputs of cost, volume, and time.

Appendix 10C outlines the major ICT capital and operating cost items that are the focus of attention for business case estimates.

The cost/benefit analysis culminates in an overall economic assessment for each option and a comparison of the relative value of each option. This assessment can be based on the net present value (NPV) method or some other appropriate method (see Appendix 10D). In the initial feasibility study it is not expected that the NPV calculation will be definitive. However, in order to submit a convincing business case, it is necessary to provide an initial NPV calculation for each option, and an initial comparison between the options even though the basis for the cost and benefit information may be approximations.

Note: Not all ICT costs will fit neatly into either one or the other of the ICT cost categories.

For cost estimation, support from the finance section can be obtained. In addition, an Internet search can deliver useful insights into the likely cost of basic items such as computer and telecommunications hardware. Industry vendors also may make non-binding submissions of a proposed cost to indicate their interest in a proposal. Consultants may be able to provide additional insights based on their experience, which you can cross-check against own research.

Step Eleven: *Review Options*. Once you have identified the costs, risks, and schedule for each of your options, you should review them and develop a brief description for each that covers key aspects such as: investment objectives likely to be met by each, level of functionality likely to be achieved, technical complexity likely to be required (for example in system integration), positive and negative implications for stakeholders (which includes related agencies), and relative value for money. A SWOT (Strength- Weakness, Opportunity and Threat) analysis (also discussed in a later chapter) can also be carried out for the options, to give an overview of the proposed system for the decision makers. Appendix 10E includes an example of a SWOT analysis.

Step Twelve: *Finalize a Concise Case*. Finally, the ICT business case should be finalized using an acceptable format, possibly using an organizational template. The format will include a brief description of each option that includes its link to the agency's policies, eGovernment strategies, the benefits the option will achieve, the financial impact, the risks, the schedule, the underlying logic and assumptions taken, any limitations that would apply, the governance and accountability arrangements, an overview of the relative value, and the pros and cons of each option.

Table 10.1 is a checklist to assist in evaluating the quality of a business case.

Table 10.1 Business Case Checklist (OGC, 2013)

1.	Is the business need clearly stated?	Y/N
2.	Have the benefits been clearly identified?	Y/N
3.	Are the reasons for and benefits of the project consistent with the organization's strategy?	Y/N
4.	Is it clear what will define a successful outcome?	Y/N
5.	Is it clear what the preferred option is?	Y/N
6.	Is it clear why this is the preferred option?	Y/N
7.	Where there is an external procurement is it clear what the sourcing option is?	Y/N
8.	Is it clear why this is the preferred sourcing option?	Y/N
9.	Is it clear how the necessary funding will be put in place?	Y/N
10.	Is it clear how the benefits will be realised?	Y/N
11.	Are the risks faced by the project explicitly stated?	Y/N
12.	Are the plans for addressing those risks explicitly stated?	Y/N

10.4.2 Presenting a Business Case

Presenting a business case convincingly is of vital importance, both as a formal written report and as an oral presentation. A professional presentation of the report speaks for the quality and dedication of the team. Writing a good executive summary is crucial - a well-written, articulate executive summary leads top management to explore the case in detail. Often busy executives do not have time to read the whole business case, and it is the executive summary that they read to form an opinion. The executive summary must cover the recommended course of action and the reasons for selecting it, a summary of the considered options, and information on key benefits, impacts, and risks.

An oral presentation of the case can often be more effective and convincing than a written report. The management board or approval authority can cross examine the presenters directly and gain assurance about the viability of the recommended project. A professional approach and attire is necessary with supporting aids such as PowerPoint presentations professionally produced.

(Photo: A. Imran)

Figure 10.2. Officials in an eGovernment Management course presenting a business case, Bangladesh Public Administration Training Centre (BPATC), 2011

10.4.3 Business Case Approval

Once a business case is presented, it needs to be formally approved by the appropriate authorities, including financial stakeholders and sponsors. An approved, signed business report then becomes a source document for subsequent phases of the project.

It is important to plan for maintenance of the business case, and how that activity links into the governance of the project as it progresses. As we can see from case studies, poor decision making during a project can be a costly exercise. As decisions rely on accurate and up-to-date information, the business case must be revisited at significant project decision points.

10.5 Project Portfolio Management

In some larger organizations the project initiation phase and the preparation of a business case report takes place in a context where there can be a number of projects competing for funding, and only those projects with the highest priority and clearest benefits will go ahead.

In this situation, a Project Portfolio Management (PPM) approach can be used to ensure that there is an optimal mix of projects to achieve organizational gaols in existing constraints (as discussed further in Chapter 14).

More in-depth treatment of this topic is available from resources such as the web site of the Project Management Institute[1].

[1] http://www.pmi.org/default.aspx

Chapter Highlights

- The first phase of the eGovernment Systems Life Cycle is the Feasibility Study, in which the feasibility of change is investigated and a business case report prepared.
- Justifying ICT investments through business cases means less likelihood of project failures and more chance of reaping greater rewards from ICT.
- Good ICT governance means ICT investments are made both for valid reasons on the basis of ongoing analysis and with clear and transparent decision making.
- A business case report gives all the necessary information for informed decision making, including a problem definition, analysis of alternative options, plus a recommended option.

Review Questions

1. What activities occur in the feasibility study phase?
2. What is the purpose of a business case?
3. Why is it important to base decisions for investments in ICT solutions on proven and reliable processes?
4. Why is it important to assess all costs associated with an investment when performing a cost/benefit analysis?
5. What are three reasons for developing a business case?
6. Why should a business case be updated periodically?
7. Why is it a good idea to include a 'do nothing' option in the options analysis section of a business case?
8. Why is it a good idea to include a list of assumptions, dependencies, and risks in a business case?
9. Why is it a good idea to include supporting documents in a business case for a large and expensive ICT investment?

Discussion Questions

1. What might occur if stakeholder needs are not identified when planning an ICT investment?
2. Why are time-based (year-by-year) budgets included in most project proposals?
3. What might occur if the creation and delivery of benefits is not monitored and evaluated during a project?
4. Why should proposed ICT investments align with an organization's policies, strategic objectives, services, and functions?

Exercises

1. Analyze a business case or project proposal using the business case review questions list in this chapter and identify any missing information. Find a case study of an implemented project: e.g., the Chittagong Custom House project (see Internet or material in a prior chapter). Identify the benefits claimed for the project and provide a qualitative or quantitative assessment of the value of each benefit.
2. Two alternative proposals are under consideration for a new system. Estimates of costs and benefits in dollars for each are given below

Year	Proposal A		Proposal B	
	Costs	Benefits	Costs	Benefits
0	25,000	0	35,000	0
1	8,000	15,000	10,000	18,000
2	6,000	20,000	10,000	24,000
3	5,000	22,000	10,000	30,000

Which proposal would you recommend using the NPV method with a discount rate of 20%? See Appendix 10D for the NPV method and answers to this exercise

Group Exercise

This exercise requires participants to work in groups to develop a business case for a project of their own choice. The business case could be for a problem situation or opportunity for their organization.

There are no right or wrong answers for an exercise such as this. The purpose of the exercise is to encourage discussion and learning about how to develop project proposals in a public sector environment. As this is an exercise rather than a real-life situation, participants will not have time to gather detailed, realistic data. Therefore, it is acceptable to provide estimates (or pragmatic guesses) about data that is needed to support the business case.

You are also encouraged to do research on the Internet on the subject matter and systems applicable to your project.

You should prepare a PowerPoint presentation of the business plan and the business case report. Remember that, in a real-life situation, your presentation of your business case could be to upper management and be aimed at gaining their support for the project.

The business case report could use the outline provided in this chapter.

Appendix 10A

The Format of a Business Case Report

The stylized format described here is adapted from the business case template of the Tasmanian Government (2008). Refer to the full document for details. A further full business case example is the FREP Handheld Business Case, BC Ministry of Forestry and Range, British Columbia, Canada (Hooper, 2007).

Title page

- Problem/project name, organization, date, authors, signatures

Table of Contents

Executive Summary

Introduction

- Sets the scene for the rationale for developing the business case

Overview

- Vision for the project - what the recommended option will deliver.
- Relationship between this project and the corporate strategic plans.

The Business Case Analysis Team

- Case analysis team, including the sponsor

Situational Assessment and Problem Statement

- Clearly establish the benefit of proceeding with the proposed project. Show the current environmental conditions, how needs are currently being met or not met, and the gap between the current state and the desired objectives.

Assumptions and Constraints

- Show assumptions about required resources or skills and any dependencies on other projects.

Identification and Analysis of Options

- List the options (e.g., (1) do nothing, (2) one alternative option, (3) the preferred option).
- For each option, give details of benefits/costs, risks, stakeholder impact, issues (details may be in appendices)
- Comparison of options
- Recommended option.

Implementation Strategy

Project Management Framework

Appendices

- Detailed cost/benefit/risk analyses.

Appendix 10B

Common ICT Project Risks

Risks can be classified into different categories. It is important to classify risks into appropriate categories in order to take proper actions on those. The following list provides some examples of ICT project risks. There could many other types of risks as well, which should be addressed according to the priority and importance.

Supplier/ Vendor Risk

- Vendor delays affect system delivery date.
- Loss of key project staff.

Administrative / Staff Risk

- Inadequate training and documentation for operations staff.
- Delays in decision-making.
- Inexperienced development staff or shortage of experienced staff.
- Lack of management support for the project.
- Unable to secure an implementation partner.
- Unauthorised changes to scope by implementation partner following sign off.

Technical Risk

- Underestimation of technology capacity requirements (server, LAN, WAN etc.).
- Unforeseen system failure during development (such as hardware, software).
- System development model not suitable for delivery of the system.
- Loss of program modules being developed/ changed due to infrastructure failure.
- Incompatibilities between products cause interface difficulties.
- Data corruption during migration or data loss during migration.
- Incomplete data capture from the old system.
- Data is rejected at migration.
- Security of working files compromised during migration.

Financial Risk

- Blow out of financial resources required.

Legal Risk

- Failure to organize required policy or legislative changes to support the proposed system or procedural changes within the required time frame.

Business risk

- Incorrect scope defined that does not match user requirements.
- Failure to achieve the anticipated project benefits.

Environmental risk

- Production environment build hampered by unforeseen problems.
- Production environment not ready for go-live.
- Training materials or environment not ready at commencement of training.
- Untested changes are made to the production environment during implementation.
- Unforeseen problems with system porting delays go-live.
- Natural disaster.
- Political unrest.

Appendix 10C

ICT Capital and Operating Costs

Capital Costs	
Hardware	Servers; Storage; Peripherals (printers, multifunction); Desktops/Mobile Computers; Network Infrastructure; Other Hardware
Systems Integration / Development	Project Management; Architect; Designing and Configuring; Programming; Testing; Technical (data, storage, hardware, etc.); Security; Other Systems Integration/Development
Other Capital Costs	Defined by business case author
Operating Costs	
Employee Expenses	Salary Costs, Training and Assistance, Salary On-Costs, Other Employee Expenses
Supplier expenses	Financing, Insurance, Legal, Marketing, Research, Training Delivery
Corporate support	Corporate support expenses
Software licensing	Application software, Development and development tools
Operating Costs	System Infrastructure Software, Other software Licensing Expenses; Other Operating cost as defined by author
System Maintenance and Support	Hardware Maintenance, software maintenance

Appendix 10D

Cost/Benefit Analysis

Evaluation of each ICT option should include both:

- Costs and benefits to end users.
- Agency costs and benefits.

The highest score should reveal the greatest return on investment for each benefit per dollar of capital investment.

Return on Investment

Return on Investment (ROI) is the ratio of value of financial benefit of an investment relative to the cost incurred. Returns may be generated by cost savings or increased income. Returns (and costs) may be stable or variable over time.

ROI = (Investment value - Investment cost) / Investment value

ROI is usually expressed as a percentage.

Net Present Value

In Net Present Value (NPV) analysis the future value of benefits is converted to their present value equivalent. This approach works well where costs and benefits can be easily converted to a financial value.

The first step is to select a target interest rate of return (the discount rate).

Each cash inflow/outflow is discounted back to its present value (PV). Then they are summed. Thus, NPV is the sum of all terms,

$R_t / (1 + i)t$

where

t = the year of the cash flow

i = the discount rate (the rate of return that could be earned on an investment in the financial markets with similar risk.)

R_t = the net cash flow (the amount of cash, inflow minus outflow) at time t.

NPV needs to be positive to support an investment.

Internal Rate of Return

Internal Rate of Return (IRR) is a figure that can be compared to the interest rate offered by financial institutions. It is sometimes called the effective interest rate of an investment.

The higher a project's IRR, the more desirable it is to undertake an investment.

Because the internal rate of return is a rate quantity, it is an indicator of the efficiency, quality, or yield of an investment. This is in contrast with the Net Present Value, which is an indicator of the value or magnitude of an investment.

Project Cost Budgeting

Most project proposals include a time based (year by year) analysis of project costs. For some project proposals a month by month financial plan may be required. Time based budgets allow both the acquirer and the supplier to plan for expense and income flows. Line items in project budgets/financial plans may include:

- Labour - permanent, contractors, outsourced
- Travel and accommodation expenses
- Equipment and software purchases and licensing
- Overhead costs such as accommodation and office costs

Answers to Exercise 2 (page 225):

(with losses in brackets)

Proposal A, NPV = 392

i.e., ((25000) + 5,833 + 9,722 + 9,837)

Proposal B, NPV = (7,138)

i.e., ((35, 000) + 6,666 + 9,722 + 11,574)

Therefore, Proposal A is to be preferred.

Appendix 10E

SWOT Analysis: Example

Strengths	Weaknesses
• Strong need due to the increasing workload and paper intensive work • Political will and top management support • Removal of big part of the routine and formal work from employees • Simplifying administrative routines • Increased efficiency, productivity and cost savings • Better decision making and control • Affordable technology options • Availability of newly established national portal and backbone	• Lack of sufficient know-how about the proposed system • Poor telecommunication infrastructure • Existing rules and regulations not compatible with ICT based business process • High investment cost • Additional level of complexity • Additional maintenance load • Lack of IT-specialised human capital • Workers and older generation are computer illiterate
Opportunities	**Threats**
• Making public administration more transparent; reduce opportunities for corruption • Increased use of ICT by the population at large will help transformation to knowledge based economy • Increased citizen participation and trust • Foster other ICT application across the government and society • Increased reputation and international competitiveness • Open the opportunity for collaboration with other organisations • Technological advances like Cloud will create new opportunities for innovation	• Increase urban/rural divides • Security breach and copyright issue/ hacking • Dependency on IT; i.e. small technical problems will disrupt the entire networks. • Fear of uncertainty or losing power • Vested interest of certain stakeholders • Potential redundancy and jobless Change of top management support • Lower functional fit • Political instability

References

AGIMO. (2008). ICT Business Case Guide Development and Review (public version). Retrieved from http://www.finance.gov.au/budget/ict-investment-framework/docs/ICT_Business_Case_Guide. pdf (accessed January 2008).

Hooper, P. (2007). FREP Handheld Business Case BC Ministry of Forests and Range FRPA Resource Evaluation Program. CGI. http://www.for.gov.bc.ca/hfp/frep/site_files/ciworkshop2007/tab10/ business-case-frep-handheld.pdf

Office of Government Commerce (OGC). The Business Case Fitness For Purpose Checklist, http:// webarchive.nationalarchives.gov.uk/20110601212617/http:/www.ogc.gov.uk/documentation_ and_templates_business_case.asp (accessed May, 2013)

Piscopo, M. (2013). Project Management Docs Business Case. http://www.projectmanagementdocs. com/project-initiation-templates/business-case.html

Tasmanian Government (2008). Project Business Case (Small to Medium Projects) Template and Guide, Version 1.1. http://www.egovernment.tas.gov.au/project_management/supporting_ resources/templates/small_to_medium_projects (accessed May, 2013)

CHAPTER 11
Build or Buy

Learning Objectives

After studying this chapter, you will be able to:

- Describe the activities that occur when obtaining a new system, either through in-house development, by purchase, or some other alternative
- Describe what occurs in the Requirements Definition Phase
- Analyze the advantages and disadvantages of different methods of obtaining or building a new system, especially "build" versus "buy"
- Describe what is meant by outsourcing, and
- Analyze the advantages and disadvantages of outsourcing.

Build vs. Buy vs. Both

Have you ever had a project begin in one direction that looked promising, but then veer off in an opposite direction that yielded remarkably better results? Of course you have. In information systems projects, there's the classic dilemma of "build vs. buy" — and unwary clients can be impaled by either the "build" horn or the "buy" horn.

Our case study in this month's e-update exemplifies a "build vs. buy" dilemma. We were originally retained by the CEO and CFO of a structural steel fabricator for a "system screening" project — that is, to review the 3 or 4 software packages that the CFO had identified, and vet the choices. We found — just as our client had — there was not an obvious choice, because:

- *Lower-end industry-specific packages would meet the needs of one — but not both — of this client's lines of business.*
- *Higher-end industry-specific packages would meet the manufacturing needs of both lines of business, but were too cumbersome for the streamlined operations of our client — they lacked sales and accounting integration, and were priced well beyond the client's project budget.*
- *General ERP (enterprise resource planning) packages were incapable of handling the inventory tracking and production planning needs unique to this industry.*

Our work did identify another lower-end package we believed had the right base and fundamental structure to support customizations for our client — and our discussions discovered that this vendor was eager to improve their software to address the needs of this client's second line of business. We provided our client with ideas for enhancements and some pointers for negotiations with the vendor — and we were done. Thus, our "system screening" project was finished.

A few months later, we received a call from the CFO, who said that, while the vendor was more than willing to develop the negotiated enhancements, our client was having trouble "speaking the language" of software development. Could we speak that language? Absolutely — in fact, that's one of the things we're well-known for! Thus began our "designing and managing systems customizations" project.

Over a period of several months, we:

- *Discussed these process changes with appropriate client personnel and obtained their agreement.*
- *Translated the revised process into functional and technical specifications that the developer could use.*
- *Managed the development work performed by the vendor.*

> - *Worked closely with the developer and end-users to understand and quickly resolve any issues during development.*
> - *Installed and tested enhanced modules, as they became available.*
> - *Resolved issues, once the software was rolled out for general usage.*
>
> *So, the rest of the story for the client is this: the project ending up costing more than they had initially budgeted - in fact, it ended up being about the same as the higher-end industry-specific packages. Our client, however, got exactly the right software for their business, and quickly realized benefits that they had not anticipated. In fact, both the CEO and the CFO said that, while they probably would not have initially undertaken this project if they had known the eventual cost, the project has already paid for itself in inventory control and usage, system accuracy and data availability, and numerous timesaving business processes.*
>
> *The moral of the story? Given the right consulting firm and the right basic package, a systems customization project could be the best possible choice.*

Source: Todd Herman Associates e-Update (2007). http://www.toddherman.com/case-study/buildbuy-both (accessed May 2013)

11.1 Introduction

In previous chapters, we explored the overall eGovernment Systems Life Cycle and the first stage of this cycle - the Feasibility Study. In this chapter, we explore two of the key stages in which a system is implemented.

These stages are:

- Stage two: requirements analysis, and
- Stage three: systems building (in-house or acquisition).

In chapter 12, we examine project management, which provides methods for planning, monitoring, and controlling the activities that occur in Stages 2 to 5 (see Figure 11.1). All stages were covered at an overview level in chapter 9.

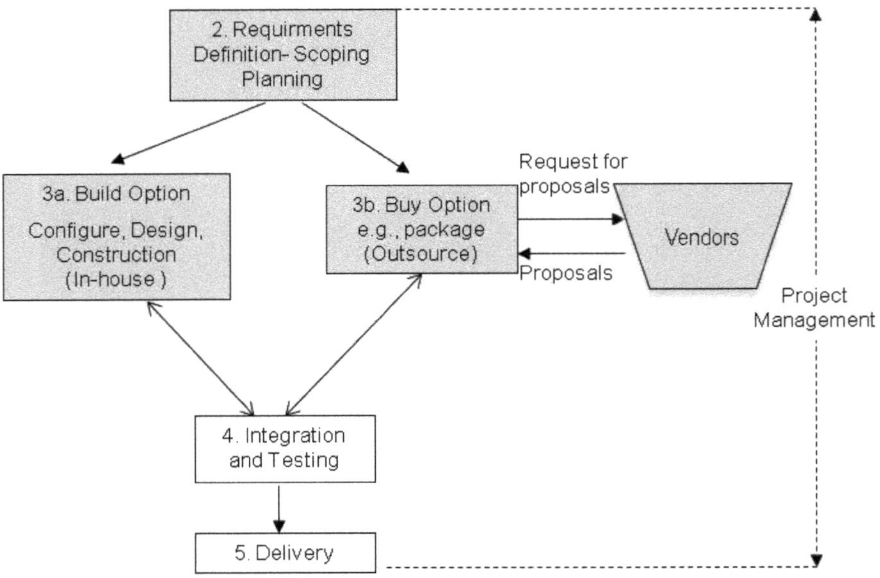

Figure 11.1. eGovernment system implementation stages

11.2 System Implementation Model

We follow the basic Waterfall Model of system implementation here, but many alternative methodologies exist, which we discuss in Appendix 11A.

The Waterfall Model is a single-pass approach to development (Figure 11.2).

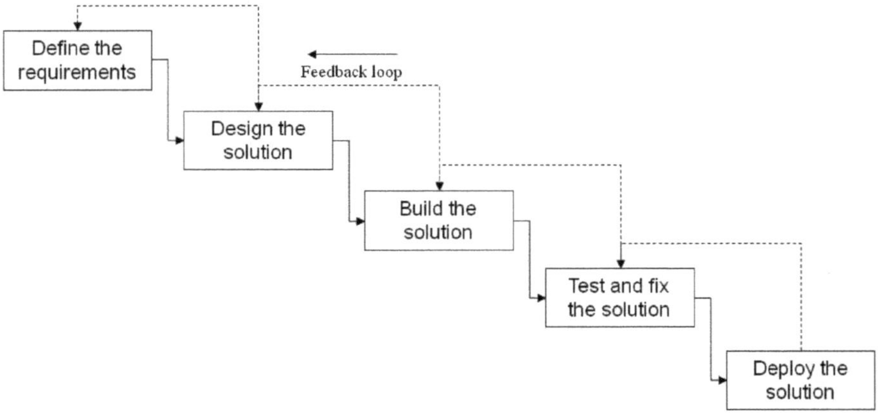

Figure 11.2. Waterfall Model of system development

Although there are feedback loops between stages, the dominant process flow moves forward and each type of activity is planned to occur only once. In simple terms, it is about:

- Analyzing once
- Designing, building, testing, and fixing once, and
- Deploying once.

With in-house system development, the effort distribution across the implementation phases is something like that shown in Table 11.1. However, there are significant variations across projects of different types.

Table 11.1 Effort distribution in Waterfall Model (Tan, Boehm, & Clark, 2011)

Phase/Activities	Effort %
Plan and requirement	7 (2-15)
Product design	17
Detailed design	27-23
Code and unit test	37-29
Integration and test	19-31
Transition	12 (0-20)

Studies in software engineering show that it is extremely important to focus on quality and defect avoidance right from the beginning of system implementation. For example, having to rework software requirement problems once the software is in operation could cost 50 to 200 times what it would cost to rework the problem in the requirements phase (Boehm & Papaccio, 1988).

11.3 Requirements Definition (Stage 2)

(Photo by F. Salam)

After the project initiation, a project team should be formed and given a charter to proceed with system implementation. Some analysis of requirements and constraints would be undertaken when exploring different alternatives for a new system in the feasibility stage. However, once the system implementation begins in earnest, it is necessary to investigate requirements more thoroughly. This is the requirements definition, or systems analysis phase.

11.3.1 Requirement issues

It is necessary to clearly specify and analyze the requirements, because it provides the foundation for future design and development of the system. This analysis includes eliciting, analyzing, specifying, and validating the requirements for a system.

Vendors often complain that many ICT systems do not succeed, because the initial requirements were not clearly specified. It takes considerable time, effort, and knowledge to carry out a good requirement analysis, which makes the developer or suppliers' job much easier. It is a challenging phase because all of the major stakeholders, and their interests, are brought in to determine the requirements. It is worth investing more time and effort in preparing requirement documents, instead of fixing the holes at a later stage of the project. The quality of the final product is highly dependent on the quality of the requirement analysis.

Requirements issues can significantly influence the success of an ICT investment. The key reasons for this are as follows:

- Business needs often derive from difficult problems that require careful analysis
- Understanding business and requirements tends to evolve over time
- Constraints and regulations that might impact on, or constrain, an ICT solution are not always apparent at the start of an investment analysis life cycle, or may change during the course of the acquisition and development of an eGovernment system, and
- Requirements gathering, analyzing, documenting, and agreeing, is often difficult and tedious work.

A sound requirement analysis phase will involve:

- Stakeholder identification
- Requirements identification
- Requirements evaluation
- Requirements agreement, and
- Requirements definition (documenting).

These activities may be revisited a number of times over the life of a project, especially when requirements are unclear or changing.

11.3.2 Key issues

The key requirements analysis issues may be that:

- There are many sources of requirements
- There are many requirements stakeholders, and
- There are many "non-functional" requirements.

Additionally:

- The requirements relevant to the full systems lifecycle (cradle to grave) should be considered, and
- The commercial and legal requirements should be analyzed.

Different requirements might arise in different phases throughout a system's life: during development, during use, and after retirement. All these lifecycle perspectives should be analyzed.

11.3.3 Requirements stakeholders

Requirements stakeholders include:

- Users - who may be many people with different roles and needs
- Customers/acquirers
- Suppliers and systems integrators
- Software engineers - developers and maintainers, and
- Regulators and evaluators.

11.3.4 Functional requirements

Functional requirements say "what" the system is actually required to do: for instance, print payslips.

11.3.5 Non-functional requirements

"Non-functional" requirements for an ICT system say more about "how" the system will do things, including:

- **Reliability** - The capability of the software to maintain its level of performance under stated conditions for a stated period of time
- **Useability** - The effort needed for use, and the individual assessment of such use, by a stated or implied set of users
- **Efficiency** - The relationship between the performance level of the software and the amount of resources used under stated conditions
- **Maintainability** - The effort needed to make specified modifications, and
- **Portability** - The ability of the software to be transferred from one environment to another.

Commercial and legal requirements (sometimes known as constraints) might include:

- Privacy and security policy and rules
- Software licensing and intellectual property rules, and
- Company financial guarantees and insurances.

11.3.6 Requirement analysis process

The following stages should be followed during requirement analysis:

1. **Preparation**. Grooming and preparation are undertaken to ensure that the project environment and team members are able to capture and analyze the system requirements.
2. **Determine business requirements**. Ensure internal and external business requirements are identified, business rules are defined and documented, and interfaces, to and from the new application, are understood.
3. **Define process model**. Draw a top-down representation of the major business processes that interact with the system and decompose into manageable functions and sub-functions until no further breakdown is feasible.
4. **Define logical data model**. Define and draw a logical model that shows data that supports the processes and business rules, and identifies all entities and their relationships to each other.
5. **Reconcile business requirements with models**. Verify that the process and logical data models accommodate all requirements and business rules.
6. **Produce functional specification**. Functionally describe how the consumer will use the application and interfaces, how processes and data are merged systematically, and how data will be retrieved, processed, and stored.

Note that if a system is to be acquired by purchase, rather than being built in-house, the requirements specification document produced at the end of this phase may be used as part of contractual arrangements.

Further Reading

For a sample of typical System Requirements Analysis, see the NYS Project Management Guidebook.

URL: http://www.cio.ny.gov/pmmp/guidebook2/SystemReq.pdf

11.4 Decision Point - Build or Buy

There are two main alternatives for the next phase of system development: build or buy.

There are several factors to consider when deciding whether to build or buy, including:

- The existing ICT development capabilities or capacity,
- The strategic ICT workforce plan
- The uniqueness of problems and solutions
- The size and complexity of required solution(s)
- The suitability of existing commercial solution(s)
- The degree of integration required
- The criticality to business operations
- The available time, and
- The total cost of ownership.

11.5 System Building (Stage 3a - In-House Option)

Even when building a system in-house, there are a number of options available, including:

- Building from scratch - usually not recommended because it is expensive and slow
- Building from components - many component routines can often be obtained, or
- Integrating applications - similar to building from components, but integrate entire applications, possibly from different units in the organization.

11.5.1 In-house development activities

If a system is developed in-house (rather than purchasing a software application or system), then the following activities may be involved:

- Architecture investigating
- Broad system designing
- Detailed designing
- Software coding
- Unit testing, and
- User interface testing.

11.5.2 System Architecture

The architecture of the system is the underlying design that links all the hardware, software, processing, outputs and human users. The eight key questions that architectural designers need to answer are (Sommerville, 2007):

- Is there a generic application architecture that can act as a template for the system that is being designed?
- How will the system be distributed across a number of processors?
- What architectural styles are appropriate for the system? (e.g., client server)
- What will be the fundamental approach used to structure the system?
- What structural units in the system will be decomposed into modules?
- What strategy will be used to control the operation of the units in the system?
- How will the architectural design be evaluated?
- How should the architecture of the system be documented?

11.5.3 Construction

Once an ICT system architecture has been decided, the elements/ components need to be created.

For hardware, the reusing and assembling of existing components is commonplace.

For software, reusing existing components is popular and increasingly common. For new or significantly modified software, construction involves the creation of software through a combination of coding, verification, unit testing, integration testing, and debugging.

11.6 System Building (Stage 3b - Buy Option)

This option is also called external sourcing or outsourcing.

Sourcing is a continuous process that starts with understanding the case for change, choosing the best sourcing option, assessing vendor offers, and transitioning to / managing the chosen sourcing solution.

There are various external sourcing options - often, a combination is selected. Sourcing options include:

- Buying an existing application package and installing it, with or without an external supplier's support, and with or without modification
- Outsourcing systems development and support services to one or more providers
- Leasing, renting, or licensing software, infrastructure, or complete systems
- Acquiring access to cloud computing services, and
- Applying a combination of the aforementioned sourcing options.

Organizations that establish a case for change should use strategic, qualitative, and quantitative analysis to arrive at the most appropriate sourcing strategy for their needs.

Organizations may also wish to investigate the market for ICT goods and services, in order to obtain a real picture of potential costs and the benefits of alternative solutions.

There are two main types of acquire/supplier relationships. The first is "commodity relationships", which are generally used when the priority is to control or reduce costs, rather than when the priority is to develop innovative ways for technology to improve performance.

The second is "partner relationships", which are based on in-depth collaboration. This suits ICT components that are strategic, particularly when the technology needs to be customized, and can play a key role in improving business performance. For these components, receiving the highest quality ICT service takes precedence over cost savings.

Between these model relationships are varying degrees of engagement, all of which involve different trade-offs between the elements that determine the real value of the arrangement.

Table 11.7 shows how a Supplier-Vendor relationship can be assessed.

Table 11.7. ICT provider satisfaction evaluation checklist (AGIMO, 2007)

Evaluation Area	Evaluation Questions
Relationship	Is your overall relationship with the vendor open and constructive?
	Is the relationship flexible and cost-effective in meeting changing volumes?
	Is the relationship flexible and cost-effective in rapidly responding to agency needs for new technology?
	Is the relationship flexible and cost-effective in rapidly responding to new ministerial and legislative requirements?
Staffing	Has the productivity of agency staff been negatively affected during the life of the contract?
	Are you happy with the vendor team's understanding of the agency's business?
	Has the vendor's team been of a consistently high quality?
	Has the vendor maintained a consistent team throughout the life of the contract?
	Has the vendor transferred knowledge to your team effectively?
	Is the agency happy with the influence it has over vendor staffing?
Contract	Has there been transparency in pricing, volumes, service level agreements (SLAs), and invoicing throughout the life of the contract?
	Has the contract stayed intact throughout the relationship?
	Were there any issues not resolved by the direct relationship management team?
	Are there any looming issues, if you decide to change to a new vendor?
Innovation	Are you comfortable that you have benefitted from natural technology evolution (such as, lower technology unit prices and technological innovation) over the period of the contract?
	Do you believe the vendor has sufficiently innovated your ICT functions?

11.7 Outsourcing

This section discusses the processes around external sourcing (outsourcing) in more detail. Outsourcing usually refers to the transfer of services from an organization to a vendor organization that might otherwise be performed by in-house employees.

Outsourcing is not limited to just ICT or infrastructure. Many business functions in an organization, including training, business processes, and logistics, can be outsourced. The concept of sourcing, or strategic alliances, works in a similar way to outsourcing, except, in this instance, there is more of a shared arrangement between the company and vendor.

IT outsourcing can be for system development purposes, maintenance purposes, or even for operation purposes. Many large companies now outsource their operations, such as call center services, e-mail services, and payroll. These jobs are handled by separate companies that specialize in each service, and are often located overseas. However, there are risks for any organization that hands over its ICT support, or other critical business functions, to another company.

11.7.1 Why Outsource?

Reasons for outsourcing will vary from company to company; however, outsourcing should be a strategic objective of the business. An organization must make this decision after a thorough analysis has provided valid reasons. The reasons to outsource can be for strategic, technical, financial, or scale considerations (Frenzel, 1999). There are many reasons why companies outsource their tasks, but saving money is the most important one. However, a decision to outsource should not be governed solely by perceived cost savings.

Bushell (2003) describes two different trajectories for outsourcing: The efficiency trajectory view and the transformational trajectory.

The efficiency trajectory outsources technology, or business applications, to achieve significant cost savings. This was the view adopted by the Australian Government in its government-wide outsourcing program, which was pursued specifically to save money. However, this argument remains controversial, because, on some occasions, cost savings were not achieved.

The transformational trajectory uses outsourcing as a tool to achieve an aggressive strategic agenda in an accelerated time frame (Bushell, 2003). This outsourcing method is often used to effect change in an organization, or to achieve significant reforms. It can be used as a method allowing organizations to gain access to better technology, or standardize existing infrastructure.

When developing an outsourcing contract, a company must carefully consider all the contractual arrangements for the outsourced agreement. There must be a clear set of performance measures and some form of service level agreement. Failure to do so may mean that issues such as operational quality cannot be quickly resolved. There are risks and benefits to outsourcing. However, any company that seeks to outsource should consider all these risks carefully, and ensure that the motivation for outsourcing is based on key strategic business drivers.

11.7.2 Procurement and Contracting

When organizations aim for an external solution, they need to implement a procurement plan, select vendor(s), and develop contract(s).

Going to market can be a lengthy process. For large projects, the timeframe can stretch to years. Of course, during this time, things may change. Thus, a means to deal with changes during the procurement process needs to be considered.

Due diligence is an important process that enables agencies to better understand legal and strategic risks, and allows tenderers to better understand an organization's requirements.

The key activities in this phase include:

- Initiating the market approach and receiving proposals
- Conducting industry briefings
- Signing confidentiality agreements
- Conducting pre-proposal "due diligence" with respect to vendors
- Selecting vendor(s)
- Reviewing proposals for completeness
- Screening/short-listing proposals
- Conducting vendor "due diligence"
- Negotiating with finalists
- Developing contract(s)
- Negotiating contract(s), and
- Executing (signing) contracts.

Contracts for ICT services will usually include service level agreements (SLAs). For each service, an SLA should specify at least:

- The name of the service
- The criticality for the business
- The importance of business continuity
- The performance metrics
- The minimum service level required
- The business impact and risks incurred if minimum service is not met
- The consequences of non-performance
- The terms for default
- The customer's obligations
- The pricing metrics and unit prices
- The likelihood of evolution on the client side
- The likelihood of evolution on the vendor side
- The exercisable options and pricing, and
- The conditions and responsibilities in case of unexpected changes.

11.7.3 Transition and Manage

Towards the end of an outsourcing arrangement, an organization needs to make transition arrangements. Transferring knowledge, assets, and staff, and migrating work-in-progress could take between three and ten months. Organizations then need to focus on managing ICT, which entails managing the relationship, managing the contract, and managing ICT operations.

Organizations at this stage need to establish processes to periodically review performance. Setting expectations and rules on how issues, risks, and problems are dealt with, early in a contractual relationship, is very important. Though, just as important is formally documenting and agreeing on these arrangements.

For further reading, see Dhar and Balakrishnan (2006).

Chapter Highlights

- Systems implementation involves defining requirements, and then either building or buying a system.
- Requirements definition, especially for large systems, is difficult and complex, but must be done properly.
- The build or buy decision rests on factors that include the in-house capabilities, the availability of off-the-shelf solutions, and the business' needs.
- Both building and buying a system can be lengthy processes that require the business owners and users to oversee and participate.
- Outsourcing requires careful attention to contractual details.

Review Questions

1. What are the factors to consider when deciding whether to build or buy a new system?
2. What are three development issues related to requirements analysis?
3. What are three things you might do to help manage development issues and risks?
4. What are five sourcing options?
5. What are the names of the two main types of acquirer/supplier relationships?
6. What is the purpose of the transition and manage phase in the outsourcing process?

Discussion Questions

1. How does the organizational enterprise architecture (discussed in Chapter 3) influence your build or buy decision?
2. Discuss the challenges and risks associated with outsourcing. How would you mitigate those challenges?

Exercise

Assume your proposal to reengineer an existing business process at your department has been approved by the appropriate authority.

- Create a list of stakeholders for the project.
- Prepare a requirement analysis document for the project.

Appendix 11A

Other Development Life Cycle Models

The system development life cycle (SDLC) is just one of many life cycles models that can be used to guide developers by explaining the way the development activities are arranged. The problem with any model is that it is a simplification of the real world; but, as long as we understand, and allow for, their limitations, models are a good way of sharing expectations of what, and when, things happen. There are many life cycle approaches available, such as incremental, evolutionary, spiral, and so on.

The key issues that influence the selection of a life cycle model are:

- The defined requirements
- The number of build or construction cycles that are required, and
- Whether interim products are to be deployed.

A recent and popular modern ICT system development approach is known as Agile Development.

Success with this approach requires close, daily cooperation between business people and developers.

Agile Development relies on small, highly effective and interactive teams to collaborate and produce useful functions, systems, or sub-systems, in short periods of time.

A normal development cycle (or sprint) is usually two to six weeks in duration, and, at the end of each sprint, a useful set of software functions is completed, tested, and accepted.

Most agile methods adhere to strict cycle time periods (sprints) - but, even though delivery dates don't move, the scope of what is delivered on that date might vary.

In simple terms:

Analyze many times, build rapidly, deploy once or many times. Repeat.

The big question is which approach (or approaches) should be used?

Most ICT solutions that support eGovernment are complex combinations of hardware and software components.

The development strategy for an ICT solution should align with, and cater for, the evolving nature of business and technical product requirements.

This requirement might mean that a combination of different lifecycle models is used.

References

Australian Government Information Management Office (2007). A guide to ICT sourcing for Australian government agencies. Retrieved from http://www.finance.gov.au/sites/default/files/ICT_Gov_B5_INT_Final.pdf

Boar, B. (2001). The Art of Strategic Planning for Information Technology. New York: John Wiley & Sons.

Boehm, B. W., & Papaccio, P. N. (1988). Understanding and controlling software costs. IEEE Transactions on Software Engineering, 14(10), 1462-1477.

Bushell, S. (2003). Agencies may "shy away" from outsourcing. CSO Online. Retrieved from http://www.cio.com.au/article/106958/report_agencies_may_shy_away_from_outsourcing/

Dhar, S., & Balakrishnan, B. (2006). Risks, benefits, and challenges in global IT outsourcing: Perspectives and practices. Journal of Global Information Management, 14(3), 39-69.

Frenzel, C.W. (1999). Management of information technology (3rd Ed.). Ontario: International Thomson Publishing.

Horrigan, D. (2003, July-August). A matter of process. CIO Government. Retrieved from http://www.cio.com.au/article/181800/matter_process/

Sommerville, I. (2007). Software engineering (8th ed.). Harrow: Addison-Wesley.

Tan, T., Boehm, B., & Clark, B. (2011). An investigation on application domains for software effort distribution patterns. Retrieved from http://www.sercuarc.org/wp-content/uploads/2014/02/15_Boehm-Domain_Effort_Distribution_Paper_v2-1-May-2011.pdf

CHAPTER 12
eGovernment Project Management Methodology

Learning Objectives

After studying this chapter, you will be able to:

- Describe the steps and methodology followed in an eGovernment project
- Determine how long a project will take and what resources it will require
- Identify the steps and actions required to ensure that the project will deliver what is required
- Ensure that an eGovernment project is going as planned
- Anticipate what might go wrong in an eGovernment project and plan mitigation measures, and
- Identify sources for additional detail on eGovernment project management

Great Wall of China and the Pyramids (Photos from Wikipedia), Mosque at Putra Jaya, Malaysia (Photo: A. Imran)

12.1 The eGovernment Project Management Methodology

> *Managing projects is one of the oldest and most respected accomplishments of mankind. We stand in awe of the achievements of the builders of the pyramids, the architects of ancient cities, the masons and craftsmen of great cathedrals and mosques; of the might and labour behind the Great Wall of China, and other wonders of the world.*
>
> *- Peter W G Morris, 1994, p.1*

A project management methodology provides a standard process for managing projects. The eGovernment Project Management Methodology (PMM) discussed in this chapter is a simple, generic, project management methodology, based on recognized project management best practice (e.g. PRINCE2[16] and the Project Management Body of Knowledge). Although it focuses on ICT and eGovernment projects, it can be used in managing all types of projects. Use of the PMM is not intended to be onerous, but is intended to provide a sufficient level of monitoring and control to prevent issues and ensure successful project completion. The project activities outlined in this chapter suggest a linear flow of activities within each phase; in practice, however, project management tends to be iterative and cyclical.

[Footnote 16: PRINCE2 (an acronym for PRojects IN Controlled Environments) is a process-based method for effective project management, used by the UK Government and recognised internationally (www.prince2.com)]

The order of steps in this chapter provides guidance about the typical order of activities, but these are not fixed (although some activities must logically occur before/after others). The project manager may choose to undertake the activities within each phase of the project lifecycle in a different order - one that suits the project and the project team better. Also, project managers using the methodology should feel free to add items to the methodology to suit the nature and complexity of their project. The key is to ensure that all of the activities in each phase are completed before moving on to the next phase. This chapter is not intended as a substitute for project management training or experience, but it can serve as a solid starting point for new project management or a quick reference for more experienced managers.

The Project Management Supplement at the end of the text provides templates that can used in the project management process.

12.2 Why Project Management?

Project management isn't rocket science - a lot of it is common sense - so why then is it so important? Projects are inherently risky and, despite the best intentions, many projects fail. Projects are unique, complex, dynamic, and highly constrained, and this creates a particularly challenging management environment.

Project management is the application of knowledge, skills, tools, and techniques to project activities to meet project requirements. Project management provides a structured approach to defining, planning, controlling, assessing, and completing project delivery in order to create the greatest chance of project success. Without proper project management, projects are more likely to run over time, over budget, and ultimately fail to deliver the benefits that they were intended to achieve.

12.2.1 Advantages of using standard PMM

The benefits of using project management include:

- Increased clarity and understanding of the project and its purpose
- A clear alignment of the project with organizational goals
- Clear roles and responsibilities
- Ensuring that the project delivery remains focused on the benefits to be achieved for the organization
- The ability to define and control the project scope
- More accurate estimation of work requirements (including resources)
- The ability to track progress throughout the project to determine if time, budget, and quality constraints will be met
- A greater ability to assess project performance
- Improved identification and handling of risks and issues
- Improved communication and stakeholder management
- Good project management practices - providing controlled project delivery
- Capturing lessons to improve future project performance
- An audit trail of project activities and decisions during a project, and
- The ability to end a project prematurely if it becomes no longer worthwhile or viable.

12.3 PMM Lifecycle

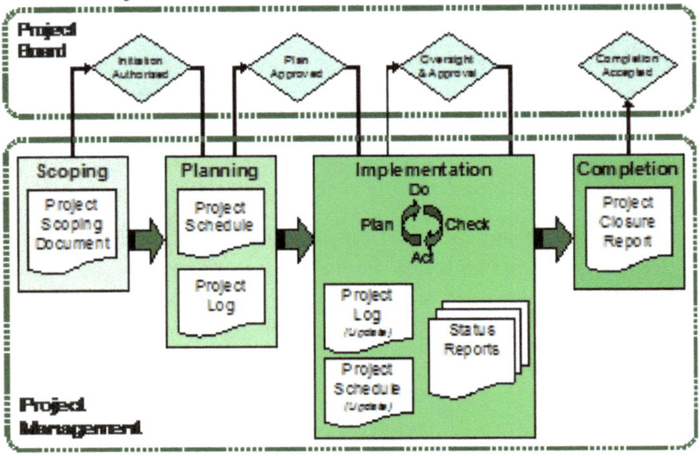

Figure 12.1. eGovernment project management methodology overview

The structure of the eGovernment PMM follows a common, four-phase project lifecycle (scoping, planning, implementation, and completion), as illustrated in Figure 12.1. The remainder of this chapter provides instructions on undertaking each of the project phases.

The project board as outlined in Figure 12.1 is a management group representing the stakeholders of the project (the organization, users, suppliers, etc), responsible for providing authorization and guidance to the project. The project board is accountable to executive management for the success of the project. It is brought together specifically to provide oversight of the project management. One member of the project board, the project sponsor (sometimes called the project executive), is ultimately responsible for the project and for ensuring it achieves its broader organizational objectives.

This chapter provides the necessary guidelines to apply the eGovernment PMM. The complete documentation comprises:

- Overview of the PMM and instructions in its application (this chapter)
- The project management supplement, with Sections A-G, containing project management document templates, their completion instructions, and useful checklists:

A. Project scoping document [scoping].

B. Project schedule [planning].

C. Status report [implementation].

D. Project closure report [completion].

E. Project log - for tracking the project.

F. Project manager's checklist.

G. Project phase completion checklist.

While PMM covers the complete project lifecycle, it is not intended to control every action that the project manager makes. Every project is different and, as such, project managers should use the PMM as a guide and consider how each document and activity applies to their particular project. The level of detail and rigor required in applying the PMM will vary according to the size and complexity of the project. However, this eGovernment PMM aims to provide a bare minimum level of project management. Consequently, while project managers using the methodology should feel free to add to the methodology to suit the nature and complexity of their project, they are discouraged from removing anything.

Hints & Tips

- The style of project management documentation is succinct and "to the point" - making use of diagrams, tables, dot-points, and so on, rather than long text.
- Do not remove anything from the eGovernment PMM templates. If you or your project sponsor believes there is a need for additional information in a document, then it should be added (preferably as an annex or appendix).
- If there is a part of an eGovernment PMM template that has no relevance to your project, this should be noted. The reader needs to be assured that you have considered the section, rather than wondering if you missed it.

12.4 Scoping

12.4.1 The Purpose of Scoping

Scoping is the first phase of the project lifecycle (see Figure 12.2). It contains a second more detailed pass through the business case process as discussed in chapter 10. The scoping phase begins after a go-ahead decision is given on the first high-level pass through the business case. It can be useful to think of the Scoping Phase as a mini-project - planned, resourced, and executed to be successful. At this stage, the project team should be selected for their abilities (e.g. technical knowledge, financial skills, and operational skills) and availability to commit to scoping the project.

The purpose of scoping is to clarify the details of the project to a sufficient level so that the Project Board can be confident about its outcome. The scoping document also gives a clear understanding and direction to the project team about their task.

Scoping is concerned with answering the questions:

- **WHY** should we be doing this project?
- **WHAT** should we be doing?
- **WHEN** should we be doing these things?
- **HOW** should we go about it?
- **WHO** should be involved?

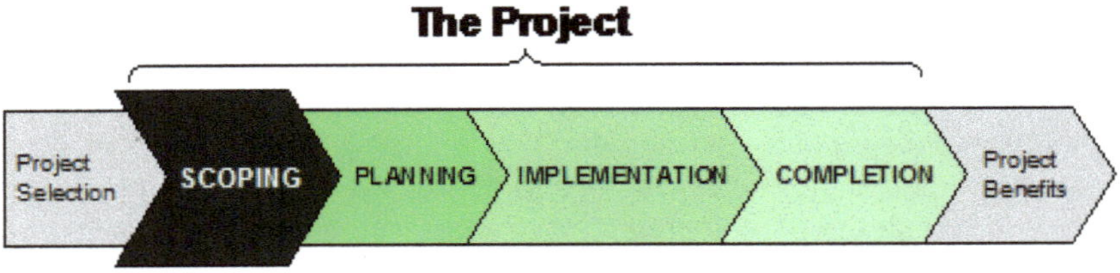

Figure 12.2. Scoping - the first phase of the project lifecycle

12.4.2 Scoping Activities

STEP 1. Clarify the project mandate & reporting schedule

The project manager should arrange a briefing on the project from the project sponsor. The project sponsor, as the head of the project board, is accountable for the realization of the benefit that will result from the project. It is important that the project manager is fully aware of the context and expectations for the project. The project manager should clarify the intent of the project and confirm the governance arrangements, including any reporting requirements in addition to the status report.

The project manager must ensure that they have a clear understanding of the project mandate before establishing the team that will work to scope the project.

Project reporting should also commence as soon as the scoping phase begins. The status report provides information on the progress and performance of the project to the project board.

The project's reporting requirements should be discussed and agreed with the Project Sponsor to ensure the levels of project risk, size, and complexity have been appropriately considered in terms of frequency of reporting. This eGovernment PMM recommends a minimum of monthly project reporting.

STEP 2. Establish the project team

The size and composition of a project team will vary across its lifecycle. At this point in the project, the project manager may be able to scope the project by themselves, and hence, the project management team will be just the project manager. Most likely however, it will be necessary to assemble a small team, with the necessary knowledge and expertise, that can work together to create the project scoping document. The project scoping document defines the business case for undertaking the project.

STEP 3. Develop the project scoping document

The project scoping document is the key document to commit resources to develop the project plan. It clearly defines the project to be undertaken (its costs, benefits, and risks) and is the document against which the organization authorizes initiation of the project. The document should be clear and succinct, making use of bullet-points, diagrams, tables etc, as appropriate.

The core areas of the scoping document to be completed are:

- Justification: Redefining the business case to show again how the project is desirable and viable. It is often a good idea to keep the business case as a separate document that can be referenced by the scoping document.
- Project Scope: Defining the work/activities that the project will include and the primary deliverables that will be produced. Constraints, assumptions, and high-level risks associated with the project are also documented. Any related work within the organization should also be identified.
- High-Level Schedule: Identifying the key milestones in the delivery of the project across the remaining phases of the project lifecycle: Planning, Implementation, and Completion.
- Key Resource Requirements: Identifying critical resources for undertaking the project. Resources may include personnel, equipment, and infrastructure.
- Project Stakeholders: Identifying stakeholders in the project. A stakeholder is any group or person that will either have an influence on the project or will be impacted by the project. The communication requirements for engaging with each stakeholder must also be decided.
- Budget Estimate: Providing a high-level breakdown of the project cost estimate. These values should be indicative only at this stage - a detailed cost estimate is developed during the Planning Phase as part of the project schedule.

For all but the smallest of projects, the project scoping document will not be able to be developed by a single person or in a single session. The scoping document will typically be developed by the project manager over a period of weeks with analysis and input from a group of people with particular skills/knowledge (the project team - see Step 1).

This text provides a project scoping document template as Section A (project management supplement). This template provides a base level of information for project scoping. The project manager may wish to add information to provide greater scoping detail (which should be done in the form of an annex or appendix). In particular, for eGovernment projects, it is sometimes necessary to include the high- level system design for the best value-for-money solution.

No sections should be removed from the project scoping document template. If the project manager believes that a section is not relevant to their particular project, they should note this on the document but not remove the section. This ensures that the Project Board is aware that the Project Manager has considered each section and made a decision on its relevance.

STEP 3a. Business case development

The project sponsor is accountable for the business case. However, the project sponsor will typically delegate responsibility for its development to the project manager following the guidelines discussed in Chapter 10.

The business case will be refined as the scoping exercise progresses. That is to say as the plans, resources, costs, risks, and so on become known in greater detail, we can refine the outline business case into the (detailed) business case.

The business case will be referred to throughout the life of the project. As we measure the project's progress against plan and manage issues and risks, it will be necessary to confirm the continued viability (or not) of the project against the business case.

Often in practice, the business case is used as the scoping document, especially for smaller projects. However, in an ideal situation a scoping document is prepared based on the outcome of the business case.

STEP 4. Obtain scoping document sign-offs and approval

Before the scoping phase can be considered complete, the project scoping document must be approved by the project sponsor on behalf of the project board. This approval authorizes the planning of the project.

Before the scoping document is presented to the project sponsor to sign, it may be necessary to have it signed-off by senior members of the organization if their area is impacted by the project. The appropriate sign-offs should be agreed with the project sponsor. This may include:

- Chief Information Officer - for highly technical ICT projects, and/or
- Chief Financial Officer - if the project involves significant cost.

Once the appropriate sign-offs have been received, the project manager should deliver the scoping document to the project sponsor in person for approval. Two copies of the scoping document should be signed: one to be kept by the project manager and one to be kept by the project sponsor.

STEP 5. Plan for the planning phase

The planning phase will typically involve significantly more time, cost, and resources than have been involved in scoping. Before starting the planning phase, the project manager needs to consider:

- What tasks need to be completed during the planning phase?
- Which additional resources will the project team require?
- How long will planning take?
- How much will it cost to plan the project?

Table 12.1. Planning phase supporting documents

Document	Input	Created	Updated	Finalized (Archived)
Project Mandate				
Project Scoping Document				

Hints & Tips

Don't spend excessive time on the scoping phase. The purpose of this phase is to do enough analysis and planning so that the project sponsor can make a decision about whether or not to commit resources and funds to the detailed planning phase - not to the project, just to the process of planning.

12.5 Planning

12.5.1 The Purpose of Planning

Planning is the second phase of the project lifecycle (see Figure 12.3). It expands on the project definition created in the Scoping Phase to develop a detailed roadmap for how the project will be implemented.

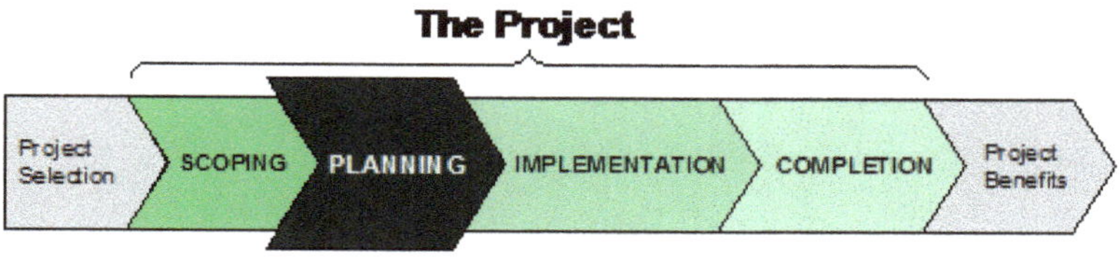

Figure 12.3. Planning - The second phase of the project lifecycle

The primary goal of the planning phase is to develop the project plan. The project plan provides the baseline against which the project can be conducted, monitored, assessed and, if necessary, adjusted. It identifies the deliverables (outputs) to be produced by the project, the tasks necessary to produce the project outputs, and estimates how long they will take, how much they will cost, what resources they will require, and any risks to the project. Without a detailed project plan to track against, it is impossible for the project manager to measure progress and determine if the project is on track for successful completion.

12.5.2 Planning Activities

STEP 1. Revise the project team

Although the project manager is ultimately responsible for planning the project (planning for both the project delivery and the project management), it is not something that should be done by an individual. A significant amount of the project management work for a project occurs during the planning phase, and the quality of the planning often determines the success of the project. The planning phase is best tackled by a team, which includes key stakeholders of the project and its outputs.

For continuity (and for the capabilities for which they were originally selected), the members of the project team from the scoping phase will typically remain on the project during the planning phase. However, it may be necessary to change or add people in order to assemble the right skills, knowledge, and background to plan the project. It is also important to make sure that there are enough people for the project team to complete the planning on time. Typically, the project team established for the planning phase will be significantly involved for the remaining life of the project.

STEP 2. Develop the project plan

The project plan is more than just the schedule for undertaking the work. It details how the project will be managed and achieved. Developing the plan requires detailed thinking and forecasting. Since projects are, by definition, unique bodies of work, it is not possible to copy a project plan from a different project.

For the eGovernment PMM, the core documents in the project plan are the project schedule and the project logs (see Steps 3 and 4). However, for an eGovernment project, the project plan may also include other documents such as requirements specifications or system designs (as discussed in Chapter 11). The project manager should add documents and information to the project plan as required in order to sufficiently plan the management and delivery of the project. This will vary depending on the size, complexity and type of project.

STEP 2a. Create the product breakdown structure

Using a technique known as product-based planning, we will first identify the outputs (products) to be created by the project. Only then will it be possible to identify the activities, dependencies, and resources required to deliver those products and hence create a Work Breakdown Structure.

Product-based planning starts with writing a project product description; that is, an overall description of what the project will deliver.

A product breakdown structure is then created; that is, the project product is then broken down into its major products, which are then successively broken down into sub-products until an appropriate level of detail is reached. As part of this process any external products will be highlighted; that is, any products (pre-existing or that need to be created) that will be sourced from outside the project team. A simple ICT example is the purchase of a server from an external vendor. It is also necessary to include reports to be developed as these also involve work.

Once all of the products have been identified, we will produce the appropriate product descriptions. The next step is to create a product flow diagram so that we can understand the sequence in which the products will be developed and the relationships between them.

STEP 2b. Create the work breakdown structure (WBS)

One of the most important aspects of the project plan is specifying the work that will be undertaken. This is typically done by creating a work breakdown structure (WBS), which identifies all of the individual tasks that must be performed to produce the project outputs/deliverables.

Once the project's products have been identified and sequenced in a product flow diagram, the high-level tasks necessary to create the products can then be identified. For each of these tasks, it may also be possible to break them down further into sub-tasks, which may also be divided further into sub-sub-tasks, etc. The WBS should continue to break down the work until a level of detail is reached where it is possible to accurately estimate the time, cost, and resource requirements for the individual activities.

Having identified the activities, the resources can then be identified including any specific skill sets required. Then the time to complete the activities needs to be estimated. There are many books and software packages that can help with estimation, but some basic guidelines include:

- Make use of your own prior experience and that of others
- Refer to similar projects completed in the past
- Be aware that people are often optimistic and therefore tend to underestimate the time required, and
- Make sure that the person creating the product is the one who prepares the effort estimates.

Resources, whether internal or external, will have cost rates applicable to them, so once we have estimated the time required to complete the activities, we will also be able to estimate the costs.

Figure 12.4 shows the basic format of a WBS. However, the actual WBS may be developed in whatever format the project manager and the project team are most comfortable with.

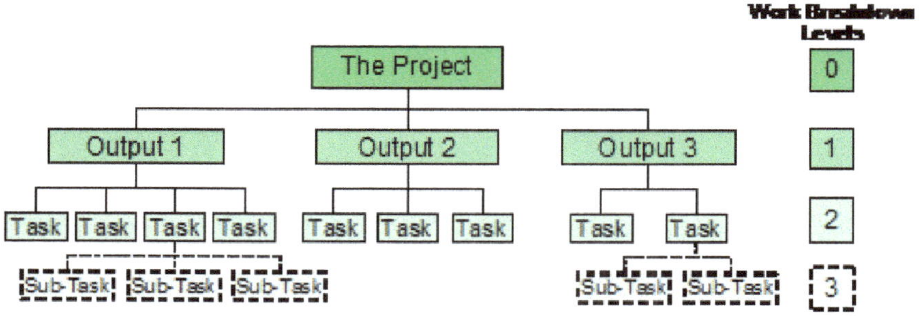

Figure 12.4. Format of a work breakdown structure (WBS)

A good WBS is fundamental to building the schedule of activities in the project plan and is a key tool in integrating the design and project management processes.

STEP 3. Create the project schedule

The project schedule summarizes the tasks involved in completing a project, including when they will be done, what resources are required to undertake them, dependencies between tasks, and the costs. The project schedule forms the work plan against which the project manager can monitor and control progress on the project. The schedule is created during the Planning Phase and updated with actual progress and revised plans during implementation and completion.

A project schedule template is given in Section B (project management supplement). The project schedule should be developed from the WBS, by estimating the time, resources, and funding required to complete each task and identifying start and finish dates for each task based on resource availability and task interdependencies (e.g., where one task cannot start until another task has finished).

The project schedule must show sufficient detail so that the people responsible for carrying out activities and producing project outputs know what they need to do and when.

The project schedule should include not only the project delivery work, but also the project management work, including:

- Planning and review meetings
- Documentation development
- Quality checks
- Reporting meetings
- Team meetings
- Training, and
- Transitioning project outputs to the organization.

The management component of project work is often overlooked during planning and is therefore often poorly scheduled and resourced, which can result in the project being both over time and over budget.

STEP 4. Creation and use of the project logs

The project logs are working documents for monitoring and controlling the following:

- Quality
- Risks
- Issues
- Changes, and
- Lessons.

The project logs are a key tool for keeping track of the project, and their value to a project manager depends on their accuracy (including being up-to-date). They should be routinely reviewed and, if necessary, updated. On a daily basis, the project manager is responsible for ensuring that quality, risks, and issues are being managed and that changes and lessons are captured.

The eGovernment PMM workbook in the book website provides templates for all of the project logs as Microsoft Word templates. The information captured in these logs is essential to monitoring project progress and preventing unpleasant surprises. The project manager should use all of the logs throughout the life of the project.

STEP 4a. Create and use the quality log

All outputs of the project should have measurable acceptance criteria established to ensure they meet the needs of the users and the organization. The tracking and assessment of these acceptance criteria through quality checks is planned and recorded in the quality log. These quality checks should also be planned in the project schedule.

STEP 4b. Create and use the risk log

Risks are uncertain events that may have an impact on the project - they might or might not happen. Because risks have the potential to affect the project (sometimes catastrophically), they need to be captured in the risk log and appropriate strategies developed for addressing them.

Common areas for risk are time, cost, quality, stakeholder management, safety, operations, and project management. Risks should be considered in terms of their:

- **Likelihood** - how likely it is that the risk will occur, and
- **Consequence** - how significant the impact would be if the risk did occur.

In general, there are five possible approaches to addressing a risk:

1. **Avoidance** - avoiding the risk completely (usually by not undertaking the activity to which the risk is associated)
2. **Reduction** - taking action to reduce the impact of the risk or the likelihood of the risk occurring
3. **Transference** - transferring the risk to another party (often through a contract in which the other party agrees to accept the risk)
4. **Contingency** - establishing a backup plan/option in case the risk does occur, and
5. **Retention** - accepting the risk (usually only appropriate where the risk is small).

Ignoring a risk is NOT a valid approach. Even risks that are retained should still be monitored and reviewed.

If the risks require action to be taken to address them, then this action should be included in the project schedule. One of the common mistakes in risk management is failure to convert the analysis and planning into actions.

STEP 4c. Create and use the issue log

Unlike risks, an issue is something that is negatively impacting the project now and must be responded to now. Issues are often the result of risks occurring. All issues should be entered into the issue log and dealt with as soon as they occur - issues that are not addressed have a tendency to grow.

If the issue is not large, it may be addressed within the existing constraints of the project (time, cost, quality, and scope), otherwise a change must be logged and approved by the project board (see step 4d) to address the issue.

STEP 4d. Create and use the change log

Changes are responses to issues that exceed the agreed constraints of the project (time, cost, quality, and scope).

At the end of the scoping phase, the project board authorizes the project because they believe that it will provide a benefit to the organization that is worth the investment (i.e., it represents value for money). This is based on the information provided in the project scoping document, which establishes the project constraints. Any change that will exceed the constraints may mean that the project will no longer benefit the organization (in which case the project should be cancelled). Consequently, all changes must be approved by the project sponsor, who effectively authorizes a new set of constraints to accommodate the change.

All changes must be recorded in the change log so that there is an information trail of the project constraints.

Changes will usually require reviewing and updating the project scoping document and project schedule. These documents will need to be approved by the project sponsor as part of the change.

STEP 4e. Create and use the lessons log

Every project is a learning experience for the project manager, the project team, and the organization. Throughout the project, as lessons are identified, they should be recorded in the lessons log. This ensures that lessons are not forgotten and provides a reference for other projects or other project managers.

Both positive lessons (the things that worked well on the project) and negative lessons (the things that didn't work well - the pitfalls to avoid) should be captured.

NOTE: It may be mentioned that for smaller projects, often one log is maintained under different headings.

STEP 5. Report project status

Throughout the life of the project, the project manager should provide at least a monthly status report to the project board. During the planning phase, the project status is reported against the plan for the planning phase.

The eGovernment PMM workbook includes a status report template, available in either a hardcopy or electronic format (as a Microsoft Word document). This status report should be delivered to the project sponsor by the project manager in person, for feedback and approval.

Producing the status report is relatively simple for project managers who are closely tracking the project progress (with the project team) and are monitoring and updating risks, issues, quality, changes, and lessons in the project logs.

In addition to the monthly status report, the project manager should also be informally reporting project events to the project sponsor, as appropriate.

STEP 6. Review and revise the project scoping document

Before finalizing the project plan, the project scoping document should be reviewed to make sure that the project plan meets the needs and constraints of the project.

The greater detail and understanding that comes through planning the project should be mapped back to the project justification in the project scoping document to ensure that it is still valid.

If changes are required to the project scoping document, it should be filed as a new version of the document and must be reviewed and approved by the project sponsor. Otherwise, the project plan should be revised until it can deliver on the project scoping document.

STEP 7. Obtain project plan sign-offs and approval

Before the planning phase can be considered complete, the project schedule and project logs (as well as any other documents included in the project plan) must be approved by the project sponsor on behalf of the project board. This approval authorizes the undertaking of the project delivery work.

Before the planning documents are presented to the project sponsor to sign, it may be necessary to have it signed-off by senior members of the organization if their area is impacted by the project. The appropriate sign-offs should be agreed with the project sponsor. This may include:

- Chief Information Officer - for highly technical ICT projects, and/or
- Chief Financial Officer - if the project involves significant cost.

Once the appropriate sign-offs have been received, the project manager should deliver the planning documents to the project sponsor in person for approval. Two copies of the documents should be signed: one to be kept by the project manager and one to be kept by the project sponsor.

Table 12.2. Planning phase supporting documents

Document	Input	Created	Updated	Finalized (Archived)
Project Mandate	✓			
Project Scoping Document	✓		✓	
Project Schedule		✓		
Project log		✓		

Hints & Tips

- The project management work in the scoping and planning phases sets the project up to succeed. Many project managers feel a need to hurry through these phases and "get on with the real work". However, this is one of the most common causes of project failure. Projects should be scoped and planned as well as possible before commencing, while recognising that planning is about forecasting and estimating and shouldn't be dragged out trying to make an estimate exact.
- While every project is unique, it is certainly possible to learn from other projects, other project managers, and technical experts throughout the organization. Don't be afraid to review lessons from previous projects or ask for input and advice.
- Don't forget to plan the project management work. Project management takes time, money, and resources - make sure this is accounted for in the plan.

12.6 Implementation

12.6.1 The Purpose of Implementation

Implementation is the third phase of the project lifecycle (see Figure 12.5), in which the project plan is executed. The implementation phase is where the delivery work happens on the project - it is where the project outputs are created. The scoping and planning phases involve project management work (not delivery work); they are involved in setting up the project to succeed.

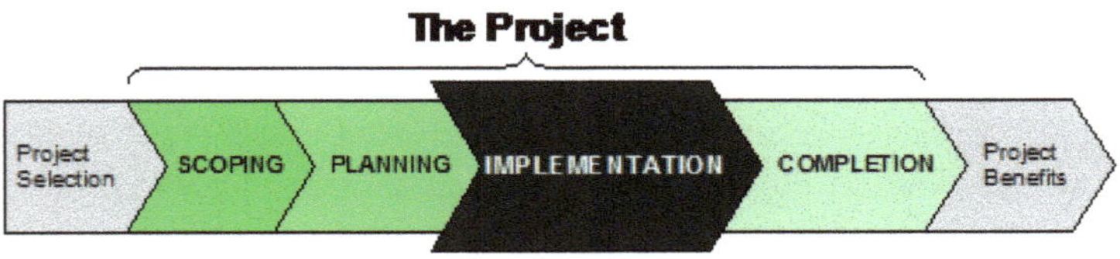

Figure 12.5. Implementation - The third phase of the project lifecycle

The implementation phase for a project manager is about monitoring and controlling the project to ensure it delivers on the plan.

NOTE: The work involved in tracking the performance of the project and taking actions to ensure it is achieving its goals is cyclic. It involves checking on progress, adjusting and re-planning as necessary, executing the new plan, and re-checking for change. The project manager will need to continuously repeat the steps described throughout the Implementation Phase until the project work is completed.

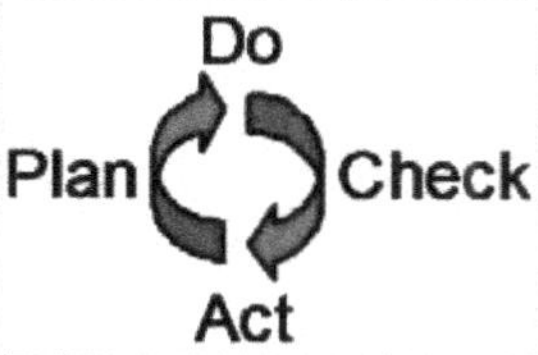

The PLAN > DO > CHECK > ACT cycle overlays just about every aspect of project management, including stakeholder management, schedule, budget, issues, risks, quality, changes, reporting, and documentation.

12.6.2 Implementation Activities

STEP 1. Revise the project team

The project team for the implementation phase will typically comprise people working full- or part-time in:

- The (design and) delivery of the project products or outputs, and/or
- The management of the project.

It is important to clearly define roles and responsibilities for each member of the team to ensure effective coordination and integration.

The members of the project team from the planning phase will typically remain on the project during the implementation phase. However, it will usually be necessary to change or add people to the team in order to assemble sufficient resources with the right skills, knowledge, and background to manage and deliver the project.

STEP 2. Implement the project plan

The project plan provides the blueprint for managing and delivering the project. In the eGovernment PMM, the project plan incorporates the project schedule and project logs, as well as any other planning documents necessitated by the size, complexity, and type of project.

The project schedule, which is one of the core documents within the project plan, should be the ultimate reference for all the planned work in the project. It provides the project manager with a single, reliable source of information on who's doing what and when.

The project manager must also ensure that stakeholders are properly engaged and informed of project progress throughout the Implementation Phase. Project managers should be proactive in seeking feedback on the information they communicate, rather than waiting for complaints about a lack of information.

NOTE: Steps 3 and 4 could be considered a part of "Step 2. Implement the project plan" as they concern the project schedule and project logs. They are elaborated here to provide more detailed guidance.

STEP 3. Execute, review, and update the project schedule

The project schedule should be reviewed and updated at appropriate intervals to ensure that it remains an accurate reflection of planned and actual progress. Any deviation in the project - whether recorded in the change log or not - must be reflected in the project schedule. This includes basic deviations such as rescheduling a meeting.

The appropriate review period will depend upon the length and complexity of the project. Each revision of the project schedule should be filed as a new version of the document.

In the eGovernment PMM, the project schedule captures not only task timing, but also resourcing and costing. Consequently, it should be updated to reflect planned and actual budget expenditure as well as resource usage.

If actual project progress does not match the planned project schedule, the remainder of the project schedule will need to be updated to reflect the new progress path and ensure that the project can still be completed within its time, cost, quality, and scope constraints.

STEP 4. Review and update the project logs

The project logs should be used to document risks, issues, changes, quality checks, and lessons as they occur throughout the life of the project. The project manager should also periodically review the logs to ensure that they are up-to-date. The project logs must be kept current for the project manager to have an accurate understanding of the status of the project.

STEP 4a. Review and update the Quality Log

The quality log is an important tool in checking and controlling the quality of project outputs. It should be reviewed and updated regularly to ensure the project is on track to deliver to the agreed level of quality (acceptance criteria).

STEP 4b. Review and update the Risk Log

The risk log is used to capture risk management information for the project. Since risk identification and analysis is an ongoing process throughout the project lifecycle, the risk log must be continually reviewed and updated to ensure it stays relevant and useful.

STEP 4c. Review and update the Issue Log

The issue log is a means of capturing, assigning, and tracking issues affecting the project. All issues should be captured in the Issue Log to ensure that they are dealt with appropriately and in a timely manner. Resource constraints often limit the project manager's capacity to deal immediately with issues, but the ongoing priority of all issues should be monitored until they are resolved.

STEP 4d. Review and update the Change Log

All proposed changes that will impact the project timeline, cost, quality, or scope must be captured and approved in the change log to ensure that the project still delivers the intended benefits for the organization.

STEP 4e. Review and update the Lessons Log

Throughout the project, as lessons are identified they should be recorded in the lessons log. Both positive lessons (the things that worked well) and negative lessons (the things that didn't) should be captured.

STEP 5. Review and revise the Project Scoping Document

Projects are conducted in dynamic environments that may change significantly over the course of a project, particularly in the ICT field. Consequently, the project scoping document should be reviewed regularly across the implementation Phase to ensure that the project is still relevant. There are three possible outcomes of the review:

- The project scoping document is still relevant and valid, and the project is on track to deliver on that project scoping document - continue with the project and keep monitoring the project scoping document; or
- The project scoping document is still relevant and valid, but the project has steered off course and is unlikely to deliver on that project scoping document - re-align the project (this may require stopping the project while re-alignment takes place); or
- The project scoping document is no longer relevant or valid, and the project should be stopped while decisions are made about its future, as the project may no longer deliver any benefit to the organization.

If changes are required to the project scoping document and the project is still viewed by the project board as worthwhile, a new version of the project scoping document should be filed and must be reviewed and approved by the project sponsor.

STEP 6. Report project status

The status report provides a snapshot of the current performance of the project. It should be completed at least monthly, but may be required more regularly depending on the size and complexity of the project - the appropriate reporting frequency should be agreed with the project sponsor. The status report provides information that can alert the project board to emerging problems before they become major issues and is a key document in the control process for the project. Status reporting is repeated periodically for the life of the project - until all project delivery work has been completed and formally approved.

Section C (project management supplement) provides a status report template. This status report should be completed and delivered in person to the project sponsor by the project manager to allow for discussion, clarification, feedback, and guidance.

Status reporting is relatively simple for project managers who are routinely tracking the project progress against the project schedule and are monitoring and updating risks, issues, quality, changes, and lessons in the project logs. However, completion of the status report still requires the project manager to collate project information, analyze it, and think about all aspects that are reported to the project sponsor.

NOTE: If problems emerge after a status report has been delivered to the project sponsor, the project manager should not wait until the next status report to raise the issue. The problem should be raised with the project sponsor as soon as possible and followed up by documenting the issues and the actions in the project logs.

Table 12.3. Implementation phase supporting documents

Document	Input	Created	Updated	Finalized (Archived)
Project Mandate	✓			
Project Scoping Document	✓			
Project Schedule	✓		✓	
Project log	✓		✓	
Project status report(s)		✓		

Hints & Tips

- Project reporting is done to inform the project sponsor's decision-making process. Project managers must think about the content of every status report - does it allow the project sponsor to make good, timely decisions?
- A project manager has a lot of things to keep on top of during the Implementation Phase - progress, risks, issues, changes, people manage-

ment - and things can quickly get out of hand if left unmanaged. Project management demands a consistent, disciplined approach.

- The project schedule is the baseline against which the performance of the project is measured. It is essential that it is current. Ensure that all changes to the project that are approved throughout its lifecycle are reflected by updating the project schedule.
- Visual management can be a great aid to team communication. Openly displaying current copies of key aspects of the plan - in particular the project schedule - allows the team to understand the priorities and interdependencies.
- Keep up-to-date with tracking project progress and maintaining the project logs. This will enable you to take corrective action as soon as issues arise and will allow you to make your status report accurate, up-to-date, and succinct. Good decisions rely on accurate, timely, appropriate information.

12.7 Completion

12.7.1 The Purpose of Completion

The completion phase confirms that the project outputs delivered during the implementation phase are complete and suitable for their intended use and that the organization is ready to accept and use these products or services to realize the intent. The project outputs are then handed over to the daily operations of the organization.

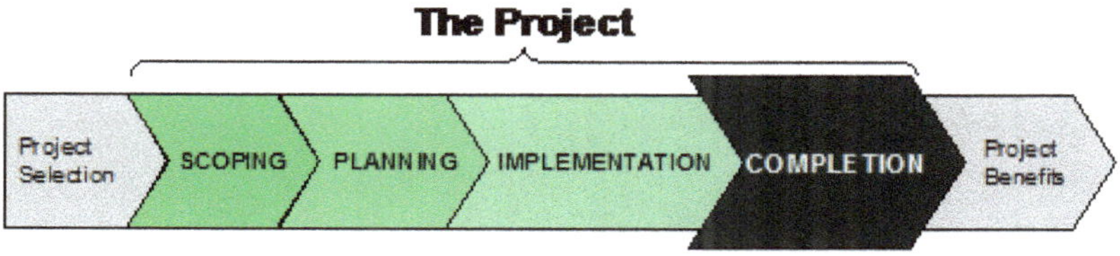

Figure 12.6. Completion - The final phase of the project lifecycle

There are two main objectives of the completion phase:

- Integrate the project products or services into the organization's operations, and
- Formally close the project and capture lessons about the management and delivery of the project.

12.7.2 Completion Activities

STEP 1. Transition project outputs to the organization

To ensure that the project outputs are used and provide the intended benefits to the organization, it is important to transition them properly to the broader organization. Handover of the project's products and services to the organization's day-to-day operations should be an activity within the project plan. It may be a straightforward handover of products (that are tested and ready for application) to an operational area or may involve a period of on-going support and/or maintenance while the change is being embedded.

Project management activities should continue throughout this transition period, including monitoring and addressing risks and issues and managing stakeholders. These activities are part of change management, which is discussed in detail in Chapter 15 of this book.

STEP 2. Prepare for project closure

Preparing for project closure involves finalizing the project documentation so that is ready for input to the closure report (Step 3).

The project manager should review the project schedule and project logs to confirm that:

- All project outputs have been produced and all tasks completed
- All risks have been dealt with or no longer exist
- All issues have been resolved or responsibility for any remaining issues has been formally accepted by someone within the organization's operations
- All quality checks were successfully completed
- All approved changes were implemented
- All lessons learnt throughout the project have been documented, and
- Appropriate stakeholders have been informed of imminent project closure.

Any outstanding activities within the logs need to be dealt with before the project can be closed.

STEP 3. Produce the project closure report

The project closure report provides a summary of the performance of the project and provides high-level lessons that could be applied in future projects. It also confirms that all project work has been completed and brings the project to a formal, controlled close.

Section D (project management supplement) provides a closure report template, which should capture:

- A short, sharp review of the project performance (in terms of time, cost, scope, quality, communications, management and team effectiveness)
- High-level lessons that can be applied to future projects
- Risk and issue management outcomes, and
- Ongoing recommendations for usage, maintenance, or review.

Ensure that the project closure report is consistent with the project plan and the final status report.

STEP 4. Obtain closure report approval

The project closure report should be presented to the project board by the project manager in person and must be authorized by the project sponsor, on behalf of the project board, before the project is considered formally closed.

Once the closure report has been authorized, all project documentation should be archived. The project manager should ensure that all project documentation is current and complete (including appropriate authorizations/approvals) before it is archived.

STEP 5. Disband remaining project team

Throughout the project lifecycle, the project team will vary in size and composition, according to the needs of the project. It is important that whenever people are released from the project, they are transitioned smoothly to their next role.

In disbanding the team and releasing them for other work, the project manager should ensure that an effort is made to celebrate the success of the project and acknowledge the contribution of people to that success.

Table 12.4. Completion phase supporting documents

Document	Input	Created	Updated	Finalized (Archived)
Project Mandate	✓			✓
Project Scoping Document	✓			✓
Project Schedule	✓		✓	✓
Project log	✓		✓	✓
Project status report(s)	✓			✓
Project closure log		✓		✓

Hints & Tips

- Project completion is not an afterthought - it needs to have been considered and planned at the outset, typically during the planning phase.
- Stakeholder engagement is every bit as important during the completion phase as it was in the preceding phases. Often, the stakeholders' last encounter with a project is the one they remember - make sure it is a good encounter.
- There is still considerable work to be done in the completion phase. However, for many on the project team it may feel like the "important" project work has already been done. Make sure motivation and enthusiasm is maintained within the team throughout this final phase. Projects that are not properly transitioned to the organization and formally closed often fail to deliver benefits to the organization due to poor uptake of the project outputs.

Chapter Highlights

- The project management methodology (PMM) is a simple, generic, project management methodology, based on recognized project management best- practices and standards.
- The project management methodology will enable a clear understanding of roles and responsibilities and a reduction in project issues through identification and management of risks.
- The structure of the eGovernment PMM follows a common, four-phase project lifecycle (scoping, planning, implementation, and completion).
- Every project is different and, as such, project managers should use the PMM as a guide and consider how each document and activity applies to their particular project.
- The project scoping document is the key document to commit resources to develop the project plan, which gives a clear understanding and direction to the project team about their task.
- Planning is the second phase of the project and develops a detailed roadmap for the project to be conducted, monitored, assessed and, if necessary, adjusted.
- Product-based planning starts with writing a project product description; that is, an overall description of what the project will deliver.
- Work breakdown structure (WBS) identifies all of the individual tasks that must be performed to produce the project outputs/deliverables.
- The project schedule forms the work plan against which the project manager can monitor and control progress on the project.
- The project logs are a key tool for keeping track of the project and their value to a project manager depends on their accuracy (including being up-to-date).
- The implementation phase is where the delivery work happens on the project - it is where the project outputs are created.
- The status report provides information that can alert the project board to emerging problems before they become major issues and is a key document in the control process for the project.
- The completion phase confirms that the project outputs delivered during the implementation phase are complete and suitable for their intended use and that the organization is ready to accept and use these products or services to realize the intent.
- Project management activities should continue throughout this transition period, including monitoring and addressing risks and issues and managing stakeholders.
- The project closure report provides a summary of the performance of the project and provides high-level lessons that could be applied in future projects.

Review Questions

1. What is a project scoping document? What are the essential elements of a project scoping document?
2. What is a project product description? Why it is important?
3. What is the best way to maintain a project schedule?
4. What is a work breakdown structure (WBS)? How does it help to better manage and forecast the project outcomes?
5. What is the purpose of a status report? How does it help to achieve success in the project?

Discussion Questions

1. Why is project management for ICT projects important? Is project management different for ICT projects compared with other projects (e.g., road building)? If so, how is it different?
2. What are the four main phases of the ICT project lifecycle? Is any phase more important than others? Is any phase more difficult than others?

Exercise

1. Find an example of a recent ICT project, possibly in your own organization. Compare what happened with the eGovernment PMM described in this chapter. Did the real- life case have similar phases to the eGovernment PMM?
2. Consider a case study provided by your instructor or obtained from a real-life case. Draw up a project schedule as specified in the eGovernment PMM.

Glossary

Benefit: The measurable improvement resulting from an outcome perceived as an advantage by one or more stakeholders.

Issue: A relevant event that has happened, was not planned, and requires management action. Project issues can be about anything to do with the project.

PMBOK: Project management body of knowledge - a project management methodology developed by the Project Management Institute in the USA.

PMM: Project management methodology - a standard process for managing projects.

PMO: Project management office - a shared competency designed to integrate project management practices within an organization. In essence, it is a centre of excellence that defines standards (such as processes, templates, and tools) and provides skills and training across a number of projects.

Program: A collection of interrelated projects - identified, planned, and managed in a co-ordinated way - which together achieves a set of objectives.

Project Board: A management group representing the stakeholders of the project (the organization, users, suppliers, etc); responsible for providing authorisation and guidance to the project.

Project Closure Report: provides a summary of the performance of the project and provides high-level lessons that could be applied in future projects.

Project Logs: a means of recording risks, issues, changes, quality, and lessons, and documenting and tracking their progress from conception to completion.

Project Manager: The individual who has responsibility and authority for the day- to-day management of the project to ensure its successful delivery.

Project Mandate: A short, written description of the project - why it is worthwhile and what it intends to achieve (also called a project brief or project charter).

The eGovernment Project Management Methodology: A brief description of the eGovernment project management methodology (PMM) and its usage.

Project Schedule: summarizes the tasks involved in completing a project, when they will be done, resources required to undertake them, and dependencies between tasks and the costs.

Project scoping document: A document that defines the justification for the project, the work to be done, the high level schedule, the key resource requirements, the budget requirements, key stakeholders, constraints, assumptions, and high level risks.

Project Sponsor: A member of the project board who is ultimately responsible for the project and ensuring it achieves its broader organizational objectives (also called the project executive).

Project Status Report: provides a snapshot of the current performance of the project.

Project Team: A group of people working together to successfully deliver a project. The project team reports to the project manager.

Project: A unique, finite body of work with a defined objective(s) and specific time, cost, and performance requirements.

Request for change: A proposal for a change to a baseline. It is a type of issue.

Risk: An uncertain event or set of events that, should it occur, will have an effect on the achievement of objectives.

Stakeholder: Any group or person that will either have an influence on, or will be impacted by, the project.

Supplement

Supplementary material for this chapter is contained at the end of the text:

A. Project scoping document [scoping]

B. Project schedule [planning]

C. Status report [implementation]

D. Project log - for tracking the project

E. Project closure report [completion]

F. Project manager's checklist

G. Project phase completion checklist.

References

Office of Government Commerce. (2009). Managing successful projects with PRINCE2. London: The Stationery Office.

Morris, P. W. G. (1994). The management of projects. London: Thomas Telford.

PMI Standards Committee (2004). A guide to the project management body of knowledge (PMBOK Guide). (3rd ed.). Newtown Square, PA: Project Management Institute (PMI).

Zimmerer, T. W., & Yasin, M. M. (1998). A leadership profile of American project managers. Project Management Journal, 29, 31-38.

John P. Kotter. (1996). Leading change. Boston, PA: Harvard Business School Press.

Further Resources for Reading

Project Management Institute http://www.pmi.org/

Project Management Case Studies http://ebookee.org/Project-Management-Case-Studies_539597.html

PART IV
MANAGING EGOVERNMENT

Part IV - Managing eGovernment

Part IV concerns the issues that must be addressed to successfully deliver eGovernment initiatives in the long term. Like all ICT project work, designing, building and implementing a new ICT system is usually considerably less than half the system's overall life and whole-of- life cost. The issues and costs of managing systems once they are in place, as well as their interaction with other systems, is a longer term on-going concern.

Part IV examines four related areas of IT management in government organisations. The areas are all at a 'higher' level; that is, they consider matters at an organisation-wide scale, rather than any single system or single service.

- **Chapter 13**, Performance Management, considers the ways of measuring whether individual systems and the whole array of systems in part III of this volume are performing to expectations. Performance management has two broad perspectives: measuring what is already happening so that assessments can be made about what is working and what needs improvement, and establishing the parameters to measure and manage the success of new projects.
- **Chapter 14**, IT Governance, Strategy and Planning, is at one management level higher than performance management. Governance is about ensuring that the right things are being done. Decisions about the right things to do are usually published as a strategy. From the strategy, business plans are created to define the work that must be done to realise the strategy.
- **Chapter 15**, People and Organisational Issues, looks at two aspects of 'the people side' of information technology. One side is the people who receive and operate new IT systems delivered as part of eGovernment initiatives. These people are typically public servants with skills and experience that are not directly related to ICT. Helping them to understand and adopt the changes that the new system represents is one key issue of people management in IT. The other key issue is the management of the IT staff in the organisation as they develop, deliver, and maintain the IT systems that make the organisation operate.
- **Chapter 16**, Political, Legal, Ethical and Environmental Issues, looks at the broadest issues surrounding eGovernment: the political environment, the legal and ethical issues in eGovernment development, and the impact on the environment that a move to increased use of information technology by government represents.

CHAPTER 13 Performance Management

Learning Objectives

After studying this chapter, you should be able to:

- Describe the different objectives of managing the performance of IT in organizations
- Identify several categories of performance indicators
- Identify several types of quantitative performance indicators
- Identify several types of qualitative performance indicators
- Describe the process of realising benefits from implementing IT in organizations
- Identify the steps involved in benefits realization management
- Recognise and interpret a benefits map
- Develop and manage a performance management strategy, and
- Recognise and complete a benefits register.

13.1 Performance Management

13.1.1 Why manage performance?

ICT is critical to most government operations. It is paid for by taxpayers, who demand appropriate expenditure. It is essential to manage the resource for best value for money. Performance management includes activities to ensure that goals are consistently being met in an effective and efficient manner. It relies on Performance Measurement, which will also be discussed in this chapter.

13.1.2 Value for money

The primary objective of performance management is different for each organization, but to most organizations, including government organizations, it will generally be to obtain value for money. Value comes from the comparison of inputs to outputs or outcomes; is the cost of attainment less than, or more than, the value of the benefits realised? Performance management seeks to ensure that the value of benefits realized exceeds the cost of investment; that is, to maximize the return on investment (ROI).

13.2 Measuring Performance

To completely manage the performance of the ICT in an organization, one must understand everything that is going on. It is rarely possible, however, to measure every aspect of the ICT investment or its return. Furthermore, attempting to measure everything would quickly become such a large activity that it would need measuring itself. So, performance management is based on selecting a range of indicators to reflect the performance overall.

There are two broad types of indicators:

- Those that are measured constantly (e.g., system up-time or website availability), and
- Those that are measured periodically (e.g., project completions or annual reports).

Critical success factors (CSFs)

Effective performance management of ICT involves monitoring things that have the most influence on success. Critical success factors (CSFs) are defined as those things that must be present for something to succeed. For example, the management commitment and end- user involvement for any ICT development initiative are CSFs for that initiative.

Key performance indicators (KPIs)

To ensure that CSFs are identified and managed, some measurement approaches for that CSF must be developed. Such measures are called key performance indicators (KPIs). An example of a KPI to support the CSF described above is the agency management's "informed" consent as demonstrated by a signed scope document for the initiative.

ICT performance management has to address both:

- Operational ICT - the mainstream day-to-day aspects of operating ICT environments, and
- ICT Projects - new initiatives that, if and when successful, will be absorbed into operational ICT (AGIMO 2006).

The indicators required for monitoring and assessing of ICT initiatives, and those required to monitor and assess operational ICT are similar but often have different data sources, timing and risk profiles (AGIMO 2006).

It is important to frame ICT KPIs in terms of the business effect of ICT. So, one would seek to measure, say, the availability of particular business services rather than simply the availability of a particular information system that may support those business services.

The trick of selecting KPIs

As mentioned earlier, there is a need to select the optimum number of appropriate KPIs to achieve the right coverage without overburdening the things being measured. The balance to draw is between the value in collecting the KPI (what can it tell you) and the cost or difficulty of measuring the KPI (what it takes to measure).

The optimum mix will vary for each project and over time for operational matters. This means that one must regularly review whether the KPIs being used are continuing to provide the value for which they were selected.

Quick Quiz

1. How do you define value for money? Why is it important for governments to achieve value for money?
2. Can you identify three critical success factors (CSFs) that might apply to any ICT project?
3. Can you identify any key performance indicators (KPIs) that might apply to both project work and operational ICT?

13.3 Performance Indicators

Performance indicators (PIs) are metrics or factors that tend to indicate the health, progress and/or success of a project, process or area of service delivery. They focus on resources and processes that lead to successful outcomes. They are usually easily described, focused, relevant, measurable, repeatable and consistent. All of these characteristics are necessary for performance indicators to function.

"Good" performance Indicators

Performance indicators can have different value. To facilitate performance management, good performance indicators have the following characteristics:

- They deliver stakeholder intelligence - insights on program uptake and understanding of program impacts and outcomes
- They identify, highlight and possibly prioritize corrective, preventative, and developmental action, and
- They enhance the value of programs by facilitating insight and optimization.

With these characteristics, PIs are integral to good ICT governance.

Styles of Performance Indicators

According to the guidance of the Australian Government, there are different styles of performance indicators (AGIMO 2006):

- **Leading** - if they are predictive of success or failure
- **Lagging** - if they reflect success or failure after the event, and
- **Coincident** - if they change at approximately the same time and in the same direction as a Project or ICT Operations as a whole.

All performance indicators are based on measurement. Those measurements might be quantitative (numbers) or qualitative (value statements). They may be precise and measurable with a high degree of "mathematical" accuracy (e.g., network traffic levels) or they may need to be based on expert or collective opinion (e.g., a customer satisfaction survey).

Types of Performance Indicators

AGIMO (2006) goes on to describe three main types of performance indicators:

- **Binary or Absolute** - these are in effect "yes" or "no" measures; indicators of whether a "desired state" is present or not; these indicators often need to be qualified by other less absolute measures.
- **Comparative** - these indicators take the situation as it is and 'measure' it against a relevant and anticipated state.
- **Trend-based** - require the collection and presentation of comparative information across a period of time, because individual instances of measurement may not provide any meaningful "performance" information, or observations of trends will make it possible to see where over- or under- performance are only temporary aberrations.

13.3.1 Categories of Performance Indicators

Performance indicators can be categorized by the broad domain of interest that they serve to measure. Categorizing performance indicators in this way is a convenience and will often simplify selection of appropriate PIs and the reporting of the meaning of their results. Table 13.1 illustrates the typical domain categories of performance indicators.

Table 13.1. Categories of performance indicators (Source: AGIMO 2006)

PI Category	Purpose
Investment	The investment category examines the returns relative to the outlays. The returns may be financial and/or economic and/or social. These indicators are of most interest to executive management in relation to "whole-of-enterprise" ICT and to sponsors in the case of ICT projects.
Financial	Financial performance indicators represent costs and revenues relative to an expected (e.g., budget or plan) or benchmarked position. While this category represents a key input to the Investment category, indicators in this category are important in their own right. This category is relevant to both ICT projects and ICT operations.
Human Resources	While there are many "human" stakeholders, these performance indicators relate primarily to ICT staff and contractors. The indicators are required to provide insights into factors such as: productivity, skill and qualification levels, retention, and attendance.
Service	The service category covers aspects of service, usually to both end users and personnel within the ICT function. These indicators seek to measure timeliness, adequacy and efficiency of service responses. Whereas these would generally be associated with ICT operations, there are instances that are highly relevant to ICT projects.
Procurement and contractual	These are intended to reflect the adequacy, efficiency, appropriateness, and financial outcomes of vendor-related tasks such as procurement and development, and management of contracts. These performance indicators are relevant to both ICT operations and ICT projects.
Development	Development performance indicators cover the full system development lifecycle. While these are most applicable to ICT projects they also apply to software maintenance and enhancement initiatives.
Training and support	The training category covers the completeness, timeliness, and effectiveness of training and support provided both to end users and to those in the ICT function. These are relevant to both ICT operations and ICT projects.
Operations	Operations performance indicators reflect the state of operations of infrastructure and systems. They are primarily concerned with performance and reliability.
Systems	These performance indicators relate to individual components of the ICT infrastructure and systems including hardware, software, and networks.

PI Category	Purpose
Risk management	The risk category is intended to measure the preparedness for and effectiveness of responses to the wide diversity of risks affecting ICT systems and the functions they support. These matters are important for both ICT projects and ICT operations although different indicators would apply to each.
Management and governance	Whereas the indicators for each of the above categories are in effect indirect "commentators" on the state of ICT Operations or ICT Projects management and governance, there are additional indicators that reveal the effectiveness, suitability and professionalism of agency approaches to these key disciplines.

13.3.2 Principles for Performance Indicators

Guidance for creating good performance indicators is encapsulated by AGIMO (2006) as principles that apply to the selection and implementation of performance indicators:

- Performance indicators must be able to lead to an action; they must be useful, not just 'interesting'
- Where "top-level" performance indicators are used, an effective "drill-down" capacity must be present to allow investigation of the drivers of changes in the top level indicator
- The collection, analysis and reporting must have integrity (this implies accuracy and completeness); a strategy to detect and remedy biases must be implemented
- The measurement and reporting cost of performance indicators should be determined; the cost of 'producing' performance measures should be orders of magnitude lower than the value of the benefits or the costs they are designed to reveal, and
- Measurement should ideally be embedded into the specific systems and process clusters, and the "administrative" systems and processes around these (e.g., human resources, financial accounting) as manual data collection can be tedious and costly, especially if collection must be repeated regularly.

For each performance indicator, it is important to determine whether to report routinely, or by exception.

It is critical to remember that performance indicators are only indicators. The problem resolution will require analysis of actual issues or data.

13.3.3 Collection of Performance Indicators

The collection of data with which to measure performance can take many forms. Table 13.2 outlines a variety of approaches available for performance indicators that are quantitative in nature—i.e. they measure some tangible thing—or qualitative in nature—i.e. they measure intangible values, such as people's views.

Table 13.2. Methods of collecting measures for different types of performance indicators (Source: Adapted from AGIMO 2006)

Quantitative	Qualitative
• Quantitative descriptive or inferential data analysis • Statistical analysis • Synthetics • Exceptions technique • Benchmarking against other similar organizations • Balanced scorecard method • Dashboard readout of business intelligence • Financial and economic analysis • Operations Research Techniques • Observation studies	• Qualitative data analysis • Surveys and/or questionaries of take-up, approval and acceptance • Telephone survey / interview • Face to face • Automated eSurvey by email • Community consultation • Diaries and activity logs • Audit using different strategies • Observation studies using check lists or other systemic forms • Behavioural analysis • Custom analysis using various methods • SWOT analysis • Case studies

Some examples of different types of performance indicators for an eGovernment initiative are suggested in Table 13.3. The table does not contain all indicators, or even the best ones, depending on the eGovernment initiative. The performance indicators shown are examples only.

Table 13.3. Examples of eGovernment performance indicators

Quantitative	Qualitative
• Number of times the eGovernment service is used per hour, day, or week • The proportion of all services delivered that are delivered through the online channel • The average time taken for a service to be delivered online • Decrease in services that include data in error •	• Citizen satisfaction with the new service, measured through an 'exit survey' attached to the service

Quick Quiz

1. What are the characteristics of "good" performance indicators?
2. Why are leading indicators so desirable? Why are they so hard to identify and measure?
3. What does it mean to "drill-down" on a "top-level" performance indicator?

13.3.4 Implementing Performance Indicators

We now turn our attention to implementing performance indicator measures. It is important to mention first for whom the indicators are collected.

Performance indicators apply to all levels of stakeholders in an organization. Which indicators to report to which stakeholders depends on:

- The stakeholder's responsibility for performance in the area being measured, and
- The stakeholder's responsibility for the business function affected by the ICT performance.

To ensure that the right stakeholder is getting the right performance indicators, important questions about the collection of data should be considered:

- Who is the custodian of the information?
- Who may have access to this information?
- How long is the information to be held for?
- What nature of "audit trails" are to be held?

Data Visualization Methods

Visualization relates to how the performance indicators are represented

Whereas a text representation is obvious, this is often not the clearest or most powerful way of showing one or a collection of performance indicators. Graphical approaches include (AGIMO 2006):

- **Dashboard** - This is an analogue of a vehicle dashboard or aircraft cockpit display (Figure 13.1). Techniques applied include digital, ribbon, and dial displays, moving bar graphs, and ticker tape analogies.
- **Traffic light** - The use of a 'green, amber, red' approach to performance indicators enables the reader to determine at a glance whether a situation is as expected (green), moving towards being below expectations (amber) or below expectations (red) (Figure 13.2).
- **Graphs** - These are particularly useful where the performance indicators are most informative when viewed as part of a trend or when compared with other linked or comparable factors (Figure 13.3).

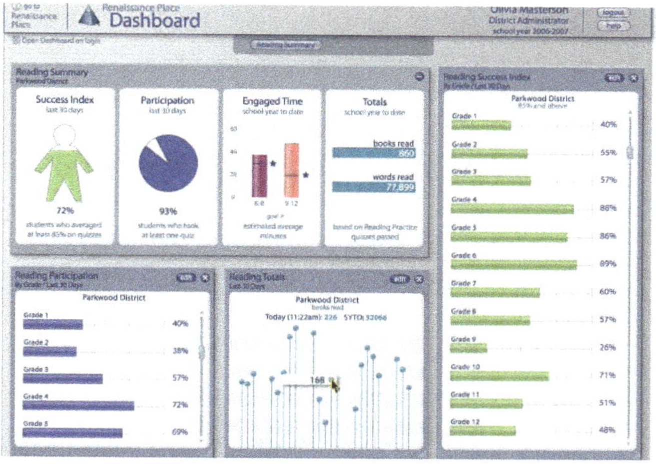

Figure 13.1 Illustrative example of a performance indicator dashboard

Month	Target	Actual
Jan-09	100	25
Feb-09	106	110
Mar-09	107	83
Apr-09	108	129
May-09	112	88
Jun-09	120	133
Jul-09	125	99
Aug-09	127	150
Sep-09	131	125
Oct-09	136	170
Nov-09	142	119
Dec-09	143	164

Figure 13.2. Example of traffic light indicators

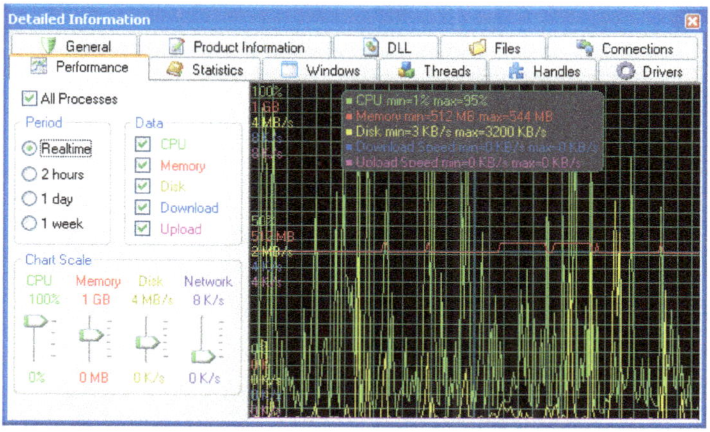

Figure 13.3. Illustrative example of a graphed performance indicator

13.3.5 Tips and Traps for Performance Indicators

The selection and use of performance indicators is as much an art as a science. The Australian Government offers the following tips and traps to consider when designing your own performance indicators (AGIMO 2006).

- Most performance indicators are intended to be indicative not conclusive.
- It is essential that indicators that are designed to compare the current "achievement" with some baseline or standard, that an "apples-with-apples" comparison is made.
- Some performance indicators may reflect a short-term anomaly that does not need corrective action.
- The potential for evaluation bias should be recognised and strategies put in place to manage this. Approaches to avoid evaluation bias include:
    - Ensuring an independent evaluation of performance indicators and the methods used to collect and report the data.
    - Ensuring the "fairness" of what is being evaluated; that is, across all the people involved in what is measured.
    - Having a balance sheet approach to performance measurement:
        - Allowing for an appropriate cluster of PIs, particularly where positive on one may balance negative on another, and
        - Look for ways of "totalling" across the cluster as a secondary test of reasonableness.
        - Using an independent external resource to conduct surveys.

13.4 Benefits Realization

Benefits realization management (BRM) monitors and guides actions taken to achieve outcomes. The steps in BRM are (NSW Audit Office 2004):

- Identifying potential benefits
- Planning and modelling those benefits
- Understanding baseline performance
- Estimating new performance
- Measuring performance
- Assigning responsibilities for review, and
- Tracking the achievement of benefits over business life cycle.

In an eGovernment project, benefits are identified and measured across the agency, or, if required, across government. Performance measures may be quantitative (e.g., the cost of a service) or qualitative (e.g., client satisfaction). Measures are documented in benefits registers.

Benefits realization acts to fight against project failure by addressing characteristics like:

- Lack of stakeholder commitment to benefits and their delivery
- Lack of focus on associated business change
- Benefits that are unrealistic

- Failure to identify the project's wider contribution
- Poor recording and tracking of achievements, and
- Absence of a clear link between the business case and ongoing improvement.

Successful BRM leads to:

- Strong governance for clear accountability
- A continuous improvement culture, and
- Investment in BRM processes, skills, and resources.

13.4.1 The Steps in Benefits Realization Management

Benefit realization management has a standard approach that will lead to an effective outcome. Like all such methods, it is a recommended outline that can be tailored to the specific needs of the organization and the project being managed. One excellent guide to implementing BRM is a better practice guide published by the Australian New South Wales Government Audit Office (NSW Audit Office 2004). The following list presents the major steps of that approach recommended by the NSW Audit Office.

Major steps in BRM

- Plan and develop the policy to implement BRM
    - Identify benefits
    - Align benefits with strategic plans and directions
    - Determine the project's contribution to business objectives
    - Set priorities, and
    - Identify beneficiaries and key stakeholders.
- Set up the governance structure
    - Determine ownership, accountability, responsibilities, roles, and functions of the process, and the benefits.
- Prepare a detailed plan.
    - Apply a methodology to identify benefits, map outcomes, develop indicators, acquire baselines, targets, and measures.

NB: this is discussed in more detail below.

- Develop measurement systems.
    - Set up data collection, monitoring, reporting and tracking mechanisms.

NB: this step is similar to performance measurement.

Do project that delivers benefits.

- Start measuring.
    - Collect data, produce and distribute reports.
- Evaluate and review measurements.
- Act on the results.

  - Use the results of the measurement to assist decision making and business improvement.
- Refine benefits and their measures.
  - Refine the measures and targets as required and capture new benefits.

Quick Quiz

1. Why is it important to explicitly identify and measure the benefits of a project?
2. For whom is benefits management most useful?
3. What are the commonalities between BRM and performance management?

13.4.2 Making Benefits Realization Work

Research conducted by the NSW Audit Office has identified **six critical success factors in BRM** (NSW Audit Office 2004):

1. Clear definition of roles, responsibilities, and accountabilities for all those involved in benefits realization.
2. Commitment to and availability of resources to develop and implement benefits realization.
3. Train participants in the process, including benefits identification, planning, analysis, and review techniques.
4. A practical methodology for benefits realization planning.
5. Systems and processes to measure, manage, and review and act on the benefits realization results.
6. Active change management.

This last success factor is the one most frequently missing in ICT projects that attempt to deliver organizational benefits. Key stakeholders in the organization can lose sight of the need to change the organization to exploit the new ICT systems to realize the benefit.

Roles and responsibility

Governance and accountability for benefits realization must be actively undertaken. Management and stakeholders must:

- Have a common understanding of the benefits realization process, and
- Determine how to govern.

Setting up a suitable benefits realization governance approach involves:

- Scoping accountabilities and responsibilities
- Assigning accountabilities, roles, responsibilities
- Determining the nature of participation, and
- Agreeing the management structure for BRM.

Commitment to resources

The resources to be applied to benefits realization planning and management must be clearly identified and a commitment made to fund BRM over the lifecycle of the program or project (NSW Audit Office 2004).

Train participants in BRM

BRM requires a rigorous methodology. Participants must be trained in that method for it to be effective. BRM is closely related to performance management and as such, the skills are transferable.

One key lesson is to not over-engineer the benefits to realise. Benefits must be understandable, recognizable and relevant for BRM to work.

Practical methodology

Benefits realization planning consists of several activities including:

- Identifying benefits
- Developing benefit maps (also known as results chains or logic models)
- Determining indicators, baselines, targets, assumptions, risks, constraints, and
- Developing ways to measure indicators (NSW Audit Office 2004).

Systems and processes for measurement

Just as in performance management, benefits realization must establish appropriate:

- Means of data collection
- Means of reporting
- Responsibility for execution, and
- Timing of measurement and reporting.

Once these decisions are made, further management is needed to determine:

- How the measures are recorded and reported, and
- How the results are used.

Active change management

BRM is an integral part of change management. An organization can only really expect to "realise benefits" from some identifiable change process. Remember that one measure of insanity is a belief that doing the same thing the same way will bring about a different result. Each change process should be able to identify the benefits that result from that process being successfully completed.

13.4.3 Benefits Realization Management Process

Step 1: Mapping the benefits

The benefits map (also known as a results chain or logic model, see Figure 13.4) provides a graphical representation of the activities, paths, assumptions, risks, and desired outcomes. It shows the chain of events connecting activities to outcomes and benefits, and the steps required towards their achievement (NSW Audit Office 2004).

Developing the benefits map will usually take a number of attempts until the benefits/outcomes are clearly and concisely described. Outcomes should be specific, measurable, achievable, and relevant and establish a time frame for achievement.

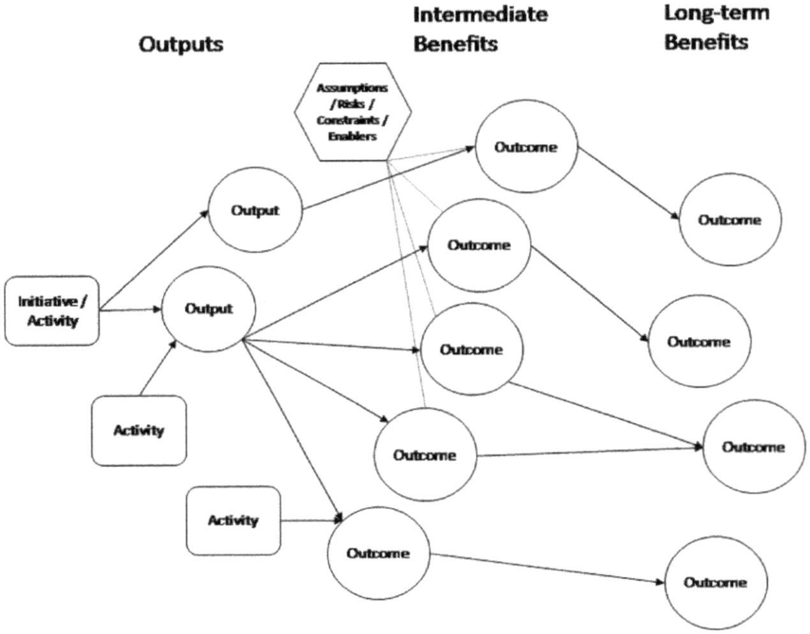

Figure 13.4. Example benefits map (Source: Adapted from NSW Audit Office 2004)

Step 2: Identifying performance indicators

The benefits management framework takes the outputs and benefits/ outcomes identified in the map and provides further information by adding indicators that will be used to show how the outputs and outcomes are being achieved (NSW Audit Office 2004). Figure 13.5 illustrates how to create a framework for indicators for a project.

Those affected by the outcomes are identified through the reach component of the framework.

Type of Project			Project Duration
Purpose			Project Budget
How?	What do we want?		Why?
Activities	Outputs	Intermediate Outcomes	Long-term Outcomes
• Xxxxx • Xxxxx • Xxxxx • Xxxxx	1.Xxxxx 2.Xxxxx 3.Xxxxx 4.Xxxxx	1.Xxxxx 2.Xxxxx	1.Xxxxx
		How do we know?	
Indicators	1.1 Xxxxx 1.2 Xxxxx 2.1 Xxxxx 3.1 Xxxxx	1.1 Xxxxx 2.1 Xxxxx 2.2 Xxxxx	1.1 Xxxxx
		What?	
Reach			
Assumptions & Risks			

Figure 13.5. Example benefits framework (Source: Adapted from NSW Audit Office 2004)

Step 3: Measuring the benefits

Each indicator identified for an output or outcome/benefit requires a measurement strategy (see Figure 13.6) which defines the:

- Type of data required (quantitative or qualitative data)
- Data source
- Methods/techniques for collection, reporting and distribution
- Timing and frequency of collection, and reporting
- Roles and responsibilities for collecting data
- Baseline and target measurements to establish the extent of change, and
- Strategies for evaluation and review (NSW Audit Office 2004)

Performance Management Strategy	Performance Indicators	Data Sources	Collection Methods	Frequency	Measurement Responsibility	Baseline	Target	Timeframe
Long-term Outcome/Benefits								
1.								
2.								
Intermediate Outcome/Benefits								
1.								
2.								
3.								
Outputs								
1.								
2.								
3.								
4.								

Figure 13.6. Example benefit measurement strategy template (Source: Adapted from NSW Audit Office 2004)

Measure the benefits, not project outputs

Importantly, it is the business outcomes that are measured, not the project outputs. Any measurement strategies must be determined in consultation with the relevant business unit.

The development of performance measures and their measurement strategy should be guided by what is practical, reasonable, and feasible to implement. The best management strategy will fail if it is impractical or resource intensive (NSW Audit Office 2004).

Benefits realization register

The benefits realization register is a reporting mechanism to track benefits achieved and monitor performance.

Benefit #/ Name/Desc	Realisation Ownership	Measure	Sources of Measurement	Measurement Ownership	Baseline	Target	Target Timeframe	Triggers/ Events	Assumptions/Risks /Comments	Actual		
										Date	Date	Date
Project nn												
Project nn												
Project nn												

Figure 13.7. An example benefits register (Source: Adapted from NSW Audit Office 2004)

Chapter Highlights

- This chapter covers two different perspectives of performance management. One involves setting expectations of success that are independent of the work going on in the organization but which measures the success of that work. The other is to design and manage work (usually project work) to specifically produce outputs that are seen as beneficial.

Performance Management	Benefits Realization
Set indicators	Predict benefits
Monitor them	Plan achievement
Reactively adjust performance	Manage realization

- Performance management is relevant for ongoing (legacy) work practices. It can allow you to refine the efficiency of existing practices. Performance management can be implemented immediately and to those elements of the business that you wish to improve.
- Benefits realization is relevant for new projects. It allows you to aim to be successful and deliberately manage towards that success. This technique is more useful when you wish to achieve new goals and not just improve current work.

Review Questions

1. Why would we attempt to specifically manage the performance of our ICT?
2. What is a "critical success factor"? Give three examples of critical success factors for ICT projects in government.
3. What is a "key performance indicator"? How does it differ from an ordinary performance indicator? What is their relationship to critical success factors?
4. What are the three main types of performance indicator? In what context would you use each?
5. The first principle of performance indicators is that "PIs must be able to lead to an action". What does this mean? How do you know you are meeting this principle?
6. Why do we attempt to specifically manage benefits in a project?
7. Why is the clear definition of roles, responsibility and accountability important for benefits realization management?
8. Why is change management important for benefits realization management?

Group Activity

Your group is tasked with developing the performance measurement system for the ICT that supports part of the business in a fictional organization.

This area of the organization provides customer service to customers who apply for permission to run small businesses in the area. The ICT provides support to this area of business in three ways:

1. The ICT infrastructure supports an electronic information resource to small business holders in the form of a web site that is available over the internet and on specially designated computers in the organization's 'shop fronts' (i.e., on kiosk computers).
2. The ICT infrastructure supports the operation of an application processing system into which applications from small business holders are entered, decisions are made by relevant authorities, and, if approved, a permit is printed on a special plastic card printing device. Each customer service person has their own PC for entering and managing applications but there is only one plastic card printing device per 'shop front' (office).
3. The ICT infrastructure supports the internal collaboration and communication within the organization's customer service staff, in the form of e-mail and file sharing servers.

The customer service part of the organization operates between 8:00am and 3:00pm each day serving customers and then between 3:00pm and 4:00pm each day the 'shop front' is closed and the customer service team complete other work.

In your team, identify at least six performance indicators for the ICT that supports this customer service part of the organization. Make sure that you only identify performance indicators for the ICT, not for the actual operations (e.g., application processing). As well as naming the indicators, describe how each would be measured, how frequently they would be monitored, and to whom they would be reported. Finally, for each indicator, briefly outline what would be done if the indicator showed that there was something wrong.

Further Resources

- The performance management element of free management library. Provides a good overview of performance management and a list of resources and related links. Retrieved from http://www.managementhelp.org/perf_mng/perf_mng.htm
- A brief introduction to key performance indicators by the RapidBI business improvement specialists. Retrieved from https://rapidbi.com/KeyPerformanceIndicatorsKPIs/#IntroductionToKPIs

- The IT metrics and productivity institute that focuses on metrics for software development, but provides insights into broader ICT performance indicators. Retrieved from http://www.itmpi.org/
- Introduction to benefits realisation management from a project management Training group in the UK. Includes some links to further references. Retrieved from http://www.pmis.co.uk/benefits_realisation.htm
- The UK Office for Government Commerce's (OGC's) Benefits Management guide. Excellent overview of Benefits management from a consistently high-quality source of government management advice. Retrieved from http://webarchive.nationalarchives.gov.uk/20110822131357/http://www.ogc.gov.uk/documents/ ManagingBenefitsV101.pdf

References

AGIMO. (2006). Performance indicator catalogue (Ver. 1.2). Australian Government. Retrieved from http://agimo.gov.au/files/2012/04/AGIMO_PerfIndicatorReport_v1_2.pdf

NSW Audit Office. (2004). Shared corporate services: realising the benefits. NSW Government. Retrieved from http://www.audit.nsw.gov.au/ArticleDocuments/197/Shared_Corporate_ Services.pdf.aspx?Embed=Y

CHAPTER 14
ICT Strategy, Planning and Governance

Learning Objectives

After studying this chapter, you will be able to:

- Recognize how ICT can play a strategic role in government organizations
- Demonstrate knowledge of ICT strategic alignment and how it can be achieved
- Demonstrate knowledge of strategic planning for ICT
- Explain what is meant by ICT governance and how to achieve sound governance
- Analyse approaches to ICT governance
- Describe a whole-of-government approach to ICT governance.
- Describe the principles underlying the ICT investment decision-making process, and
- Describe project management governance structures.

Forget about mere IT-business alignment

At many companies, the new name of the game is melding together technology and business operations, with CIOs getting a say in setting not only IT plans but business strategies as well.

For example, when Anthony Hill was asked to lead an eBusiness initiative at Golden Gate University several years ago, what the US-based school's academic leaders actually were asking him to do was transform its entire operating model along business-to-consumer lines, he said.

Instead of the IT department simply supporting business operations, "we now talk about how IT gets in front of the business" and drives it into new ways of doing things, said Hill, who is Golden Gate's CIO.

"IT should no longer be viewed as just an enabler of somebody else's business strategy," he added. "We need to change the dialogue to really eliminate the lines between IT and the business."

Peter Walton, CIO at Hess, has literally altered the dialogue at the US-based petroleum products company by banning IT staffers from referring to its business units as customers or even users. Instead, Walton said he wants his team to treat their fellow employees simply as "company-mates and peers". He even tries to avoid using the word "alignment" internally. It goes deeper than that now, he said: "We're trying to fuse with the business."

Source: Hoffman, T., & Stedman, C. (2008, March 14). CIOs: Forget IT-business alignment; it's all about fusion. Computerworld. Retrieved from http://www.computerworld.com/article/2537775/it-management/forget-it-business-alignment---it-s-all-about-fusion-now--cios-say.html /

It's gotten to the point where it's almost impossible to distinguish between the business strategy and the IT strategy of any successful enterprise. Approximately half of the investments that customers make in IT are now driven by line-of-business managers, not chief information officers.

Louis Gerstner, IBM chairman of the board, IBM Annual Report, 2001

Discussion

The need for a very close relationship (i.e., alignment) between planning for a business as a whole and planning for the ICT in the organization is stressed in the vignette above. Does there need to be such a close relationship in government organizations, as compared with commercial organizations? Why?

The answer for many government organizations is "yes". As discussed in the first chapter of this book, benefits from ICT may be assessed differently in government organizations because they aim to provide services for citizens rather than realizing profits. Yet, there is still the need to have a mission, goal, and objectives for each government organization, and to have mechanisms in place to ensure that ICT strategy is aligned with the overall mission and goals of the organization.

Do you agree? Please revisit this topic at the end of the chapter and after you have looked at case studies from public sector organizations.

14.1 ICT Management

At the beginning of this book, it was shown how ICT, if used effectively, can add considerable value to organizations of all types, including government organizations.

You have learned about the technical underpinnings of ICT, important ICT systems in common use and the methods that can be used to acquire and develop ICT systems in the chapters in Parts II and III of this book.

At this point we are returning to a higher-level view of ICT in the organization to look at how ICT is managed effectively to give value.

In order to understand how ICT is best managed, it is necessary to understand the concepts of:

- ICT strategic alignment
- ICT strategic planning, and
- ICT governance.

Each of these concepts will be covered in this chapter.

14.2 ICT Strategic Alignment

ICT strategic alignment refers to the degree to which the aims and activities of ICT units are aligned, or are in step with, organizational strategy. When there is a state of good alignment, the plans and projects of the ICT units are fully integrated with the plans and priorities of the organization overall.

Evidence suggests that businesses cannot be competitive if their business and ICT system are not aligned, and ICT managers and chief information officers (CIOs) continue to quote ICT/Business Alignment as one of their key concerns.

Table 14.1 shows the 2011 results of a survey performed each year by the Society for Information Management to gather information about ICT priorities from ICT leaders around the globe. ICT and business alignment is the most pressing issue for ICT managers in this survey and has been on the list of key issues for 30 years (Luftman & Ben-Zvi, 2010).

Luftman and Ben-Zvi (2010) believe that ICT and business alignment continues to be a problem because:

- Management looks for a single option (a "silver bullet") to facilitate alignment, whereas there is a need to address many aspects of alignment: partnership, communications, governance, ICT metrics, technology and human resources
- It is not just how ICT is aligned with the organization, it is how ICT and the organization are aligned with each other
- Organizational management needs to advance past a focus that is just on ICT infrastructures, and
- ICT leaders do not send clear messages, using confusing "buzz words" to refer to the alignment need, such as linkage, fusion, integration and fit.

In order to facilitate alignment, the following eight dimensions of alignment should be addressed (Scott, 2005, pp. 916-920):

1. Shared understanding by ICT and senior executive of planning processes. ICT planners need to understand the organization's planning and processes, just as the organizational planners need to understand ICT planning and processes.
2. CIO a member of the senior executive team. Communication and knowledge sharing are enhanced when the CIO is a member of senior management and there is public recognition of the importance of ICT and the need for ICT and the organization to work together.
3. Shared culture and good communications. There should be a collective understanding and commitment to working towards organizational goals and working in the "company way". Communication is vital, for instance in regular meetings across the organization. Communication may be improved by structural changes such as embedding some ICT staff in business units.
4. Deep commitment to ICT planning by senior management. The organization's senior management should be aware of how ICT can assist the organization to reach its goals. Having a steering committee with senior executive members for projects, or a powerful project sponsor who champions projects, is useful.
5. Shared plan goals. An explicit effort should be made to link the ICT and organizational plans. The ICT plans should be consistent with the goals of the organizational plan.

6. Deep end-user involvement. Linkages should be established between end users and IT analysts and planners so that vital information about systems to be developed is shared. These linkages could be via service-level agreements, or by joint leadership of development projects, with both a business and an ICT sponsor for projects.
7. Jointarchitecture/portfolioselection.Planningtheoverallarchitecture for ICT is important as it sets directions for ICT infrastructure into the mid and distant future. Senior management must understand this, and although enterprise architecture planning is complex, they should engage in the architectural planning.
8. Identity of plan factors. There should be a direct linkage between the organization and ICT plans at the operational level, for instance in terms of budget cycles, review terms, and project justification techniques.

Table 14.1. Five top issues for ICT management 2011 (Luftman & Ben-Zvi, 2011)

Rank	Issue
1	ICT and business alignment
2	Business agility and speed to market
3	Business process re-engineering
4	Business productivity and cost reduction
5	ICT strategic planning

14.2.1 Organizational Strategy

The discussion of alignment between the organization and the ICT units stresses the importance of strategic planning at both the organizational level and for ICT units. What is a strategy and why is strategic planning important?

Strategy definition

A strategy is a collection of statements that express or propose a means through which an organization can fulfill its primary purpose or mission (Frenzel & Frenzel, 2004, p. 65).

Setting a strategy for an organization is important to ensure there is, throughout the organization:

- A focus on the organizational mission
- Consistent direction within the organization's divisions
- Reduced uncertainty in decision making, and
- Help in providing definition and meaning to the organization.

In today's world, effective organizational management means that the importance of ICT is recognized at the top levels of the organization, and that strategy setting for ICT is integrated with strategy setting for the whole organization.

14.2.2 Strategy Development

Developing a strategic plan requires a thorough understanding of the current environment of the organization, both internal and external. Both opportunities and risks need to be identified.

Types of strategic planning

Organizational approaches to strategic planning vary widely and it is hard to find a "best-practice" approach. The planning approaches can differ in terms of being "planned" versus "seat-of-the-pants" (no planning), formal versus informal, incremental versus transformational, static versus dynamic, and so on (Scott, 2005).

SWOT analysis

A well-known example of a "planned" approach that can be used is a SWOT analysis (also covered in Chapter 10). The organization first identifies the objectives of the organization and then for each objective examines:

- Strengths: features of the organization that are helpful in achieving the objective
- Weaknesses: features of the organization that are harmful to achieving the objective
- Opportunities: external conditions that could assist in achieving the objective, and
- Threats: external conditions that could hinder the organization's performance.

The SWOT analysis can help in the creative generation of strategies to achieve the objective or, in contrast, it could show that with some objectives the threats are too large and the objective should be abandoned or amended. With ICT, because of the rate of change, strategic planning needs to be carried out on an ongoing basis, with possible revision of strategies as conditions change.

Further, strategies set directions, but for strategies to work, they need to be turned into detailed plans, which have enough information for them to be acted upon. As an example, the Australian Bureau of Statistics Corporate Plan contains a comprehensive strategy document. Brief excerpts from the ABS show the different types of statements at different levels (Exhibit 14.1.).

Exhibit 14.1. ABS Strategy document excerpts

Mission statement	We assist and encourage informed decision making, research and discussion within governments and the community, by leading a high-quality, objective and responsive national statistical service.
Objective (1)	An expanded and improved national statistical service.
Strategy for objective (1) (in part)	ABS will develop and communicate a shared understanding of Australia's statistical service and lead the implementation of this vision. To achieve this we will:
	• Work in partnership with other organizations to develop an agreement on how the national statistical system should operate, and • Build support within government for a national statistical policy and lead the policy's development and implementation.
Measures of outcome	We will be successful when:
	• A national statistical policy exists that is adopted across the national statistical system.

Source: ABS. (2008). Retrieved from http://www.abs.gov.au/websitedbs/d3310114.nsf/Home/About+Us?OpenDocument (accessed 2008)

14.3 ICT Governance

In addition to strategy setting and planning, organizations need to ensure they have good ICT governance. A useful **definition of ICT governance** is adapted from Standards Australia (2005).

> *ICT Governance is the system for the direction and control of the current and future use of ICT. It includes the evaluation and direction of the plans for the use of ICT so as to support the organization. The plans must be monitored to ensure their achievement. ICT governance includes the policies and strategy for the use of ICT in an organization.*

ICT governance is the responsibility of top-level senior management.

14.3.1 Governance principles

Standards Australia (2005) offers principles for achieving sound ICT governance:

1. Establish responsibilities for ICT that are clearly understood.

   Individuals and groups within the organization should understand and accept their responsibilities for ICT.

2. Plan ICT so it supports the needs of the organization as well as possible.

   ICT plans should fit the current and continuing needs of the organization and the ICT plans should support the corporate plans.

3. Acquire ICT by valid processes and methods.

   ICT acquisitions should be made for approved reasons in an authorized manner and on the basis of suitable and continuing analysis, and there should be appropriate balance between costs, long-term and short-term benefits and risks.

4. Ensure ICT has good performance whenever required.

   ICT should be fit for its purpose in supporting the organization, should be responsive to changing business requirements, and should provide support to the business at all times.

5. Ensure ICT conforms with applicable rules and regulations.

   ICT should conform to applicable regulations and policies, both internal and external.

6. Ensure ICT is used so that human factors are respected.

   ICT should meet the current and evolving needs of all people involved.

Figure 14.1 illustrates this model of ICT governance.

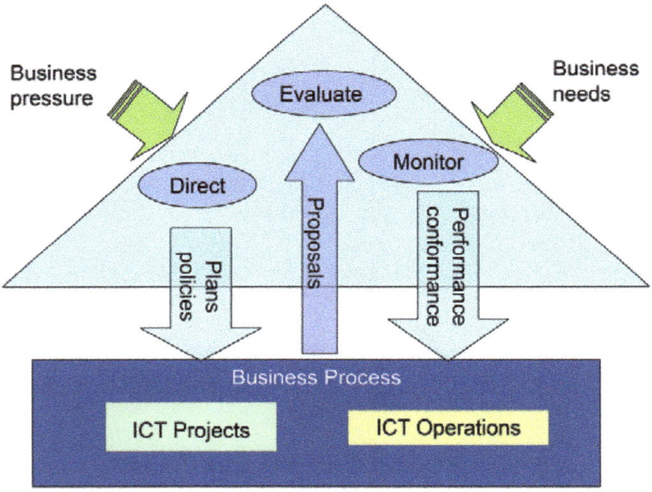

Figure 14.1. Model for ICT governance (adapted from Standards Australia, 2005, p. 9)

14.3.2 A Whole-of-Government Approach

For a large organization, or a government that has many different departments that all deal with ICT, it can be advantageous to consider if some degree of standardization in governing and using ICT is helpful. Having a coordinated whole-of-government approach can assist with transfer of skills across departments, greater purchasing power when acquiring ICT resources, standardization that allows information to be exchanged more easily across organizations, and in reducing duplication where several departments keep the same information or carry out the same functions.

An example is provided in the Australian Government, which has a central coordinating body to achieve a whole-of-government approach to ICT. This body is the Australian Government Information Management Office (AGIMO), now in the Ministry of Finance and Deregulation (AGIMO, 2013). Material from this agency has been used in preparing this book. In a sense, AGIMO helps to provides ICT governance for the government as a whole.

The principles which AGIMO follows are (AGIMO, 2006):

- That there is central oversighting of funding
- Departments (agencies) must have good governance in place
- Departments must justify investments through cost/benefit analysis
- Departments must measure outcomes
- AGIMO helps departments achieve re-use and interoperability standards
- AGIMO helps departments with education, tools and training, and
- AGIMO will help to achieve its roles by providing standards, handbooks, best-practice guides, and so on for government departments and others.

Note that in Australia the placement of the central coordinating body and its manner of operation has changed over time. As in many organizations, there are arguments for and against centralization versus decentralization of decision making in general, and with respect to ICT governance in particular. It is expected that governments in each country would consider their own context carefully when considering any central coordination of ICT.

Apart from AGIMO, another body that provides useful guidance at the whole-of-government level is the Australian National Audit Office (http://www.anao.gov.au/). For example, it publishes guides for developing and managing contracts and templates for contract management.

14.4 ICT Investment Principles

The principles underlying ICT investment should be understood as part of overall good governance of the organization.

The need for responsible decision making, oversight and management of ICT investments is widely accepted as a best-practice approach. The other reason ICT investments need to be carefully planned and managed is that failure when implementing ICT often has serious consequences for all parties that are involved. Because government organizations are accountable for their actions it is important that decisions on investing in ICT solutions are based on proven, reliable and repeatable processes.

The Australian Government Information Management Office (AGIMO) has developed a set of eGovernment ICT investment principles and these have been used as the basis for the eGovernment ICT investment principles (see Table 14.2).

Table 14.2. The eGovernment ICT investment principles

Principle 1	Government organizations should be provided with sufficient information to enable appropriate assessment of the allocation of funds for ICT-enabled business-change programs and projects.
Principle 2	Government organizations should be responsible for the effective, efficient and ethical use of resources.
Principle 3	Investments in new business capability involving ICT should be justified by and measured against costs and benefits.
Principle 4	Government organizations should be responsible for measuring the outcomes achieved by ICT and the return on the investment in ICT.

Source: http://agimo.gov.au/files/2012/04/ICT_INVESTMENT_ PRINCIPLES.pdf

14.4.1 Project Governance

Projects are the means by which investments in ICT are realized. As such the management of projects is a further important aspect of ICT governance. Projects do not exist in isolation. All projects must be delivered in the context of the organization in which they exist. Figure 14.2 shows a typical governance context and management roles for a project. These roles are described below:

- *Executive management*: the organization's top-level management; responsible for setting strategic objectives and determining the direction for the organization. As strategic objectives often require organizational change that cannot be achieved through normal business operations, projects (or groups of projects) are often developed for this purpose.
- *Project program management*: high-level management; responsible for a program of interrelated projects. Within an organization, this role may typically be fulfilled by senior management (such as business unit management or functional management) or a dedicated program management office.
- *Project board*: a management group representing the stakeholders of the project (the organization, users, suppliers, etc.); responsible for providing authorization and guidance to the project. The project board is accountable to executive management for the success of the project. It is brought together specifically to provide oversight of the project management. One member of the project board, the project sponsor (sometimes called the project executive), is ultimately responsible for the project and ensuring it achieves its broader organizational objectives.
- *Project management*: the project manager (and their project management team); responsible for day-to-day management of the project to ensure its successful delivery.

- *Project Delivery*: the team members responsible for performing the actual project work.

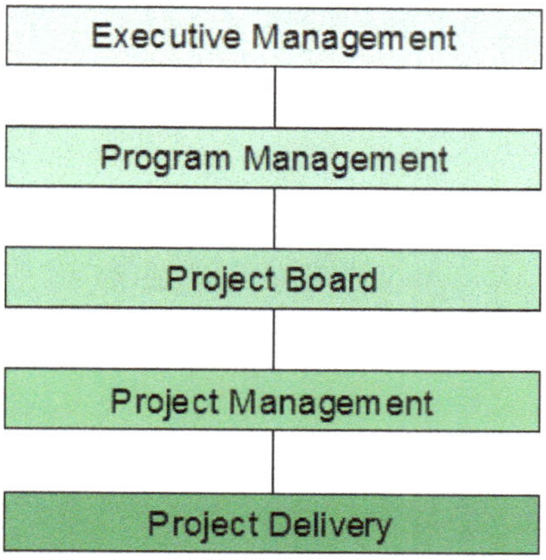

Figure 14.2. Typical project governance structure

The relationship between the project management and the project board is central to effective governance. Through the work of the project manager and the project team, the project sponsor can achieve their responsibility of ensuring that the project provides the intended benefits to the organization. Expectations of the project sponsor and the project manager should be clarified in their first meeting.

General responsibilities of the project board include:

- Appointment of the project manager
- Authorization of the project (objectives, scope, schedule, budget and quality)
- Review and approval of project documentation (including status reports)
- Authorisation of stages within the project
- Addressing high-level project risks and issues
- Reporting to program management and the broader organisation
- Provision of guidance and direction of the project
- Provision of advice to the project manager
- Authorising any changes to the project, and
- Approval of project completion.

Chapter Highlights

- To get the full benefit from ICT, organizational strategies and plans, and ICT strategies and plans, need to be integrated; that is, in a state of alignment.
- The achievement of alignment has a number of dimensions, such as shared understanding by ICT and organizational managers of the importance of ICT to the organization.
- There are a number of approaches to the development of strategies for the organization and ICT, including SWOT analysis.
- ICT governance is the system by which ICT use and development in the organization is directed and controlled.
- Sound ICT governance means adherence to principles such as the establishment of clearly understood responsibilities for ICT.
- A whole-of-government approach to ICT governance can be adopted.
- A sound approach to ICT investments is part of good ICT governance.
- Project governance and project program management are also important aspects of ICT governance.

Review Questions

1. Define the following terms: ICT alignment, organizational strategy, ICT governance, project program management.
2. How can ICT alignment be facilitated? Suggest eight dimensions of the facilitation of ICT alignment.
3. Describe the SWOT analysis approach to strategic planning.
4. List five principles of sound ICT governance.
5. List four principles for sound ICT investments.
6. Describe management structures that can be adopted to achieve good project governance.

Discussion Questions

Consider the four high-level components of the ABS Governance Framework in the appendix to this chapter:

1. Strategic management forum
2. Information resources management committee
3. Investment review board, and
4. Technical services division executive.

Does your organization have something similar? If not, would something similar work for you?

Appendix 14A

ABS Case Study of Good Governance

A case study of good governance is provided to illustrate some of the mechanisms that can be used to achieve good ICT governance (case study adapted from Gregor, Hart, & Martin, 2007). The Australian Bureau of Statistics (ABS) is used as it is respected within government as a best-practice organization and has received international recognition as a world leader in statistics delivery. This government department has existed since 1905 and collects, processes and disseminates accurate and timely economic and community information (e.g., census data). It has been given a high rating for ICT use by the Gartner Group.

Features of the governance arrangement in the ABS include:

- A formal IT Governance Framework (see Figure 14A.1)
- Alignment of ICT with business needs, through:
    - executives interested in ICT
    - establishment of a learning environment with a culture of continuous improvement
    - collaboration among stakeholders in developing business and ICT plans
    - good communication of ICT plans to staff, and
    - feedback on ICT investments through advisory groups and external committees
- A well-developed enterprise architecture, a framework that relates and documents all components of ICT in the organization, including mission, business processes, ICT operation, human processes, lifecycle phases, technologies, development methodologies.

NOTE: that there are four important bodies at four different levels for managing and coordinating in the ABS Governance Framework. These are:

- Strategic Management Forum:
    - A peak decision-making body for the whole of the ABS (chief executive officer- level) provides the IRMC chairman at the next level down.
- Information Resources Management Committee (IRMC):
    - Meets twice a year. Ensures ICT resources are managed to achieve best corporate outcomes.
    - Reviews ICT strategies, oversees resource usage, and agrees on the business cases for large investments.
- Investment Review Board:
    - Meets as the governance board requires for Technical Services Division projects to ensure value for money and to approve business cases for minor investments
- Technical Services Division Executive:

- Consists of the chief information officer, chief technical officer and three IT workshop or branch heads. It makes tactical IT decisions and implements technology directives.

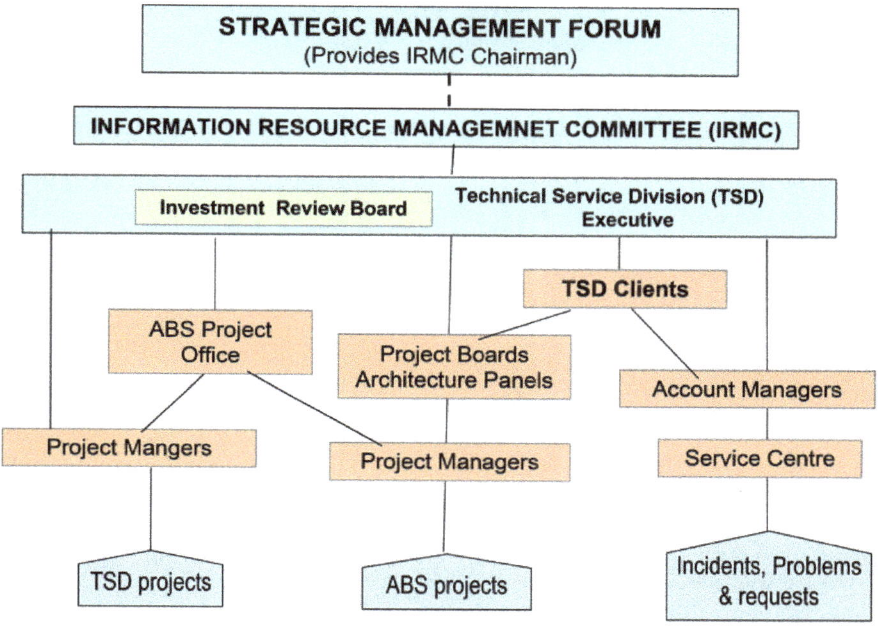

Figure 14A.1. The governance framework in the Australian Bureau of Statistics (adapted from Gregor, Hart and Martin 2007)

References

AGIMO. (2006). ICT Investment Framework. Retrieved from http://www.finance.gov.au/policy-guides-procurement/ict-investment-framework/

AGIMO. (2013). About the CIO and CTO/Procurement Coordinator. http://www.finance.gov.au/archive/about/

Avison, D., Gregor, S., & Wilson, D. (2006). Managerial IT unconsciousness. Communications of the ACM, 49(7), 88-93.

Avison, D., Jones, J., Powell, P., & Wilson, D. (2004). Using and validating the strategic alignment model. Journal of Strategic Information Systems, 13, 223-246.

Gregor. S., Hart, D., & Martin, N. (2007) Enterprise architectures: Enablers of business strategy and IS/ IT alignment in government. Information Technology & People, 20(2), 96-120.

Frenzel, C., & Frenzel, J. (2004). Management of information technology. Boston, MA: Thomson Course Technology.

Hoffman, T., & Stedman, C. (2008, March 14). CIOs: Forget IT-business alignment; it's all about fusion. Computerworld.

Luftman, J., & Ben-Zvi, T. (2010). Key issues for IT executives 2010: Judicious IT investments continue post-recession. MISQ Executive, 9(4), 263-273.

Luftman, J., & Ben-Zvi, T. (2011). Key issues for IT executives 2011: Cautious optimism in uncertain economic times. MIS Quarterly Executive, 10(4), 203-212.

Scott, G. M. (2005). Still not solved: The persistent problem of IT strategic planning. Communications of the AIS, 16(47).

Standards Australia. (2005). AS 8015-2005 corporate governance of information and communication technology. Sydney: Standards Australia.

CHAPTER 15 People and Organizational Issues

Learning Objectives

After studying this chapter, you will be able to:

- Discuss potential problems with ICT-enabled change
- Discuss change management and associated issues, which includes overcoming user resistance, fear of job losses, and so on.
- Describe the nature and structure of the ICT department
- Discuss issues associated with staffing ICT functions
- Discuss the role of the ICT Manager (Chief Information Officer)
- Explain how ICT skills can be developed and sourced
- Explain the concept of frameworks for ICT skills classification, and
- Discuss the concepts of ICT Service management and ITIL.

Why man behind the machine matters

(Photo credit: Rafiqul Islam)

While eGovernment systems have huge potential, they can significantly impact an organization's existing corporate culture, which encompasses the personal values, skills, and habits of the employees, as well as the organization's work patterns. Anxiety about the changes that a new system will bring to an organization can severely affect the system's expected outcomes. Adapting to new systems in an organization's culture is important because no system can function smoothly without the cooperation and support of the employees.

Change is often hard to accept, and people take time to become accustomed to new changes. On the other hand, implementers commonly feel that the major task is over once a new system is installed successfully. A project's success is commonly viewed in terms of whether it delivers on time and on budget. However, in reality, the ultimate success largely depends on how effectively the new system is adopted and accepted in the organization.

In modern organizations, change management itself has become an important stage of the implementation process. Recognizing this reality, organizations today often form a separate change management team that is comprised of people with special skills and which is led by a change manager. When the project manager delivers the project, the change manager takes over to actually realize the outcome and to merge the new system with the organization's corporate culture, which can be a challenging task. In fact, the change management process can often usefully begin even before a system becomes operational.

The evolution of a separate professional group, the Change Management Institute (CMI) (similar to the Project management Institute (PMI)) emphasizes the increasing importance of change management professionals in today's world.

Change management not only includes training about new systems and practices, but also shows employees how to adjust to new systems instead of fearing change. It involves cultural adaptation to facilitate the introduction of the new system into existing practices and to deal with resistance from employees.

> *"What is the cost to an organization of a system that is forced upon people, and with which they feel little ownership? They will either sink it, or ensure it never reaches its potential. Either way, the organization will never get the return on investment it imagined" (Turbit, 2005, p. 3)*

15.1 Resistance to Change

The introduction of new ICT systems is a major undertaking and requires careful attention to people factors as well as to technology.

People can resist change for many reasons. The most common reasons are:

- Resistance to change in general - This is a universal psychological phenomenon - people attempts to resist any new changes merely because they prefer the familiar.
- Fear of the unknown - There can be different fears for different people. Some may fear technology.
- Fear of losing their job - New automated systems may make some jobs redundant, may cause employees to be assigned new roles or may mean transfers throughout a company.
- Perceptions of loss of power and changes in employee relationships - EGovernment systems will probably change the way many employees interact with one another.
- A switch in focus - eGovernment systems transform the focus from a task-oriented approach to a process-oriented one, which may concern employees.
- Uncertainty about personal capacity to learn new things - Learning and developing new skills means burden in terms of cost, effort, and time.

15.2 Change Management

We often fail to appreciate that change is not a single event, but rather a process, managed with due consideration to the fact that employees are people, not machines. Thus, people should be the main focus for any successful business change. Understanding the people in organizations - their motivations, leadership skills, and past performance - and the current company culture is essential to recognize, understand, and integrate the vision and implementation of a new system. The first step towards any successful transformation effort is to convey the necessity for change to people such as the stakeholders who are likely to be affected by change (Dooley & Johnson, 2001). The system's success also depends on how thoroughly management conveys the new cultural messages to the organization (Campbell & Kleiner, 1997). These messages provide people in the organization with guidelines to predict the outcome of acceptable behaviour patterns and prepare them to adapt to changing circumstances.

15.2.1 Principles of Change Management

Many change management models in use today are developed through trial and error and are based on experiences of experts in the field of change management. In some cases, these experts have created a standard process based on their consultancy experiences and models.

There is no simple recipe for change management, and it is not a matter of simply following steps because each organization's requirements are not the same. The right approach will depend on the unique characteristics of the change and the attributes of the impacted organization. Research with hundreds of project teams has shown that a one-size-fits-all approach is not appropriate.

However, understanding the psychology of change and the key guiding principles helps adjust your own approach according to the size and nature of the change. Booz Allen Hamilton, a global strategy and technology consulting company, suggests ten principles for change management (Jones, Aguirre, & Calderone, 2004):

1. *Address the "human side" systematically*. A formal plan for managing change should be developed early with engagement from all key stakeholders. This change management plan must be fully integrated with the whole change process.
2. *Start at the top*. The top management leadership team must fully and publicly support the change and must be involved in it. Lack of strong executive support is a good predictor for failure. Thus, it is important to coach sponsors and managers about the critical nature of their engagement in different stages of the project and to provide them with the guidelines and tools to be successful.
3. *Involve every layer*. The change management plan must identify key individuals throughout the organization who can be trained to act as champions and supporters of the change at each layer of the organization.
4. *Make the formal case*. Writing a document with the formal case for change provides a basis for communication and alignment around the change. This document can show the convincing need for change, the vision for the future, and the road map to guide change behavior.
5. *Create ownership*. Change is more successful when those involved feel a sense of ownership of the change. Ownership can be promoted by involving people in identifying problems and suggesting solutions, and by incentives and rewards. The rewards can be intrinsic (recognition) or extrinsic (monetary) at both the organizational and individual level. It is important to instill values of empowerment and ownership of day-to-day work among employees.
6. *Communicate the message*. Core messages about the change must be communicated and reinforced regularly. Managers must also listen to employees to understand how their messages are being received. The communications can come from all levels, involve many communication channels, and may even involve "over-kill" with the same message delivered in different ways.

7. *Assess the cultural landscape.* The culture of the organization with respect to change needs to be understood and assessed early on and thoroughly. There is a need to assess readiness to change and to identify potential conflicts and sources of resistance.
8. *Address culture explicitly.* When the culture is understood, it can be confronted explicitly as part of the change program.
9. *Prepare for the unexpected.* No change program will go completely according to plan and there is a need to continually monitor the change and take action if needed to address problems.
10. *Speak to the individual.* Individuals and their personal fears, feelings, and wants must be central in the change process. Management should be honest about what the change means for individuals. Supporters of change can be visibly rewarded and those blocking change may need remedial action of some type. For employees whose roles change, it can be helpful to remind them that this is a chance to add new skills to an already impressive career, and that the change can help move the organization and the individual in a forward direction.

15.2.2 Change Manager

A change manager must be prepared for the worst and for negative reactions from users about new processes. Their role is to prepare employees and executives for the changes that come with the new system. These changes are often not easy to tackle, but making sure employees are comfortable with the new system is a worthwhile investment of time and money. A well-crafted change management system can smoothly steer changes over a period of time and can tackle the shift in people's expectations.

As a manager, it is important to build personal relationships with employees so that they feel comfortable. It is important to listen to employees' concerns. If a manager is too busy, he can assign the responsibility to another responsible individual or can set up a team or system to handle questions and feedback, which will allow employees to express their opinions. To be an efficient change manager it is important to understand people, accept their diversity and choices and understand the existing culture of the organizations.

Change Management Toolkit: A comprehensive change management process, including templates, worksheets, assessments, checklists and guidelines. A valuable resource for change management team members and consultants.

Retrieved from http://www.change-management.com/change-management-toolkit.htm

Change Management Guide for Managers and Supervisors: A guide specifically designed for managers and supervisors dealing with change - complete with team and individual coaching activities, best practices findings and frequently asked questions.

Retrieved from http://www.change-management.com/managers-guide.htm

Group Exercise

Consider the10 principles for managing organizational change in the Booz Allen Hamilton report (Jones et al., 2004).

1. How well do you think these steps address resistance to change with ICT? How will these steps address the factors leading to resistance to change identified above, which includes the fear of job losses?
2. Think of a change process that you have been involved in. Did it work well? Was a lack of success due to some of the 10 principles being missed?

15.3 The ICT Department

While ICT is an integral part of employees' activities throughout an organization, a dedicated ICT department is often necessary to manage and operate the organization's central ICT systems and assets. Many medium to large organizations have an ICT department that provides specialized expertise, develops new applications, and supports the end-users' ICT needs.

Previous chapters deal with several functions of the ICT department, which includes the business case chapter, the governance chapter, and the project management chapter.

The ICT department is part of ICT governance for the overall organization, and it typically maintains the project portfolio for all ICT projects across the organization.

Case Study: Ratio of IT Support Staff to Employees Falls Short of Ideal

Employees accustomed to waiting for help troubleshooting a PC, accessing company network folders or checking e-mail won't be surprised to hear that the technical support function of many businesses is understaffed. In a new survey, chief information officers (CIOs) polled said their companies' technical support teams are, on average, 40% smaller than they optimally should be.

The national poll includes interviews with more than 1,400 CIOs from a stratified random sample of U.S. companies with 100 or more employees. It was conducted by an independent research firm and developed by Robert Half Technology, a leading provider of information technology professionals on a project and full-time basis.

CIOs were asked, "What is the ratio of internal end-users to technical support employees at your company?" The mean response was 136:1.

CIOs also were asked, "What would be the ideal ratio of internal end-users to technical support employees at your company?" The mean response was 82:1.

"Many managers, particularly those with organizations experiencing growth, are realizing their technical support or help desk teams can no longer keep up with increasing end-user needs," said Katherine Spencer Lee, executive director of Robert Half Technology. "An understaffed technical support function can lead to a frustrated and less productive workforce, which ultimately affects the company's bottom line."

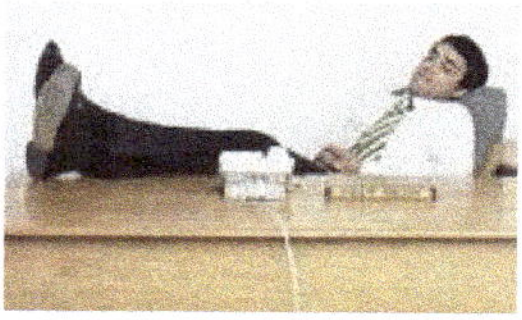

(photo source: www.fotosearch.com/)

Source: Robert Half Technology. (2007, August 29). Please continue to hold. Retrieved from http://rht.mediaroom.com/index.php?s=131&item=127

Discuss

What ratio of technical support staff to end-users do you have in your organization? What problems do you see resulting if there are too few support staff? What actions can be taken to address the problems?

15.3.1 ICT Department activities

The ICT department's activities are many and varied, and depend in part on the size and type of organization to which they belong. Once, the ICT department had an important role in the development of applications and could employ many programmers. Nowadays, application software is more likely to be purchased off-the-shelf rather than developed in-house. The wide use of desktop computers means that more people are dealing with the ICT department on a regular basis. As such, ICT staff members have more of a service role. ICT staff are expected to help users with hardware and software problems, with installation, and with their ICT purchase decisions. They are also expected to educate, control, and implement standards for end-users.

The list of possible ICT department's activities includes:

- Purchasing and installing hardware (and updates/maintenance) for both end-users and enterprise systems
- Purchasing and installing software (and updates/maintenance) for both end-users and enterprise central systems
- Supporting end-users (a help desk)
- Educating end-users
- Developing organizational web sites
- Doing in-house development when required
- Managing a project portfolio for all ICT projects in the organization

- Providing and managing the enterprise architecture
- Managing outsourcing
- Ensuring that back-up, security, risk management, and disaster recovery procedures are in place
- Promoting standards for the effective use and management of ICT
- Ensuring compliance with software licensing policies and ethical usage of computing equipment, and
- Assisting with ICT strategic planning and governance.

15.3.2 Structure of the ICT department

The structure and organization of typical IT departments depends on organizational size, scope, function, jurisdiction and many other external factors such as government policies, budget, backbone infrastructure, external service support, and outsourcing opportunities. So a structure should be developed based on an organization's own context to meet its own circumstances. Gartner (2003) suggests four basic steps to design an organization's ICT department. These steps are 1) Business Driver Assessment, 2) Organization Readiness Assessment, 3) Structure Model Assessment (the strengths and weaknesses of centralized, decentralized, or hybrid), and 4) Business Impact Assessment. Below are some best-practice steps to prepare an ICT structure for a new organization (Yesser, 2007):

- Define the functions of organization
- Map roles to these functions
- Work out how to manage your activities
- Build a structure that will help to effect that management
- Align the organization structure with the IT strategy
- Focus on "customer-centric" service design
- Design the organization based on required services, functions, and the estimated workload
- Keep the end results in mind
- Consider the external environment
- Implement the structure, and
- Review and modify for reality.

Schiesser (2010) mentions three key factors as the basis of ICT structure decisions. These are departmental responsibilities, planning orientation, and infrastructure processes. Many organizations initially form their ICT unit with a basic organizational structure: one component for application development and maintenance (software), and an infrastructure component (network and hardware). As the department grows and IT begins to expand its services, more and more components are added to the basic structure, which will likely evolve into an organization similar to one shown in Figure 15.1.

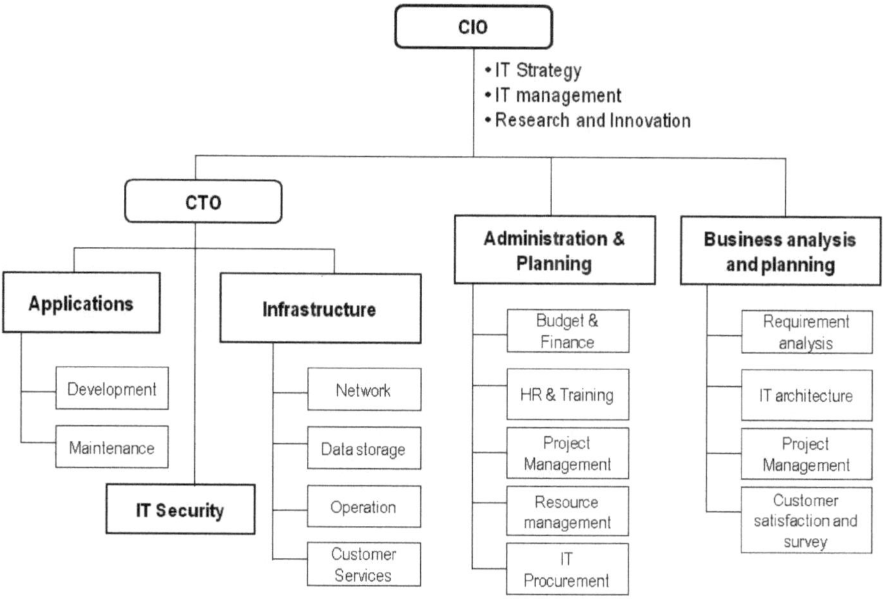

Figure 15.1. A typical structure of a standard IT department

While the CIO is the organizational head of the ICT department, in some large organizations, a chief technical officer (CTO) with sound technical knowledge may be introduced to lead the technical team. A CIO is responsible for the overall IT strategy and its alignment with business, management and innovation, new ventures, design, and administration and training of staff.

However, the placement of different components often varies from organization to organization based on their unique circumstances and need.

15.3.3 ICT staff roles

The ICT department can include staff with many different responsibilities. This includes project managers, database managers, system administrators, network managers, systems analysts and designers, and information architects. IT professionals often have to face the challenges of being part of the most dynamic technology industry in which people often have to play different role and always continue the development of their expertise to suit and survive in the environment.

In small organizations especially, ICT staff can wear many hats and be responsible for a range of the activities. In larger organizations, staff duties will often be divided and the staff will be located to specific roles. In very large organizations, ICT functions may be distributed, with ICT staff in business units and a central ICT department. Obviously, management in these circumstances can be very difficult, especially when the subsidiary units have incompatible software, systems, and standards. Thus, the role of the manager or director of the ICT department, often termed the chief information officer (CIO), is particularly important and this role is discussed further below.

15.3.4 Staffing the ICT department and ICT skills

Few other industries are as diverse as ICT, and few other skills are so flexible and universal. ICT is professional, quirky, creative and fast- paced. It's an industry that just keeps growing, and has a booming global sector.

Careers for ICT professionals are extremely varied. They include network engineers, game designers, business analysts, application developers, 3D artists, security specialists, and more.

There is a growing need for skilled ICT professionals and there is a current global ICT skills shortage.

Typical IT service roles

A typical IT service organization will use a four-tier support staff solution:

1. Level one: Help desk personnel, who handle calls for help and provide basic support.
2. Level two: Computer support technicians, computer support analysts, and desktop specialists.
3. Level three: Network administrators/system administrators, who work on break and fix issues that could not be resolved at the lower levels.
4. Level four: The highest level of IT personnel, the network engineer/system engineers and designers.

In order for an organization to be successful, it must proactively manage ICT skills.

Staffing challenges

ICT industry challenges include:

- The need to define and codify ICT skills
- The need to identify the skills required for each specific ICT role
- The need to be able to evaluate and improve the skills of individuals, and
- The need to be able to obtain required staff.

Skills Framework for an information Age (SFIA)

One means of addressing the problem of ICT staffing is to use a "skills framework" in conjunction with the Human Resources department to define the skills needed for different ICT positions and to classify the positions that are possibly already filled with existing staff with the organization.

The Appendix to this chapter outlines one such skills framework as an example: the Skills Framework for an Information Age (SFIA).

> *"Importantly, the role of CIO is not being looked on as 'Chief IT Mechanic.' It is recognised as a means to extract value from technology and gain insight from complex systems"*
>
> *Mark Hale, Director of IS for Food Retail, The Essentials CIO, Global CIO study by IBM, p. 62*

Chief Information Officer (CIO)

The manager of the IT department has a particularly important role. This manager is commonly termed the Chief Information Officer (CIO).

The CIO is often the link between the IT department and the other units of the organization. For this reason, it is important for CIOs to have both business and technical knowledge. CIOs help organizations to cope with complexity by simplifying operations, business process, products, and services.

CIO roles

Important roles that the CIO undertakes include being (Smaltz, S., Sambamurthy,V., and Agarwal, R., 2006):

- *A strategist*: CIOs assist their organizations to gain valuable business opportunities with IT-based innovation and business process re-design. CIOs need to understand and be involved in organizational strategic planning.
- *A relationship architect*: CIOs must liaise and build partnerships with other business units and service providers inside and outside the organization. The external liaison becomes more important as ICT outsourcing grows.
- *An integrator*: The CIO provides leadership in enterprise- wide integration of processes, data storage, and information provision.
- *An IT educator*: An important feature of the CIO role is the requirement to help other managers learn about IT and appreciate the opportunities that are offered. That is, the CIO must assist in making management and staff more "IT savvy". Greater knowledge of IT opportunities across the organization is a first step towards acceptance of innovation with IT.
- *A utility provider*: A fundamental role of the CIO is to ensure that IT services and infrastructures are reliable and fit-for- purpose. This role requires the effective management of the IT department itself and is a foundation for fulfillment of the other roles. The IT department and the CIO lose credibility if they cannot provide essential services.
- *An information steward*: The CIO must ensure that the organization has high-quality data available and that operational systems are secure. There must be high levels of data quality, security, and integrity, and privacy must be safeguarded. External and internal threats from malicious acts and accidents must be guarded against.

CIO success factor

Based on a CIO opinion survey, Austin, Nolan, & O'Donnell (2009, p. 36) outline the following key success factor for future CIOs:

- Enhance and maintain relationship with other business leaders
- Develop a team of expert technologists within the organization who understand the business, and
- Educate top management and peer executives on new possibilities enabled by IT and about the major trade off implicit in technology choices.

15.4 Standards for ICT Service Management

> *"Effective IT management ... deals with everyday challenges of the job, respond to major crises, and remakes the company's technology capability into a vital strategic asset"*
>
> *Austin et al., 2009, The Adventure of an IT Leader*

A fuller understanding of the ICT department's activities can be obtained by looking at well-known guides to best practice for ICT service management.

15.4.1 IT infrastructure library (ITIL)

One best practice guide is ITIL or the IT Infrastructure Library, both registered trademarks of the United Kingdom's Office of Government Commerce. Individuals can study to become certified under the ITIL scheme. ITIL provides details of major ICT practices, with checklists, tasks, and procedures that can be adapted to the organizational context. See https://www.axelos.com/itil, http://www.itlibrary.org, http://www.itsmfi.org/

ITIL is broadly compatible with ISO/IEC 20000, the first international standard for IT service management.

See the following exhibit for more information.

Exhibit 15.2. The ITIL Open Guide

The information technology infrastructure library (ITIL) defines the organizational structure and skill requirements of an information technology organization and a set of standard operational management procedures and practices to allow the organization to manage an ICT operation and associated infrastructure. The operational procedures and practices are supplier independent and apply to all aspects within the ICT Infrastructure.

Future organisations will need to achieve an edge in the extremely competitive environment of IT Services. As such, establishing a standard to enhance interoperability, effectiveness, business value while reducing operational overhead and risk is critical.

ITIL concept emerged in 1980s by the Central Computer and Telecommunications Agency (CCTA), now called the Office of Government Commerce (OGC) of the British Government to provide a systematic and professional approach to the management of IT services based on expert advice and best practices. Large companies and government agencies in Europe adopted the framework very quickly in the early 1990s and it became popular both in the UK and across the world. In year 2000, Microsoft used ITIL as the basis to develop their proprietary Microsoft Operations Framework (MOF).

As IT has changed and evolved over the period, and so did ITIL with its version three, known as ITIL v3, being the current release. The current version is detailed within five core publications enabling organizations to deliver appropriate services and to achieve business goals and benefits. These five volumes are: Service Strategy; Service Design; Service Transition; Service Operation; and Continual Service Improvement.

Further Resources:

The ITIL Open Guide—a collaborative community "version" of ITIL (see http://www.itlibrary.org)

The IT Service Management Forum (ITSMf), the primary "professional" body for ITIL practitioners, is closely aligned with the OGC in developing and promulgating ITIL (see http://www.itsmfi.org/)

Activity

Research the composition of ICT departments by examining examples in government agencies that show their organizational structure on the Internet.

- What appear to be the functions of these departments? What type of personnel do they employ?
- Are they integrated with business units or separate?
- To whom does the CIO report?
- Investigate the pros and cons of different placements of the ICT department in the organizational structure.

Class Exercise

Study the article by Misra (2007). The chief information officer concept in eGovernment: Lessons for developing countries.

1. Summarize the main points made in this article and discuss.
2. What differences do you see between the CIO roles in developed versus developing countries?

Chapter Highlights

- The introduction of new ICT systems is a major undertaking and requires careful attention to both people and technology factors.
- When the project manager finishes his tasks through the delivery of the project, the change manager takes over to actually realize the outcome and to merge the new system with organization's corporate culture.
- Change management not only comprises training about new system and practices, but it also provides a kind of mentoring for employees to adjust to the new system instead of fearing their changes.
- A change manager's role is to prepare employees and executives for the changes that come with the new system.
- To be an efficient change manager, it is important to understand the people and accept their diversity and choices, and to understand the sensitivity of the existing culture of organizations.
- The ICT department has the specialized expertise to operate central ICT systems, develop new applications, and support the use of ICT in organizations.
- The ICT department's responsibilities are varied and include strategic planning, purchasing, maintenance, providing a help desk, and promoting standards and security.
- The service role of the ICT department is of increasing importance.
- The ITIL best practice guide provides detailed guidance for ICT service management.
- The chief information officer (CIO) is the link between the ICT department and the organization and the CIO requires both business and technical knowledge.
- Many parts of the world are experiencing an ICT skills shortage. ICT managers need to be proactive in training and recruiting ICT staff.
- The skills framework for an information age (SFIA) provides a means for defining and classifying the skills required of ICT professionals.

Review Questions

1. What are six important job positions in the ICT department?
2. What are ten important activities the ICT department engages in?
3. What is ITIL? What is its purpose?
4. What are the main roles of the CIO?
5. What steps can be taken to overcome resistance to change with new ICT initiatives?

Discussion Questions

1. What type of training prepares someone for the CIO role? How can someone with a technical educational background (e.g., engineering, computer science) build up the right skills set for promotion to a CIO?
2. How can a CIO obtain strategic influence in an organization? Is this a difficult task?
3. How can the CIO foster ICT alignment with business strategy?

Exercise

Project: Special Challenges in the Public Sector of Developing Countries

Prepare a report addressing the following questions:

- Are there special challenges for organizational change in the public sector in developing countries?
- Is a fear of job losses likely to be a major source of resistance to change? The argument is made that ICT does not lead to job losses but rather to the provision of better services to clients and citizens with the same staff working more efficiently. Can you find evidence to support this argument?
- Are there special challenges because of the existing cultures in the public sector, hierarchical organizations, and public sector rules and legislation? Discuss.

Appendix 15A

Skills Framework for the Information Age (SFIA)

The skills framework for the information age (SFIA) provides a common reference model for the identification of the skills needed to develop effective information systems (IS) that use information technologies (IT).

SFIA provides a standardized view of the wide range of professional skills needed by people working in information technology. These skills are generic and, therefore, independent of any specific underlying technology. For example, "network design" is a required skill but SFIA is not concerned whether a particular network is to be designed using CISCO or Juniper technologies.

The overall purpose of SFIA is to assist organizations that employ IT professionals to:

- Reduce IT project risk
- Retain staff
- Make recruitment effective, and
- Enhance the effectiveness and efficiency of the IT function by developing the right skills, by deploying them to their best effect and, by providing appropriate development and career paths for IT professionals.

SFIA's focus on professional skills rather than technological information means that the framework is readily understood by a wide community. This includes:

- IT professionals and their managers in industry and Government
- HR managers, professionals, and training staff, and
- Non-technical managers.

SFIA is suitable for use in any organization that employs IT professionals. It is now used worldwide in industry and government as a standard way of describing IT skills. Evidence of its global use is the fact that it has already been translated into Chinese and Japanese.

SFIA Structure

The SFIA approach is to define the skill categories required in order to successfully develop and deliver effective information systems. It uses a two-dimensional framework that defines skill categories in one dimension and responsibility levels in the other.

The skill categories have been given practical descriptions that should make them familiar. These categories are then broken down into sub-categories, which are then further broken down into individual skills. It is important to remember that these skills are not position or role descriptions but rather define skill sets or capabilities. What they provide is the set of IT capabilities required by a particular job holder. These capabilities can then be included as the "person" description section in a job/position/role description.

The Responsibility Levels define the levels of responsibility and accountability associated with any given skill across the roles in which that particular skill applies.

SFIA Skills

As mentioned earlier, SFIA defines a set of skill categories. These categories are logical groupings of capabilities (skills) that are required for the ICT organization to be able to deliver effective ICT services that can meet business requirements. The categories are:

- Strategy and architecture: This includes the capabilities required to align the overall ICT strategy to the business, definition of appropriate enterprise and technical architectures, innovation, business process improvement, risk management, sustainability, and the evaluation of emerging technologies.
- Business change: This includes portfolio/programme/project management, organization design & implementation, change implementation planning and management, benefits management and stakeholder relationship management.
- Solution development and implementation: This describes the capabilities required to develop and implement highly effective, usable, and sustainable ICT systems.
- Service management: This considers the end to end delivery of ICT services, which include design, transition to the production environment, and operational delivery and support. These particular capabilities are aligned to the ITIL framework.
- Procurement and management support: This includes the sourcing of external goods/services, quality management, resource management, and learning and development.
- Client interface: This describes the capabilities required to market and sell the ICT services and to provide an effective account management function.

These categories are then divided into subcategories. Finally, the subcategories are broken down into individual skills. The skills can then be applied to a job function or role. Remember, however, that a skill must be applied at a responsibility level appropriate to that role. SFIA defines a total of 90 separate skills.

References

Austin, R. D., Nolan, R. L., & O'Donnell, S. (2009). The adventures of an IT leader. Cambridge: Harvard Business Press.

Campbell, S., & Kleiner, B. H. (1997). New developments in re-engineering organizations. Work Study, 46(3), 99-103.

Dooley, K., & Johnson, D. (2001). Changing the new product development process: Reengineering or continuous quality improvement? Measuring Business Excellence, 5(4), 32-38.

Gartner. (2003). Structuring for success: Building blocks for IT organization design. Retrieved from http://www.gartner.com/newsroom/

Jones, J., Aguirre, D., & Calderone, M. (2004). 10 principles of change management. Retrieved from http://www.strategy-business.com/article/rr00006?gko=643d0

Misra, D. C. (2007). The chief information officer concept in eGovernment: Lessons for Developing Countries. Retrieved from http://www.docstoc.com/docs/67900924/The-Chief-Information- Officer-(CIO)-Concept-in-EGovernment

Schiesser, R. (2010). IT systems management (Second ed.). IN: Prentice Hall.

Smaltz, D. H., Sambamurthy, V., & Agarwal, R. (2006). The antecedents of CIO role effectivness in organizations: An empirical study in the healthcare sector. IEEE Transactions on Engineering Management, 53(2), 207-223.

Turbit, N. (2005). ERP implementation - the traps. www.projectperfect.com.au. Retrieved from http://www.projectperfect.com.au/downloads/Info/info_erp_imp.pdf

Yesser. (2007). Best practices of IT organization design (Ver. 1). Retrieved from http://www.yesser.gov.sa/en/Methodologies/Methodologies%20and%20Best%20Practices/Best%20Practices%20of%20IT%20Organization%20Design/Best_Practices_of_IT_Organization_Design_en.pdf.

CHAPTER 16
Political, Legal, Ethical and Environmental Issues

Learning Objectives

After studying this chapter, you will be able to:

- Understand how the political environment should be taken into account when conceptualizing and formulating eGovernment measures and policies
- Identify the key ethical/legal issues in eGovernment
- Recognize the environmental issues that should be considered when planning and implementing eGovernment, and
- Provide a practical ICT sustainability assessment by applying Green ICT "readiness" principles.

Managing the environment

eGovernment implementation and management involves a range of managerial and technical skills. These skills must be applied to address various ideological and cultural environments that surround and underpin eGovernment activity. Some of these external environmental factors can override other major issues such as know-how, attitude, and infrastructure. Understanding various environmental influences and their interactions is important for eGovernment managers. The extent of these environmental issues is often vast and complex. This chapter introduces some of these issues with further pointers to their wider dimensions on eGovernment implementation.

Managing the ICT in a particular environment is challenging because the contextual factors vary from one country to another, in different locations in the same country, and in the same location at different times. Internal factors such as organizational culture, local practice, and staff skill may even differ from one department to another in the same government or industry. eGovernment managers must tackle these realities by using their knowledge and responding appropriately to the situation.

(Photo credit : F. Salam)

16.1 LDC Environment - A Researcher's View

The academic literature suggests that "the environment in LDCs [least developed countries] is volatile, and particularly with IT constantly changing" (Kelegai and Middleton, 2004, p.60). As such, the implementation strategies are also different and there is no "one size fits all" approach. Understanding the overall environment is crucial in determining its effects and also in formulating strategies to deal with any inherent problems.

The first step in information systems and eGovernment project design is to draw a contextual map. The environment dimensions that are unique to the developing country's concerns must be addressed during the planning stage. Figure 16.1 shows a contextual environment of eGovernment in Bangladesh, an LDC (Imran, Turner, & Gregor, 2008).

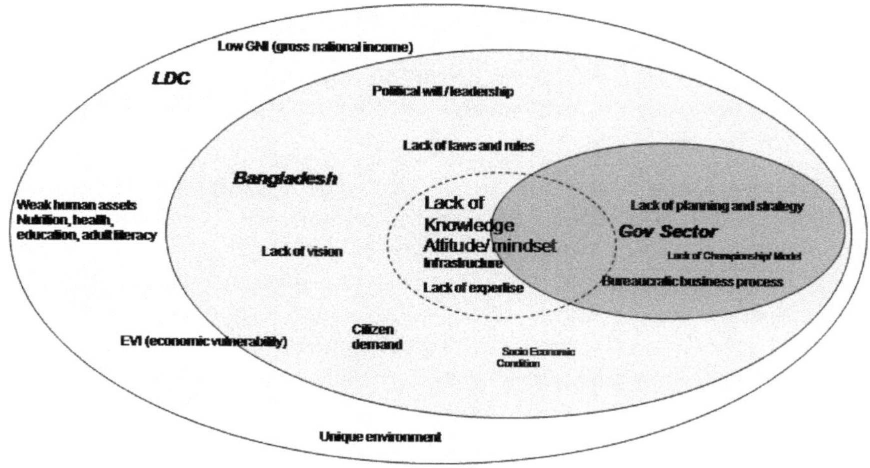

Figure 16.1. eGovernment environment in Bangladesh (Imran et al., 2008, p. 33)

Several intangible factors dominate this environment, such as the lack of knowledge, expertise, and planning and strategy. Other significant factors include the decision makers' attitudes and mindsets, and the political will and leadership.

Additionally, contextual issues, such as the country's socio-economic condition, citizen demand, the state of the country's legal system, and the country's overall standing and capacity, play important roles in creating a conducive environment for eGovernment adoption. Public bureaucracies increasingly operate in a global environment, which requires greater communication and cooperation between nations.

16.2 The Political Environment

The political environment surrounding eGovernment is no different from that of which any innovation is likely to face in a developing country.

Research argues that eGovernment technologies have positive influences on politics and democracy by improving citizens' engagement with their government. In the developed world, eGovernment is continuing to enhance the efficiency and productivity of the government, as well as its ability to deliver better services to its citizens.

The leaders of a country often include eGovernment on the national agenda. International and donor pressures also influence political leaders to move in this direction. Often the political will does not translate into action because there is no clear, consistent, and long-term strategy. Furthermore, strong political support for eGovernment cannot be sustained if it does not benefit the poor, the vulnerable, or the majority of the country's citizens.

Like any other government reform initiative, an eGovernment project requires strong political will to implement. Without strong political leadership and sufficient financial resources, eGovernment will not be sustainable. Horrocks (2009) argues that, since eGovernment has increasingly dominated the policy agenda for better delivery of public services, the eGovernment experts and their supporters are becoming powerful enough to influence the policies in public services.

eGovernment adoption patterns are different in different countries because of the differences in their political systems. For example, the US and China are different in their structure and inter-governmental relationship. In China, governments are highly centralized. But, in the US, state governments operate differently from and independently of the federal (national) government (which means that they often act against the federal government). The decision-making process of the Chinese Government may be seen to be somewhat easier than in the US because of the centralized decision-making process, which often makes it easier to implement large interconnected systems across the country (Hao, 2007).

Some of the ramifications of eGovernment are sensitive in nature. eGovernment projects often promote transparency, which reduces the opportunity for corruption. They also often seek to remove bureaucratic layers as part of administrative reform. These issues often directly threaten the powerful stakeholders in the status quo because their vested interests are affected. eGovernment has been used as a tool for administrative reform and to bring good governance, but true reform is only possible with strong political will and commitment.

16.2.1 Access to information

When we think about human rights over the last century, access to information was unlikely to arise until relatively recently. There is now much debate on this issue across the world. Countries list information access as one of the basic human rights. However, this is not just about access by and for individuals. ICT can be used for empowerment through information; for example, to educate people where teachers physically cannot. Governments are also extending and facilitating access in different forms to ensure equal opportunity and democratic rights for citizens. For example, Australia plans to roll out national high-speed broadband for all Australians by 2017 at the cost of $43 billion (AUD). Such an initiative is driven by the belief that it makes a huge difference whether or not you are information rich or information poor in this modern, knowledge-based economy. That belief applies in business, education, and in social life.

Worldwide, today's citizens are quickly transforming to digital citizens. They are enjoying eServices from government, business, and welfare agencies. The overwhelming impact of social networking sites such as Facebook and Twitter in setting citizens' expectations cannot be overemphasized.

While correct and abundant information can help to build a good society, incorrect information and half-truths can cause great damage to the society. It is common these days to feel bombarded with information, be it from the Internet, TV, radio, or other media. Citizens are struggling to develop coping mechanisms for filtering and analyzing information.

The adage says that "information is power", and those who can control the information have more political power and authority. Believing this, some governments are unwilling to initiate information access reforms for fear of empowering people and facing consequent threats to the authority of the establishment. The political fallout from the WikiLeaks dissemination of previously secret government cables and the so- called "Arab Spring" event, apparently facilitated by Twitter and other social media in 2011, are seen as evidence for the potential political empowerment offered by the information age and social media in particular.

In contrast, however, some of the world's authoritarian governments enthusiastically embrace new technical standards because they can trace people with opinions that are opposite to official governmental views (Kalathil & Boas, 2001). In many instances, projects and initiatives on eGovernment get political support when they match the dominant political interest, or when they exert control over access to information (Nidumolu, Goodman, Vogel, & Danowitz, 1996).

WikiLeaks - Consequence Analysis

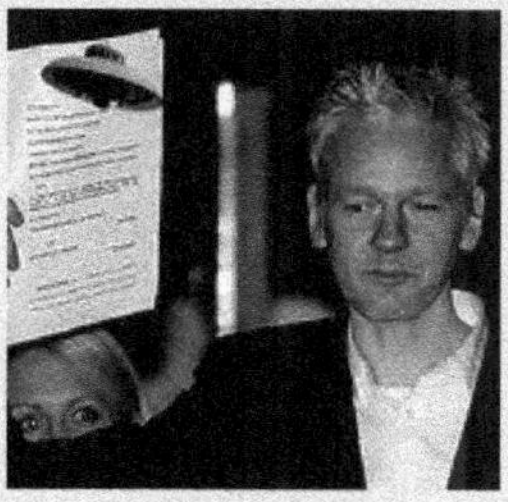

Wikileaks founder Julian Assange (Photo credit: A. Azikiwe)

WikiLeaks (http://www.wikileaks.org/) has been in operation since 2006. It came to wide public notice only in 2010 with the staged release of leaked information from U.S. diplomatic cables. The leaked information is disseminated through WikiLeaks' website and passed to major newspaper publishers, radio, television, and social networking sites. The spread of information on such mass scale would not happen without the use of ICT.

WikiLeaks' revelations have embarrassed a lot of countries and their leaders. Heads of state are becoming concerned that these revelations may decide their political futures in their own countries. Often these leaks could be a game-changer in case of foreign relations and diplomacy.

WikiLeaks' founder, Julian Assange, has been accused of illegal activities, unethical behaviour, and even treason, but no charges have been laid against him for his activities with WikiLeaks. People who leak material to

> *WikiLeaks are "whistleblowers", who may have different motives. However, the legal and ethical implications of these activities are still under question and debate. For example, under the Australian Standard AS8004-2003, whistle blowing is an important element in detecting corrupt, illegal, and other undesirable conduct, which is necessary to achieve good corporate governance.*
>
> *While Assange claims to wish to achieve more transparency to stimulate investigations and reforms through WikiLeaks' activities, it remains unclear and un-investigated how far the site and its activities were able to create pressure on the governments to attain that goal. Rather, governments may react by putting more restrictions on access to reduce the risk of future leaks.*
>
> *However, the leaks have also sent a message to the governments around the world that they should become more transparent to reduce the potential for and effect of future leaks.*

Source: Bowern, M. (2011, May). The Information Age. Australian Computer Society.

16.2.2 Organizational Level Politics

Many LDCs that are struggling to build political and social systems are also yet to have a clear structure of organizational systems. The core activities of any information system are in coordinating and integrating the processes that take place at an organizational level. The interaction between people and organizations and internal politics strongly influences organizational operation and management.

At the organizational level, there are two-way pressures on managers using ICT. One is from the political leaders and top management, who want to see more programs handled by the managers. The other is from citizens and businesses, who push for better performance and accountability of the public officials and their programs. However, research has found that, particularly in LDCs, the top executives of most organizations still lack understanding of ICT. With the introduction of ICT systems and the easy communication and dissemination of information that they provide, the old hierarchical command and control model is no longer the most appropriate way to run a modern organization.

ICT systems allow the devolution of decision making to staff members who are closer to where the actual services are delivered. Ultimately, the implementation of self-serve eGovernment services transfers responsibility to the citizen. With this impetus to shift authority, the world is fast moving towards flatter structures with team-based approaches that are delivered through ICT networks. Managers now derive power from how connected they are because fewer things are secret and influence is crucial.

16.2.3 Leadership/Championship

Many researchers and practitioners strongly emphasize leadership drive and political will as the key factors for ICT diffusion in developing countries (Kandelin, Lin, & Muntoro, 1998; Taifur, 2004; Zaitun, Mashkuri, & Wood-Harper, 2000). According to Wilson (2004), "Leaders who fail to seize ICT opportunities may produce the same results as leaders who failed to build factories or railroads in the early stages of the industrial revolution" (p. 5).

Like any ICT undertaking, eGovernment programs face many challenges. It was often found that there was a visionary leader who pushed the change against many challenges behind every successful eGovernment project. A leader should not only be convinced and believe in eGovernment, but they should be willing to take risks, and publicly sponsor and promote change.

Kaufeld, Chari, and Freeme (2009) argue that an effective ICT leader needs a wide variety of competencies on operational, tactical, and strategic levels. The leader must use these different management competencies at different levels based on the need.

Leadership is critical in ICT success. In eGovernment, this frequently requires political leadership and organizational leadership. The nation's political culture can enable or inhibit eGovernment projects just as much as socio-economic or technological infrastructure issues do. The interest and support of political leaders will vary over time and depend on their political agenda. Finally, strong leadership is needed in the government organization when implementing eGovernment projects. There will always be competing priorities, both political and managerial, and strong leadership is needed to complete eGovernment projects.

N. Chandrababu Naidu: IT Leader and Champion

A range of IT initiatives in the state of Andhra Pradesh (AP) in India are largely the result of Chief Minister N. Chandrababu Naidu's vision and determination. His knowledge and enthusiasm about IT and a long-term commitment to the change process was instrumental in driving the ICT revolution across the country. He not only took a detailed interest in implementation, but was willing to accept and learn from mistakes.

N. Chandrababu Naidu (Photo credit: WorldNews Network)

Quick Quiz

1. How do you define value for money? Why is it important for governments to achieve value for money?
2. Can you identify three critical success factors (CSFs) that might apply to any ICT project?
3. Can you identify any key performance indicators (KPIs) that might apply to both project work and operational ICT?

16.3 The Ethical Issues

Every society has a set of rules and beliefs about right and wrong, which are expressed through code and conduct regarding how people should behave and react.

While some attitudes, values, and beliefs are more or less universal, many ethical standards vary from society to society based on their culture and tradition.

At the organizational level, there are several important reasons to promote ethical behaviour in decision making, such as to gain confidence of the community, to foster best practices, and to provide legal cover to the organization (Reynolds, 2010). A U.S. Treasury department study found that 60% of its computer security breaches occurred from lapses in the organization, which emphasizes the need to develop ethical IT behaviour among employees (Stone & Henry, 2003). There are many examples around the world where unethical use of information and information systems has had negative consequences on individuals, organizations, and the respective countries.

Ethics in relation to information systems is increasingly becoming important because the risk associated with its improper use can be significant. Stone and Henry (cited in Rocheleau, 2006, p. 237) identify three major factors that influence ethical behaviours in IT decision making. These are:

- Personal - the individual's personal code of ethics
- Informal - the influence of co-workers' expectations, and
- Formal company policies - the company's formal code of ethics.

While eGovernment, as a type of information system, provides an opportunity for governments to reach out to people, it also demonstrates a government's commitment to transparency and legitimacy. Through more accessible and complete information with improved and convenient channels of communication, eGovernment has the potential not only to increase citizens' satisfaction and trust in government, but also to reduce the information gap between citizens and governments.

The ethical issues surrounding eGovernment may deal with:

- Ensuring transparency and accountability

- Using content in documents and forms that are suitable for citizen needs and culture
- Ensuring social justice
- Ensuring freedom of expression and censorship
- Protecting children from illegal uses of ICT
- Protecting intellectual property
- Preserving cultural diversity and harmony
- Maintaining standards in dealings and service delivery, and
- Earning trust and confidence.

Examples of some general unethical uses of ICT in the public service could be:

- Misusing (i.e., for personal gain) official IT resources
- Breaching citizens' privacy through the abuse of personal data under custody
- Downloading unauthorized content using official resources, and
- Participating in criminal activities such as hacking or electronically stealing material by copying it.

From the citizens' perspective, one of the core issues in electronic environments is the question of trust. Examples of how that trust is tested are (Chopra & Wallace, 2003; Mullen & Horner, 2004):

- Can we trust the information we obtain from the Internet or other electronic sources?
- Are the computing systems upon which we rely trustworthy?
- Can we trust the people with whom we form relationships through electronic means?

Therefore, it is important to ensure that the benefits and services are delivered on time, accurately, and completely, without compromising ethical norms. The government needs to set an example by designing appropriate eGovernment services to benefit its citizens. The government should also ensure a good level of data protection and should educate its citizens on matters of computer security and privacy.

It is also important to make information easily accessible to both the media and the public. Suppression of information can embarrass countries and their leaders when that information later comes to light (e.g., from websites such as WikiLeaks).

eGovernment strategies must, therefore, include ethical issues that directly affect eGovernment satisfaction and trust among citizens. In most cultures, the government has a moral obligation to maintain transparency when providing government services to citizens and businesses. This objective can be reached through simplifying and streamlining the existing business processes through eGovernment.

Overall, the eGovernment approach should not be limited to the technological capabilities of ICT, but rather seek to empower citizens to improve the quality of their lives, while ensuring their ethical rights as human beings. Table 16.1 illustrates some ethical principles associated with government implementation in Africa.

Table 16.1. Principles of ethics associated with eGovernment implementation (adapted from e-Africa, p. 5)

Ethical Principle	Application in eGovernment implementation
Treating citizens equally in terms of government service delivery	Online and digital relationship between the government and citizens
Legal entity of decisions	Standard procedures, portals, and legal disclaimers for online services
Neutrality and transparency of the government agencies	Reduce human error and intervention through automated services and transactions ; better control and accountability of resources and files
Proximity and accessibility to the government services	Cutting the cost, distance and time; avoid intermediary channels and hierarchy
Democratic participation in decision making process	Use of social media, Gov 2.0 and online forum participation on government policies and plans
Quality, efficiency and continuity of services	Fast, accurate and improved service delivery through provision of 24/7 automated and online services
Evaluation and measurement of performances and services	Better control and management helps to quantify and evaluate performance matrix more clearly
Privacy and security of citizens data and rights	Secure authentication process and maintaining high level of data security can prevent unauthorized disclosure of private documents

Quick Quiz

1. Why it is important to promote ethical behavior in decision making at the organizational level?
2. What factors influence ethical behaviors in IT decision making?
3. How can you establish trust among citizens on an eGovernment system?

16.4 The Legal Issues

Smooth eGovernment operation requires adequate and up-to-date legal cover. Obsolete laws and regulations can seriously impede eGovernment operations and their take off. Changing and reforming the existing laws and regulations is a daunting and time-consuming task that requires careful planning, coordination, and negotiations with a range of stakeholders. Thus, eGovernment and legal reform should take place hand-in-hand. It is also important to educate citizens and users about the legislation in respect to eGovernment through an awareness campaign.

The legal reform should aim to create equal opportunities for everyone to participate in the eGovernance process. This will encourage public organizations and the wider society's participation, and will facilitate planning and coordination between the agencies responsible for the development of eGovernment. The law must facilitate a smooth transition and its management from paper-based to electronic documentation.

Many legal issues related to eGovernment are similar to those in eCommerce because eGovernment is essentially derived from eCommerce (except for service providers, who are the government agencies in eGovernment). In both the cases, the Internet is the primary vehicle for service delivery to customers, citizens, and businesses.

16.4.1 Legal challenges

Because of the way that the Internet operates through routers, servers are located at different jurisdictions that are often out of national boundaries, and data is despatched following various routes and technology protocols such as TCP/IP, SMTP, and so on. Legal issues associated with this thus get complicated.

Again, while the seamless flow of information between department and entities is a major advantage of eGovernment, it also poses a legal challenge in terms of responsibility, custody, and so on. For example, questions may arise about why, for example, the agriculture department has access to the health department's information and data (Leith, 2002). A lack of understanding of such legal implications and technical limitations/capabilities between technical and legal people is potentially a barrier against resolving these issues.

Amoussou-Guenou (2004) identifies three main categories of legal issues in relation to eGovernment. These are:

- The **legal validity** of eGovernment acts is the first thing to ensure through adoption and recognition of associated laws, establishment of rights, and titles on eGovernment. For example, Association of Southeast Asian Nations (ASEAN) countries such as Singapore, Thailand, Malaysia, and the Philippines resolved the problem of the legal validity of eGovernment through drafting similar provisions in the legal acts and constitution of these countries.
- An environment of **trust** and confidence is the second step toward establishing legal protection through various means such as authentication, identity management, privacy and data protection, network and information security, the fight against cybercrime, and so on; and

- According to international conventions on human rights and national constitutions, governments' obligation to citizens and citizens' access to state justice and **legal remedies** must be ensured. This may be achieved through various means and policies such as online dispute resolution.

Some of the critical factors surrounding the legal area of eGovernment are discussed briefly below.

Jurisdiction beyond boundary

Since eGovernment services through the Internet extend beyond traditional boundaries and modes, it is subject to more laws than normal face-to-face transactions. Also, citizens who currently reside beyond national boundaries (i.e., in other countries) may also interact with government through the World Wide Web. On the management side, the complexity increases due to the multinational and international involvement in online operations, including administering World Wide Web domains, system hosting, international copyright protection, and so on. Some common global issues on the Web may have to be dealt by the international court of justice or an international criminal court. However, these organizations are yet to attain the capability to tackle many legal issues related to cyber-crime and issues beyond geographical boundaries. Even the implementations of digital signatures vary between countries because some of the national regulatory framework may conflict with other national and international laws.

Email

While email is increasingly becoming an important means of communication for government business, legislation pertaining to e-mail is still pending in many developing countries. A dilemma exists in many government organizations about the liability, misuse, and storage of e-mail. Every official email is important, and is of historic and legal value. There is a requirement to manage e-mails throughout their lifecycle. According to the Australian Electronic Transactions Act 1999, emails are to be given the same treatment as paper records. Deleting emails that contain business, historic, or legal information can be illegal. IT managers must ensure that a comprehensive email policy is in place and that all employees of the organization are made aware of these policies.

Electronic record

It is important to ensure that laws are updated to recognize all types of electronic documents and transactions. The regulations in the field of records management are developed, based on the experiences over the last decade, to deal with all the issues in relation to electronic records management. Many international standards and laws have been enacted, such as the "Data Protection and Electronic Evidence Act" and the "United Nations Model Law on Electronic Commerce", to indicate the validity of the records procedures in the electronic environment (Barata, 2004).

Digital signature

A digital signature is the substitute of an ink signature that embeds a special kind of electronic identity in an electronic document. Digital signatures cannot be copied to another document and can be applied to an entire document. Digital signatures reveal any attempts to tamper with documents.

A record is authentic if it is created or sent by the person who claims to have sent it. A record has integrity if it is complete and unaltered. A digital signature proves the authenticity and integrity of a digital document (Boudrez, 2007).

Additionally, the identification of parties involved is essential in electronic transactions. Legal requirements need proof that the signature was made by the person or by the authority concerned. However, the risk of digital certificates being obtained by gaining access to a victim's email inbox remains.

In some developing countries, while the legal issues of digital signatures have been included in their ICT acts, follow-up steps have not been taken to implement the act.

Digital rights management

There is huge concern about how to preserve and establish the rights and titles of online materials and services. It is often challenging to maintain and protect all government transactions and information against the rights and freedoms people enjoy in cyberspace. Protecting intellectual property and copyright in web-based information services should be dealt with diligently, because governments often deal with sensitive information, and the legal implication when such information is breached can be disastrous.

Cybercrime

With the development of technology, the range of cyber-related crime and threats has also increased. Managing these add to the challenges for eGovernment managers. Legal implications for these crimes are also evolving with changing circumstances, some of which are often complicated due to the global jurisdiction. Issues related with the misuse of eGovernment channels to threaten or harass organizations or people should be adequately covered through legal frameworks. Accordingly, the terms and conditions of using government websites should clearly cover the risk of costly lawsuits. Often an appropriate disclaimer can save an organization from liability. Also, some of the typical eCommerce related legal issues equally apply in eGovernment, such as false announcements and claims, defamation or product disparagement, IP infringement, breach of privacy, or the disclosure of private data. Engaging with different types and age groups of citizens, which include children and disabled persons, requires clear policy and procedures to avoid serious legal consequences for the government.

Further Reading

Basu, S. (2007). *Legal issues for eGovernment in developing countries. In A. Anttiroiko & M. Malkia (Eds.), encyclopaedia of digital government (pp. 1154-1160). Hershey, PA. .*

Chissick, M., & Harrington, J. (2003). *EGovernment: A practical guide to the legal issues. UK: Sweet & Maxwell.*

Quick Quiz

1. What are the three steps to implement legal infrastructure in eGovernment?
2. What does the legal validity of eGovernment mean?
3. What are the essential characteristics of a reliable record?

16.5 The Environmental Issues

Many developing countries are constantly faced with the possibilities and challenges of natural calamities such as floods, earthquakes, torrential rains, and tsunamis. The frequency of the threats related to climate change is increasing and they will influence every sphere of life, which includes the use of ICT.

The innovative use of media on a massive scale for climate change campaigns has led to many people becoming aware of the issues and taking appropriate measures to help fix them. There is a growing education and awareness scheme in schools, cultural associations, and societies.

However, the exploitation of hype around climate change for political and vested interests has created much debate and confusion. Many people are torn between the viewpoints of the climate sceptics and scientists, and barraged by jargon words such as "carbon footprint" and "CFC" [19]. The ongoing political conflict about climate change has not only confused the real issues but also caused a dilemma in people's minds. Nonetheless, climate change is not an isolated issue. It encompasses a multi-level involvement in the social, economic, and political spheres. Such a global problem can only be dealt with effectively when societies are better informed and prepared, in which ICT can play a greater role through information dissemination, education, and technical investigation.

16.5.1 Green ICT

Innovative use of information technology can be an effective tool for knowledge-based societies to address environmental issues. "Green IT" practices and policies are likely to contribute to preserving the environment for future generations. (Worthington, 2011, p.10)[1]

The Green Effect of ICT

ICT also uses a considerable amount of energy, paper, and water, and has other environmental impacts. Government agencies are major consumers of ICT products and services. To better administer and reduce the environmental impacts of ICT use, different governments have chosen to adopt different policies and initiatives to encourage their agencies to mitigate the effect of ICT on the environment.

Government organizations can lower the impact of their ICT activities on the environment by adopting sound operating principles and practices and by measuring their performance against checklists.

ICT has the potential not only to improve environmental performance in eGovernment and the ICT industry itself, but ICTs can also address climate change across the whole economy. The biggest gains for smarter environmental and economic strategies and applications are in three areas that contribute to the bulk of greenhouse gases: power generation and distribution, buildings, and transportation. Further environmental benefits of ICT applications are evident in areas such as water management, biodiversity protection, and pollution reduction. ICT innovation is a key element to spur green growth in eGovernment and in the economic crisis and recovery. The OECD suggests that most of its member governments are still following business-as-usual paths and have not adequately tapped the innovation potential of this area.[2]

Nevertheless, a global declaration by both developed and developing countries at the recent UN Forum on Climate Change Conference in Cancun, Mexico, suggests that there is a greater consensus that ICT is a vital tool to address climate change[3]. This was also fully supported by the ICT industry[4].

Sources: Murugesan, S. (2008). Harnessing green IT: Principles and practices. IEEE IT Professional, 10(1), 24-33.

Towards green ICT strategies: Assessing policies and programmes on ICT and the Environment, Working Party on the Information Economy (WPIE). (2009, May). Paper presented at the OECD Conference on ICTs, the environment and climate change, Helsingør, Denmark. Retrieved from

---

[1] Chlorofluorocarbon (CFC) is an organic compound that contains carbon, chlorine, hydrogen, and fluorine, produced as a volatile derivative of methane and ethane.

[2] See http://www.oecd.org/sti/ieconomy/ictstheenvironmentandclimatechange.htm

[3] See http://www.itu.int/themes/climate/events/un-climate.html

[4] The ICT industry coordinated the "Guadalajara ICT Declaration for Transformative Low-Carbon Solutions", the main contents of which were adopted in the UNFCCC-CoP16 Declaration. This is a result of a public private dialogue in Guadalajara, Mexico prior to the Conference. http://gesi.org/portfolio/project/10

http://www.oecd.org/sti/ieconomy/ictstheenvirohttp://www.oecd.org/sti/ict/green-ictnmentandclimatechange.htm

The Climate Group. (2008). Smart 2020 Report.

Key terms and concepts in green ICT

There are a number of specific terms that are important in the area of Green ICT, not least the term itself. The list below presents some of the most common terms and their commonly accepted meanings.

- ***Green IT, Green ICT, or Green Computing** - "The study and practice of designing, manufacturing, using, and disposing of computers, servers, and associated subsystems - such as monitors, printers, storage devices, and networking and communications systems – efficiently and effectively with minimal or no impact on the environment".*
- ***Environmental programs and initiatives by governments,** which often translate to eGovernment programs and initiatives, can be classified by the following three criteria: direct or enabling effects (explained below), environmental impact category, and life cycle phase.*
- ***Direct effects ("Green for IT or ICT"):** "Policies and programs that can focus on direct effects when targeting the environmental impacts of ICTs". ICT is responsible for 2 - 3% of global emissions of CO2, which is on par with the aviation industry, and both are growing rapidly.*
- ***Enabling effects ("Green by IT" or "ICT for Green"):** "Policies and programmes can focus on enabling effects when using ICT applications to reduce environmental impacts across economic and social activities (97 - 98% of global emissions of CO2)". ICT is NOT responsible for 98% of global emissions of CO2, but ICT could deliver a 15% reduction in global CO2 by 2020 to deliver cost savings of over a trillion dollars on fuel and energy and the cost of carbon.*
- ***ICT sustainability in government operations:** this is about how to manage ICT, with the aim being more sustainable use of ICT[5].*

16.5.2 The Effects of ICT on Environmental Sustainability

The effects of ICT on environmental sustainability can be best understood using a three-level effects framework. The first-order effects are where most attention is focused today. These are the direct impact of ICT on the environment, such as contamination throughout the life cycle, greenhouse gas emission from electricity generation, and so on.

[5]See example, the Australian Government ICT Sustainability Plan 2010-2015 http://www.environment.gov.au/sustainability/%20government/ictplan/index.htm; and https://www-s.fujitsu.com/au/whitepapers/greenict_sotn_form.html

ICT has substantial second-order effects, which indirectly contribute to the environment. ICT has the ability to change business processes to improve or otherwise increase the environmental impacts of those processes. For example, the use of eBusiness approaches reduces the consumption of transport by customers, and the use of video- conferencing reduces the travel of business people.

The third-order effects are longer term and result from changes to behaviors or economic structures. One investigation of these effects was reported in the Prospective Technological Studies for the European Commission in the 2004 report, The Future Impact of ICTs on Environmental Sustainability (as cited in Gartner, 2007).

First-order effects are understood reasonably well; second-order effects are somewhat understood, but the coverage is still patchy; and third order effects are understood very little. Several studies show that ICT's potential to reduce the environmental impact through reduction of business operations costs and products is substantial (Hilty, 2008). As government agencies are major consumers of ICT products and services, they must be conscious of the potential second-order and third-order effects their ICT initiatives may have.

16.5.3 Distributed versus Non-distributed computing

Although there is a great deal of focus on energy management and environmental impact of data centers (or servers), relatively little attention is paid to the energy used by distributed computing. Research suggests that there is a roughly even split between the two in terms of energy use (more detail on energy use is outlined below).

One source contends that the reason why there is such a focus on data centers is that they represent a "centralization" of the problem. Furthermore, much funding has been spent on data center environments, and decisions connected to them represent a large and long-term capital investment (Aldrich & Parello, 2011).

Distributed computing or non-data-center environments are possibly the way to go, where virtualization and cloud computing model likely to have little effect on linear energy use.

16.5.4 Energy Use in the Government Agencies

Data centers, networking infrastructure, printing, and distributing computing ICT infrastructure typically accounts for more than 20% of the energy used in an office building, with up to 70% attributed to ICT in typical government office (Greening IT, 2009).

As the costs of energy - and carbon - rise, government agencies have an obvious incentive to reduce these figures. Various experts and studies have shown that ICT-related emissions can be easily cut by around 15 - 30% just by implementing simple behavioral changes, such as switching off computers at the end of the day.

Furthermore, once integrated energy management can be made to combine mainframe system management, telephony management, PC management, and building management, energy efficiency improvements of more than 50% can be made (Aldrich & Parello, 2011).

Once such integrated systems are in place, the switching off function can be automated by deploying centralized desktop power management, which can vastly improve energy efficiency. By using the information supply chain more efficiently overall - from the desktop computer to printers and to server farms, as well as employing new, more energy efficient systems - reductions of over 50% are possible.

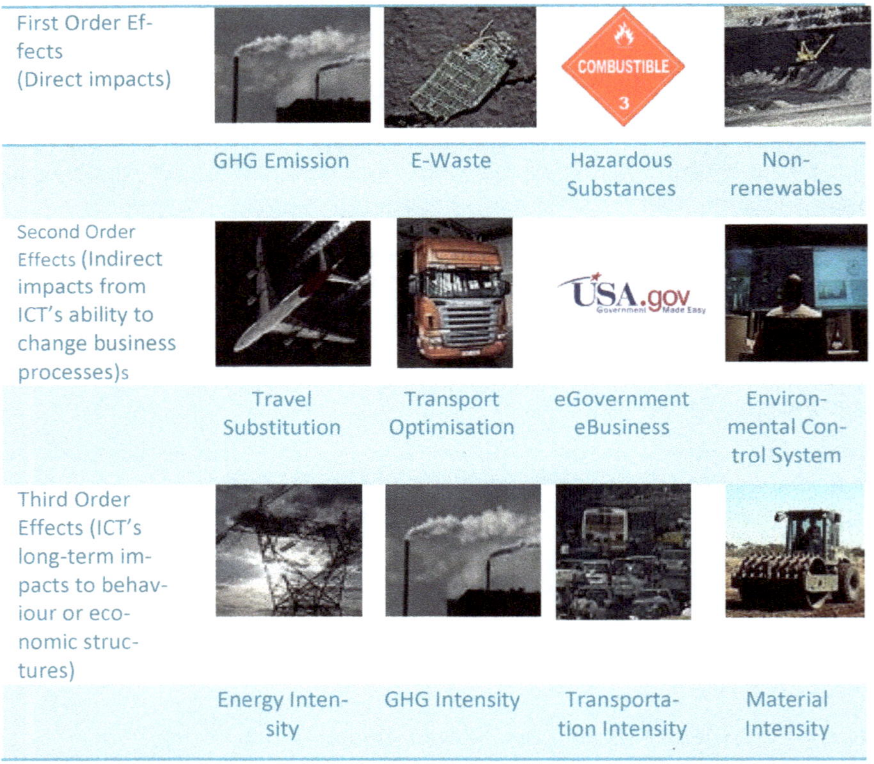

First Order Effects (Direct impacts)
COMBUSTIBLE
3
GHG Emission
E-Waste
Hazardous Substances
Non-renewables
Second Order Effects (Indirect impacts from ICT's ability to change business processes)s
USA.gov
Travel Substitution
Transport Optimisation
eGovernment eBusiness
Environmental Control System
Third Order Effects (ICT's long-term impacts to behaviour or economic structures)
Energy Intensity
GHG Intensity
Transportation Intensity
Material Intensity

Images: 1. Creative Commons (CC) Attribution to FreeFoto.Com; 2. CC Attribution to Guinnog; 5. CC Attribution to Sergey Kustov; 6. CC Atribution to Zaphod; 9. CC Atribution to JGkatz; 10. CC Atribution to NOMAD; and 3, 4, 7, 8 and 11. Public Domain Images.

Figure 16.2. The effects of ICT on environmental sustainability (adapted from IPTS, 2004)

Note: Figure is based on the findings of a report by Institute for Prospective Technological Studies (IPTS) for the European Commission, "The Future Impact of the ICTs on Environmental Sustainability". Technical Report EUR 21384 EN, ECSC-EEC-EAEC, Brussels, Luxembourg, 2004, (http://ftp.jrc.es/EURdoc/eur21384en.pdf)

16.5.5 The Effects of ICT's Global CO_2 Emissions

The "dirty little secret" of ICT's global CO2 emissions, (a largely unknown fact prior to 2007, when analyst Gartner stated that the ICT sector was responsible for 2% of global carbon emissions) is that ICT's global greenhouse gas emissions resulting from electrical use are equivalent to those of the airline industry. The distribution of emissions of the major categories of ICT equipment is as follows:

- 39% is due to computers and monitors (all figures are excluding embodied energy - i.e., the energy to manufacture, package, and transport)
- 31% is due to telecoms (LAN & Office telecom - 7%, Mobile telecom - 9%. Fixed-line telecoms - 5%), and
- 23% is due to servers (including cooling of various storage facilities from server rooms to data centres) (Gartner, 2007). The Vital Role that ICTs Can Play in Addressing Climate Change

16.5.6 The Vital Role that ICTs Can Play in Addressing Climate Change

In response to the recommendations of the United Nations Framework Convention on Climate Change (UNFCCC, www.unfccc.int) on the need to cap global greenhouse gas (GHG) emissions, governments around the world are looking at internationally-agreed standards and policies that governments and the ICT industry can apply to tackle climate change. Various international industry bodies as well as international bodies such as the ITU, GeSI and APECTEL have issued declarations that illustrate the enormous potential of ICT solutions to cut their own emissions.[6]

The seminal SMART2020 report illustrates well the potential of ICTs to enable energy efficiency in the key opportunity areas - travel/transport, buildings, grids, and industry systems - to help turn potential CO2 reductions into reality. This will include opportunities offered through these systems as well as ICT dematerialization, such that the energy efficiency gain achieved in these sectors can produce an outcome whereby ICTs can save five times their own emissions, comparing the baseline of 2002 with 2020.

The Smart2020 report further stated that while some ICT growth in mature developed markets can be expected, the most rapid growth of ICT use will be due to the rising demand for ICT in developing countries (Fig. 16.3.). The report

---

[6] International Telecommunications Union (ITU) and the Global eSustainability Initiative (GeSI) have issued a joint publication on how ICTs can address various problems that all countries (particularly developing countries) face with respect to Climate Change. ICT s can be used to mitigate the impact of other sectors on greenhouse gas (GHG) emissions and to help countries adapt to climate change. (See www.itu.int/dms_pub/itu-t/oth/4B/01/T4B010000010001PDFE.pdf). The 44th Meeting of the APEC Telecommunications and Information Working Group (APECTEL) in Kuala Lumpur, Malaysia (September, 2011) discussed ways to implement the TEL 2010-2015 Strategic Action Plan, which contains the development of ICT applications in Green ICT for Sustainable Growth (www.apec.org).

stated that "just one in 10 people owns a PC in China today (2008); by 2020, that will rise to seven in 10, comparable to current ownership rates in the US. In just 12 years' time, one in two Chinese people will own a mobile phone and half of all households will be connected by broadband. It will be a similar story in India. By 2020, almost a third of the global population will own a PC (currently one in 50), 50% will own a mobile phone, and one in 20 households will have a broadband connection (GeSI, 2008).

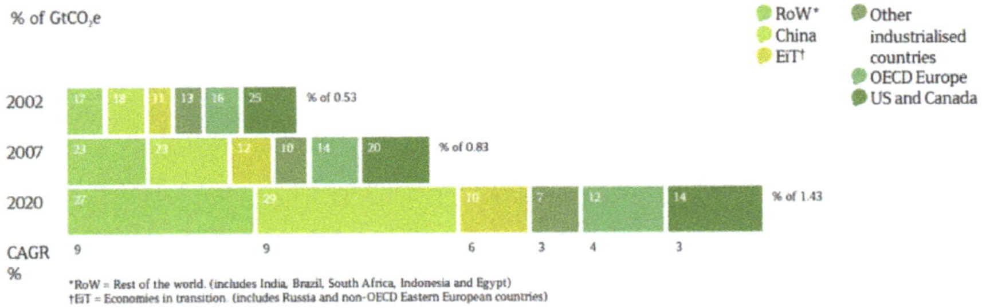

Figure 16.3. The ICT global footprint by geography (2002, 2007, and 2020)

Fast Facts from the United Kingdom: ICT Energy Consumption

Energy consumption of ICT is considerable and it is rapidly growing.

- *ICT equipment makes up for 10% of the UK's electricity consumption*
- *Non-domestic energy consumption from ICT equipment rose by 70% from 2000 - 2006 and is forecast to rise a further 40% by 2020*
- *Data centers account for about a quarter of the ICT sector's emissions,*
- *In the US, electricity demand from data centers doubled in the five years up to 2006, meaning 1.5% of the total electricity demand in the US was from data centers, and it is predicted to double again by 2011. This would result in an annual electricity cost of $7.4 billion.*

However, there are real potential savings and quick wins for organizations that are greening their ICT infrastructure.

- *30% of the overall energy consumed by PCs is wasted by leaving them switched on when not in use.*
- *1,000 PCs running 24/7 cost around £70,000 in electricity over a year.*
- *A third of employees in the UK do not switch off their PCs when they leave the office at the end of the day, costing the UK £123 million a year in electricity.*

Why is "switching off" PCs important?

More than 6 million PCs were left on over Christmas 2006, consuming nearly 40 million kW of electricity - enough to cook 30 million turkeys. Together with the printers and other hardware, this would have produced 19,000 tons of CO2, at a cost of around £8.6 million.

Source: Global Action Plan (2009) Green ICT Handbook: A Guide to Green ICT, Global Action Plan (creating the climate for change), URL: http://www.globalactionplan.org.uk/

16.5.7 The ICT Sustainability or Green IT "Readiness" Framework

Different people can understand ICT sustainability differently. Too many definitions have led to a lack of clarity that has made it difficult to measure the effectiveness or the extent of an organization's implementation of Green ICT measures (or "readiness"). Just as an organization "can't manage what it can't measure", equally, the organization "can't measure what it can't define."

The ICT sustainability "readiness" framework - which is used as the basis for the checklist below as well as for on-going global benchmarking (Connection Research for Fujitsu Limited, 2011) - is a way of defining ICT sustainability and measuring its many components. The framework defines four general areas or "pillars" of ICT sustainability:

- Equipment lifecycle
- End user/distributed computing
- Enterprise and data center, and
- ICT as a low-carbon enabler

The first three cover an area generally called "Green for ICT" or "greening the ICT infrastructure" while the last pillar is often loosely described as "Green by ICT" or "ICT for Green".

This framework can also be used for further ICT sustainability benchmarking for an individual government agency across time or for a cross-sectional study of various sectors comparing components of the private sector and government agencies as a whole.

16.5.8 The ICT "Readiness" Checklist

The checklist (adapted from AGIMO, 2007) is aimed at raising awareness among stakeholders about the impact of government ICT resources on the environment. It provides information and guidelines to people responsible for managing government ICT products and services. The checklist can help to:

- Identify existing practices within the agency that influence management of the environmental impact
- Identify priority areas for improvements, and

- Develop policies and plans to implement improvements in managing the environmental impact.

Step1. Formulate an ICT sustainability plan

Has your agency formulated an ICT sustainability plan that outlines the details of the policies and practices that your agency will adopt?

Government agencies can reduce the impact of their ICT activities by formulating:

- A list of Green ICT "quick wins" that includes high, medium, and longer priority option practices in the agency
- Procurement policy guidance, and
- A government data center strategy.

Step 2. Procurement of ICT products and services

Has your agency considered the environmental impact of ICT products and services in business plans and procurement plans?

- The use of environmental standards or energy ratings for ICT products and services that are being procured
- The environmental performance of the suppliers of ICT products and services that are being procured, and
- An environmentally sound disposal plan for ICT products and services no longer required.

Step 3. Re-use, recycling, and disposal of products and services

Has your agency identified methods or means by which ICT products and services can be re-used or recycled?

When considering the disposal of ICT products, agencies should identify opportunities for recycling or re-use.

- Make recycling decisions by considering your national government waste reduction, and adopting or putting together an official guideline on this matter
- Consider programs that provide free or subsidized computers to the community
- Consider recycling toner cartridges and using recycled toner cartridges rather than purchasing new cartridges
- Recycle ICT equipment packaging, and
- Monitor contract performance in relation to re-use and recycling clauses in your contract for ICT products and services and ensure that there is a clause for the vendors to enter into a used equipment take-back arrangement program in the procurement contract.

Has your agency identified the hazardous material in your ICT products and services and the means by which they will be disposed?

- Put in place a strategy to communicate what is hazardous waste in ICT products and how it should be disposed
- Dispose of waste in accordance with your national guidance on electronic scrap/eWwaste and hazardous waste material, and
- Ensure that any hazardous waste produced by your agency is disposed of appropriately, and that it does not contravene your national hazardous waste regulations for exports and imports of waste products.

Step 4. End-user operation of ICT products and services

Has your agency implemented policies and practices that encourage good environmental awareness and practice in the environmentally friendly use of ICT?

- Switch off all ICT equipment (including printing equipment) outside of work hours and issue posters and directives to encourage staff to implement this policy. In addition, if possible, use ICT to automate the power switch-off process of as much equipment as possible (including printing equipment).

Has your agency considered setting all desktop PCs to black screens or static screen savers instead of active screensavers?

Has your agency considered deploying software that can automatically switch off computers, monitors, and other IP-based equipment in your building when they are not in use? Has it considered implementing automatic software patching for computers, or providing you with reports of the energy or carbon emissions of this equipment?

- If your agency is not yet able to acquire such software, consider some free software (e.g., Microsoft Server Active Windows "script" or open source alternatives) that can just switch off computers when not in use during the day.

Has your agency considered implementing a policy such that all staff computers or associated monitors will have an internal setting such that, if they are in an "idle" state (when not in use) for longer than 10 minutes, they will be switched off, or, if ICT equipment cannot be switched off, activate standby or sleep mode?

Has your agency considered a policy to regularly measure the power consumption of all ICT equipment as a component of total power use?

Step 5. Enterprise and data center operation of ICT products and services

Has your agency considered implementing a medium and long-term data center strategy as a way to reduce the environmental impacts of commuting?

There are at least three major aims of such a strategy:

- Your agency might consider adopting, as soon as is practicable, modern technologies and practices that will improve the effectiveness and efficiency of the data center use.

- Your agency might consider adopting a practice where data center sites and services can be shared in ways that reduce the duplication and unnecessary cost of base infrastructure.
- Your agency might consider adopting a practice where your government data center sites can optimally match the business needs and requirements of the agency. Only those systems that have a genuine business need to operate on a 24/7 basis should be located in expensive, high-end data centers.

Step 6. ICT as a low carbon enabler

Has your agency considered implementing "ICT for Green" or "Green for ICT" measures to use ICT as an enabling technology to help your agency and the wider community to reduce their carbon emissions?

The key areas are:

- Using ICT for teleconferencing rather than face-to-face meetings to reduce the environmental impact associated with commuting
- Implementing a policy of using tele-networking and online collaboration, such as office social networking software, as a way to reduce environmental impacts of commuting, and
- Adopting an integrated energy management for the buildings that your agency occupies that would enable the automatic switching off of all IP-based equipment in the building (including computers, switching/networking, printing, heating, ventilation air-conditioning (HVAC), and lighting equipment) outside of work hours and when they are not in use.

Using an integrated client/server architecture, your agency can:

- Manage/report the energy requirements/use of Power over Ethernet (PoE) of all IP-based devices
- Extend enterprise power management to desktop and laptop PCs, and
- Allow integration with the ecosystem partner solutions to control building management systems (through the IP-based HVAC and lighting systems).

Step 7. Undertake energy/carbon auditing and quality assurance, and develop executive summary/reporting

Has your agency considered a policy of implementing environmental impact reporting on the use of ICT equipment?

- Government agencies can make significant cost savings from reduced energy costs, increased efficiency, and greater recycling and/or reduction of electronic waste by adopting an Environmental Management System (EMS) or energy/carbon emission measurement software (CEMS). An EMS/CEMS is a tool for measuring and improving an organization's compliance with regulations and management of environmental risks.

Has your agency considered an evaluation of the factors that may inhibit it from implementing an ICT Sustainability (or "Green IT") Policy?

While government agencies can make significant cost savings from reduced energy costs, there are well documented inhibiting factors such as:

- The absence of enforceable government regulations
- The lack of senior management leadership on Green IT
- The cost of Green IT solutions
- The extent (or lack) of Green IT solutions
- The unclear business value of Green IT, and
- The extent (or lack) of Green ICT training in your agency.

Quick Quiz

1. How do you define value for money? Why is it important for governments to achieve value for money?
2. Can you identify three Critical Success Factors (CSFs) that might apply to any ICT project?
3. Can you identify any Key Performance Indicators (KPIs) that might apply to both project work and operational ICT?

Chapter Highlights

- Contextual dimensions such as politics, ethics, and environment that are unique to a country's concern often override other major issues surrounding eGovernment implementation and management.
- Starting from the planning stage of eGovernment systems, environmental factors need to be tackled by managers through their knowledge and appropriate response to the situation.
- Several intangible factors dominate this environment, such as the lack of knowledge, expertise, and planning and strategy. Other significant factors include the decision makers' attitudes and mindsets, and the political will and leadership.
- Leadership drive and political will are often the key factors for ICT diffusion in developing countries, but, due to the lack of a clear, consistent, and long-term strategy and vision, political will does often not translate into action.
- Unethical use of ICT in the public service could compromise official/public interest, breach citizens' privacy, and abuse personal data under custody.
- The government has a moral obligation to maintain transparency when providing government services through eGovernment, and also to uphold people's ethical rights.
- There is a close relationship between eGovernment and administrative reform, and both should take place hand-in-hand.
- A global climate change can only be effective when each society is better informed and prepared. For this, ICT can play a greater role in information dissemination, education, and technical investigation.
- Green IT practices and policies are likely to contribute in preserving the better environment for future generations.
- ICT's role in helping the environment can be classified into three categories: (1). Direct effects or the first-order effects - impact of ICT on the environment, such as contamination by greenhouse gas emissions; (2). Second-order effects - ability to change business processes to improve the environmental impacts; and (3). Third-order effects - long-term effects that bring about changes to behaviors or economic structures.
- Data centers and networking infrastructure typically account for more than 20% of the energy used in an office building, with up to 70% attributed to ICT in typical government offices.
- Studies have shown that ICT-related emissions can easily be cut by around 15 - 30% just by implementing simple behavior change such as switching off computers at the end of the day.
- The ICT Sustainability Readiness Framework stands on four pillars: 1. Equipment lifecycle, 2. End user/distributed computing, 3. Enterprise and data center, and 4. ICT as a low-carbon enabler.

Review Questions

1. What are the environmental constraints that impact eGovernment implementation and management?
2. How can eGovernment help to establish some of the basic human rights, such as access to information?
3. Why do vested interest groups or authoritarian regimes want to resist eGovernment?
4. What does "whistleblower" mean? Is this legally accepted?
5. How do organizational politics influence eGovernment?
6. What is IT leadership? What are the traits of IT leadership?
7. What are the ethical issues surrounding eGovernment?
8. Give three examples of ethical principles applied in eGovernment implementation.
9. What is a digital signature? What legal implications does it have?
10. What is the purpose of an ICT sustainability (or "Green IT" or "Green Computing") policy?
11. List three actions in which ICT sustainability can improve energy efficiency.
12. Why is it important to assess all costs associated with an investment or to perform a cost/benefit analysis before implementing any ICT sustainability measures?
13. What is the approximate percentage of the overall energy consumed by PCs that is wasted by leaving on when not in use?
14. Who offers the "greenest" eGear (desktops and workstations) now?
15. Who offers ENERGY STAR certified PCs now?
16. Who offers ENERGY STAR Servers now?

Discussion questions

1. Why and how does political environment influence eGovernment implementation?
2. As an eGovernment manager, what should be your role in managing political effects/influences?
3. There is a close relationship between eGovernment and administrative reform - justify this statement.
4. How do you apply the principles of ethics at different levels (toward citizens, in the administration, and among the administrators) through eGovernment?
5. Why is it important to invest in ICT Sustainable solutions?
6. Review the lesson learnt from the initial ICT Energy Audit report and identify any problems that may arise due to management or staff resistance to the Green IT "quick win" relating to behavioural changes in the business-as-usual scenario in your agency.

Exercises

1. Analyze a case or a proposal for formulating and adopting an ICT sustainability plan for your agency, either as a stand-alone strategy or as part of the environment management plan, using the checklist questions in this chapter and identify any missing information.
2. Create a list of benefits in terms of energy cost savings and environmental accreditation (ISO14000 series, or other systems that might be applicable in your country), sustainability credibility acknowledgements, or CSR publicity for the ICT Sustainability Proposal for your agency.
3. Create a set of "Quick Win" cost-saving measures for the ICT Sustainability Plan. For example, the cost savings from conducting an inventory to conduct a periodic ICT energy audit. This audit will involve the measurement of all ICT equipment before and after the implementation of energy efficiency ("quick win") measures. Below is a guide to the equipment you should look to measure. The list is not exhaustive and should be prepared according to your agency's requirements.
   Desktop end user environment:
   - Desktops
   - Laptops
   - Monitors
   - Thin clients
   - Printers, and
   - Multi-functional devices
4. How much can your agency save in terms of energy costs and carbon dioxide emissions of your PC desktops? Please use energy calculators offered by IT equipment vendors or non-profit organizations (e.g., FFITS.org, ClimateSaversComputing.org, and others offered by IT vendors).

Further Reading

AGIMO. (2009). Australian Government ICT Sustainability Plan 2010-2015.
The Architecture Journal/Microsoft. (2011, May). Green Computing.
GreenICT.org.uk. (2009). Green ICT Handbook.
AGIMO. (2010). Green ICT Procurement Toolkit.
Green ICT Quick Wins. Retrieved from http://www.finance.gov.au/eGovernment/ strategy-and-governance/sustainable-ict/quick-wins.html
OGC. (2008). Green ICT: UK Government Greening ICT Strategy.

References

AGIMO (2007). Better Practice Checklist, Managing the environmental impact of information and communications technology (ICT) URL http://www.finance.gov.au/agimo-archive/better-practice-checklists/environmental-impact.html

Aldrich, R., & Parello, J. (2011). IP-enabled energy management: A proven strategy for administering energy as a service. Indiana: Sybex-Wiley.

Amoussou-Guenou, R. (2004). Legal aspects of eGovernment. Paper presented at the Regional Workshop on Implementing eGovernment, United Nations Conference Center, Bangkok.

Barata, K. (2004). Archives in the digital age. Journal of the Society of Archivists, 25(1), 63-70. Boudrez, F. (2007). Digital signatures and electronic records. Archival Science 7, 179-193.

Chopra, K., & Wallace, W. A. (2003). Trust in electronic environments. Paper presented at the Proceedings of the 36th Hawaii International Conference on Systems Sciences.

Connection Research for Fujitsu Limited. (2011). ICT Sustainability: The Global Benchmark.

e-Africa. (n.d.). In the Regional Workshop on Building eGovernance capacity in Africa. Retrieved from http://unpan1.un.org/intradoc/groups/public/documents/cafrad/unpan006497.pdf

Ecos Magazine. (2009, Aug-Sep). Greening IT. 9, 24-27. Retrieved from http://www.ecosmagazine. com/?paper=EC150p24

Gartner. (2007, April). Green IT: The New Industry Shockwave. Presented at Symposium/ITXPO Conference, April 2007.

Gartner. (2007). Green IT: Dealing with the shock wave. Paper presented at the Gartner Symposium/ ITxpo Sydney November.

Global eSustainability Initiative (GeSI). (2008). SMART2020: Enabling the Low- Carbon Economy in the Information Age. Retrieved from http://gesi.org/files/Reports/Smart%202020%20report%20in%20English.pdf

Hao, W. (2007). A comparative study of how political mechanism influence digital government between united states and china. Paper presented at the 8th Annual Association of Pacific Rim Universities Doctoral Students Conference Tokyo, Japan.

Hilty, L. M. (2008). Information technology and sustainability. Essays on the relationship between ICT and sustainable development. Books on demand. ISBN: 9783837019704

Horrocks, I. (2009). Experts and eGovernment: Power, influence and the capture of a policy domain in the UK. . Information, Communication and Society, 12(1), 110-127.

Imran, A., Turner, T., & Gregor, S. (2008). Educate to innovate - fast tracking ICT management capabilities amongst the key government officials for eGovernment implementation in Bangladesh. Paper presented at the SIG GlobDev Workshop, Paris, France.

IPTS. (2004). The future impact of the ICTs on environmental sustainability. Retrieved from http://ftp.jrc. es/EURdoc/eur21384en.pdf

Kalathil, S., & Boas, T. C. (2001). The Internet and state control in authoritarian regimes: China, Cuba, and the counterrevolution. Information Revolution and World Politics Project. Retrieved from http://carnegieendowment.org/files/21KalathilBoas.pdf

Kandelin, N. A., Lin, T. W., & Muntoro , K. R. (1998). A study of the attitudes of Indonesian managers toward key factors in information system development and implementation. Journal of Global Information Management, 6(3), 17-26.

Kaufeld, N. v. U., Chari, V., & Freeme, D. (2009). Critical success factors for effective IT leadership. Electronic Journal Information Systems Evaluation, 12(1), 119-128.

Kelegai, L. and Middleton, M. (2004). Factors influencing information systems success in Papua New Guinea organisations: A case analysis. Australasian Journal of Information Systems, 11(2), 57-69.

Leith, P. (2002). Legal issues in eGovernment. Paper presented at the JURIX Workshop on eGovernment ,15th Annual International Conference on Legal Knowledge and Information Systems, London, UK.

Mullen, H., and Horner, D. S. (2004). Ethical problems for eGovernment: An evaluative framework. Electronic Journal of eGovernment, 2(3), 187-196.

Nidumolu, S. R., Goodman, S. E., Vogel, D. R., & Danowitz, A. K. (1996). Information technology for local administration support: The governorates project in Egypt. MIS Quarterly, 20(2), 197-224.

Reynolds, G. W. (2010). Ethics in Information Technology. Boston: Cengage.

Rocheleau, B. (2006). Information management and ethical issues in government. Hershey PA: Idea Group.

Stone, R. W., & Henry, J. W. (2003). Identifying and developing measures of information technology ethical work climates. Journal of Business Ethics, 46(4), 337-350.

Taifur, S. (2004). Comprehensive study of egovernment initiatives in Bangladesh. Planning Division, Ministry of Planning, Government of Bangladesh.

Wilson, E. J. (2004). The information revolution and developing countries. London: MIT Press.

Worthington, T. (2011). ICT sustainability: Assessment and strategies for a low carbon future. North Carolina: LuLu Press.

Zaitun, A. B., Mashkuri, Y., & Wood-Harper, A. T. (2000). Systems integration for a developing country: Failure or success? A Malaysian case study. The Electronic Journal of Information Systems in Developing Countries, 3(5), 1-10.

PART V - SUPPLEMENT

Part V - Supplement

This part provides report templates that supplement the project management chapter.

CHAPTER 17
eGovernment Project Management Supplement

This chapter contains material that supplements the project management methodology in Chapter 12. It contains templates that can be used to produce project management reports. It contains:

- Project Scoping Document Template
- Project Schedule Template
- Status Report
- Project Logs
- Project Closure Report
- eGovernment Project Manager's Checklist
- eGovernment Project Phase Completion Checklist

17.1 Project Scoping Document Template

1. Project Title			
Keywords			
Project Manager		**Contact**	P: E:
Date Raised		**Estimated Cost**	
Expected Start Date		**Estimated Completion Date**	
2. Project Manager Sign-off			
Name	**Signature**	**Date**	
3. Justification			
Background			
Project Summary			
Consideration of Alternatives			
4. Project Scope			
Scope Definition			
Primary Deliverables			
Constraints			
Assumptions			
Related Work			
Exclusions			
Primary Risks			

5. High-Level Schedule			
Phase	Deliverable	Start	Finish

6. Key Resource Requirements			
Role/Resource	Description	Required Skills/Attributes	Utilisation

7. Project Stakeholders				
Stakeholder	Influence Level (L, M, H)	Impact Level (L, M, H)	Communication Requirements	Communication Methods

8. Budget Estimate	
Materials & Equipment	
Personnel (Internal & External)	
Operating Costs	
Other	
TOTAL	

9. Project Authorisation			
	Name	Signature	Date
Project Sponsor			
CIO (if required)			
CFO (if required)			

17.2 Project Schedule Template

1. Project Title		Date Created		Last Updated	
Project Manager		Contact	P:	E:

2. Overall Project Summary	Start date	End date	Duration	Task Costs	Overhead Costs	Total Cost
Planned						
Actual						
Variance (Planned – Actual)						

Work Breakdown

ID	Deliverable/Task	hType (D, T)	Status (N, U, C)	Responsible	Resources		Cost	Start	End	Duration	1	2	3	4	5	6	7	8	9	10	11	12	..
						Plan																	
						Actual																	
						Plan																	
						Actual																	
						Plan																	
						Actual																	
						Plan																	
						Actual																	
						Plan																	
						Actual																	
						Plan																	
						Actual																	
						Plan																	
						Actual																	
						Plan																	
						Actual																	

17.3 Status Report

17.3.1 Completion Instructions

The Project Status Report provides a snapshot of the current performance of the project. It should be completed at intervals appropriate for the length and complexity of the project – at least monthly. The Project Status Report provides information that can inform the Project Sponsor's decision making and is a key document in the control process for the project. The document should be clear and succinct, making use of bullet-points, diagrams, tables etc, as appropriate.

17.3.2 Determining Traffic-Light Status

Throughout the Project Status Report, the status of project aspects is indicated visually through the use of traffic-light colours (green, orange and red) and face symbols. Wherever a 'Traffic-light Status' is required, the appropriate colour and symbol can be determined using the table below.

Colour	Description	Reporting Action
GREEN	The project (project aspect) is progressing as planned, with no significant issues.	Status update only. No issues/ risks/ scope changes for advice or approval.
ORANGE	There are one or more issues which threaten the project (project aspect); however, the project manager believes they are recoverable and an approach has been developed to deal with them.	Issues briefly outlined along with their planned treatment. For advice only – no Project Sponsor involvement/support anticipated.
RED	There are one or more significant issues which threaten the success of the project (i.e. they will prevent meeting the approved schedule, budget, quality, scope or strategic intent, if they are not addressed).	Issues briefly outlined in this report along with recommended action and rationale. Advice/decisions required of the Project Sponsor

17.3.3 Project Title

This section provides the primary reference details that identify the project. These details can be cross-referenced to the other documentation created throughout the project.

Field	Instructions	Example
Project Title	Record the title of the project. This should match the title established by the Project Scoping Document.	Implementation of an Electronic Document Management System
Project Manager	The name of the project manager.	Mr P. Sarkhel
Contact	Contact details (phone and email) for the project manager.	P: 880-2-8311111 psarkhel@bangladesh.gov.bd
Reporting Period Start	The start date for the period of time covered by this Status Report.	1 Apr 2012
Reporting Period Finish	The end date for the period of time covered by this Status Report.	30 Apr 2012

17.3.4 Status Overview

The Status Overview provides an at-a-glance summary of the status of the overall project. Although it is on the first page, this section is usually completed after sections 3 to 6, as it provides a high-level overview of the rest of the document.

Field	Instructions	Example
Status Overview	Provide a brief summary of the overall status of the project.	Project is within 5% of budget and 10% of schedule. Issues have arisen but are under control.
Overall Status	Enter the overall Traffic-light Status of the project, based on the definitions in Table 1. The overall Traffic-light Status of the project should be the most severe of the status fields from the remainder of the document. For example, if the Budget Status is ORANGE, then the Overall Status cannot be GREEN.	ORANGE
Percentage Work Complete	Indicate what percentage of the project work has been completed. This can be calculated from the Project Schedule.	10%
Budget Spent	Indicate the amount of the project budget that has been spent. This can be calculated from either the Project Schedule or from the financial records for the project.	$26,010
Time Spent	Indicate how much time has been spent on	6 weeks

Field	Instructions	Example
	the project. (The difference between the reporting period finish date and the date that the project actually started.)	
Planned Work Complete	Indicate what percentage of the project work was originally planned to be completed. This can be calculated from the Project Schedule.	11%
Planned Budget Spent	Indicate the amount of the project budget that was originally planned to be spent by now. This can be calculated from the baseline Project Schedule.	$25,000
Planned Time Spent	Indicate how much time was planned to have been spent on the project. (The difference between the reporting period finish date and the date that the project was planned to start.)	6 weeks

17.3.5 Schedule Status

This section provides information on all deliverables that were planned (expected) to be completed during the reporting period.

Field	Instructions	Example
Deliverables Expected - ID	The ID of the deliverable, taken from the Project Schedule.	1.0
Deliverables Expected - Deliverable	The name and/or description of the deliverable, taken from the Project Schedule.	System Requirements Specification
Achieved	Enter YES if the deliverable was completed during the reporting period or NO if the deliverable has not been completed.	NO
Status	Enter the Traffic-light Status of the deliverable based on the definitions in Table 1.	**ORANGE**
Explanation	If the Status is not GREEN, provide a brief explanation for the status and indicate any likely impacts on the overall schedule.	Awaiting CIO review of Requirements Specification document. CIO contacted 30/4/12 – review due by 2/5/12 with no issues. Should not impact the overall schedule.

17.3.6 Budget Status

The Budget Status has two main sections:

- Current - provides a budget summary for the project to date.
- Forecast - provides an updated budget forecast for the whole of the project based on the current status of the project.

Current

Field	Instructions	Example
Budget (A)	Enter the amount of the project budget that was originally planned to be spent by now. This can be calculated from the Project Schedule.	$25,000
Actual (B)	Enter the amount of the project budget that has actually been spent. This can be calculated from either the Project Schedule or from the financial records for the project.	$26,010
Variance (C=A-B)	Calculate the difference between the amount of the project budget that was originally planned to be spent and the amount that has actually been spent.	-$1,010

Forecast

Field	Instructions	Example
Budget (A)	Enter the amount of the project budget that was originally planned to be spent by now. This can be calculated from the Project Schedule.	$25,000
Actual (B)	Enter the amount of the project budget that has actually been spent. This can be calculated from either the Project Schedule or from the financial records for the project.	$26,010
Variance (C=A-B)	Calculate the difference between the amount of the project budget that was originally planned to be spent and the amount that has actually been spent.	-$1,010
Explanation	If the current Variance exceeds ±10% of the approved budget to date, comment on the reasons and likely impacts on the overall budget.	Current Variance <5%. No budget issues.
Status	Enter the Traffic-light Status of the budget, based on the definitions in Table 1.	**GREEN**

17.3.7 Risk Status

This section identifies any risks that have arisen or changed during this reporting period. Do not include risks that have already been dealt with in previous status reports and have not changed. If no risks have arisen or changed, this should be noted.

Field	Instructions	Example
Risk ID	The ID of the risk, taken from the Risk Log.	R7
Risk	The description of the risk, taken from the Risk Log.	Reviews involving members of the organisation outside of the project team may take longer than expected. Additional review time has been allowed in the Project Schedule to reduce the risk.
Status	Enter the Traffic-light Status of the risk, based on the definitions in Table 1.	GREEN

17.3.8 Issue Status

This section identifies any issues that have arisen or changed during this reporting period. Do not include issues that have already been dealt with in previous status reports and have not changed. If no issues have arisen or changed, this should be noted.

Field	Instructions	Example
Issue ID	The ID of the issue, taken from the Issue Log.	I3
Issue	The description of the issue, taken from the Issue Log.	Some members of the project team have been ill lately, which threatened the Project Schedule. Other team members have been working overtime to compensate.
Status	Enter the Traffic-light Status of the issue, based on the definitions in Table 1.	ORANGE

17.3.9 Project Sponsor Comment

This section acknowledges that the Project Sponsor has discussed the Status Report with the project manager and is comfortable with the information provided. It is important that any outcomes of the

Status Report discussion are captured so that appropriate action can be taken.

Field	Instructions	Example
Project Sponsor Comment	Record any actions/decisions that arise from presenting the Status Report to the Project Sponsor.	Project is on track. Project Sponsor will undertake to explain the importance of timely reviews to non-project team members, to speed up review process.
Signature	Signature of the Project Sponsor accepting the Status Report and the comment recorded on their behalf.	
Date	The date that the Project Sponsor signed the document	1 May 2012

17.4 Project Status Report Template

Project Status Report Template

1. Project Title				
Project Manager			Contact	P: E:
Reporting Period	Start:		Finish:	

2. Status Overview			Overall Status	
Actual		Planned		
Percentage Work Complete		Planned Work Complete		
Budget Spent		Planned Budget Spent		
Time Spent		Planned Time Spent		

3. Schedule Status				
Deliverables Expected		Achieved	Status	Explanation (For Red and Orange status only)
ID	Deliverable			

4. Budget Status							
Current				Forecast			
Period	Budget	Actual	Variance	Period	Budget	Forecast	Variance
	A	B	C = A - B		D	E	F = D - E

Project to Date				Whole of Project			
Explanation							**Status**

5. Risk Status		
Risk ID	**Risk**	**Status**
R		
R		
R		
R		

6. Issue Status		
Issue ID	**Issue**	**Status**
I		
I		
I		
I		

7. Project Sponsor Comment	
Signature	**Date**

17.5 Project Logs

17.5.1 Project Title

This section provides the primary reference details that identify the project. These details can be cross-referenced to the other documentation created throughout the project.

Field	Instructions	Example
Project Title	Record the title of the project. This should match the title established by the Project Scoping Document.	Implementation of an Electronic Document Management System
Date Created	Date that the Log was created.	11 Mar 2012
Last Updated	Date that the Log was last updated.	16 Jun 2012
Project Manager	The name of the project manager.	Mr P. Sarker
Contact	Contact details (phone and email) for the project manager.	P: 880-2-8311111 psarkhel@bangladesh.gov.bd

17.5.2 Quality Log Completion Instructions

The Quality Log lists each of the project deliverables (product, service or data) and documents the level of quality required, the quality control (i.e. review) details and quality assurance (i.e. sign-off) approvals. It is a very important document in ensuring that the product outputs meet the end-users' needs. All project deliverables should have quality criteria.

Deliverable Quality

This section provides the quality requirements and review details.

Field	Instructions	Example
ID	The ID for referencing the quality criteria. These should be numerically ordered and prefixed with a 'Q' to distinguish them from other IDs.	Q3
Deliverable (ID; Name)	The ID and name/description of the deliverable (from the Project Schedule) to which the quality criteria relate.	1.0 System Requirements Specification
Quality Criteria	Identify the criteria that will be used to determine the quality of the deliverable. This should be based on the intended use of the deliverable and the needs of the users. Quality criteria must be clear and measurable.	Document must capture: System context Business requirements Functional requirements

Field	Instructions	Example
Responsible	The name of the person responsible for checking the quality of the deliverable once it is completed.	Mrs T. Binkley
Review Date	The date that the quality of the deliverable was reviewed by the person responsible.	4 Jun 2012
Result	The outcome of the quality review (i.e. did the deliverable meet the quality criteria).	Pass. Document captures all necessary requirements.
Action(s)	If the quality of the deliverable is unacceptable, document the action(s) taken to address the quality issue.	Not applicable.
Sign-off Date	The date that the quality of the deliverable was approved.	6 Jun 2012
Approver	The name of the person who approved the quality of the deliverable. This should be someone with sufficient authority to approve project outputs (often the project manager).	Mr P. Sarker

17.5.3 Risk Log Completion Instructions

The Risks Log lists all identified risks for the project and the related mitigation strategies. As far as possible, project risks should be identified during the Planning Phase of the project; however additional risks may become apparent during the Implementation Phase and should be documented and managed.

Determining Risk Rating

In order to visually identify the relative importance/threat of different risks, each risk is given a colour- coded rating (green, orange or red) based on its likelihood and consequence. The risk rating can be determined using Table 17.2.

Table 17.2: Determining the rating of a risk

Likelihood / Consequence	Low	Medium	High
Low	Green	Green	Orange
Medium	Green	Orange	Orange
High	Orange	Orange	Red

For any risks where the rating is Orange or Red, a detailed mitigation strategy should be developed and may need to be documented separately.

Risks

This section captures all risks identified throughout the project.

Field	Instructions	Example
ID	The ID for referencing the risk. These should be numerically ordered and prefixed with an 'R' to distinguish them from other IDs.	R1
Risk	Describe the risk to the project. Risks are often documented as "If X happens, then the result is likely to be Y".	Project servers are being upgraded during the Implementation Phase, which may impact testing of the pilot system.
Mitigation	Identify how the risk will be dealt with (mitigated). Mitigation strategies commonly attempt to avoid the risk, transfer the risk to another party, reduce the risk or, if the risk is low enough, accept the risk.	Additional time has been allowed in the schedule to accommodate slight delays in pilot testing and contingency funds have been identified to hire additional hardware for the pilot testing if necessary.
Likelihood	The likelihood of the risk occurring: **High** - If no action is taken, the risk will almost certainly eventuate. **Medium** - If no action is taken, there is a good chance that the risk will eventuate. **Low** - The risk is not likely to eventuate, even if no action is taken.	Medium
Consequence	The consequence for the project (or organisation) if the risk does occur: **High** - If the risk eventuates, the project will not deliver on time/budget/quality or there may be damage to the organisation's reputation. **Medium** - If the risk eventuates, the project may not deliver on time/budget/quality but there is no risk of damage to company reputation. **Low** - If the risk eventuates, the project may not achieve an ideal outcome, but it is not critical to project success.	Medium
Rating	Identify the rating of the risk, based on the likelihood and consequence using	Orange

Field	Instructions	Example
	Table 2. For any risks where the rating is Orange or Red, a detailed mitigation strategy should be developed and may need to be documented separately.	
Date Raised	The date that the risk was raised and entered into the Risk Log.	10 Mar 2012
Status	Identify the status of the risk, according to:	O
	O (Open) – the risk is still valid and may still occur.	
	I (In progress) – the risk has occurred and is being managed (in which case the risk is now an issue and should be captured in the Issue Log).	
	C (Closed) – the risk has either been dealt with or can no longer occur.	
Responsible	The name of the person responsible for monitoring the risk and its mitigation strategy.	Mrs T. Carrow

17.5.4 Issue Log Completion Instructions

The Issue Log captures all issues arising during the course of the project. Issues often arise when a risk eventuates. It is important that all issues are documented, as they will often form the basis for any deviations in the project (scope, budget, schedule, etc) and provide valuable lessons, which also need to be captured and reported.

Issues

This section captures all issues that occur throughout the project.

Field	Instructions	Example
ID	The ID for referencing the issue. These should be numerically ordered and prefixed with an 'I' to distinguish them from other IDs.	I3
Issue	Identify the issue that is affecting the project.	Some members of the project team have been ill lately, which threatened the project schedule.
Priority	Determine the priority of the issue:	Medium

Field	Instructions	Example
	High - High potential of the project not delivering on time/budget/quality or damage to the organisation's reputation if the issue is not addressed.	
	Medium - Some potential of the project not delivering on time/budget/quality but no damage to the organisation's reputation if the issue is not addressed.	
	Low - Resolution of issue could lead to a better project outcome but is not critical to project success.	
Status	Identify the status of the issue, according to:	C
	O (Open) – the issue is affecting the project.	
	I (In Progress) – resolution of the issue is underway.	
	C (Closed) – the issue has been addressed.	
Date Raised	The date that the issue was identified and entered into the Issue Log.	2 May 2012
Raised By	The name of the person who raised the issue.	Mr P. Sarkhel
Responsible	The person responsible for monitoring the issue and its resolution.	Mr P. Sarker
Action(s)	Document the action(s) taken to address the issue.	Other team members worked overtime to keep the project on schedule.

17.5.5 Change Log Completion Instructions

The Change Log charts all changes to the project (scope, budget, schedule, resourcing, etc) throughout its lifecycle. This is often important to allow project stakeholders to understand the reasons for variations in project conduct and outcomes. Changes are commonly required in response to an issue or risk, or as a result of changes to the project environment.

Whenever a change is required to the project, it should be entered into the Change Log. Depending on the complexity of the change, a separated document may also be prepared to adequately describe the change, summarise impacts and seek approval.

Changes

This section captures all changes that are made to the project (scope, time, budget, etc) throughout its lifecycle.

Field	Instructions	Example
ID	The ID for referencing the change. These should be numerically ordered and prefixed with a 'C' to distinguish them from other IDs.	C1
Change	Describe the proposed change to the project.	The original Project Schedule allowed for 2 days of training per person in the use of the new system. It is now apparent that 5 days of training are required. Suggest increasing the duration of the project by 3 days to allow for the additional training.
Priority	Determine the priority of the change:	Low
	High - Failure to implement the change would lead to an inability to deliver project benefits or cause significant damage to the organisation's reputation.	
	Medium - Failure to implement the change may compromise project cost, quality or time.	
	Low - The proposed change could potentially lead to a better outcome but is not necessary for the project to achieve its planned outcomes.	
Status	Identify the status of the change, according to:	A
	P (Proposed) – the change has been identified.	
	I (Investigating) – the change is being investigated to determine if it should be implemented.	

Field	Instructions	Example
	A (Accepted) – the change has been accepted (and will be implemented).	
	R (Rejected) – the change has been rejected (and will not be implemented).	
Date Raised	The date the change was proposed and entered into the Change Log.	13 Apr 2012
Raised By	The name of the person who proposed the change.	Mr P. Sarker
Responsible	The name of the person responsible for monitoring the change and its implementation.	Mrs T. Binkley
Decision Reasoning	Document the decision that was made regarding the change (was it implemented or not) and the reason for the decision.	The schedule was extended by 3 days, as it was felt that the additional benefits of having properly trained users outweighed the slight delay.

17.5.6 Lessons Log Completion Instructions

The Lessons Log is a repository of any lessons learned during the project that can be usefully applied to other projects. Lessons can include both things that went well and should be done again, as well as things that went badly and should be avoided. The Issue Log should be reviewed for potential lessons learned throughout the project lifecycle.

Lessons Learned

This section captures all lessons learnt throughout the project.

Field	Instructions	Example
ID	The ID for referencing the lesson. These should be numerically ordered and prefixed with an 'L' to distinguish them from other IDs.	L5
Lesson	Describe the lesson that has been learnt and how it should be applied to future projects.	Time allowances for reviews of project outputs by members of the organisation external to the project team, should be defined up front and strictly enforced;

Field	Instructions	Example
		otherwise they can significantly affect the project schedule.
Project Phase	Identify the project phase to which the lesson relates: Scoping, Planning, Implementation or Completion (or 'General' for lessons that are not specific to a project phase).	General
Date	The date that the lesson was identified and entered into the Lessons Log.	22 May 2012
Author	The name of the person who captured the project lesson.	Mr P. Sarker

17.5.7 Quality Log Template

Quality Log Template

1. Project Title			Date Created		Last Updated	
Project Manager		Contact	P:		E:	

2. Deliverable Quality

ID	Deliverable (ID; Name)	Quality Criteria	Responsible	Review Date	Result	Action(s)	Sign-off Date	Approver
Q1								
Q2								
Q3								
Q4								
Q5								

Risk Log Template

1. Project Title			Date Created		Last Updated	
Project Manager		Contact	P:		E:	

2. Risks

ID	Risk	Mitigation	Likelihood (H, M, L)	Consequence (H, M, L)	Rating	Date Raised	Status (O, I, P)	Responsible
R1								
R2								
R3								
R4								
R5								

Issue Log Template

1. Project Title			Date Created		Last Updated	
Project Manager		Contact	P:		E:	

2. Issues

ID	Issue	Priority (H, M, L)	Status (O, I, C)	Date Raised	Raised By	Responsible	Action(s)
I1							
I2							
I3							
I4							
I5							

Change Log Template

1. Project Title			Date Created		Last Updated	
Project Manager		Contact	P:		E:	

2. Changes

ID	Change	Priority (H, M, L)	Status (P, I, A, R)	Date Raised	Raised By	Responsible	Decision Reasoning
C1							
C2							
C3							
C4							
C5							

Lessons Log Template

1. Project Title				Date Created		Last Updated	
Project Manager		Contact	P:		E:		

2. Lessons Learned

ID	Lesson	Project Phase	Date	Author
L1				
L2				
L3				
L4				
L5				

17.6 Project Closure Report

17.6.1 Completion Instructions

The Project Closure Report provides a summary of the performance of the project and identifies high-level lessons that could be applied in future projects. It also brings the project to a formal, controlled close. The final Project Schedule, completed Project Logs and the most recent Project

Status Report can all provide useful input to the Closure Report. The document should be clear and succinct, making use of bullet-points, diagrams, tables etc, as appropriate.

Project Title

This section provides the primary reference details that identify the project. These details can be cross-referenced to the other documentation created throughout the project.

Field	Instructions	Example
Project Title	Record the title of the project. This should match the title established by the Project Scoping Document.	Implementation of an Electronic Document Management System
Project Manager	The name of the project manager.	Mr P. Sarker
Contact	Contact details (phone and email) for the project manager.	P: 880-2-8311111 psarkhel@bangladesh.gov.bd

Project Performance Summary

This section provides an overall, high-level summary of the outcome(s) of the project.

Field	Instructions	Example
Commencement Date	The date that work on the project commenced, taken from the Project Schedule.	15 Mar 2012
Completion Date	The date that work on the project was completed, taken from the Project Schedule.	6 Nov 2012
Budget Cost	Indicate the total amount that the project was initially budgeted to cost, taken from the baseline Project Schedule.	$335,200
Actual Cost	Indicate the total amount that the project actually cost, taken from the final Project Schedule.	$339,450
Planned Duration	Indicate how long the project was initially planned to take, taken from the baseline Project Schedule.	7 months 2 weeks
Actual Duration	Indicate how long the project actually took, taken from the final Project Schedule.	7 months 3 weeks
Objectives Achievement	Comment on the success of the project. How well did the project deliver on the original intent? How was this measured?	Project was completed successfully. All outputs were delivered to the required quality. Initial user feedback regarding the new system is very positive.
Project Impact	Comment on the impact of the project on the organisation. If possible, quantify the impact in dollars. If the impact of the project cannot be determined at this stage, explain the anticipated impact and outline a schedule and method for reviewing the impact at a later date.	The organisation's manual document handling process has been completely replaced by the new electronic document management system. Initial analysis indicates that this has reduced document handling time by 80% and increased document visibility and accessibility.

Project Manager Sign-off

This section indicates the project manager's assertion that the Project Closure Document is complete and accurate. Although it is on the front page of the document, this section should be signed by the project manager once the Project Closure Document is complete to indicate that it has been finished and is ready for submission to the Project Board for approval.

Field	Instructions	Example
Name	The name of the project manager.	Mr P. Sarker
Signature	Signature of the project manager.	
Date	The date that the project manager signed the document.	9 Nov 2012

Schedule Performance

This section provides information on the delivery of the primary project deliverables.

Field	Instructions	Example
ID	The ID of the deliverable, taken from the Project Schedule.	1.0
Deliverable	The name and/or description of the deliverable, taken from the Project Schedule.	System Requirements Specification
Planned Delivery	The date that the deliverable was planned for completion.	30 Apr 2012
Actual Delivery	The date that the deliverable was actually completed.	2 May 2012
Deviation (Days)	The difference between the planned delivery date and the actual delivery date.	2 days
Comments	Comment on the adherence to the delivery schedule. Were there particular reasons for any deviation? How could schedule adherence be improved for future projects?	Delivered slightly late due to the review by the CIO taking longer than anticipated. Additional time should be allowed in the schedule for external reviews in the future.

Budget Performance

This section summarises how well the project performed against the budget.

Field	Instructions	Example
Budget Cost (A)	Enter the amount that the project was originally budgeted to cost. This can be determined from the baseline Project Schedule.	$335,200
Actual Cost (B)	Enter the amount that the project actually cost. This can be determined from either the final Project Schedule or from the financial records for the project.	$339,450
Variance (C=A-B)	Calculate the difference between the amount that the project was budgeted to cost and the amount that it actually cost.	-$4250
Comment	Comment on the project's overall adherence to the budget. Were there particular reasons for any variance? How could budget adherence be improved for future projects?	The project was delivered almost exactly on budget (budget variance was less than 1.3%).

Risk & Issue Management Performance

This section summarises the key risks and issues. Only include significant risks and issues, which had an impact on the overall project.

Field	Instructions	Example
Risk/Issue ID	The ID of the risk/issue, taken from the Project Logs.	R1
Risk/Issue	The description of the risk/issue, taken from the Project Logs.	Project servers are being upgraded during the Implementation Phase, which may impact testing of the pilot system.
Impact	Describe the risk/issue's impact on the project (scope, schedule, budget, quality, outcomes).	Due to a timing conflict with the server upgrade program, pilot testing could not take place on the main system. Contingency funds were allocated to hire additional hardware for the pilot testing so that the project could remain on schedule.
Management Approach and	Describe the approach used to address the risk/issue. How ef-	Contingency funds were flagged at the project outset to address

Field	Instructions	Example
Effectiveness	fective was it? How could it have been improved?	the risk and the risk was monitored throughout its life. The decision was made to hire additional hardware for the pilot testing early enough that the schedule was not impacted.
Comments	Comment on the overall project risk and issue management performance. Did issues arise that weren't on the Risk Log? Why? Did risks on the Risk Log become issues? Why? How effective were mitigating actions?	Overall risk and issue management was effective, allowing the project to deliver the intended outcomes. Risks were generally identified early and regularly tracked. Only one issue arose that was not anticipated in the Risk Log and this was due to an organisational event that was not known to the project team. All issues were addressed successfully.

Scope Management Performance

This section summarises the management of changes to the project's scope. Only include significant changes, which had an impact on the project outcomes.

Field	Instructions	Example
Change ID	The ID of the change, taken from the Change Log.	C1
Change	The description of the change, taken from the Change Log.	The original Project Schedule allowed for 2 days of training per person in the use of the new system. It is now apparent that 5 days of training are required. Suggest increasing the duration of the project by 3 days to allow for the additional training.
Impact	Describe the change's impact on the project (schedule, budget, quality, outcomes).	The project was completed 6 days behind the original schedule, largely due to additional training and administration requirements.

Field	Instructions	Example
Comments	Comment on the overall scope management performance. Were all changes managed effectively through the Change Log? Did the scope changes impact on the project's ability to deliver on its strategic intent? Were changes required that could have been avoided with greater planning or foresight? How?	There were very few changes to the project scope and these did not impact the project outcomes.

Lessons Learned

This section captures the key lessons that were identified throughout the project. Only include important lessons, which have an impact on how future projects should be conducted. Remember, lessons should include both things that went well and should be done again, as well as things that went badly and should be avoided.

Field	Instructions	Example
Lesson ID	The ID of the lesson, taken from the Lessons Log.	L5
Lesson	The description of the lesson, taken from the Lessons Logs.	Time allowances for reviews of project outputs by members of the organisation external to the project team should be defined up front and strictly enforced; otherwise they can significantly affect the Project Schedule.
Impact	Describe the impact that learning the lesson had on the project.	Realisation of this lesson early in the project caused the project team to change the way external reviews were approached by setting a deadline for accepting feedback, so that other project work was not delayed.
Recommendation	Recommendation for how the lesson should be incorporated into the conduct of future projects.	Establish a review timeline for project outputs during planning and have it agreed to by all external reviewers, then control the review deadlines throughout the project.

Quality Performance

This section summarises how well the project performed against the quality criteria.

Field	Instructions	Example
Quality Performance	Review the Quality Log and comment on the deliverable quality. How did the acceptance criteria for each deliverable serve the project? Were high-quality outputs delivered? If not, what were the quality shortcomings and how could they be avoided in future projects?	All project outputs were delivered to the required quality Some quality criteria were not initially clear enough and this caused some slight delays in the quality reviews. All criteria should be clear and measurable in the future.

Communications & Stakeholder Management Performance

This section summarises how well stakeholders were engaged and managed throughout the project.

Field	Instructions	Example
Communications & Stakeholder Management Performance	Comment on the engagement and management of stakeholders in the project. How could this have been done better? Did all stakeholders receive the information that they needed when they needed it? Was all information available to stakeholders timely and up-to-date?	Overall stakeholder management was well done, with very few complaints received. Display of the Project Schedule on the wall during team meetings was particularly effective in making the team aware of deadlines and task interdependencies. Launch of the final system could have been better publicised to reduce issues with the initial roll-out.

Performance of People and Teams

This section summarises how well the project team performed together throughout the project.

Field	Instructions	Example
Performance of People and Teams	Comment on the engagement and management of people and teams in the project. How could this be done better? Did any significant conflicts occur? If so, please describe briefly and note impact on the project. Were any specific people/team management approaches particularly effective?	The project team worked very effectively together, with no major issues. The monthly team newsletter was very effective in creating a team bond and sharing general project information. Mrs T. Binkley in particular showed excellent leadership potential and attention to detail and should be considered for further project roles.

Ongoing Recommendations

This section captures any recommendations that the project manager wishes to make.

Field	Instructions	Example
Ongoing Recommendations	List any recommendations for ongoing maintenance and operations related to the project outputs and any follow-up actions necessary to review project impacts at a later date.	Technical support staff has already been trained in the use and maintenance of the new system. A minor update to the software is being released by the vendor next year and should be installed as part of the licence. A complete review of project impact is recommended for 6 months time to evaluate the uptake of the system and its overall impact on workloads and document handling errors.

General Comments

This section is a general section for any comments that the project manager feels are important and have not been recorded elsewhere in the document.

Field	Instructions	Example
General Comments	List any additional comments that should be recorded; such as technical matters, economic or environmental issues that impacted the project or commendations to individuals.	The system has been set up to manage document files only, however the software selected has the capability to manage other file types if this functionality is required at a later date.

Project Completion Acceptance

This section authorises the completion of the project. It is completed once the rest of the document has been prepared by the project manager (with the assistance of the project team). Project completion must be formally approved before the project can be finalised and the documentation archived.

Field	Instructions	Example
Name	The name of the person authorising completion of the project.	Mr A. Jones
Signature	Signature of the person authorising completion of the project.	
Date	The date that the person signed the document to authorise completion of the project.	11 Nov 2012

17.6.2 Project Closure Report Template

1. Project Title							
Project Manager				**Contact**		P: E:	
2. Project Performance Summary							
Commencement Date				**Completion Date**			
Budget Cost		**Actual Cost**		**Planned Duration**		**Actual Duration**	
Objectives Achievement							
Project Impact							
3. Project Manager Sign-off							
Name			**Signature**			**Date**	

4. Schedule Performance

ID	Deliverable	Planned Delivery	Actual Delivery	Deviation	Comments

5. Budget Performance

Budget Cost (A)	Actual Cost (B)	Variance (C = A – B)	Comment

6. Risk & Issue Management Performance

Risk/ Issue ID	Risk/Issue	Impact	Management Approach & Effectiveness

Comments

7. Scope Management Performance		
Change ID	Change	Impact
C		
C		
Comments		

8. Lessons Learned			
Lesson ID	Lesson	Impact	Recommendation
L			

9. Quality Performance			
10. Communications & Stakeholder Management Performance			
11. Performance of People and Teams			
12. Ongoing Recommendations			
13. General Comments			
14. Project Completion Acceptance			
	Name	Signature	Date
Project Sponsor			

17.7 eGovernment Project Manager's Checklist

This section provides a checklist of the common activities that the project manager should be performing throughout the project. The activities are organised according to how often they should be performed. These frequencies however, are only a guide - activities may need to be completed more or less often depending upon the needs of the project. This is not a complete list of every activity that a project manager will perform during a project, but is meant to aid the project manager in keeping track of some of their more common responsibilities. Please note that while these activities are the responsibility of the project manager, the project manager should seek input/ support from the project team as required.

17.7.1 Daily

Activity	Related Document(s)
Read and respond to emails - project issues, updates and proposed changes may emerge via daily emails	Emails
Check for today's meetings and appointments and ensure adequate preparation	Project Schedule; project manager's diary or calendar
Check for tasks to be started or due for completion	Project Schedule
Check and update the status of tasks	Project Schedule
Raise or update issues	Issue Log
Review and capture risks	Risk Log
Capture lessons that arise	Lessons Log

17.7.2 Weekly

Activity	Related Document(s)
Check for this week's meetings, appointments and communications requirements and, prepare as necessary	Project Schedule; project manager's diary or calendar
Confirm that resources are available for any tasks to be started in the coming week	Project Schedule
Check status of project deliverables	Project Schedule; Quality Log
Review and update actual project progress	Project Schedule
Conduct project team meetings	Meeting Minutes
Raise or update risks and issues	Risk Log; Issue Log
Raise, document and implement changes as required	Change Log
Inform Project Sponsor of progress/issues as required	

17.7.3 Monthly

Activity	Related Document(s)
Manage project stakeholders - check for and conduct this month's significant communications requirements	Project Scoping Document; Project Schedule
Confirm resource requirements for the month	Project Schedule
Check status of deliverables	Project Schedule; Quality Log
Review any related work occurring within the organisation	Project Scoping Document, Project Schedule, Issue Log, Risk Log
Update project financials (estimates, actuals & forecasts)	Project Schedule
Review risks (open and new)	Risk Log
Review issues (unresolved and new)	Issue Log
Consolidate & analyse project information - prepare Project Status Report	Status Report
Deliver Status Report to Project Sponsor	Status Report
Update plans with actuals and approved changes	Project Schedule, Quality Log

17.7.4 Each Project Phase

Activity	Related Document(s)
Manage stakeholders – update stakeholder information and provide communication	Project Scoping Document; Project Schedule
Prepare for next phase or project completion	Project Mandate; Project Scoping Document; Project Schedule; Project Logs; Status Reports; Project Closure Report
Confirm resource requirements and availability	Project Schedule
Arrange acceptance and handover of project deliverables	Project Schedule; Quality Log
Receive approval for next phase or project completion	Project Mandate; Project Scoping Document; Project Schedule; Project Logs; Status Reports; Project Closure Report

17.8 eGovernment Project Phase Completion Checklist

This document provides a checklist of activities that should be completed during each phase of the standard project lifecycle: Scoping, Planning, Implementation and Completion. This is not a complete list of every activity that will take place during a project, but is meant to identify the key items that the project manager should confirm have been completed before finishing a phase and beginning the next.

Scoping Phase	Complete
Clarify Project Mandate with Project Sponsor	
Establish Project Team	
Complete Project Scoping Document	
Project Scoping Document approved	
Prepare/plan for Planning Phase	

Planning Phase	Complete
Revise Project Team	
Complete Work Breakdown Structure (break work into manageable tasks)	
Complete Project Schedule	
Plan project delivery work	
Plan project management work	
Create Project Logs:	
Create Quality Log	
Create Risk Log	
Create Issues Log	
Create Change Log	
Create Lessons Log	
Manage project stakeholders	
Report project status to Project Sponsor	
Review Project Mandate	
Revise Project Scoping Document	
Project Plan (Project Schedule and Project Logs) approved	

Implementation Phase	Complete
Revise Project Team	
Deliver project outputs	
Complete monthly Status Reports	
Monitor and update Project Schedule	
Monitor and update Project Logs:	
Update Quality Log	
Update Risk Log	
Update Issues Log	
Update Change Log	
Update Lessons Log	
Manage project stakeholders	
Review Project Mandate	
Review Project Scoping Document	

Completion Phase	Complete
Handover project outputs to organisation	
Finalise Project Schedule	
Finalise Project Logs:	
Finalise Quality Log	
Finalise Risk Log	
Finalise Issues Log	
Finalise Change Log	
Finalise Lessons Log	
Complete Project Closure Report	
Recommend any follow-on actions	
Project Closure Report approved	
Archive project documentation	
Disband Project Team (transition members to other work)	

Author Biographies

Dr Ahmed Imran

Dr Ahmed Imran is an Information System (IS) researcher whose research interest largely emerged from his personal experience that includes ICT adoption in public sector, eGovernment and ICT in developing countries. Ahmed had a versatile and challenging experience before his transition to academia. He served in the defence force and held important positions in the IT sector. Ahmed's past experience is invaluable for research in understanding and providing rich insight of the context in least developed courtiers. His PhD research gained an in-depth understanding of impediments to eGovernment adoption in LDCs, which led to a process model for successful ICT adoption in public sectors within a LDC environment. Part of Ahmed's research has been successfully implemented as an applied international research project through a competitive AusAID grant, which also received prestigious Vice Chancellor's award for Community outreach in 2010. Ahmed is actively involved in number of research projects and has published and presented his research in distinguished forums around the world. Ahmed is currently a lecturer of information System in the School of Engineering and IT at UNSW Canberra, at the Australian Defence Force Academy and a Visiting Fellow at Research School of Accounting and Business Information Systems at the Australian National University.

Professor Shirley Gregor, AO

Shirley Gregor is Professor of Information Systems at the Australian National University, Canberra, where she is a Director of the National Centre for Information Systems Research. Professor Gregor's current research interests include the adoption and strategic use of information and communications technologies, intelligent systems, human-computer interaction and the philosophy of technology. Dr Gregor has published in journals such as MIS Quarterly, Journal of the Association of Information Systems, International Journal of Electronic Commerce, International Journal of Human Computer Studies, European Journal of Information Systems and Information Technology & People. Professor Gregor was made an Officer of the Order of Australia in the Queen's Birthday Honour's list in June 2005 for services as an educator and researcher in the field of information systems and for work in eCommerce in the agribusiness sector. She is a Fellow of the Australian Computer Society and a Fellow of the Association for Information Systems. She was a Senior Editor of MIS Quarterly 2008-2010 and is Editor-in-Chief of the Journal of the Association of Information Systems 2010-2013.

Dr Tim Turner, FACS

Dr Tim Turner has been involved in the IT industry for over 30 years, with the focus on eCommerce, and particularly eGovernment, for over 18 years. He has concentrated his attention on assisting governments at all levels to understand how information technology can be used to enhance effectiveness and efficiency. Recently, that focus has shifted to aiding the governments of least-developed countries. He has played significant roles in several of Australia's leading eGovernment projects and consults to peak government and industry bodies in the eGovernment arena. Tim has also delivered significant projects in the private sector in information technology generally and electronic commerce specifically.

Tim is a Senior Lecturer in IT in the School of Engineering and IT at UNSW Canberra, at the Australian Defence Force Academy. As a senior lecturer, he is teaching Australia's future military leaders to understand and exploit information technology. His PhD developed a theory of eGovernment service design grounded in his experience and that of Australian governments at the Federal, State and Local levels. Tim is a Fellow of the Australian Computer Society and has held executive roles in that professional society.

Index

www.ingramcontent.com/pod-product-compliance
Lightning Source LLC
Chambersburg PA
CBHW051441270326
41932CB00025B/3389
9781911218234